# Uncharted Territory

# Uncharted Territory

## What Numbers Tell Us about the Biggest Hit Songs and Ourselves

## Chris Dalla Riva

BLOOMSBURY ACADEMIC

NEW YORK · LONDON · OXFORD · NEW DELHI · SYDNEY

BLOOMSBURY ACADEMIC
Bloomsbury Publishing Inc, 1385 Broadway, New York, NY 10018, USA
Bloomsbury Publishing Plc, 50 Bedford Square, London, WC1B 3DP, UK
Bloomsbury Publishing Ireland, 29 Earlsfort Terrace, Dublin 2, D02 AY28, Ireland

BLOOMSBURY, BLOOMSBURY ACADEMIC and the Diana logo are trademarks of
Bloomsbury Publishing Plc

First published in the United States of America 2025
Reprinted by Bloomsbury Academic 2025

Library of Congress Cataloging-in-Publication Data

Names: Dalla Riva, Chris, author.
Title: Uncharted territory: what numbers tell us about the biggest hit
songs and ourselves / Chris Dalla Riva.
Description: New York : Bloomsbury Publishing, 2025. | Includes
bibliographical references and index. | Summary: "This insightful and
surprising history based on data and numbers will reframe everything you
thought you knew about popular music over the last 6 decades"-- Provided by publisher.
Identifiers: LCCN 2025015155 (print) | LCCN 2025015156 (ebook) | ISBN
9798765149843 (hardback) | ISBN 9798765149904 (pdf) | ISBN 9798765149911 (epub)
Subjects: LCSH: Popular music–History and criticism.
Classification: LCC ML3470 .D34 2025 (print) | LCC ML3470 (ebook) | DDC
782.4216409–dc23/eng/20250409
LC record available at https://lccn.loc.gov/2025015155
LC ebook record available at https://lccn.loc.gov/2025015156

Typeset by Deanta Global Publishing Services, Chennai, India
Printed and bound in the United States of America

For product safety related questions contact productsafety@bloomsbury.com.

To find out more about our authors and books visit www.bloomsbury.com and
sign up for our newsletters.

*To Mom, Dad, Natalie, Emily, and Devin*
*Thank you for encouraging my wide array of interests*

# *Contents*

*Acknowledgments* ix

**That Poor Little Fool Fell into the Moody River** 1
August 4, 1958—June 19, 1961

**Meet Me at Quarter to Three with Your Sugar Pie** 21
June 26, 1961—June 19, 1965

**Mr. Tambourine Man and the Raindrops on His Head** 43
June 26, 1965—January 3, 1970

**I Want You Back in the Sweet Sunshine on My Shoulders** 65
January 31, 1970—March 30, 1974

**When You're Hooked on Feeling with a Dancing Queen** 89
April 6, 1974—April 9, 1977

**Don't Give Up on Us Just as It's Time for a Celebration** 111
April 16, 1977—February 7, 1981

**Rocking from 9 to 5 with My Buddy Amadeus** 133
February 21, 1981—March 29, 1986

**You Already Got My Kiss, So Don't Forget My Number** 155
April 19, 1986—July 1, 1989

**It's a Damn Good Thing We Danced the Macarena** 177
July 8, 1989—August 3, 1996

**I Mean It, No Diggity, I Like the Way You Move** 201
November 9, 1996—February 14, 2004

**Slow Jamz Run Down to the Deepest Part of Me** 229
February 21, 2004—March 3, 2012

**All I Know Is That We Are Young, Dumb Suckers** 257
March 17, 2012—March 16, 2019

**On That Dusty Old Town Road, I Died with a Smile** 281
April 13, 2019—January 11, 2025

*Bibliography* 305
*Index* 324
*About the Author* 340

# *Acknowledgments*

The words in this book would not exist without Vinnie Christopher or George O'Har. Though we went to high school together, Vinnie and I didn't become friends until we struck up an unexpected friendship while working at a summer camp together. Years later, when I mentioned that I was going to listen to every number one hit, he asked if he could join me. I obliged, and I'm lucky that I did. Not only does Vinnie have vast knowledge of popular music, but he was an ever-present sounding board for all my theories and ideas that became the lifeblood of this book.

My friendship with George O'Har was also unexpected. He was my English professor at Boston College. Given how honest he was about my writing in his class, I knew that I was onto something when I sent him an early version of the first chapter of this book, and he told me to keep at it. This book would not exist without his encouragement and feedback.[1]

Though the words in this book would not exist without those two, the words would not have been printed without Fred Bronson or Michael Tan. Fred is a longtime writer and one of the premier authorities on *Billboard* number one hits. We became friendly after he came across a TikTok that I'd posted about Honey Cone's criminally underrated chart-topper, "Want Ads." After years of pitching this book to no avail, Fred connected me with Michael Tan, an editor he was working with. I will always be grateful to Michael and the team at Bloomsbury for taking a chance on me.

The words in this book would be far worse without Cailley LaPara, Devin Portilla, Bob Dalla Riva, Matthew Meehan, and Andrew Goodman. They were

---

[1] Also, thank you for introducing me to Jorge Luis Borges.

the first people to read this musical volume in full. Their feedback made it much better.

The graphics in the book would not only be worse without Caileigh Nerney, but they wouldn't exist at all. She made every chart contained in these pages. Data analytics without good data visualization is like Elton John without Bernie Taupin. Sure, it works, but not as well as it could.

The musical analysis in this book would be much worse without Ande Flavelle, my longtime music teacher. Only acknowledging Ande as my teacher provides an incomplete picture, though. Of course, I'm glad that he taught me how to play the guitar, but I'm equally grateful for our friendship and the fact that he took my creative ideas seriously from the time I was eleven.

I have no idea why Walt Hickey answered a cold email that I sent him years ago, but Chapter 6 would be much worse if he didn't reply. Frankly, this whole book would be much worse without Walt. Few people have done more for the niche but vibrant community that combines culture with numbers than he has.

Thank you to Max Rauch, Ken De Poto, John Cozz, and Kevin Donnelly for teaching me the true power of musical collaboration.[2]

Thank you to God for making the major chord and man for making the minor chord.

Thank you to Dave Macli, Charlie Kaplan, Jack Driscoll, Vanessa Wilkins, and my colleagues at Audiomack for giving me the chance to work in the music business.

Thank you to everyone who subscribes to my newsletter, *Can't Get Much Higher*. I wouldn't be getting a book published without you.

Thank you to Evan P. Raftes for taking the pictures that appear in this book.

Thank you to the wonderful public school educators in West Caldwell, New Jersey, who instilled a love for mathematics, music, and writing deep in my soul.

Thank you to the cast and crew of *How I Met Your Mother*, the show that played in the background while I edited this book.

---

[2] Your endless lessons about the intricacies of emo music have also not gone unnoticed.

Thank you to Richard Tresch, Richard McGowan, Chris Maxwell, Mary Beth Savio, and Bill Crook for teaching me more about economics, statistics, and data analytics than I could ever ask for.

Thank you to the Internet Archive, Hoboken Public Library, and countless editors of Wikipedia. There is almost nothing I value more than information being freely available.

Thank you to Matt Daniels and Ernie Smith for being the first people to publish my writing.

Thank you to Hank Williams, Ella Marija Lani Yelich-O'Connor, Paul Westerberg, Jack White, Jim Croce, Bruce Springsteen, Loretta Lynn, Johnny Cash, Big Bill Broonzy, Brian Fallon, Jack Antonoff, Stevland Hardaway Morris, Robert Zimmerman, Kacey Musgraves, and Margaret Debay Rogers for endless musical inspiration.

Thank you to Monica Wojtal and Seamus Magee for being down to go to almost any concert at a moment's notice.

Thank you to John Franklin for laughter, creative inspiration, singing old doo-wop songs with me, and being the brother I never had.

Finally, thank you to the absurd number of people who gave me feedback on parts of this book, rated songs, answered my emails, or have come out to see me play in the dingiest of venues. I will now list you all by the length of your name because I'm tired of alphabetical order: David Kim, Joe Vango, Neil Shah, Sean Dyer, Ted Gioia, Will Page, Fiona Shea, Bob Davison, Chey Watson, Evan Bogart, Imani Brown, Kara Reilly, Katie Walsh, Lenny Russo, Richie Todd, Tom Rowland, Alexa Migton, Alisha Kabir, Aliyah Lopez, Annie Borman, Brian Zisook, Dave Edwards, Jake Travers, Joey Krieger, Val Coughlin, Amanda Bettin, Chris Hreniuk, Dan Gallagher, Erik Almquist, Jamie Carroll, Katie Petrino, Steve Knopper, Claire Messina, Liliana Zeolla, Mark Mattheiss, Michael Nufrio, Mark Richardson, Patrick Crorkin, Abigail Sokolsky, Thomas G. Hanley, Melissa Stiefbold, Allison Battinelli, Michael Pelczynski, Dr. Edouard Nicaise, Donna-Claire Chesman, Vinnie Christopher Sr., Donald Dennis Lynch III, and Luke "Lou Christie" Lograno.

And, once again, thank you to Mom, Dad, Natalie, Emily, and Devin. You don't write a book like this unless people have been encouraging you for a long time.

"Writing about music is like dancing about architecture"

I have no idea who said this quote. In fact, I've seen it credited to everyone from Elvis Costello to Frank Zappa. While I've written this book so that it can be enjoyed if you are familiar with any of the songs mentioned or not, the quote is a good reminder that you could spill thousands of pages of ink and never capture the first note of a song. Because of that, I hope you check out some of the music mentioned in these pages. To assist in that process, I've built playlists that contain every song mentioned in this book in the order they appear. You can find those playlists at https://chrisdallariva.com/uncharted.

# *That Poor Little Fool Fell into the Moody River*

## August 4, 1958—June 19, 1961

### Smoke Gets in Your Eyes

In 2017, I stumbled upon a Spotify playlist called "Every Number One Song on Billboard," created by a presumed Batman lover named harveydent,da. As a musician and a data junkie, I'd always been fascinated with *Billboard* Hot 100 number one hits, but harveydent,da gave me a tool to search through and listen to them. So, that's what I did. I started searching and listening. Not methodically but randomly. And I was surprised with what even cursory searches turned up.

- There have been 12 number one hits where the lead artist was named "Bob"—13 if you count B.o.B—but none by Bob Dylan.

- The only US states to appear in the title of a number one are California, Georgia, Kansas, and Texas.[1] My home state, New Jersey, has sadly never had the pleasure.

- At 96 seconds, Maurice Williams and the Zodiacs' hit "Stay" (November 21, 1960) is the shortest song to ever get to number one.

---

[1] For the curious, here are the number ones: "Hotel California" by the Eagles (1977), "California Love" by 2Pac ft. Dr. Dre (1996), "California Gurls" by Katy Perry ft. Snoop Dogg (2010), "Georgia on My Mind" by Ray Charles (November 14, 1960), "Midnight Train to Georgia" by Gladys Knight and the Pips (1973), "The Night the Lights Went Out in Georgia" by Vicki Lawrence (1973), "Kansas City" by Wilbert Harrison (May 18, 1959), and "TEXAS HOLD 'EM" by Beyoncé (2024).

- Thanks to Queen and XXXTentacion, chart-topping artist names have spanned the entire alphabet.

- The second song to top the charts—"Nel Blu Dipinto Di Blu (Volare)" by Domenico Modugno (August 18, 1958)—is unlike almost all number ones in that it contains no English lyrics.

But where was Bruce Springsteen? How did Ringo Starr top the charts twice before John Lennon did it once? And why were many of Elton John's number ones not that good? I was confused. I felt like the misty-eyed lover in The Platters' powerful number one "Smoke Gets in Your Eyes" (January 19, 1959), my vision clouded by the passage of time. I hadn't realized that public tastes had shifted so dramatically over the decades, once-unpopular works now hailed as masterpieces and ubiquitous hits of yesteryear fading from our consciousness by the day.

To get a better grasp on this, I decided to listen to every song to ever top the *Billboard* Hot 100, working chronologically from the beginning. To color my listening, I would build a dataset that tracked a variety of facts and figures about the songs in hopes of writing about my journey, eventually assembling everything I wrote into a book.[2]

Each chapter would be written through musical, historical, and analytical lenses, using data to tell the story of American popular music. The years covered in each chapter would be denoted an "era." Each chapter would be titled by smashing together the names of the first and last number ones of the era. The major sections in every chapter would be named from a relevant lyric of the era's chart-toppers. This is the first era. It covers 53 songs, starting with Ricky Nelson's "Poor Little Fool" (August 4, 1958) and progressing week-by-week to Pat Boone's "Moody River" (June 19, 1961).

---

[2] You are holding such. Ideally, you have paid for it. If not, I hope you've told someone with higher morals about it.

# A Primer on Musical Data and Musical Eras

I've collected a ton of data as I've journeyed through these songs, including everything from songwriters and producers to key signatures and lyrical complexity. The first time I mention a number one from the current era, I'll list the date it reached number one in parentheses after the song title or artist (e.g., "It's All in the Game" by Tommy Edwards (September 29, 1958)).[3] If I mention a number one from another era, I'll only include the year it topped the charts (e.g., "drivers license" by Olivia Rodrigo (2021)). Though I might mention dates associated with non-number ones, those dates will not be in parentheses.

On top of this, I've developed a simple metric to assess a song's quality. It boils down to averaging three independent ratings on a scale between one and ten. Two of the people rating songs were consistent throughout this entire process: me[4] and a pop-culturally savvy friend of mine. The third rater changed regularly, usually after a stint of 25 songs. I wanted to rotate people through this third position so that I could get different perspectives on the music. While I won't list the ratings explicitly, you will always be able to find the era's highest- and lowest-rated songs at the end of each chapter.

This raises a question: Why have I defined the first era to be from August 4, 1958, to June 19, 1961? Mostly because the *Billboard* Hot 100 did not exist before August 4, 1958. Since it has been the foremost popular music chart for decades, its inception seems like a nice start date. Because of that, "Big Hunk o' Love" (August 10, 1959) is Elvis Presley's first number one and not "Jailhouse Rock" or "Hound Dog" or one of his earlier hits. It's also why we don't see Frank Sinatra appear until the late 1960s and why famous big-band leaders like Glenn Miller and Benny Goodman are absent.

But why did I stop at the week of June 19, 1961, for this chapter? The 53rd song seems kind of random. And it is. We generally think of popular music history by decade because (a) we use base ten arithmetic and (b) it's easier to compartmentalize in our minds, but decadal divisions make as

---

[3] As this melody was composed by Charles C. Dawes, vice president in the Calvin Coolidge administration, it is the only number one written by a US vice president.

[4] Obviously.

much sense as random dates. When a year or a decade ends, trends don't stop. Indeed, we can look back and identify popular styles over stretches of time, but rarely are things created or destroyed on certain dates. Things evolve. It may be as useful to think of August 4, 1958, through June 19, 1961, as a musical era as it is to think about 1950 to 1959 as a musical era.

Still, I tried to concoct some reason for my stopping point. I chose Pat Boone's "Moody River" because it exemplifies a few different tropes of this period that we're going to discuss. Additionally, Boone proves a natural pair with Ricky Nelson, the era's first chart-topping artist. Both were once massively popular but have largely seen their stars fade as time has gone on. Bookending this era with those two illustrates an important lesson in both popular music and life: time shows no mercy.[5]

## This Time Tomorrow, Reckon Where I'll Be

*Billboard* was founded in 1894 as a trade magazine that covered advertising via posters, flyers, and, of course, billboards. Over time, they began to report on entertainment and celebrity gossip, eventually shifting almost all their coverage to the music industry.

Throughout the 1930s and 1940s, they began to publish a variety of charts, including Best Sellers in Stores, Most Played by DJs, and Most Played in Jukeboxes, to track the most popular records in the United States. In late 1958, they introduced the Hot 100, which aggregated music data across all formats to determine the true most popular singles in America each week. The number one record was the most popular, the number two record was the second most popular, and so on.

Throughout the decades, the Hot 100 has evolved, accounting for streams and digital sales, among many other sources, and while it has faced scrutiny (see Chapters 5 and 9), it remains the premier authority on the most popular songs in the United States. But as everybody knows, you don't have to look far

---

[5] For songs that time has been merciful to, see The Rolling Stones. For faces that time has not been merciful to, see The Rolling Stones.

to find things that were once popular that show their age. This isn't necessarily a bad thing. Everything ages. But we can break time's weathering of popular songs into a few different categories: tastelessness, technological evolution, saturation, and of-its-era.

## Tastelessness: That's Not Politically Correct!

This book covers August 1958 to January 2025. That's only 67.5 years, well below the average American lifespan. But in another sense, 67.5 years is a *very* long time. The world changes fast, and so does our perception of what is acceptable. For example, there's a predatory undertone when Elvis Presley sings the following in his jaunty rocker "Stuck on You" (April 25, 1960): "Hide in the kitchen, hide in the hall / Ain't gonna do you no good at all / Cause once I catch you, and the kissing starts / A team of wild horses couldn't tear us apart."

Additionally, Ricky Nelson reducing the world's women to their ethnicities on "Travelin' Man" (May 29, 1961) (e.g., "China Doll," "pretty señorita," "cute little Eskimo") is inappropriate, along with the stereotypical Native American chanting throughout Johnny Preston's otherwise serviceable rock 'n' roller "Running Bear" (January 18, 1960). For many, this type of aging is the hardest to look past as it conflicts with contemporary notions of race and gender.

## Technological Evolution: That's Archaic!

"Alley Oop" (July 11, 1960) is one of the more intriguing number ones of this era. Performed by a ragtag group of studio musicians dubbed "The Hollywood Argyles," it's a song about a cartoon caveman that sounds like it was recorded in a garage in a chaotic 15 minutes. That last part is important. The low fidelity of "Alley Oop" announces its age. Of course, artists today can simulate that sound quality with digital recording software, but most opt for the pristine sound available to them.

Technology doesn't just affect how we record, though. It also affects how we listen. We used to listen to vinyl records. Then we listened to cassettes. Then CDs. Then digital downloads. Now, we listen on streaming services. Vinyl has physical limits to how much sound it can hold without losing quality. The longest number one in this era was "El Paso" by Marty Robbins (January 4, 1960) at about four-and-a-half minutes. While it's safe to generalize that the most number ones are under five minutes, you can now theoretically record a ten-and-a-half-hour epic on a cheap computer in your bedroom. More on that in Chapter 10.

## Saturation: That's Been Done Before!

There's an old joke that goes something like, "I don't understand why everybody makes such a big deal about *Hamlet*. It's just a bunch of famous sayings strung together by a stupid plot." In other words, *Hamlet* is cliché. Of course, *Hamlet* isn't cliché. But it can feel cliché given that others have copied it endlessly.

Certain songs age this way too. The prime example from this era is Chubby Checker's "The Twist" (September 19, 1960). First, "The Twist" suffers from genre saturation. Rock 'n' roll, a once cutting-edge sound, has gone from counterculture to mainstream culture. Decades after its dominance, much popular music in America remains informed by the rock tradition.

On top of this, "The Twist" itself is saturated. Not only did Checker release a sequel, "Let's Twist Again," but scores of artists, from Frank Sinatra to The Beatles, recorded their own twists. Though versions by Hank Ballard and Chubby Checker simultaneously charted in 1960, the craze reached its apex in 1962 when Checker's version made a second run to the top of the charts. As you can see in Figure 1.1, 22 different twists debuted on the Hot 100 that year. By 1965, there were zero. "The Twist" became so ubiquitous so fast that by the end of the 1960s, it felt like it could have been released 100 years earlier.

## Of-Its-Era: That's Grandma's Favorite!

While saturated songs also sound like they are of a specific era, the difference here is that of-its-era songs haven't been absorbed into the mainstream. They seem aged because they are using musical and lyrical motifs that are no longer popular. When you hear ornate, playful strings on "Save the Last Dance for Me" by The Drifters (October 17, 1960) and "Will You Love Me Tomorrow" by The Shirelles (January 30, 1961), you know that you aren't listening to

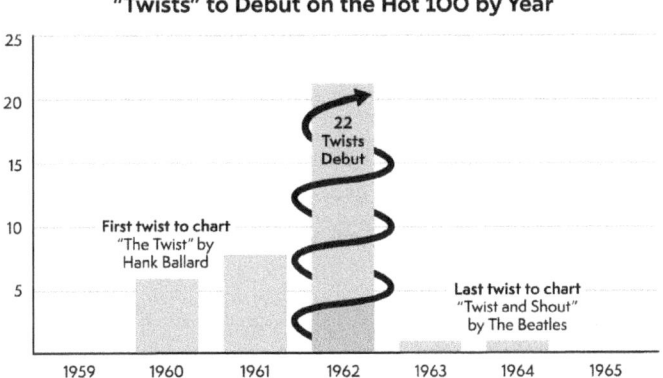

**Figure 1.1**

something from the last two weeks. Those elements are era-specific. Let's talk about two of-its-era motifs that date songs to this time: death narratives and lyrical introductions.

## *Of-Its Era: Death Narratives*

While most songs have a lyrical throughline, there were ten number ones in this era that had narratives (i.e., a plot with a loose beginning, middle, and end). Of those ten narrative-driven songs, at least eight were about death.

Take The Kingston Trio's "Tom Dooley" (November 17, 1958) as an example. Opening with a spoken monologue, it's a folk number notable for its weaving of three voices that recounts Tom Dooley murdering a woman, his attempted escape, and his subsequent sentence to hang.

While I can't deem eight songs notable in absolute terms, it's still more than I was expecting given the dismal nature of the topic. What's interesting is that within this bleak tradition, there is a notable subgenre that made up half of this era's death narratives: teenage tragedy songs. These songs usually feature two teens in a doomed relationship that results in one dying and the other longing to see them again.

During the seven-week period from January 4, 1960, to February 21, 1960, three consecutive teenage tragedy songs topped the charts. The first was the aforementioned "El Paso," a sprawling Tex-Mex epic that follows the blood-soaked love triangle of two cowboys and Feleena, a dancer at Rosa's Cantina. The second was Johnny Preston's "Running Bear," a Native American teenage tragedy that we spoke about a couple pages ago. The third was Mark Dinning's "Teen Angel" (February 8, 1960), a song so depressing—it's about a couple who escapes from a car stalled on a railroad track only for the 16-year-old girl to die trying to recover her boyfriend's high school ring—that it was allegedly banned by some radio stations.

So where did this depressing trope come from? It's unlikely that there is a single explanation, but we can ruminate on some influential factors.

- **The Birth of the Teenager**: The word "teenager" can only be traced back to the early 1900s, and it didn't become commonplace until the 1950s. The concept of teenage years likely grew from the decline in child labor, compulsory education, the proliferation of the automobile, and the increase in leisure time enabled by the economic boom following the Second World War. With the rise of the teenager quickly came panics about teenage crime, delinquency, and rebelliousness. Deaths in teenage tragedy songs are sometimes romanticized as a noble or rebellious act.

- **Musical Deaths**: Many famous musicians died prematurely in the years leading up to and during this era, including Jimmie Rodgers, Hank Williams, Johnny Ace, Eddie Cochran, Ritchie Valens, The Big Bopper, and Buddy Holly.

- **Religion**: While music heard in houses of worship can be uplifting, many worshipful songs also focus on death and the afterlife. As America remained highly religious in this era, we'd expect some of those religious beliefs and practices to influence popular music.

- **Death and Disease**: Throughout the first half of the twentieth century, there were a variety of deadly tragedies, including the First World War, the Influenza Pandemic, the Great Depression, the Second World War, the Holocaust, and the Korean War.

Nevertheless, this plot device goes back centuries in both literature (e.g., *Romeo and Juliet*) and music (e.g., "Barbara Allen").[6] "So-called *execution ballads* and *murder ballads*," Ted Gioia notes in his book *Music: A Subversive History*, "were especially popular with the public." He goes on, "I doubt if anything in our current culture can match the combination of the macabre and the celebratory achieved in these songs." Given the historical ubiquity of childhood mortality, economic depression, and violence, the simplest explanation might be that tragic death used to be more common. This would also provide context for why death and destruction feature in songs of this era that aren't about teens. As an example, take Larry Verne's "Mr. Custer" (October 10, 1960), a record recounting a terrified American soldier trying to avoid a "redskin a-waiting out there" who is "fixing to take [his] hair" during the Battle of Little Big Horn.

Though it has never been as prevalent as during this era, this device has occasionally been resurrected. Meat Loaf's "Bat Out of Hell" is probably the most grandiose take on the teenage tragedy song, an extravagant, nine-minute rock epic about two lovers and a motorcycle crash. Eminem's "Stan," not about romantic passion but rather a deranged fan, could also be deemed of the teenage tragedy variety. Additionally, hits from the late 2010s, including Billie Eilish's "bury a friend," XXXTentacion's "SAD!" (2018), and Powfu's "death bed (coffee for your head)," readily use morbid imagery to evoke emotion. More on that in Chapter 12.

## *Of-Its-Era: Lyrical Introductions*

Along with the death narrative, this era is also characterized by the lyrical introduction. We'll talk about song structure in more detail in Chapter 5, but all you need to know now is that an introduction is a section that starts a song that isn't repeated. A lyrical introduction is an introduction that—you guessed it—contains lyrics.

13 percent of number ones in this era have lyrical introductions. The Fleetwoods' somber lullaby "Mr. Blue" (November 16, 1959) and Lloyd Price's

---

[6] If there were such thing as a hit song in the 1700s, then "Barbara Allen" was one of the century's biggest smashes. It would later be recorded by Joan Baez, Dolly Parton, and Green Day's Billie Joe Armstrong, among others.

murderous rocker "Stagger Lee" (August 25, 1958) each illustrate this idea. Both open with a drifting vocal passage before entering their main repeated sections of verses and choruses.

Lyrical introductions were a staple of popular music throughout the early 1900s. While you can trace their lineage back centuries, the twentieth-century incarnation was driven by the intimate connection between popular music, the theater, and Hollywood. Many hit songs between 1910 and 1950 were originally written for the stage or screen. In those contexts, it would be jarring for a character to break into the heat of a song if they had just been speaking. A slow, free-flowing, half-spoken musical section was a more natural way to make this transition.

As the connection between the theater, Hollywood, and popular music weakened, lyrical introductions went with it. In fact, this era is really the last where we hear them with any regularity. In a 2017 conversation with Bob Dylan, interviewer Bill Flanagan observed exactly this: "A lot of singers leave off the intros when they record these songs [from the 1920s to the 1950s] . . . The Beatles occasionally wrote an intro to a song ('to lead a better life, I need my love to be here . . .') but hardly any other composers of your [Dylan's] generation or after did." Flanagan is correct. Not only have lyrical introductions become exceedingly rare since 1960, but when old songs that contain them are performed, those sections are sometimes ignored. For example, the eternal "Over the Rainbow" from *The Wizard of Oz* has an introduction. It wasn't included in the film and is often left out of performances.

# When He Knows You're Tellin' Lies

If you've ever read a brief history of popular music of the 1950s and 1960s, it usually goes something like this. Evolving from earlier styles, rock 'n' roll established itself as a distinct genre in the early 1950s. And this early rock 'n' roll music was earth-shaking. From Bill Haley and Elvis Presley to Fats Domino and Chuck Berry, this music created such fervor among teens that it was seen as a threat. In 1956, *The New York Times* reported on a psychiatrist that called rock 'n' roll a "communicable disease." Certain cities went on to ban the music in their concert halls while segregationists bemoaned how it led to racial integration among young people. In short, this music was revolutionary for not just how it sounded but how it united people across racial, gender, and geographic lines.

Then the revolution came to a halt. In 1957, Little Richard turned his back on music for the church. In March 1958, Elvis Presley was drafted into the army. Two months later, Jerry Lee Lewis faced backlash when it was revealed that he had married his 13-year-old cousin. In February 1959, Buddy Holly died in a plane crash. Ten months after that, Chuck Berry was arrested for transporting a minor across state lines. With all these stars out of commission, the musical dark ages were upon us. But this age wasn't meant to last. The Beatles soon landed on American shores, the first of many groundbreaking British bands to find success in the United States in the mid-1960s in what came to be known as the "British Invasion."

In his book *Retromania*, critic Simon Reynolds summed up this perspective while talking about the early 1960s: "But culturally these were the dying days of the fifties, just before Beatlemania hit American shores and rock got serious with [Bob] Dylan." Dylan himself would agree with this sentiment in his autobiography, albeit not citing himself as one of pop music's saviors: "Things were pretty sleepy on the Americana radio scene in the late '50s and early '60s. Popular radio was sort of at a standstill and filled with empty pleasantries. It was years before The Beatles, The Who or The Rolling Stones would breathe new life and excitement into it."

Of course, there is some truth to this narrative. But the number ones from August 4, 1958, through June 19, 1961, are testament to the fact that it isn't the full story. Not only was there incredible music during these supposed dark ages, but there was also incredible variety. Because we're going to talk about the bests of this era in the next section, let's focus on variety here. To do this, we'll look at the four number ones from July through September 1959.

This foursome began with Paul Anka's waltzing pop song "Lonely Boy" (July 13, 1959). Then Elvis Presley's relentless rock 'n' roller "Big Hunk o' Love" (August 10, 1959) took over. After that, The Browns' plainspoken folk song "The Three Bells" (August 24, 1959) topped the charts. Finally, Santo and Johnny's semi-conscious instrumental "Sleep Walk" (September 21, 1959) wore pop music's crown. Across these four songs, we encounter multiple time signatures, an array of genres, and an assortment of vocal stylings. Frankly, having both Paul Anka's stately annunciation and Elvis Presley's wild yawp find mass appeal in such a short period speaks to the variety of this era. This foursome also brings up two other important things about this period: Elvis Presley and instrumentals.

## Elvis Presley Rules the Land

Of the 43 artists to top the charts in this era, only seven did it more than once. For six of those seven artists, "more than once" means twice. The outlier was Elvis Presley, who did it five times. While his first two number ones—"Big Hunk o' Love" and "Stuck on You"—harken back but pale in comparison to the raucous rock 'n' roll before his conscription, the last three—"It's Now or Never" (August 15, 1960), "Are You Lonesome Tonight?" (November 28, 1960), and "Surrender" (March 20, 1961)—are stunning. They pull from an array of influences, including the music of Italy and vaudeville, and showcase Presley's vocal range both within and across genres. Given Presley's mythic status, it's easy to forget why he is considered such a giant.

## Instrumentals Rule a Piece of the Land

Of the 53 chart-toppers in this era, five were instrumentals. I didn't expect more than one in such a short period. This expectation wasn't just overturned by the amount of instrumental number ones but also by their time atop the charts. In fact, two spent more weeks at number one than the average song in this era. Bert Kaempfert's trumpet-driven reverie "Wonderland by Night" (January 9, 1961) did it for three. Percy Faith's lush beauty "Theme from *A Summer Place*" (February 22, 1960) did it for nine. We'll talk a little bit more about this phenomenon in the next chapter.

As I'm at the beginning of my journey through the number ones, I can't say if this era shows more comparative variety than others—we'll have to wait for Chapter 9 for that—but I feel comfortable celebrating what I've seen, especially given the blandness that people often characterize this era with. But what drove that variety?

To emphasize an earlier point, you don't have to go back that far to see a wildly different world. On top of different social mores and structures, how we think about, consume, and transmit popular music has changed. Those changes drove much of this variety.

Before the advent of recorded music in the 1870s, a song's popularity was tracked via sales of sheet music, or pieces of paper that had songs notated on them. So, if you wanted to jam to "Oh! Susanna"—one of the biggest hits of the 1840s—you couldn't tune your radio to your local pop station or queue it up on your favorite streaming service. You either had to find someone who knew how to read sheet music to play it for you or learn it yourself. Because of this, songs weren't necessarily associated with a single performer. They were associated with whoever was playing it for you at that moment. In an interview with Conan O'Brien, singer-songwriter Elvis Costello captured how this idea lived well into the age of recorded music when talking about how his mother worked in a record shop:

> [People] thought in terms of interpretations of songs. People would quite often come in and sing to my mother in the shop . . . And they wouldn't know any of the words. They wouldn't know the title. They would just sing the melody of the song, and she would have to try to decode it and then recommend a rendition.

Costello's observation illustrates why covers were not only still common in this era but expected. For example, while The Browns' "The Three Bells" was at the top of the charts in 1959, another version of the song by Dick Flood reached number 23.[7] Go back to 1946, and three different versions of the song "To Each His Own" all topped *Billboard*'s National Best Selling Retail Records chart. A modern equivalent of this would be if when Snoop Dogg put out "Drop it Like It's Hot" (2004), other rappers—like Eminem and Kanye West—recorded their own versions that rivaled Snoop's version in popularity. Though this world no longer exists, it did well into the 1960s. Thus, it's not surprising that 42 percent of songs in this era are either covers or clearly based off another work.

---

[7] Dick Flood might be the most unfortunate name in the history of popular music.

- Dave "Baby" Cortez's "The Happy Organ" (May 11, 1959) interpolates the melody from the traditional song "Shortnin' Bread."

- The Elegants' "Little Star" (August 25, 1958) turns the nursery rhyme "Twinkle, Twinkle Little Star" into a half-rocking, half-doo-wopping song.

- Brenda Lee's "I Want to Be Wanted" (October 24, 1960) is an English rewrite of the Italian song "Per Tutta La Vita."

It might seem counterintuitive, but this reuse of music from other songs generated a ton of variety. The reason for this is that if a bunch of artists were lifting a riff or covering a song, you had to make sure your version stood out. The song "Blue Moon" illustrates this well.

"Blue Moon" was originally a ballad written by Richard Rodgers and Lorenz Hart in 1934. Over the years, it has been covered many times, appearing as the instrumental theme on the 1930s radio show *Hollywood Hotel*, adorned with ornate strings by Mel Tormé in 1949, and injected with jazzy flair by Billie Holiday three years after that. When The Marcels joined this lineage in 1961, they pushed "Blue Moon" in a completely different direction, using their vocal acrobatics to reimagine the tune in the doo-wop idiom.

This also illustrates how artists could interpret songs outside of the genres they typically worked in. Even if a song were originally operatic, that didn't mean you couldn't swing it, like Bobby Darin did with *The Threepenny Opera*'s "Mack the Knife" (October 5, 1959). This genre cross-pollination was especially potent in this era because these years were a musical juncture of sorts. While rock 'n' roll and folk were climbing the charts, jazz was receding. That's part of the reason we see a mind-numbing instrumental like Lawrence Welk's "Calcutta" (February 13, 1961) replaced at the top of the charts by an electrifying song like Chubby Checker's "Pony Time" (February 27, 1961).

Finally, you could argue that popular music was less monolithic in this era. Not everyone had televisions, the internet did not exist, and the recording and telecommunications industries were less concentrated. These factors made it possible for popular music not to be dominated by singular ideas.[8]

---

[8] We'll address some of these ideas in Chapters 7 and 13, but it's worth a word on the deregulation of telecommunications because it falls outside the scope of this book. The Telecommunications Act of

# Tears Are Falling, and I Feel the Pain

As noted at the beginning of this chapter, I had three people rate each chart-topping song on a scale between one and ten. I then averaged those ratings, so we could talk about the highest-rated, lowest-rated, and most divisive number ones at the end of each chapter. This exercise raises a few questions.

First, is it possible to measure the quality of a song? I'm not sure. But regardless of if it's possible, it's valuable to try to understand how we feel about art. Plus, these things aren't set in stone. I might think that Brenda Lee's ballad "I'm Sorry" (July 18, 1960) is better than Guy Mitchell's twangy tale of lost love, "Heartaches by the Number" (December 14, 1959). You might think otherwise. That's okay. Some of my favorite conversations are when people and I disagree about songs. Even if those conversations don't leave either party with a new opinion, they usually give you a deeper understanding of yourself and the music you're talking about.

Still, is there really a point to me talking about songs that I don't think are very good? Yes. I'll turn to my favorite music critic Socrates to explain why: "For if he does not know the bad, neither will he know the good when the same topic is being discussed." Again, it's important to try to understand our feelings about art, whether good and bad. Those feelings can often illuminate things we didn't know about ourselves. Furthermore, when people talk about music of the past, they usually only talk about the best stuff. This is a pernicious bias that can convince us that music is getting worse by the year. That's not the case. There's always been good stuff and bad stuff. We just don't listen to the bad stuff anymore. But in this book, we will. The lows will be celebrated as frequently as the highs.

---

1996 was the first major overhaul of telecommunication law since 1934. The law was supposed to incite more competition, but it ended up having the opposite effect, especially in radio, which saw a ton of consolidation. Some argue that this led to less regional programming variety.

# Highlights

1. **"Runaway" by Del Shannon (April 24, 1961)**[9]—Allegedly when Del Shannon recorded this song, he was so nervous that he sang flat. It was up to producer Harry Balk to speed the tape up to get the vocal in the right key. But I can understand why Del Shannon was nervous. From the fuzzy guitar to the cascading piano and the twisting proto-synth, "Runaway" makes a breakup feel like the end of the world. And if you are to properly capture the romantic apocalypse of the lyric "Tears are falling and I feel the pain / Wishing you were here by me / To end this misery," you probably shouldn't be able to control your nerves.

2. **"Georgia on My Mind" by Ray Charles (November 14, 1960)**—The reason this song has been recorded hundreds of times is because the melody sounds like it was delivered from the high heavens. That's not a shock. That melody was written by Hoagie Carmichael, the man behind classics like "Stardust" and "Heart and Soul." But the reason you know this version of "Georgia on My Mind" rather than any other comes down to a different person: Ray Charles.

   To state the obvious, Ray Charles was a talented piano player. You can hear that talent shine on the jazzy fills he sprinkles throughout this song. But his greatest instrument was his voice, a voice whose subtle slides and slurs could make Georgia feel like your home even if you'd never been within a thousand miles of it.

3. **"Running Scared" by Roy Orbison (June 5, 1961)**—Roy Orbison is filled with fear at the beginning of this song. "Just running scared each place we go / So afraid that he might show," he sings over a lone acoustic guitar. Though he repeats the fearful title at the top of each of the first four verses, there's also a fire burning within him. And that fire grows stronger as new production elements emerge section by section. First, it's percussion. Then strings. Then wistful back-up vocals. When the song reaches its climax, Orbison's voice is quavering over a full band.

---

[9] The Shirelles' "Will You Love Me Tomorrow" and The Drifters' "Save the Last Dance for Me" both ranked high enough to be included here. They were mentioned earlier.

"My heart was breaking, which one would it be?" he bellows. "You turned around and walked away with me." As the song fades, someone is running scared. But it's not Roy Orbison.

# Lowlights

1. **"Itsy Bitsy Teenie Weenie Yellow Polka Dot Bikini" by Brian Hyland (August 8, 1960)**—Earlier, I said at least eight narrative-based songs were about death. This is arguably the ninth. It's about a girl who is embarrassed by the yellow polka dot bikini she is wearing and runs from place to place to stay covered up. She starts in a changing room, then runs to a blanket, and then into the water. While in the water, she's described as "turning blue" before the final line declares that there isn't anywhere else for her to go. Call me crazy, but I think this irritating song is more sinister than it seems.

2. **"The Battle of New Orleans" by Johnny Horton (June 1, 1960)**—Jimmy Driftwood, an Arkansan educator, wrote this song to pique his students' interest in American history. It must have worked. The composition went on to win Song of the Year at the Grammys in 1960 after being popularized by Johnny Horton. As some of President Andrew Jackson's exploits have become widely recognized as horrific (e.g., Indian Removal Act), hearing about his military triumphs set to a rollicking banjo isn't something your average person would voluntarily subject themselves to.

3. **"Moody River" by Pat Boone (June 19, 1961)**—Written about a girl who drowns herself out of shame for her infidelity, "Moody River" fits squarely within the teenage tragedy tradition. Sort of. The lyrics of "Moody River" do tell of a tragedy, but the music does not. The arrangement is built around a piano that lives at the intersection of cheery and jangly. There is no law dictating that music and lyrics align, but having those two things at odds in this song makes the narrator sound more like a sociopath than a high schooler experiencing unspeakable trauma.

## Argument Starters

I've developed a metric to measure which songs sparked the most disagreement among the three judges.[10] This era's crown was worn by Mark Dinning's aforementioned "Teen Angel." Again, "Teen Angel" is a teenage tragedy song. In his book *Death Discs*, Alan Clayson describes songs of this type as "ridiculously sentimental, frequently corny but nearly always completely sincere." Your opinion of "Teen Angel" comes down to whether you think the sincerity overrides the sentimental corniness. If so, then it's a soul-crushing dirge. If not, then it's unlistenable dreck. I fall into the latter camp.

## Odds and Ends

This is a space for me to call out some songs that didn't make it into the body of the text. It doesn't mean they are good or bad, though. I just think they are noteworthy for some reason. Like *Highlights* and *Lowlights*, I will keep this to three songs.

1. **"To Know Him is to Love Him" by The Teddy Bears (December 1, 1958)**—A vocal trio composed of Marshall Leib, Annette Kleinbard, and Phil Spector, The Teddy Bears would spawn an odd array of musical careers despite not lasting much longer than their lone number one hit. Leib would go on to work as record executive. Kleinbard would soon take the name Carol Connors and become an Oscar-nominated lyricist. Spector would outstrip the two in both fame and infamy, though.

   After establishing himself as one of the most successful and respected producers of the 1960s, Spector became increasingly reclusive. After decades of allegations of abuse by his collaborators, he was convicted of murdering actress Lana Clarkson in 2003. He died in prison in 2021, a shell of the precocious young man who once took his father's epitaph (i.e., "To Know Him Was to Love Him") and turned it into a gentle love song. More on him in the next chapter.

---

[10] Nerd alert: This metric is calculated as the average absolute pairwise distance among each judge's rating.

2. **"Come Softly to Me" by The Fleetwoods (April 13, 1959)**—The reason that you might miss "Come Softly to Me" is the same reason you'll remember it. It's quiet, the trio barely whispering over a gentle bass and guitar. But if your ears can latch onto that quiet beauty, you will be entranced, soon wishing every band would turn the volume down a few decibels.

3. **"Cathy's Clown" by The Everly Brothers (May 23, 1960)**—"It is the *sound* of 'Cathy's Clown' that is so gripping," Daniel J. Levitin wrote for the Library of Congress when The Everly Brothers' classic was named to the National Recording Registry. And he is correct. While the composition itself is fantastic—the refrain "There he goes, he's Cathy's clown" containing the devastation of a Greek tragedy—it is the details and sonic quality of that performance that raise "Cathy's Clown" above the lot.

   Listen to the duo's vocals drift apart as they hang onto the word "love." Listen to the short guitar arpeggio at the end of the chorus as they sing "I die each time I hear this sound." Listen to the difference in atmosphere around the stately snare and flavorful cymbal work on the chorus and verse, respectively. These details are why Levitin describes "Cathy's Clown" as "a line of demarcation for the increasingly important role that timbre (tonal color) would play in the 20th and 21st century popular music."

## Everything Else

This is where I'll chronologically list all the other number ones that still haven't been mentioned, albeit without the date they first topped the charts. Please note that even though they don't make it into the body of the text, these songs are still included in the data that peppers each chapter. Furthermore, the songs aren't worth disregarding. Some are quite good. But your time is valuable, and I have a word count to stay under.

"It's Only Make Believe" by Conway Twitty. "The Chipmunk Song" by The Chipmunks. "Venus" by Frankie Avalon. "Why" by Frankie Avalon. "Everybody's Somebody's Fool" by Connie Francis. "My Heart Has A Mind of Its Own" by Connie Francis. "Mother-in-Law" by Ernie K-Doe.

# Meet Me at Quarter to Three with Your Sugar Pie

## June 26, 1961—June 19, 1965

### There Isn't an Ocean Too Deep

The other day I was talking to a friend about this book, and he expressed concern that number ones were too fluky a category of songs to draw conclusions from. He thought that I needed a larger sample of songs if I wanted to say anything substantive about popular music.

This made me question the entire premise of this project. Throughout the first chapter, I used the number ones to make broader claims about the state of American popular music. But if number ones aren't representative of popular music, then I shouldn't be using them to do that.

But the more I thought about it, the more I disagreed. Yes, there are number ones that my friend's claim applied to. Take Roy Orbison's "Running Scared" (1961) as an example. "Running Scared" wasn't part of some larger movement. It's more indebted to classical music and opera than anything that was bubbling on the charts at the time. In other words, its success was sort of a fluke. So was The Tornados' "Telstar" (December 22, 1962). Experimental instrumentals that sound like you're hurtling through space in a cartoonish future weren't getting to number one regularly in the 1960s.[1] Nevertheless, I do believe that

---

[1] Though these sounds were not topping the charts often, they weren't produced in a vacuum. The brainchild of Joe Meek, an inventive but troubled producer who would later die in a murder-suicide,

*Billboard* number ones are usually instances of larger trends. I'll illustrate this with my "High-Tide/Low-Tide Theory of Popular Music."

## The High-Tide/Low-Tide Theory of Popular Music

Imagine that songs float in the middle of the ocean. There are a few brave sailors that venture into the sea in search of novel sounds, but most people only become aware of music as it gets closer to the shore. And while certain songs catch rogue waves and ride them in alone (e.g., "Telstar"), most similar songs journey in groups as the tide rises and falls. Thus, if a song in a certain style makes it all the way to land, the sea is usually littered with similar songs. Furthermore, if a song in a certain style makes it to shore, it was usually preceded by similar songs that the tide had dragged toward the beachgoers. The tide will then go out and bring certain genres back to the distant sonic whirlpool in the middle of the ocean. We can see this idea more concretely by looking at surf rock.

Surf rock is a subgenre of rock music that grew out of southern California beach culture in the late 1950s. While today it's associated with the doo-wop-infused rock 'n' roll of The Beach Boys,[2] it started as an instrumental genre characterized by reverb-soaked guitar that approximated the crashing of waves. Dick Dale remains the seminal figure in instrumental surf rock; his machine-gun riffs heard on classics like "Miserlou" undulating with such fury that you can almost smell the salt of the sea.

Dale brought surf rock to the national scene when his song "Let's Go Trippin'" entered the Hot 100 on November 25, 1961, eventually peaking at number 67. After "Let's Go Trippin'" caught a small swell, an onslaught of surf-related songs found their way onto the charts. In December 1961, The Marketts' instrumental "Surfer's Stomp" made it to number 31. Not long after, The Beach Boys charted "Surfin' Safari" and "Surfin' U.S.A." at numbers 14 and

---

"Telstar" was part of a short-lived style sometimes dubbed "space age pop" that used new audio technology to construct futuristic sounds.

[2] Dennis Wilson was the only member of The Beach Boys that actually surfed. He drowned to death.

three, respectively. Finally, "Surf City" by Jan and Dean made it all the way to number one on July 20, 1963.

While no other surf rocker found its way to the top of the charts, 13 songs with "surf" in their title or by an artist whose name contained the word would crack the Hot 100 in 1963 alone. But by 1965, the style was effectively dead. In summary, though it may have been a fluke that "Surf City" was the only surf rock song to reach number one, it was indicative of a larger style. This characterizes most chart-toppers.

## The Fluky-ness of Number Two Hits

I want to take a moment to acknowledge that this book is not trying to tell a complete history of popular music. That should be obvious, given that the Hot 100 started in 1958. But I think a song from this era will clarify my point: "Sugar Shack" by Jimmy Gilmer and the Fireballs (October 12, 1963).

"Sugar Shack" is a doubly egregious number one. First, it's painful to listen to. Built around a keyboard line that could give you ear damage, it tells the strange tale of a "crazy little shack beyond the tracks" that serves mighty good

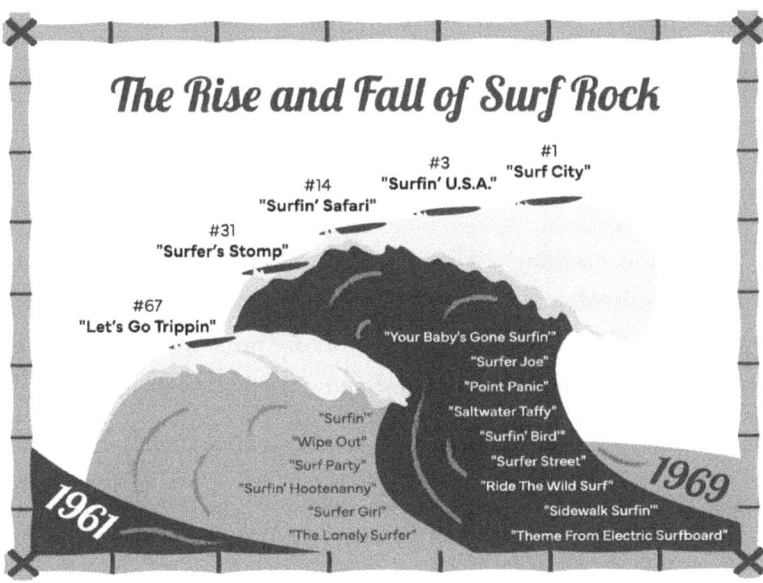

Figure 2.1

espresso. The narrator meets a "cute little girlie" employed by the shop and falls in love with her. Though they get married, they long to return to that sweet sugar shack.

Secondly, during its five-week run atop the charts, it prevented "Be My Baby" by The Ronettes from making it to number one. Unlike "Sugar Shack," "Be My Baby" is such a masterpiece that Brian Wilson of The Beach Boys described it to *The New York Times* in 2013 as "the greatest record ever produced." Its opening *boom boom-boom pow* drumbeat has been quoted in hundreds of other songs, and it might be the quintessential example of Phil Spector's "wall of sound" production style.[3]

So, yes, I'm happy to admit that it's a fluke that "Sugar Shack" wasn't only a five-week number one but also the best-selling song of 1963. But would I be remiss not to mention "Be My Baby"? No. While it's a seminal piece of popular music, I am not here to catalog the entirety of such. I'm here to tease out the trends that the number ones highlight.

If "Be My Baby" summited the charts, I might have written more about the production process of Phil Spector. But since it didn't, and "Sugar Shack" did, I'll probably talk about how popular music between June 26, 1961, and June 19, 1965, was bursting with syrupy joy. Neither discussion is wrong. They are both just incomplete. And I'm okay with that. But before we treat ourselves to that discussion, let's talk about something else: death.

## I Love You, I Will to the End

Death? Yes, death. It's time to talk about the great equalizer. Again. I know you might be all death-ed out from the teenage tragedy song talk in Chapter 1. But this time, we're going to use the term a bit more broadly. We'll talk about one actual death, namely that of John F. Kennedy. We'll also talk about a figurative

---

[3] We mentioned Phil Spector at the end of the last chapter. Initially part of the group that topped the charts with "To Know Him Is to Love Him" (1958), Spector soon traded the stage for the studio, in turn becoming one of the most influential producers of the 1960s. His "wall of sound" style—best exemplified by "Be My Baby" and The Righteous Brothers' "You've Lost That Lovin' Feelin'" (February 6, 1965)—saw him create dense, orchestral records that he described as "a Wagnerian approach to rock 'n' roll: little symphonies for the kids."

death, namely that of a musical style. But our third "death" isn't really a death. It's how songs end. But pretend song endings are deaths for these next few pages. I don't think you'll have too much trouble with that. If you're reading this book, you probably agree that when a song is as good as something like "Where Did Our Love Go" by The Supremes (August 22, 1964), then grief is the appropriate feeling when it's over.

## The Death of the Instrumental

In the first era, there were five instrumentals across 53 songs. If this pace continued, we would expect to see eight instrumentals in this era. We didn't. In addition to "Telstar," there were two others: Mr. Acker Bilk's clarinet-driven dream "Stranger on the Shore" (May 26, 1962) and David Rose's burlesque romp "The Stripper" (July 7, 1962). In many ways, "The Stripper" is the instrumental's death knell, a sexy vestige of the bygone big-band era. That's not to say we won't see other instrumentals top the charts. But other than a few times during the 1970s, they will be less clustered.

I wanted to look back to the past to see how prevalent non-vocal music once was. To do this, I gathered the number ones that topped *Billboard*'s National Best Selling Retail Records chart between July 1940 and July 1958. As I mentioned in Chapter 1, the Hot 100 did not exist before August 1958. So, the National Best Selling Retail Records chart is the best resource to get a handle on this earlier era.[4] While I could simply count the instrumentals in this period—there were 16—that wouldn't tell the full story. Jimmy Dorsey's "Blue Champagne" is a good example as to why.

"Blue Champagne" was a single-week chart-leader in September 1941. While the song is not an instrumental, 60 percent of it has no vocals. To account for music like this, I dusted off an old stopwatch and timed the instrumental

---

[4] Unless otherwise noted, anytime I mention number ones after August 1958, I am talking about number ones on the Hot 100. Anytime I mention number ones before August 1958, I am talking about number ones on the National Best Selling Retail Records chart.

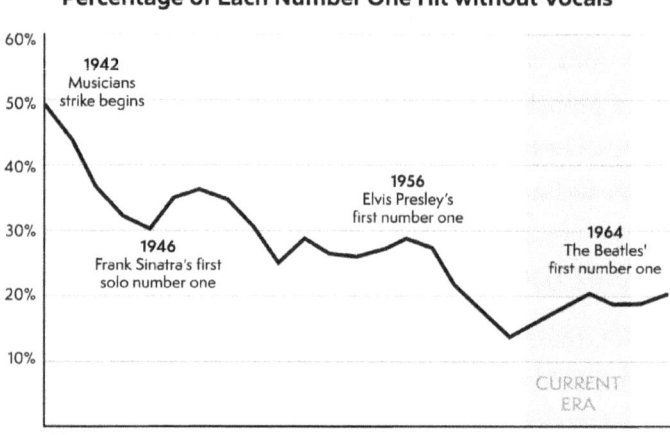

**Figure 2.2**

sections of each *Billboard* number one from July 1940 through the end of this era. The results are displayed in Figure 2.2.[5]

During the 1940s, 37 percent of your average number one hit was vocal-free, meaning that for every minute of music you heard, about 22 seconds contained no vocals. That non-vocal music level would begin dipping in the early 1950s before taking a nosedive between 1958 and 1960. From 1962 to the end of this era, 19 percent of your average number one hit was vocal-free. That decline signifies a fundamental change in the music that we listen to. As instrumentalists faded into the background, vocalists became the stars. Let's understand this reversal.

Between the beginning of the Hot 100 (i.e., August 4, 1958) and June 19, 1965, 104 artists reached the top of the Hot 100. If we ignore the eight artists who had instrumental chart-toppers and Manfred Mann—the keyboardist namesake of the band behind "Do Wah Diddy Diddy" (October 17, 1964)— every other artist is identified by one of the following: a group name (e.g.,

---

[5] Nerd alert: Unless specified otherwise, every line chart in this book shows a three-year moving average. This means that the value of the line in 1963, for example, represents the average across 1961, 1962, and 1963. Similarly, the value of the line in 1964, represents the average across 1962, 1963, and 1964. I used this methodology because it makes trends a bit clearer.

"Easier Said Than Done" by The Essex (July 6, 1963)), the lead singer's name (e.g., "Tossin' and Turnin'" by Bobby Lewis (July 10, 1961)), or both (e.g., "Our Day Will Come" by Ruby and the Romantics (March 23, 1963)). This stands in contrast to the artist names in the 1940s.

Moments ago, I mentioned Jimmy Dorsey's "Blue Champagne." While vocals on the track were handled by Bob Eberly, nobody would call it Eberly's song. It was Jimmy Dorsey's song. It was Jimmy Dorsey's band. And Jimmy Dorsey didn't sing. He played the clarinet and saxophone.

This is not unique. Of the songs that topped the charts between 1940 and 1945, 72 percent had a lead artist who wasn't a singer. Tommy Dorsey was a trombonist. Artie Shaw was a clarinetist. Harry James was a trumpet player. But this world didn't last. The vocalist would soon take center stage. Why?

First, The Second World War raged throughout the 1940s. Over 400,000 Americans, and tens of millions globally, were killed in the conflict. Some that died were musicians. And I'm not just talking about unknown tuba players. I'm talking about stars. Take Glenn Miller as an example. The trombonist and bandleader had seven songs top the charts between 1941 and 1943 before he went missing in action while entertaining troops overseas during the conflict. With musicians' careers derailed or ended by the war, a new flock of stars was able to take over.

Those that were now in the spotlight were also standing there with cutting-edge microphone and amplification technology. In a world before those two things, it was hard for an audience to hear what someone was singing, especially if they were competing with the roar of an orchestra. This new technology not only made it easier for vocalists to share the stage with bombastic brass and wind instruments, but it also made it possible to develop new vocal stylings, like the intimate croons of Frank Sinatra and Bing Crosby.

Amplification wasn't only good for the vocalist, though. It was also good for some other instruments, like the guitar. While some big bands of the 1930s had guitar players, an acoustic guitar or a poorly amplified guitar was easily drowned out by those same orchestras that were overpowering vocalists. Thus, amplification allowed the guitar to bust out beyond the solo, acoustic contexts it was often associated with at the turn of the twentieth century. Additionally, unlike brass and wind instruments, guitarists can sing while they play. That's why the rise of the electric guitar, rock music, and vocal star are all intimately connected.

Beyond these improvements, the 1942 musicians' strike also proved a subtle influence on this transition. Between August 1942 and November 1944, James C. Petrillo, the zealous head of the American Federation of Musicians (AFM), the largest musical labor union in the United States, organized a work stoppage. Petrillo was worried that the growing popularity of records, radio, and jukeboxes would lead to fewer lucrative live performances. Against the odds, the biggest labels eventually met the AFM's demands, but by the time they did, there had been some unexpected consequences for vocalists.

Vocalists were not eligible to be members of the AFM. Along with reissuing old songs and releasing a backlog of new songs, labels used this fact to fight back against the recording ban. For example, during this period, there were some popular songs recorded a cappella, like Dinah Shore's "I'll Walk Alone." By the time the strike was over, bandleaders no longer got top billing. Vocalists did. A new era was upon us.

## The Death of John F. Kennedy

On November 22, 1963, President John F. Kennedy was assassinated in Dallas, Texas. For many, Kennedy—a man brimming with charisma—was a symbol of hope. Whether you believed his message or not, his murder left every American shocked. In the world of pop music, the story that is frequently told is that in the wake of this national tragedy, four Kennedy-level-charismatic, mop-topped Liverpudlians crossed the Atlantic with their jangling guitars and Everly Brothers-esque harmonies and pulled America from its widespread melancholy. Yes, I'm talking about The Beatles. If this tale is correct, then The Beatles' early success was partly a function of timing equal parts grim and great.

Before diving into this claim, I want to start with a qualification. I love The Beatles. I've nearly always loved them. In fact, my mother sang me "Eight Days a Week" (March 13, 1965) as a lullaby, so this infatuation is quite ingrained.[6]

---

[6] When she would sing the same song to my sisters, they told her to stop. So, Beatles fandom doesn't come naturally to everyone.

But this book is not about The Beatles. It's about numbers and number one hits. And though The Beatles did top the charts an absurd number of times, I refuse to turn this into a John-Paul-George-Ringo hagiography. Thus, when writing about them, I will try to take the attitude that John Lennon voices in a sound bite on The Beatles' retrospective *Anthology*: "We were just a band who made it very, very big. That's all."

Still, The Beatles were quite popular. Unprecedentedly so. You can see that with some wild facts about their success in 1964.

- Songs written by John Lennon and Paul McCartney occupied the top of the charts in 38 percent of weeks.

- On April 4, 1964, The Beatles locked down the first five positions of the Hot 100 with "Can't Buy Me Love" (April 4, 1963), "Twist And Shout," "She Loves You" (March 21, 1964), "I Want To Hold Your Hand" (February 1, 1964), and "Please Please Me."

- Two songs *about* The Beatles—"We Love You Beatles" by The Carefrees and "A Letter to The Beatles" by The Four Preps—snuck their way onto the charts.

- At the end of the year, Lorne Greene topped the charts with "Ringo" (December 5, 1964), an outlaw saga whose titular character shares a name with The Beatles' drummer Ringo Starr.[7]

Now that we have some grasp on The Beatles' popularity, let's get back to this Kennedy-Beatles narrative and why it's bogus. When The Beatles came to the United States, they were already moving millions of units in the United Kingdom and beginning to get more press stateside. *The New York Times*, for example, first wrote about them on November 4, 1963. *Time* did a piece eleven days later. NBC covered them three days after that. Still, you might argue that The Beatles had released a couple of songs in the United States to little acclaim

---

[7] This song had nothing to do with Ringo Starr. It's about an outlaw named Johnny Ringo. While I'm sure many teens bought the tune thinking it was about Starr, it wasn't unprecedented for songs like "Ringo" to top the charts. Three years earlier, Jimmy Dean sent the similar "Big Bad John" (November 6, 1961) to number one. Both are spoken-word narratives about the death of a mythic figure that build tension with related key changes.

earlier in 1963. None of those caught on until after the president was killed. "It was no accident," critic Lester Bangs wrote in *The Rolling Stone Illustrated History of Rock and Roll*, "that the Beatles had their overwhelmingly successful *Ed Sullivan Show* debut shortly after JFK was shot."

Again, nice theory, but it doesn't stand up to scrutiny. The Beatles' singles released in the United States in early 1963 were put out by tiny labels because Capitol Records, the American partner of their label at home, had little interest in them. When The Beatles' manager, Brian Epstein, finally convinced Capitol to promote "I Want To Hold Your Hand" shortly after Kennedy's death, it was backed by a large budget and a swell of interest in the band by young fans and stodgy newsmen. Beatlemania was coming to the United States no matter who was in the White House. I think Kennedy's death did impact popular musicians, though. It just wasn't British rockers. It was a Belgian nun.

Jeanne-Paule Marie Deckers was a member of the Catholic Dominican Order, born in 1933. As a form of entertainment, Deckers would write and perform folk songs for her fellow sisters. With the approval of her superiors, she approached Philips Records to see if the convent could pay to have some recordings pressed. The label demurred, but Deckers wasn't to be discouraged. A few months later, they changed their tune after hearing some of her songs. Billing her as Sœur Sourire, or The Singing Nun, her self-titled album sold millions of copies backed by the single "Dominique" (December 7, 1963), a simple acoustic number that tells the story of the pious St. Dominic.

I can't claim that "Dominique" would have been some obscure record in America without Kennedy's death. It had entered the Hot 100 in the United States two weeks before his assassination. But it seems a bit coincidental that in the wake of the murder of the first Catholic president that a gentle song by a Catholic nun about a Catholic saint would make it to number one. W. J. Rorabaugh notes as much in his book *Kennedy and the Promise of the Sixties*: "Although few Americans could follow the lyrics, the beautiful melodies were not an inappropriate form of mourning for a Catholic president and his francophone wife."

While this claim may seem similar to the claim about The Beatles, it's smaller in scope. I simply think that JFK's death helped "Dominique" make the final push to the top of the charts. And that push is no easy task. During

The Singing Nun's run at number one, she held off The Kingsmen's garage rock classic "Louie Louie" from reaching the musical promised land. Sure, big budgets and sex appeal are a tried-and-true ways to sell a pop song, but sometimes it helps to have God on your side.

## The Death of a Song . . . Okay, We're Talking About Fade Outs

When people talk about hit songs, they often talk about one of a few things: chords, melody, lyrics, and production. But songs have other qualities that are so implicit that we rarely think about them. Take the length of a song as an example. "Stay" (1960) by Maurice Williams and the Zodiacs is effective because it runs less than two minutes long. It only makes sense that a song beckoning a lover to "stay just a little bit longer" would end sooner than the listener wanted.

I think song endings work in the same way. We don't think about them too often, but they are a vital piece of what makes a song tick. Within both eras thus far, the most popular way to end a song—occurring about 55 percent of the time—is the fade out. And that's too bad. I hate the fade out.

Take a song like "Come See About Me" by The Supremes (December 19, 1964) as an example. From the subtle vibraphone accents to the brief saxophone solo, each element of this track was crafted and recorded with great care. Then you get to the end, and it's as if the geniuses at Motown faded the song out so they could get an early dinner. It's an unsatisfactory exit. Most of the time, at least.

Occasionally, the fade out makes sense. Take Gary U.S. Bonds' party-starting "Quarter to Three" (June 26, 1961) as an example. This is a fuzzy, scuzzy record that distills an all-night get-together into a swinging two-and-a-half minutes. The fade out works because a party like the one Gary U.S. Bonds is singing about never really ends. It fades into your memory in a nostalgia-soaked haze.

The fade out also works on Frankie Valli and the Four Seasons' "Rag Doll" (July 18, 1964), a song that tells the sad tale of a love broken up by socioeconomic class. Everything on this record is shaking. The lead vocal quavers. The guitars oscillate. The snare hits are a bit off-kilter. At the end, Valli's voice soars in falsetto. It feels like he's walking the streets alone, wishing things could change but knowing they never will. The fade out works because a pain like that endures. In fact, that's what fade outs do best. They signify an endlessness. If the song isn't trying to do that, the fade out starts to feel like a cop-out.

I would be remiss not to acknowledge that the prevalence of the fade out in this era is partially connected to two things beyond the control of artists and producers: radio programming formats and the technical constraints of vinyl records. First, radio stations were skeptical of longer songs because every additional minute of music meant less time for advertisements. Second, as mentioned in the last chapter, vinyl records—and all physical media for that matter—can only hold so much sound. The 7-inch, this era's most popular single format, could fit around four minutes of high-fidelity music per side. So, even if radio stations were drawn to the eight-minute epic you wrote, there wasn't anything you could sell it on. Your best option was to fade the single out early and leave the full rendition for the album.

The Animals had to do that when they released "House of the Rising Sun" (September 5, 1964). The four-and-a-half-minute run-time was pushing the limits of both the 7-inch single and commercial radio customs. Rather than getting the haunting ending that grinds to a halt on the album, the first pressing of the single fades out around the three-minute mark as Eric Burdon howls over a pulsing organ.

If you ever insist on recording a song with a fade out, all I ask is that you do it with the deliberateness of something like The Beatles' "A Hard Day's Night" (August 1, 1964). After a rapturous opening chord, the band works through three verses and a bridge before launching into a short, suggestive guitar solo. After another bridge and verse, John Lennon repeats, "You know I feel alright" twice before the guitars fade out in a blissful, relaxed loop, two lovers coming down from their high. That's a lofty benchmark, but writing songs is a serious business, sometimes as serious as death itself.

## We're So Happy and That's How We're Gonna Stay

After all this talk of death and destruction and endings, you might think that nothing joyous was going on in American popular music at this time. You would be wrong. As I noted earlier, I was struck by the cheer of a large majority of number ones in this era. On top of that, I was excited by the diversity we were beginning to see. White American men still dominated the top of the charts, but there was a surge of artists who were Black, women, and non-Americans winning over the ears of the record-buying public.

## Music That Makes You Feel Good

I was out to eat with George O'Har, an author and English professor from my alma mater, and he told me, "I find myself listening to mostly Latin music these days because American pop music is so depressing. Pop music is supposed to bring people together and make you feel good." While you'll hear more about twenty-first century pop in Chapter 12, I think O'Har's opinion was shaped by the gleeful music of this era. I attribute this glee to love songs, cheerful arrangements masking depressing lyrics, and an assortment of handclaps, snaps, and stomps.

In our first era, only 6 percent of number ones utilize handclaps to fill out the percussion arrangement. In this era, 28 percent do. Since most people can clap, when they are used in an arrangement, they make it feel like you're surrounded by friends enjoying music together.[8] In a certain sense, there's nothing more uplifting than two hands being smashed together at a regular interval.

Beyond anecdotal evidence, we can see the joy of handclaps with data from Spotify. To power its algorithmic curation, Spotify gives every song a happiness score between 0 and 100. While you can find some examples of this metric being wrong—like The Tymes' heart-warming "So Much in Love" (August 3, 1963) being rated as less happy than Bobby Vinton's maudlin "Roses are Red (My Love)" (July 14, 1962)—it's typically spot on. Using this metric, we see that songs in this era without handclaps average a happiness score of 66, while songs with them average a score of 79, over 19 percent higher.

---

[8] Like I'm not actually sitting alone in my bedroom being empowered by The Angels' fierce, clap-laden "My Boyfriend's Back" (August 31, 1963).

On top of songs with handclaps, we also see a glut of songs about love. From era one to era two, the share of love-related songs increased from 66 percent to 80 percent. While this love-related category also includes songs about break-ups (e.g., "Baby Love" by The Supremes (October 31, 1964)), many of these break-up songs—about 63 percent, if you can trust my ears—are disguised by cheery arrangements. Take Neil Sedaka's "Breaking Up Is Hard to Do" (August 11, 1962) as an example.

Though Sedaka is begging his lover to stay with him throughout this track, you wouldn't know it. The doo-wopping *down-dooby-doo-down-down* back-up vocals, handclaps, and snaps make it feel like a celebration. Many other songs in this era display the same lyrical-musical confusion. It's this confusion that allows glee to permeate a larger sample of songs than the lyrical content would initially suggest.

## Music That Makes You Feel Included

While I was gathering the data that powered the earlier section about the decline of instrumentals, I thought it would also be interesting to build a simple demographic profile of each artist that topped the charts.

Using obituaries, interviews, and Wikipedia, I categorized each chart-topping artist's race and gender. Racial categories only included "White," "Black," and "Other," each of which was defined according to the US Census Bureau. "White" meant the artist was descended from "any of the original peoples of Europe, the Middle East, or North Africa." "Black" meant the artist was descended from people "having origins in any of the Black racial groups of Africa." Finally, "Other" was a catchall for peoples of the rest of the Earth. I used this catchall because racial groups that weren't White or Black had little to no presence atop the charts through this era.

Imperfect methodology? Sure. Notions of race and gender have shifted substantially over the years. Plus, things can get distorted when you reduce complex identities to binary categories. But even with these issues in mind, the data still presents an illuminating picture of the evolving demography of the most popular musical artists.

In Figure 2.3, you'll notice that Black artists very rarely topped the charts before 1960. More specifically, between 1940 and 1958, only 6.9 percent of number one hits on *Billboard*'s National Best Selling Retail Records chart were by Black artists. As we'll see in Chapter 6, this was to no fault of their own. From the dawn of recording, Black musicians were either ignored or prevented from releasing music. It wasn't until the 1920s that early record labels realized that there was a market for music made by Black musicians. Labels, often run by White executives, started marketing this music to Black people under the moniker "race records." Despite limited budgets, the music crossed over with White audiences and the term "race records" was replaced with "Rhythm & Blues," eventually shortened to "R&B."

Though by the early 1960s a slew of labels were recording and marketing Black artists with fervor, the success of a fledgling label helped lift those artists to even greater heights: Motown. Founded by Berry Gordy in 1959, the label took its name and inspiration from the Motor City, the nickname for Gordy's hometown of Detroit, as they pumped out pop smashes from their Hitsville US headquarters like cars on an assembly line.

Gordy was both a talented songwriter and businessman. He cowrote some of Motown's early hits and sought to make the label a self-sufficient entity,

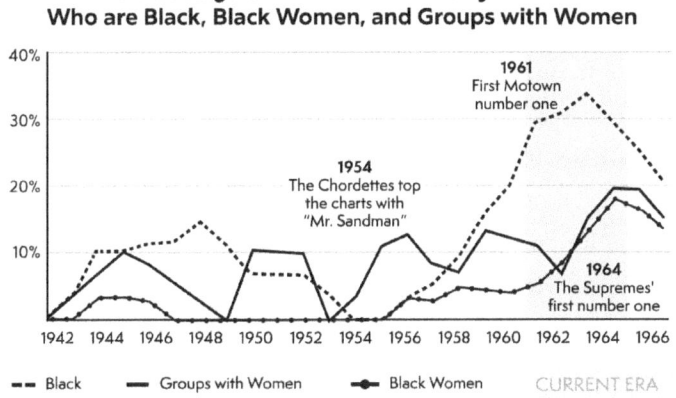

Figure 2.3

handling writing, recording, marketing, and publishing for every act on his roster. In 1960, Motown had its first million-seller with The Miracles' "Shop Around." A year later, they hit number one with The Marvelettes' infectious "Please Mr. Postman" (December 11, 1961). From there, they couldn't be stopped, topping the charts nine more times before the end of this era. Of the six Motown acts behind those chart-toppers, all were Black and half were women.

This brings up an important point. Though much of Motown's early history is focused on the men who wrote the songs and had powerful positions at the label, women were vital in turning it into a musical powerhouse. Many of Motown's early successes, like The Supremes, Marvelettes, Vandellas, and Velvelettes, were groups of women. And Gordy wasn't afraid to put women in important business roles. His four sisters and then-wife worked in notable roles at the company, and certain departments—like quality control, the department that selected which recordings to release—were headed by women.

Motown's focus on women-fronted groups was part of a larger trend, though. While solo women vocalists have always had a degree of prominence since the dawn of recorded music, women-fronted groups became more common during the 1940s and 1950s with popular acts like The Andrews Sisters, The Bobbettes, The Chantels, and The Chordettes. Along with Motown, other labels jumped on this girl group bandwagon.

After climbing the charts with "Will You Love Me Tomorrow" (1961), The Shirelles got to number one in this era with "Soldier Boy" (May 5, 1962), another song released on Scepter Records, one of the few labels run by a woman, in this case, Florence Greenberg. Laurie Records, a small label that was also home to Dion DiMucci and his swinging, hey-hey-bum-da-hey-da-hey-da-singing "Runaround Sue" (October 23, 1961), scored a number one with The Chiffons' "He's So Fine" (March 30, 1963). Red Bird, a short-lived label founded by legendary songwriters Jerry Leiber and Mike Stoller, also topped the charts with The Dixie Cups' wedding-day classic "Chapel of Love" (June 6, 1964).

These groups, along with the stable of Motown stars, were undeniable proof that Americans were willing to listen to artists across race and gender. That's not to say that Black artists didn't face racism. In his autobiography, Berry Gordy recalled how a Motown tour bus was shot at while driving in Alabama in the early 1960s. Martha Reeves also noted in a 2011 interview with NPR that her group the Vandellas weren't pictured on their debut album out of fear that DJs wouldn't play their songs had they known the group was composed of Black women. Still, as the civil rights movement resulted in tangible gains for Black citizens, it was clear that attitudes were shifting, and artists atop the charts were not only a reflection of that but also an influence on it.

Outside of girl groups, we also saw non-Americans top the charts more frequently in this era. In the first era, we only saw two songs by non-American artists reach number one: "Nel Blu Dipinto Di Blu" (1958) by Italian crooner Domenico Modugno and "Wonderland by Night" (1961) by German bandleader Bert Kaempfert. In this era, we saw 19. Though this was mostly driven by the British Invasion, we also saw the melodically gorgeous "Sukiyaki" by Japanese artist Kyu Sakamoto (June 15, 1963) and the aforementioned "Dominique" by the Belgian Singing Nun top the charts. Thus, in under 20 years since the end of the Second World War, songs by artists from all three Axis powers won over American ears.

# I've Got Sunshine on a Cloudy Day

When I started getting into the history of popular music in the 2000s, one thing that was expressed to me was that everything began with The Beatles. Over the first two chapters of this book, I've taken great pains to show how that isn't true. There was a rich musical world before The Beatles picked up their instruments, so rich that it was able to inspire much of what they did.

Nevertheless, it would be misleading if I acted like The Beatles, the British Invasion, and 1964 generally did not signal a sea change in popular music. In fact, when The Beatles' "I Want To Hold Your Hand" unseated Bobby Vinton's sentimental "There! I've Said It Again" (January 4, 1964) from the top of the charts, you could almost feel a rip in the spacetime continuum. Critic Ian MacDonald wrote of this moment, "Every American artist, black or white, asked about 'I Want to Hold Your Hand' has said much the same: It altered everything, ushering in a new era and changing their lives." Listening to the number ones, you can see what MacDonald is saying. During the rest of 1964, it's as if the old world and the new world were wrestling with one another.

After 13 weeks at number one, The Beatles were replaced at the top of the charts by a 62-year-old Louis Armstrong singing "Hello, Dolly!" (May 9, 1964), a vaudeville-inspired showtune. A few months later, The Beatles were again displaced at number one by another old-timer: Dean Martin. The 47-year-old singer took his waltzing, schmaltzing "Everybody Loves Somebody" (August 15, 1964) to the top of the charts for one week. With Motown and The Beatles and Phil Spector and The Beach Boys firing on all cylinders at the same time, 1964 was a banner year for popular music. But as with every era, the highest highs were paired with dismal lows.

## Highlights

1. **"My Girl" by The Temptations (March 6, 1965)**[9]—When Smokey Robinson wrote "My Guy" for Mary Wells (May 16, 1964), I imagine he thought he'd never write a better song. "My Guy" is just so expertly crafted that burgeoning songwriters should study it. But then a year later, he decided to write a response to "My Guy" for The Temptations. Response songs were very common during the 1960s. Chubby Checker hits it big with "The Twist" (1960). Joey Dee jumps on the bandwagon with the "Peppermint Twist" (June 27, 1962).[10] Only one name made sense for Smokey's response: "My Girl."

   "My Girl" is not just the greatest response song of all time, it might be the greatest song period. I'd go so far as to argue that if a random DJ in the twenty-first century cut off whatever booty-shaking track they were playing at the club on Friday night and put on "My Girl," nobody

---

[9] Both "A Hard Day's Night" and "I Want To Hold Your Hand" by The Beatles were rated high enough to be included here. I mentioned them earlier.

[10] Joey Dee was backed by a group called The Starliters. They are certainly the only group to have had both future rockstar Jimi Hendrix and actor Joe Pesci as members at one time. Neither was involved with this track, though.

would complain. Decades later, the ascending guitar riff and finger-snapping rhythm that drive this track remain as fresh as ever.

2. **"Ticket to Ride" by The Beatles (May 22, 1965)**—The Beatles' most miraculous skill might be how they could smash together disparate styles. That skill is on full display in "Ticket to Ride." The verses are a jangling pop song with a droning guitar note throughout, reminiscent of an Indian raga. The bridge is strait-laced rock 'n' roll. The outro is a country and western hootenanny with a looping, falsetto vocal. You wouldn't notice these stylistic differences without paying close attention, though. The Fab Four make them sound like they've always gone together.

3. **"He's a Rebel" by The Crystals (November 3, 1962)**—The music industry has been filled with shady characters since its inception. "He's a Rebel" is a good example of this because, despite what every copy of the record says, it's not actually by The Crystals. The Crystals were on tour when Phil Spector decided that he wanted to record the song. So, he brought in a different group called The Blossoms to do it. The Crystals had no idea until they heard it on the radio. Because of a questionable contract, Spector was able to use their name without their consent.

    Even through all that trickery and deception, there's no denying that "He's a Rebel" is a musical achievement. When the song opens, it sounds thin, a circular piano riff barely twinkling over some drums. But somehow when you get to the chorus, the song is humongous, sax-wailing, and voices swirling. I've listened to this song countless times, and I'm still not sure how Spector and "The Crystals" were able to pull it off.

# Lowlights

1. **"Wooden Heart" by Joe Dowell (August 28, 1961)**—This song is a cover of a waltzing German tune that Elvis Presley took to the top of the British charts. I guess the thought process was that if it were a hit for Elvis in the United Kingdom, then somebody in the United States needed to record it. That somebody turned out to be Joe Dowell. While

Dowell's voice is bland, "Wooden Heart" isn't helping him out. It's built around a keyboard that's in a constant struggle with the keyboard from "Sugar Shack" for the most annoying recorded sound in the twentieth century.

2. **"Go Away Little Girl" by Steve Lawrence (January 12, 1963)**—My sister Natalie was walking through the room while I was listening to this song. 27-year-old Steve Lawrence crooning the words "Go away, little girl / I'm not supposed to be alone with you" stopped her dead in her tracks. "Is this by a pedophile?" she asked.

   Despite how creepy that couplet might sound, the lyrics are not anything criminal. The song was composed by Carole King and Gerry Goffin about a man tempted to cheat on his lover. Albeit patronizing, the term "little girl" was common fare in pop songs at the time. In this era alone, it's used in five additional songs, including The Beatles' "I Feel Fine" (December 12, 1964) (e.g., "I'm so glad that she's my little girl") and Tommy Roe's "Sheila" (September 8, 1962) (e.g., "Man this little girl is fine"). But when you need this many words to explain why a creepy-sounding song actually isn't creepy, you're probably not going to have people lining up to listen to it.

3. **"Mrs. Brown, You've Got a Lovely Daughter" by Herman's Hermits (May 1, 1965)**—While the palm-muted guitar on this track does create some interesting texture, any interest you might have in that texture is destroyed by a painfully plain vocal singing about how "it ain't no good to pine" for a girl like Mrs. Brown's daughter.

## Argument Starters

I was shocked that "The Game of Love" by Wayne Fontana and the Mindbenders (April 24, 1965) sparked the most disagreement in this era. I thought it was a fun, bluesy rock record with inventive back-up vocals and silly, sex-infused lyrics. I was the outlier, though. The other judges thought that if you were looking for the sound Wayne Fontana was going for, there were a hundred other places you could turn.

"If you want a bluesy record with a good driving rhythm and dynamite back-up vocals," my friend who rated this song told me, "throw on 'Hit the Road Jack' by Ray Charles (October 9, 1961)." I thought it was a questionable comparison, but you're not going to hear any complaints from me if you put Ray Charles on the turntable.

## Odds and Ends

1. **"Leader of the Pack" by The Shangri-Las (November 28, 1964)**— On many days, The Shangri-Las are my favorite women-led group to emerge from this era. And "Leader of the Pack" is a good example as to why. With spoken dialogue, over-the-top sound effects, and a chugging guitar, this is not only the teenage tragedy songs to end all teenage tragedy songs but an entire movie unfolding in your ears.

2. **"I'm Telling You Now" by Freddie and the Dreamers (April 10, 1965)**—In the wake of "The Twist" (1960), many other songs tried to start dance crazes. "The Jerk." "The Loco-Motion" (August 25, 1962). "The Wah-Watusi." "The Monster Mash" (October 20, 1962).

   The silliest of these crazes was The Freddie, a dance created by the wacky British group Freddie and the Dreamers. To do The Freddie, stand in place and kick your extended legs straight out one after another in rhythm with "I'm Telling You Now." If you don't feel stupid after 30 seconds, I at least hope you're stretched out.

3. **"If You Wanna Be Happy" by Jimmy Soul (April 27, 1963)**—I've heard a lot of crazy lyrics in pop songs, but the craziest might be Jimmy Soul advising that the only way to guarantee a lifetime of happiness is by marrying an ugly woman. If I'm married by the time this book is published, I want to make it clear to my wife that I haven't heeded this advice. You are very beautiful, honey.

## Everything Else

"Michael" by The Highwaymen. "Take Good Care of My Baby" by Bobby Vee. "The Lion Sleeps Tonight" by The Tokens. "Duke of Earl" by Gene Chandler.

"Hey! Baby" by Bruce Channel. "Don't Break the Heart that Loves You" by Connie Francis. "Johnny Angel" by Shelley Fabares. "Good Luck Charm" by Elvis Presley. "I Can't Stop Loving You" by Ray Charles. "Sherry" by Frankie Valli and the Four Seasons. "Big Girls Don't Cry" by Frankie Valli & the Four Seasons. "Walk Right In" by The Rooftop Singers. "Hey Paula" by Paul and Paula. "Walk Like a Man" by Frankie Valli and the Four Seasons. "I Will Follow Him" by Little Peggy March. "It's My Party" by Lesley Gore. "Fingertips Pt. 2" by Stevie Wonder. "Blue Velvet" by Bobby Vinton. "Deep Purple" by Nino Tempo and April Stevens. "I'm Leaving it Up to You" by Dale and Grace. "Love Me Do" by The Beatles. "A World Without Love" by Peter and Gordon. "I Get Around" by The Beach Boys. "Oh, Pretty Woman" by Roy Orbison. "Mr. Lonely" by Bobby Vinton. "Downtown" by Petula Clark. "This Diamond Ring" by Gary Lewis and the Playboys. "Stop! In the Name of Love" by The Supremes. "Help Me, Rhonda" by The Beach Boys. "Back in My Arms Again" by The Supremes. "I Can't Help Myself (Sugar Pie Honey Bunch)" by Four Tops.

# Mr. Tambourine Man and the Raindrops on His Head

## June 26, 1965—January 3, 1970

### He'd Change the World for the Good
### Thing He's Found

People have argued for centuries about who invented calculus: Sir Isaac Newton or Gottfried Leibniz.[1] In truth, the answer is not either one of them but "neither" and "both." "Neither" because mathematicians had discovered ideas reminiscent of calculus before Newton and Leibniz. "Both" because they independently happened upon similar ideas at roughly the same time.

It seems far-fetched that two men in different countries would discover such a difficult discipline at roughly the same time. What's far stranger is that simultaneous, independent discovery, or what sociologist Robert K. Merton termed "multiple discovery," is somewhat common.

Multiple discovery is antithetical to what is sometimes dubbed the "heroic theory of invention," which posits that inventions and ideas are conceived by great individuals. By contrast, multiple discovery argues that the individual was in the right place at the right time. If the mechanism of discovery is more influenced by the environment than some unexpected insight, then we

---

[1] I'm told that litigating a centuries-old debate about calculus is the worst way to keep your readers interested.

shouldn't be surprised to see multiple people coming up with the same things around the same time. Often applied to scientific and technological ideas, we can also apply this Mertonian thinking to popular music.

# Multiple Discovery and Music

In November 2007, critic J. Hoberman reviewed Todd Haynes' experimental Bob Dylan biopic *I'm Not There* in *The Village Voice*. Near the end of the piece, he wrote two fascinating paragraphs that I think about regularly:

> Certain cultural figures have a particular inevitability. Charles Chaplin and Elvis Presley rode technological waves, surfing to superstardom on powerful socio-economic currents. Had Chaplin never come to America, another slapstick comic would have emerged to reign over the nation's nickelodeons; Elvis might never have been born, but someone else would surely have brought the world rock 'n' roll.
>
> No such logic accounts for Bob Dylan. No iron law of history demanded that a would-be Elvis from Hibbing, Minnesota, would swerve through the Greenwich Village folk revival to become the world's first and greatest rock 'n' roll beatnik bard and then—having achieved fame and adoration beyond reckoning—vanish into a folk tradition of his own making.

Hoberman is ruminating on some Mertonian ideas here. In his words, the musical innovations of Elvis Presley were an "inevitability."[2] The times made him, not the other way around. Bob Dylan, by contrast, was a heroic figure that shaped an era, inventing the idea of the singer-songwriter, bringing lyrical complexity to the pop song, and so much more.

People often talk about The Beatles in the same way that Hoberman talks about Dylan. "No such logic," I could see someone writing, "accounts for The Beatles. No iron law of history demanded that would-be Little Richards and

---

[2] In the last chapter, I talked about my dislike for fade outs. In this era, Elvis Presley's "Suspicious Minds" (November 1, 1969), an otherwise flawless song about crumbling love, commits a sin worse than the fade out. It fades out twice! The first one is false, the song fading back in, before fading out for real.

Buddy Hollys from Liverpool would swerve through the Hamburg, Germany rock clubs to become the world's greatest rock 'n' roll band and then—having achieved fame and adoration beyond reckoning—break up and set forth into a musical world they'd remade in less than a decade."

Though rock music was a vital force in the last era, it became all-conquering in this one. Every genre, from folk to soul to jazz, was appropriating pieces of the guitar-based genre. At the same time, the genre itself was beginning to splinter. Some rockers leaned into a spacey, psychedelic form of the genre. Others pared it back to its roots. Still, others cranked up their amps to make it as loud and abrasive as possible.

What it meant to be a popular artist was also changing. By the end of this era, artists were regularly writing their own music, the studio became as important as the stage in making a career, the album superseded the single as the most important format for serious artists, and so much more. The reason for these changes is usually pinned on heroic figures, like The Beatles and Bob Dylan.[3] These were not Mertonian figures. They seemed larger than life itself, bending popular culture to their respective wills.

As I made clear at the end of the last chapter, I adore The Beatles. On most days, I consider their song "Yesterday" (October 9, 1965) to be the finest composition of the twentieth century. And my love for Dylan is at least as great as my love for those Liverpool lads. So, I am amenable to the heroic figures-driven history of this era. In fact, there's a lot of truth to it.

Still, I think both The Beatles and Bob Dylan are prime examples of a related Mertonian idea: the Matthew Effect, or when prominent people or groups in a field are given disproportionate credit for things as compared to unknown people who made similar contributions. In this chapter, I want to explore how two changes in this era, namely the growing complexity of lyrics and artists writing their own songs, are often pinned on Bob Dylan and The Beatles, but were being explored by many others.

---

[3] Sending ten songs to number one for 32 weeks, The Beatles remained the most popular artist in this era. While Dylan was also popular, as noted in Chapter 1, he never had a number one himself. The closest he got was "Like a Rolling Stone" and "Rainy Day Women #12 & 35" each peaking at number two. The former was blocked by The Beatles' "Help!" (September 4, 1965). The latter got stuck behind The Mamas and the Papas' "Monday, Monday" (May 7, 1966).

# Hear My Words That I Might Teach You

Before interviewing Bob Dylan for *Playboy* in 1966, critic Nat Hentoff captured the two perspectives people have on the singer's voice: "Some found its flat Midwestern tones gratingly mesmeric; others agreed with a Missouri folk singer who had likened the Dylan sound to that of 'a dog with his leg caught in barbed wire.'" To this day, Dylan's vocals are no less controversial. My mom, for example, likes to remind me whenever I put on his music that she can't stand his voice. Still, she is happy to concede that he writes nice songs.

Hentoff's piece goes on to highlight this exact idea in the very next sentence: "All agreed, however, that [Dylan's] songs were strangely personal and often disturbing, a pungent mixture of loneliness and defiance laced with traces of Guthrie, echoes of the Negro blues singers and more than a suggestion of country-and-western; but essentially Dylan was developing his own penetratingly distinctive style."

If you don't trust my mom or an old *Playboy* piece to inform you on Dylan's skills as a songwriter and lyricist, you don't have to look far for more evidence. He won the 2016 Nobel Prize in literature "for having created new poetic expressions within the great American song tradition."

If that's not enough, I downloaded the lyrics to every original song from Bob Dylan's 1960s studio albums and compared them to the number ones across the first three eras. By nearly any metric you can conceive, Dylan's lyrics are more complex than your typical chart-topper thus far. They have 40 percent more words and 25 percent more unique words on average. Also, if you apply any well-known formula for measuring text difficulty, Dylan's songs are notably more complex.

In short, it's clear that Bob Dylan was doing something different with his lyrics than the average musician. But were the lyrics in the number ones changing too? And if so, did that have anything to do with Dylan?

## Are Number One Hit Lyrics Changing?

If you were to ask me which chart-topping artist had the shortest name in this era, I'd get you an answer very quickly: Lulu. The four-letter Scottish singer got to number one with "To Sir With Love" (October 21, 1967), a song from a film of the same name starring Sidney Poitier. The reason I can find this answer quickly is because (a) we can agree on a metric to measure it, and (b) calculating that metric is easy. All you need to do is count the number of characters in each artist's name.

Measuring the complexity of a set of lyrics is not like this. Your best bet is to look at a bunch of metrics and see if they all agree. That's what I did when comparing Bob Dylan's lyrics to the number ones, and it's also what I did when looking at the number ones over time.

Again, this is not a straightforward task. There is no agreed-upon way to determine changes in lyrical complexity. That's why in Figure 3.1, I look at eight different metrics. While I will relegate a more in-depth discussion to a footnote, the high-level summary is that there is a small but perceptible increase in lyrical complexity throughout the 1960s.[4] Can we attribute this change to Bob Dylan's growing influence?

During the 1960s, artists as far-flung as Elvis Presley, Jimi Hendrix, and Stevie Wonder covered Dylan's music. Praise from his songwriting contemporaries was also effusive.

- In *Yeah! Yeah! Yeah!: The Story of Pop Music from Bill Haley to Beyoncé*, Bob Stanley recounts how famed lyricist Gerry Goffin "lost his mind once he heard Dylan, deciding everything he'd ever written was shallow and worthless, trashing his old tapes and acetates, to the horror of his friends."

---

[4] Nerd alert: To measure lyrical complexity I looked at average word length and the percentage of unique words in each song, along with six measures of text difficulty: Flesch-Kincaid, Gunning FOG, Dale-Chall, SMOG, Linsear Write, and Coleman-Liau. Percentage of unique words, word length, Coleman-Liau, and Dale-Chall decline between 1958 and 1964-ish before rising throughout the rest of the 1960s. Flesh-Kincaid and SMOG are relatively steady between 1958 and 1964-ish before rising steadily throughout the rest of the 1960s. Gunning Fog and Linsear Write rise throughout the entire period.

Again, Dylan never had a number one himself, but if you run t-tests comparing the period before and after The Byrds' cover of his "Mr. Tambourine Man" (June 26, 1965) topped the charts—maybe the height of his creative influence—the difference in Flesh-Kincaid, SMOG, Linsear Write, and Gunning FOG are significant at the 0.01 level. Dale-Chall is significant at the 0.05 level. Percent of unique words, word length, and Coleman-Liau are insignificant.

## Measuring the Lyrical Complexity
## of Number One Hits

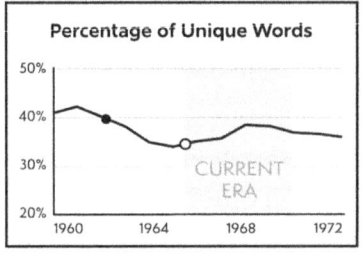
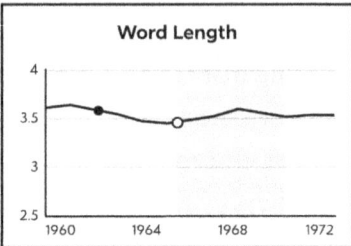

*Various readability tests measuring the years of education
required for the average person to understand a text:*

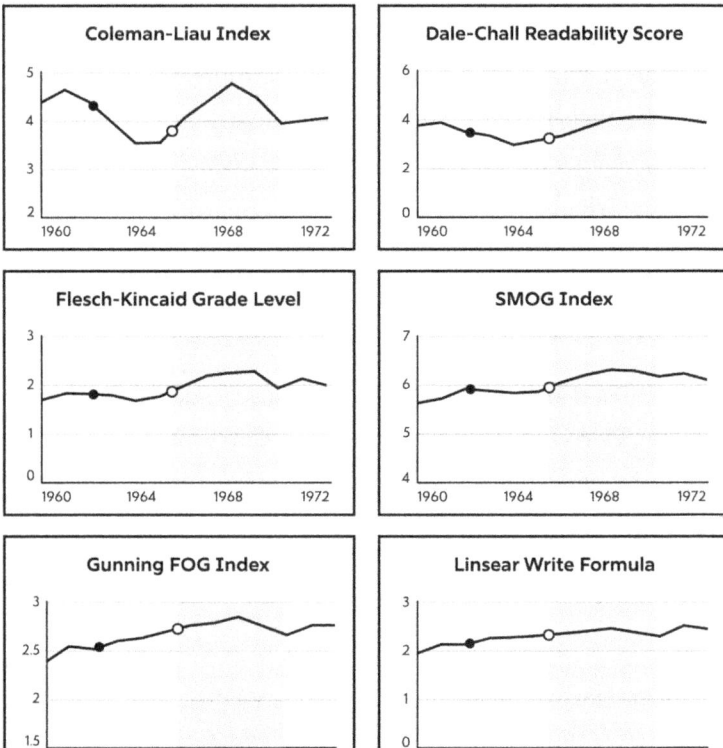

● **1962** Bob Dylan releases his debut album

○ **1965** The Byrds' cover of Dylan's "Mr. Tambourine Man" goes to number one

Figure 3.1

- "Bob Dylan," Sly Stone relates in his memoir, "he was only one guy, working with just voice, guitar, and harmonica. It was so little to go on, or at least that's what people thought, but they didn't hear how dead serious he was about what he was doing . . . He pushed his mind at you through his music."

- When asked how he went from "writing what were essentially pop songs . . . to more artistic songs," in the book *Songwriters on Songwriting*, Paul Simon responded, "I'm trying to find out if there's anyone besides Bob Dylan who could have influenced me. But I really can't imagine . . . that there was."

So, the lyrical changes in popular music were all due to Bob Dylan, right? Not exactly. I cut off that Paul Simon quote in the middle of his answer. Here's the rest of it: "It might not have been Dylan directly but it was the folk scene of Bleecker and MacDougal [in Manhattan's Greenwich Village]. But [Dylan] was so dominant a force in it that in a way you can attribute it to him. Although, I'm sure that he was influenced by the street, too. That scene probably influenced that kind of writing." Simon is situating Dylan as an influential figure in a much larger scene. In that same book, Dylan concurs when asked if folk and rock music would have been united had he not existed: "Somebody else would have done it in some other kind of way."

When considering Dylan and Simon's thoughts together, you get a very Mertonian perspective on lyrical shifts during the 1960s. Yes, Dylan was wildly important, but he was also the beneficiary of the Matthew Effect, with many people, places, and events also driving changes in popular lyrics. In general, these shifts can be categorized into two groups: songs with lyrics about new topics and songs with lyrics of a more literary nature.

## *Lyrical Evolution: New Topics*

While there were notable events in the last era, like the Cuban Missile Crisis and the assassination of John F. Kennedy, in this era, it felt like American society was upended every few weeks. The war in Vietnam was escalating. Martin Luther King, Jr. was assassinated. The Civil Rights Act was passed. Robert F.

Kennedy was assassinated. The women's rights movement began to grow. All this tumult had a notable impact on the words that songwriters wrote.

We see songs meant to empower women, like Nancy Sinatra's psychedelic folk tune "These Boots Are Made for Walkin'" (February 26, 1966),[5] Aretha Franklin's explosive "Respect" (June 3, 1967), and Jeannie C. Riley's twangy "Harper Valley PTA" (September 21, 1968). That final song is about a woman named Mrs. Johnson who receives a letter from the local PTA complaining that she is raising her daughter poorly because she is "wearing [her] dresses way too high" and "drinking and a-running around with men." Mrs. Johnson then shows up at a PTA meeting and eviscerates every hypocrite in Harper Valley.[6]

Only highlighting Aretha Franklin's "Respect" as a women's rights anthem is unfair, though. It also doubled as a Civil Rights anthem. We also see The Rascals' "People Got to Be Free" (August 17, 1968) and Sly and the Family Stone's "Everyday People" (November 15, 1969) demanding respect for humans of every race and gender in this era.

Before this era, there were songs that used war as a subtext, like "Soldier Boy" by The Shirelles (1962) and "Mr. Lonely" by Bobby Vinton (1964). In this era, we get overt Vietnam War references via Barry McGuire's "Eve of Destruction" (September 25, 1965). Opening with the line "The eastern world, it is exploding / Violence flaring, bullets loading" over a bellowing drum, the song proceeds to capture a world where "human respect is disintegrating."

As before, war also remained in the background of some other chart-toppers, like the sublime "Leaving on a Jet Plane" by Peter, Paul, and Mary (December 20, 1967), The Monkees' barn-burning "Last Train to Clarksville" (November 5, 1966), and The Byrds' biblically-inspired "Turn! Turn! Turn!" (December 4, 1965).[7]

There were also songs whose lyrical topics were new but not necessarily tied to a particular event. Some of these topics are easy to identify—like The Beatles

---

[5] Yes, she is Frank's daughter. In fact, she shared a number one with him: "Somethin' Stupid" (July 2, 1966), a cutesy, Spanish-inspired tune that represents the only time parent and child have dueted on a number one.

[6] Interestingly, these three empowering songs were respectively written by Lee Hazlewood, Otis Redding, and Tom T. Hall, all of whom were men.

[7] Songwriter Pete Seeger neglected to give God a credit on this one.

"Paperback Writer" (June 25, 1966) chronicling a journeyman author and The Supremes' "Love Child" (November 30, 1968), a meditation on illegitimacy and the cycle of poverty—while others proved a bit more difficult to pin down.

The Rolling Stones' first three number ones—"(I Can't Get No) Satisfaction" (July 10, 1965), "Get Off of My Cloud" (November 6, 1965), and "Paint It, Black" (July 11, 1966)—illustrate this idea. "(I Can't Get No) Satisfaction" and "Get Off of My Cloud" are restless rockers, Jagger shouting about everyday annoyances, like television advertisers trying to pawn the latest trendy product off on him. "Paint It, Black," by contrast, is a brooding acoustic number built around a sitar and propulsive percussion. It sees Jagger falling deeper and deeper into darkness (i.e., "I look inside myself and see my heart is black"). These sentiments would never have found their way onto pop radio even a few years earlier.

## *Lyrical Evolution: Literary Devices*

When Bob Dylan first heard The Byrds' cover of his "Mr. Tambourine Man" (June 26, 1965)—a more pop-oriented version of his drifting folk song— he allegedly said, "Wow, you can dance to that!" And even though The Byrds removed some of Dylan's verses to streamline the song, it remains a quintessential example of the literary devices that took over lyrics in this era. Rife with metaphor and repeated rhymes (e.g., "Take me for a trip upon your magic swirling ship / All my senses have been stripped"), "Mr. Tambourine Man" captures a hazy state of consciousness, possibly even something religious (e.g., "In the jingle jangle morning, I'll come following you").

Simon and Garfunkel's "The Sound of Silence" (January 1, 1966) also has similar literary elements. Using juxtaposition to create vivid, ambiguous imagery (e.g., "People talking without speaking / People hearing without listening"), the song has a sense of hopelessness lurking in the lyrics and the duo's dirge-like close-harmonies (e.g., "The words of the prophets are written on the subway walls and tenement halls / And whispered in the sound of silence").

Though there were scores of great verses written throughout this era, the finest set might belong to Bobbie Gentry's "Ode to Billie Joe" (August 26,

1967). Though it falls into the broad folk tradition like "Mr. Tambourine Man" and "The Sound of Silence," "Ode to Billie Joe" stands apart for its warbling vocals from Gentry and mysterious strings arranged by Jimmie Haskell.

The lyrics take us to Mississippi dinner table where a family is talking about how Billie Joe MacAllister died by jumping off the Tallahatchie Bridge. Gentry's narrative isn't straightforward, though. You've got family members passing judgment on the deceased while also passing food around the table (e.g., "Well Billie Joe never had a lick of sense. Pass the biscuits please.") It also seems like everyone at the table knows something but can't bring themselves to say it (e.g., "He said he saw a girl that looked a lot like you up on Choctaw Ridge / And she and Billie Joe was throwing something off the Tallahatchie Bridge"). Filled with enough intrigue that the song was adapted into a movie of the same name, you might never hear a popular song with a narrative as complex as "Ode to Billie Joe."

With all this talk about lyrical shifts during this era, I should also note that we do continue to see standard lyrical fare atop the charts. The sentimental words in Herb Alpert's "This Guy's in Love with You" (June 22, 1968) and The Association's "Cherish" (September 24, 1966), for example, could have been written in any decade of the twentieth century. Love songs always sell. But between the influence of Bob Dylan, folk music, and the tumult of the 1960s, lyricists were willing to experiment.

## It Took Me Years to Write, Will You Take a Look?

Let's imagine bands are businesses. The front person is the CEO. The other members are employees. Though this is a lame way to look at a band, successful groups eventually amount to corporate entities. From this perspective, a band breaking up for creative differences is a business dispute. In the *1843* magazine article "A rocker's guide to management," Ian Leslie captures this idea:

> Rock groups are mini-corporations . . . Bands such as Coldplay or Kings
> of Leon operate sophisticated corporate machines that are responsible for
> multiple revenue streams . . . Yet the music machine ultimately depends

on a small group of talented individuals working closely together to create something magical. Once members of a group decide that they can't stand to be in the same room as each other, the magic stops and the money dries up.

If bands are businesses, then like businesses, they can vertically integrate. Vertical integration is when a business owns each piece of its supply chain. For example, a vertically integrated eyewear business would own the factories that produce the frames and lenses, the distribution network that gets the product to stores, and the stores themselves. Tommy James and the Shondells prove a good example of vertical integration in popular music-making, one of the most profound musical shifts of the twentieth century.

In 1966, The Shondells topped the charts with "Hanky Panky" (July 16, 1966), a hormonal garage rocker. It was written by the famed songwriting duo Jeff Barry and Ellie Greenwich. It was produced by Henry Glover. And it was performed by Tommy James and his group. Three years later, The Shondells found their way to the top of the charts with the shimmering "Crimson and Clover" (February 1, 1969), a love song that exists at the intersection delicate and unrestrained. Unlike "Hanky Panky," Tommy James and his group cowrote, produced, and performed the song. Thus, in three short years, Tommy James had taken creative control by vertically integrating his group.

The 1960s is typically seen as the decade where artists began to wrest creative control from professional songwriters and producers. Often, that change is associated with the decade's most popular group: The Beatles. Here's what that same article from *1843* magazine says about such: "The Beatles invented the idea of the band as a creative unit in the 1960s. John Lennon's and Paul McCartney's artistic partnership enabled them to vertically integrate the hitherto separate functions of songwriting and performing." Using the number ones, I wanted to investigate this claim. Were more artists vertically integrating in the 1960s? And, if so, was it because of The Beatles?

## Are More Artists Writing and Producing Their Own Material?

Before understanding the evolution of artists writing and producing their own work, let's clarify the meaning of each of those terms. We'll use The

Troggs' eternally cool "Wild Thing" (July 30, 1966) as an example. "Wild Thing" was written by Chip Taylor, meaning he chose the words, melody, and underlying chord progression. It was then produced by Larry Page, who oversaw the recording process and might have helped the group choose a specific arrangement for Taylor's chords, lyrics, and melody. In this case, Page and the band chose to make a scuzzy record, only the brief ocarina solo taking your attention away from the thumping electric guitar and half-spoken, sex-infused vocals.

In Figure 3.2, you can see that from 1940 through 1956, fewer than 8 percent of number ones were written by the performing artist. In that same time, less than 2 percent of number ones were produced by the performing artist. From 1957 through 1962, both of those percentages rise sharply with 35 percent of number ones written by the artist and 11 percent produced by the artist. Though the numbers fall a bit after that, they respectively surpass 48 percent and 32 percent by the end of this era.

Before assessing how much of this shift was due to The Beatles, I need to stress its wide-reaching impact. In his 2021 book *Major Labels*, critic Kelefa Sanneh noted, "For the biggest names in music, identifying as a singer-songwriter meant embracing a certain seriousness of purpose." This idea that

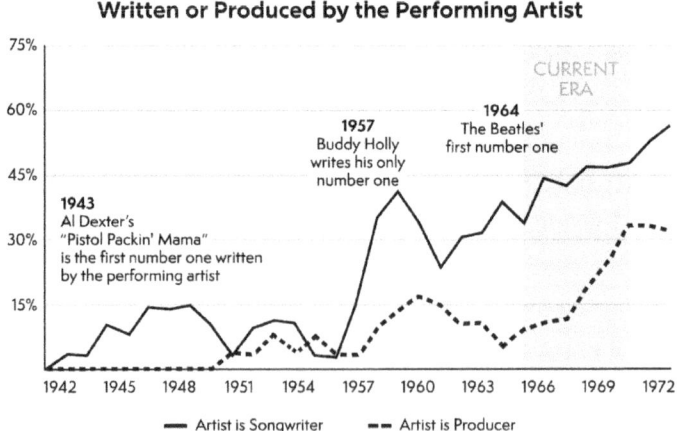

**Figure 3.2**

Sanneh is getting at—that we take musical works more seriously if they are written or produced by the performing artist—emerged during this era. It's part of the reason why, as we will discuss in Chapter 11, the performing artist almost always had a songwriting credit on their releases by the 2000s. It's also part of the reason why artists go to great lengths to prove that they write their own songs. Nevertheless, was this shift due to The Beatles?

Not exactly. Of course, The Beatles inspired countless artists to pen their own songs. But by the time The Beatles topped the Hot 100 in 1964, artists had more regularly been writing and producing their own work for almost a decade. The beginnings of this change came down to increased competition in the music industry of the 1940s.

First, in 1941, the major radio broadcasters in the United States refused to play any compositions represented by ASCAP, an organization that collected performance royalties for songwriters. After a decade of royalty rate increases, the broadcasters decided to boycott the organization's large catalog rather than stomach another rate hike. To fill airtime, they not only played compositions that were in the public domain, but decided to start their own ASCAP-competitor, BMI.

While ASCAP had focused on songwriters who worked with big bands, Hollywood studios, and Broadway productions, BMI set its sights on genres that ASCAP had ignored, like R&B, country, and gospel. Unlike the big-band model where artists performed compositions written by others, artists in these genres more regularly wrote their own songs. By the time ASCAP and radio broadcasters came to a royalty rate agreement, singer-songwriters were getting much more airplay.

While ASCAP lost some power in the performance rights space, a similar thing happened in the recorded music space. At the time, the industry was dominated by three labels: RCA, Columbia, and Decca. And these labels were largely selling music to adults. As the decade wore on, some insurgent labels began to emerge. Some of these, like Apollo and Savoy, cropped up during the musicians' strike we spoke about in the last chapter because they were willing to meet the demands of the American Federation of Musicians before the bigger companies. Others, like Atlantic, Chess, and Sun, were founded during the economic boom after the Second World War when returning soldiers and their families had money to spend. In his book *All Shook Up*, Glenn Altschuler goes so far as to say that "Between 1948 and 1954, a thousand [independent labels] went into business."

Many of these labels were recording music that the bigger companies had little interest in, like rock 'n' roll. Art Rupe, who founded Specialty Records in 1946 and released music by Little Richard and Lloyd Price, noted exactly that: "I looked for an area neglected by the majors and in essence took the crumbs off the table of the record industry." Part of the reason those bigger labels had little interest in those "crumbs" was because they didn't understand the audience: teenagers. As noted in Chapter 1, teenagers were a new phenomenon at the time. Up until then, there was no distinct demographic period between childhood and adulthood. But now this new demographic group was growing, and they too had some money to spend.

So, if you were an upstart label trying to market music to teenagers, what would you do? Hire middle-aged songwriters and producers to make songs for entire orchestras to play? Or have young people write and record music for their peers with a couple instruments? The latter was probably a better bet. It was simpler and cheaper.

Many of the artists that came to dominate the 1960s, including The Beatles, grew up idolizing Little Richard, Eddie Cochran, Buddy Holly, Chuck Berry, and others that grew famous under this new paradigm. The songwriting partnership of John Lennon and Paul McCartney solidified the lineage that they belonged to.

## Should We Take Artists That Write Their Music More Seriously?

I need to take a moment to dispel the common notion that artists who don't write, produce, and perform their own material should be taken less seriously than those that do. The problem with this notion is that it's often applied inconsistently. For example, you will seldom meet a person who claims that Frank Sinatra's music lacked seriousness even though he wrote almost nothing that he sang, including this era's lush "Strangers in the Night" (July 2, 1966).

The Beach Boys are another interesting case study. They went to number one once in this era with "Good Vibrations" (December 10, 1966). "Good Vibrations" is a masterclass in songwriting and production. It rejects typical structure and is more akin to a "pocket symphony"—a term The Beach Boys' publicist Derek Taylor allegedly used to describe the song—with at least four distinct sections. At the time it was the most expensive song ever recorded and helped pave the way for other structurally atypical popular songs, like The Beatles' "A Day in the Life," Queen's "Bohemian Rhapsody," Paul McCartney's "Band on the Run" (1974) and Travis Scott's "SICKO MODE" (2018).

While Brian Wilson wrote and produced the music and Mike Love wrote the lyrics, The Beach Boys didn't contribute too much to the performance of the song beyond the vocals. In fact, The Wrecking Crew, a loose conglomerate of Los Angeles studio musicians, played nearly every instrument. In other words, "Good Vibrations" is a profound work even though it was largely performed by hired guns.

Compare both The Beach Boys and Sinatra to The Monkees, a group that achieved commercial success without critical praise.[8] Their music wasn't taken as seriously because (a) the group was originally assembled for a television show and (b) they didn't write or perform their early songs. Nevertheless, this notion of seriousness starts to feel silly when you listen to those songs.

Along with the aforementioned "Last Train to Clarksville," their similarly titled number ones "I'm a Believer" (December 31, 1966) and "Daydream Believer" (December 2, 1967) are on par with some of the best popular songs of the 1960s. Sure, the group and their songs were packaged for mass appeal, but nearly all popular music is, even the popular music that is deemed "serious." It makes more sense to say you don't like The Monkees' rather than claiming that they've committed some grave musical sin. As Kelefa Sanneh notes in the aforementioned *Major Labels*, "Writing and singing your own songs is just one approach to music making."

---

[8] One thing you can 100 percent attribute to The Beatles is bands naming themselves after misspelled animals, like The Monkees, The Byrds, and Def Leppard, among others. The Turtles—who topped the charts with "Happy Together" (March 25, 1967)—also sort of fit the bill as they once replaced the "u" in their name with a "y" (i.e., The Tyrtles).

# People Say Believe Half of What You See

It's strange that in the last two chapters, I've claimed to love Bob Dylan and The Beatles while also spilling pages of ink trying to convince you that we're too quick to ascribe certain innovations to them. I assure you that I really do love them. But the thing I love about them and The Supremes and any other endlessly celebrated artist is not the things they've supposedly changed about popular culture. It's their songs.

Decades later, the glorious crescendo in The Beatles' "Hey Jude" (September 28, 1968) hits as hard as it did in 1968. The bass grooving on "You Can't Hurry Love" (September 10, 1966) right after The Supremes shout, "Now break!" likewise remains as captivating as ever. Though I wax on about music, great songs often don't require any background knowledge. For better or worse, bad songs don't either.

## Highlights

1. **"I Heard It Through the Grapevine" by Marvin Gaye (December 14, 1968)**[9]—This song is about humiliating heartache. It's about finding out your lover is done with you indirectly, through rumors circulating on the streets, rumors you are the last to be privy to.

   That rumor starts with the keyboard playing a circular riff in its lower register. Then it moves to the drums, a soft thump, your heartbeat. Then it finds its way to the guitar and strings echoing the initial whisper of the keyboard. With each step, the truth becomes more apparent. Then Marvin Gaye arrives, the pain dripping from his voice, a voice whose range and control are nearly inhuman. He knows the truth, and even if "a man ain't supposed to cry," he can't hide his pain.

2. **"(Sittin' On) The Dock of The Bay" by Otis Redding (March 16, 1968)**—Topping the charts in the wake of Redding's death, this is a record that can trick you. The rise and fall of the melody, the nautical

---

[9] "Paperback Writer" by The Beatles, "Good Vibrations" by The Beach Boys, "Love Child" by The Supremes, "Respect" by Aretha Franklin, and both "(I Can't Get No) Satisfaction" and "Paint It, Black" by The Rolling Stones were all rated high enough to be included here. I mentioned them earlier.

sound effects, and the whistling all capture a tranquil day by the water. But that's only part of the story. Listening to the lyrics and Redding's delicate delivery, we see a lost narrator. Part of the reason he is "wasting time" on the dock of the bay is because he has nowhere else to go and wants to forget it. No matter how many miles you roam, certain things are inescapable.

3. **"You Keep Me Hangin' On" by The Supremes (November 19, 1966)**— Even if there were no vocals on this track, you'd feel the uncertainty. The key shifts back and forth between sections. The guitar riff sounds like a telegraph signal that you can't decode. And it might be. Because at the beginning of this song, Diana Ross can't make sense of anything. "Set me free, why don't you, babe?" she pleads with her lover. Though anxiety persists throughout, her questions turn to demands at the end: "Go on, get out, get out of my life." Sometimes you need to take matters into your own hands.

# Lowlights

1. **"Honey" by Bobby Goldsboro (April 13, 1968)**—Telling the story of a man whose wife died, "Honey" falls within the maudlin tragedy song tradition. But what makes this sappy song stand out is that it's not clear whether the narrator ever really liked his wife. He describes her as "Kind of dumb and kind of smart," while also recounting how he laughed himself to tears when she almost hurt herself falling in the snow. With lines like, "She wrecked the car and she was sad / And so afraid that I'd be mad, but what the heck," the only thing you should feel after "Honey" is hope that you'll never be in a relationship like this.

2. **"The Ballad of the Green Berets" by SSgt. Barry Sadler (March 5, 1966)**—When looking back at the 1960s, we often remember the scores of artists who wrote songs in protest of the Vietnam War. But there really were people who supported it. "The Ballad of the Green Berets" is proof of that. Topping the charts for five weeks on its way to becoming

the tenth best-selling single of 1966, SSgt. Barry Sadler's military march is an unabashed celebration of the armed forces, the soldier in his song dying with only one final request for his wife, namely that their son also serve. Now knowing about the endless, pointless destruction of the Vietnam War, this musical wish is hard to stomach.

3. **"In the Year 2525 (Exordium & Terminus)" by Zagar and Evans (July 12, 1969)**—In Dave Barry's novel *Tricky Business*, he describes a band that is forced to work the party circuit after they fail to make it big. When the group is asked to play a song that they don't like, Barry describes how they then perform a retaliation song to punish the audience. "In the Year 2525" is described as the "hydrogen bomb" of retaliation songs. While I don't know if I'd go that far, it's a strange song that predicts the future in thousand-year increments. If Zagar and Evans are correct, then in the year 4545 you'll no longer need your teeth because "You won't find a thing to chew." Dentists, please beware!

## Argument Starters

The most divisive song in this era was "Incense and Peppermints" by Strawberry Alarm Clock (November 25, 1967). The loudest complaint was that it was a half-rate psychedelic rock song with lyrics that read like Mad Libs: "Good sense innocence crippling mankind / Dead kings many things I can't define."

Mad-Libs-ing lyrics can work, though. The Beatles' "Come Together" (November 29, 1969), for example, mostly comes across as gibberish: "He got toe jam football / He got monkey finger / He shoot Coca-Cola." But that gibberish works well. I think part of the reason is that the bluesy musical arrangement is so strong. You could sing almost anything over good music, and people will listen. The opposite is not true. Even the greatest lyricist can't save bad chords, melodies, and production.

## Odds and Ends

1. **"I'm Henry VIII, I Am" by Herman's Hermits (August 7, 1965)**—I've got to tip my cap to Herman's Hermits. "I'm Henry VIII, I Am"—an

old British tune about a widow who has had seven husbands named Henry die on her and is now about to marry her eighth Henry—might be the most annoying song I've ever heard. Sung at breakneck pace in a cockney accent, you'll probably have had your fill before the song hits the 30-second mark. But as that happens, Hermits' frontman Peter Noone shouts, "Second verse, same as the first!" and proceeds to sing the exact same verse again. A team of musical scientists could spend a thousand years in a lab and never cook up something as irritating as this song.

2. **"Wedding Bell Blues" by The 5th Dimension (November 8, 1969)**— This is a soulful piano number about a woman pleading with her lover Bill to propose. I adore this song, but how was the name Bill immortalized in a popular song before my name? My name has been around for thousands of years. Lots of Christ songs. Not many Chris songs. We shall overcome.

3. **"All You Need Is Love" by The Beatles (August 19, 1967)**—When I was forced to sing in the fifth-grade choir, the music teacher told us that we were going to perform two Beatles songs. Having just gotten into the music of the famed quartet, I was pumped. Then she announced her selections: "When I'm Sixty-Four" and "All You Need Is Love." I didn't like these songs, and being forced to sing them only made me hate them more.

But as I grew, my relationship with "All You Need Is Love" began to change. When I started playing the guitar, I was intrigued by the bizarre time signatures that John Lennon incidentally utilized in his plea for peace. Soon after, I learned more about the song. It was written for a television program called *Our World* that was broadcast to hundreds of millions of people. The Beatles had to craft a song that had lyrics simple enough that anyone with a rudimentary understanding of English could grasp them. To further expand the appeal, they also inserted pieces of other well-known works into the song, like the French National Anthem and Glenn Miller's "In the Mood." It's a tall order to write a song for the entire world. But even with all this knowledge, it still sounded like hippie-ish garble to me.

That changed recently. I was in my bedroom fiddling with the radio when I heard "All You Need Is Love" start coming through the speaker. I paused to see what the station was. But the signal wasn't great, and a news broadcast began interfering. The newscaster was recounting the details from the May 31, 2019, Virginia Beach shooting where 12 people were killed and five were injured. But then Lennon's voice cut through again. I was listening to this disheartening newscast while also hearing Lennon repeat his song's refrain: "All you need is love."

It was an odd experience. Somewhere between hopeful and dystopic. But I think I finally understood what John Lennon was getting at. The lyrics are simple, but sometimes love really is all you need.

# Everything Else

"I Got You Babe" by Sonny and Cher. "Hang on Sloopy" by The McCoys. "I Hear a Symphony" by The Supremes. "Over and Over" by The Dave Clark Five. "We Can Work It Out" by The Beatles. "My Love" by Petula Clark. "Lightnin' Strikes" by Lou Christie. "(You're My) Soul and Inspiration" by The Righteous Brothers. "Good Lovin'" by The Rascals. "When a Man Loves a Woman" by Percy Sledge. "Summer in the City" by The Lovin' Spoonful. "Sunshine Superman" by Donovan. "Reach Out I'll Be There" by Four Tops. "96 Tears" by ? and the Mysterians. "Poor Side of Town" by Johnny Rivers. "Winchester Cathedral" by The New Vaudeville Band. "Kind of a Drag" by The Buckinghams. "Ruby Tuesday" by The Rolling Stones. "Love is Here and Now You're Gone" by The Supremes. "Penny Lane" by The Beatles. "The Happening" by The Supremes. "Groovin'" by The Rascals. "Windy" by The Association. "Light My Fire" by The Doors. "The Letter" by The Box Tops. "Hello, Goodbye" by The Beatles. "Judy in Disguise (With Glasses)" by John Fred and His Playboy Band. "Green Tambourine" by The Lemon Pipers. "Love is Blue" by Paul Mauriat. "Tighten Up" by Archie Bell and the Drells. "Mrs. Robinson" by Simon and Garfunkel. "Grazing in the Grass" by Hugh Masekela. "Hello, I Love You" by The Doors. "Dizzy" by Tommy Roe. "Aquarius/Let the Sunshine In (The Flesh Failures)" by The 5th Dimension. "Get Back" by The Beatles. "Love Theme from *Romeo and Juliet*" by Henri Mancini and His Orchestra. "Honky Tonk Women" by The Rolling Stones. "Sugar, Sugar" by The Archies. "I Can't Get Next to You" by The Temptations. "Na Na Hey Hey Kiss Him Goodbye" by Steam. "Someday We'll Be Together" by Diana Ross and the Supremes. "Raindrops Keep Falling on My Head" by B. J. Thomas.

# I Want You Back in the Sweet Sunshine on My Shoulders

# January 31, 1970—March 30, 1974

## At the Edge of the Bar Sat a Gal Named Doris

I spent most of my weekends during the summer of 2019 bouncing around the Jersey Shore's various bars.[1] While I have a soft spot for many of New Jersey's beach hangouts, my favorite place during that summer was the Parker House. The Parker House is a nineteenth-century seaside mansion open during the summer months that combines upstairs residences with a first-floor restaurant and basement bar, colloquially known as "God's Basement." The basement, sprawling in every direction, always has live music and is packed with college graduates trying to hang onto their youth.

One weekend when my friends and I were drinking at the Parker House, the night's band busted into Bruce Springsteen's "Rosalita (Come Out Tonight)." "Rosalita"—released in the middle of this era—is a rowdy, seven-minute rock 'n' soul epic from Springsteen's second record, *The Wild, The Innocent & the E Street Shuffle*. Though it didn't get anywhere near the charts, it's a fan favorite that I've heard at least a thousand times between the radio, the record, and various Springsteen concerts. But on that humid, New Jersey night, packed

---

[1] I also spent a fair share of time on the beach arguing about who should be on New Jersey's musical Mt. Rushmore. I've settled on Frank Sinatra, Bruce Springsteen, Whitney Houston, and Count Basie.

shoulder-to-shoulder, sipping Red Bull vodkas with a splash of pineapple through bamboo straws in that swampy basement, I witnessed a cover band play the world's greatest version of "Rosalita."

How is this possible? How could I have seen Springsteen—one of rock music's great live performers—play the song, yet suggest that a cover band bested him and his E Street compatriots? The reason I make this assertion is one fact: my grimy location. And when I say "my grimy location," I'm not talking specifically about being at the Parker House drinking with my friends. I'm talking about seeing a live band in a packed bar.

## The Importance of Musical Context

Before he'd achieved any level of celebrity, Bruce Springsteen built his musical chops as a popular bar act in New Jersey and the surrounding area. When you're playing in bars, your goal is to capture anybody who wanders in, so they stick around and buy drinks. But entertaining people is hard work, especially when nobody knows who you are. Because of this, some of Springsteen's early work was written with a bar in mind.

"Rosalita," for example, is long, which is necessary if you're playing four-hour sets. It's packed with energy and has a few tempo changes, which keep listeners engaged. Lyrically, it's a humorous profession of love, injected with a few moments—like the repeated "Your papa says he knows that I don't have any money"—that have audience participation in mind. In his autobiography, he noted that the song was "arranged to leave the band and the audience . . . gasping for breath. Just when you thought the song was over, you'd be surprised by another section . . . When you left the stage . . . you'd worked to be remembered."

When I saw that cover band perform "Rosalita" at the Parker House, it wasn't great because the band was great. It was great because I was hearing it in a bar, the place it was intended to be heard. Of course, I've enjoyed hearing "Rosalita" in stadiums, but it wasn't written with that space in mind. Compare "Rosalita" to a later Springsteen composition, like "Born in the U.S.A." With its slower tempo, monstrous riff, repetitive chorus, and structural simplicity, it was clearly written to be heard in an open-air stadium.

This connection between music and intended context isn't limited to Springsteen's bar band epics, though. In his book *How Music Works*, the Talking Heads frontman David Byrne writes about this relationship:

> Context largely determines what is written, painted, sculpted, sung, or performed. That doesn't sound like much of an insight, but it's actually the opposite of conventional wisdom, which maintains that creation emerges out of some interior emotion, from an upwelling of passion or feeling . . . This is the romantic notion of how creative work comes to be, but I think the path of creation is almost 180° from this model. I believe that we unconsciously and instinctively make work to fit preexisting formats.

Byrne illustrates this idea by describing the emergence of different genres. Jazz, he writes, "was a pragmatic way of solving a problem that had emerged: the 'written' melody would run out while the musicians were playing, and in order to keep a popular section continuing longer for the dancers who wanted to keep moving, the players would jam over those chord changes while maintaining the same groove." Yes, this is a simplification, but it's insightful. Artists work within the constraints of technology and their environment. These constraints are not deterministic, but they are influential.

This insight has reshaped how I think about music. If you think Love Unlimited Orchestra's glitzy, Barry White-penned, instrumental "Love's Theme" (February 9, 1974) is a big, beautiful nothing, get a DJ to crank up the volume in a club and you'll have no choice but to start moving your feet. Should you find Isaac Hayes's spoken monologue in "Theme from *Shaft*" (November 20, 1971) over-the-top, go watch it play behind the opening credits of the movie that it was made for. You'll be convinced that no piece of cinema has ever been better soundtracked.

Context isn't everything, but it matters deeply. Songs written for nightclubs won't necessarily hit the same if you're listening to them through your headphones. A propulsive rhythm created for a car stereo, might fall flat in your living room. In this chapter, I want to talk about the structures that shape popular music. While physical spaces, social context, and technological advancement all play a role, I'm going to focus on how changing demographics shaped the number ones of this era and how changing legal attitudes came to shape popular music for decades after.

# You Know the World Gets a Little Bit Older

Almost five months before he topped the charts with "You've Got a Friend" (July 31, 1971), James Taylor graced the cover of *Time* magazine. Here's how the publication captured rock music at the time: "The '70s have brought a startling change. Over the last year a far gentler variety of rock sound has begun to soothe the land." Decades later, this characterization has persisted. This era remains closely associated with mellow, acoustic music.

It's not that we don't see any loose rockers. The Guess Who's "American Woman" (May 9, 1970), Grand Funk's "We're an American Band" (September 29, 1973), and Edgar Winter's "Frankenstein" (May 26, 1973), three of the heaviest songs to date, all topped the charts. But there were fewer of them compared to the last two eras. That's kind of strange given that nearly every artist in this era was making music in those previous eras.

Of course, mellow music has always been popular. "The Three Bells" by The Browns (1959), "Roses are Red (My Love)" (1962) by Bobby Vinton, and "This Guy's in Love with You" by Herb Alpert (1968) are three of the mellowest songs you'll ever hear, and they all spent multiple weeks atop the charts before this era. But given the mellow characterization that this era often has, I wanted to see (a) if the data gives any credence to it and (b) if so, then what structures helped shape it.

## Are Songs Getting Softer?

If we define acoustic music as any song largely driven by an acoustic guitar or a piano, then we do indeed see many acoustic songs in this era. For example, Jim Croce's posthumous "Time in a Bottle" (December 29, 1973), The Rolling Stone's mournful "Angie" (October 20, 1973), and George Harrison's divine plea "Give Me Love (Give Me Peace on Earth)" (June 30, 1973) all topped the charts.[2] In fact, from February 19, 1972 to April 15, 1972, four exceedingly acoustic songs followed each other at number one: Harry Nilsson's "Without You" (February 19, 1972), Neil Young's "Heart of Gold" (March 18, 1972), America's "A Horse With No Name" (March 25, 1972), and Roberta Flack's "The First Time Ever I Saw Your Face" (April 15, 1972).

Calling the music of this era "acoustic" is limited, though. I think you need to use a word that's a bit more encompassing, like "soft" or "smooth." Roberta Flack's "The First Time Ever I Saw Your Face" is undoubtedly acoustic, her voice floating atop an arpeggiated acoustic guitar. But with a rhythm section barely rising above a whisper, the song is also characterized by its soft, smooth atmosphere. No piece of it is reminiscent of something like Janis Joplin's "Me and Bobby McGee" (March 20, 1971). Joplin's song starts off with an acoustic guitar, wandering along like the nomad in the lyrics, but then builds into an explosive blues jam. Her gravelly voice is the antithesis of Flack's and the acoustic qualities of each song are leagues apart.

Many songs in this era aren't acoustic but have the same soft quality of "The First Time Ever I Saw Your Face." Take The Carpenters' "Top of the World" (December 1, 1973) as an example. A song with a strong country influence, Karen Carpenter's crystalline voice is backed by a clip-clopping bass, Wurlitzer electric piano, pedal steel, and clean electric guitar. You couldn't call it acoustic, but it has many qualities that acoustic songs do. This notion of softness allows us to recognize, for example, that Stevie Wonder's "You Are the Sunshine of My Life" (May 19, 1973) and the Bee Gee's "How Can You Mend a Broken Heart" (August 7, 1971) are similar in texture even though the latter is more traditionally acoustic.

To test if this notion is more than anecdotal, I looked at two metrics from Spotify: loudness and acousticness. Loudness is the average intensity of the sound in a song, measured in decibels. Acousticness is Spotify's estimate, between 0 percent and 100 percent, if a song is acoustic. Since my idea of softness is imprecise, I figured these could provide clarification. I posited that

---

[2] Harrison's song was preceded by Paul McCartney meandering ballad "My Love" (June 2, 1973), the only time members of The Beatles would replace each other atop the charts. Coincidentally, "My Love" was followed by "Will it Go Round in Circles" by Billy Preston (July 7, 1973), the keyboardist who featured on The Beatles' "Get Back" (1969).

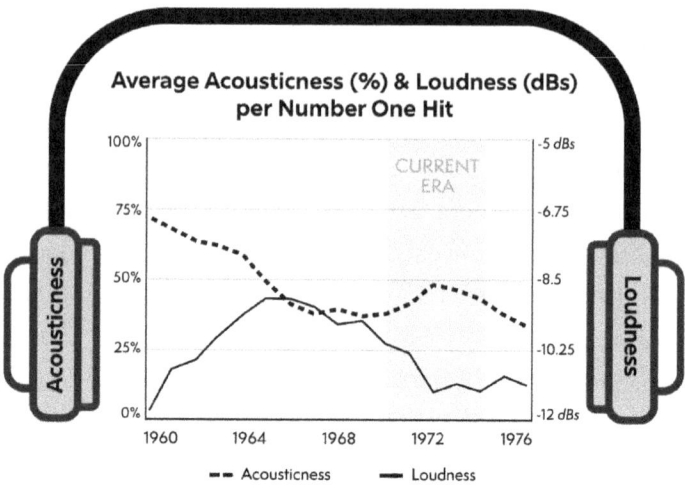

**Figure 4.1**

"soft music" would be quieter and that the acousticness metric would pick up some soft, non-acoustic numbers. And it does. For example, despite the fact the aforementioned "Top of the World" is built around an electric guitar and electronic keyboards, it clocks in at −13 decibels with an acousticness score of 81 percent.

In Figure 4.1, we see that these metrics are near mirror images of one another. This tells a consistent story. Music was quieter and more acoustic at the beginning of the first era, it grew louder and less acoustic throughout the 1960s, and then in the early-1970s became quieter and more acoustic again, though not as much as during the first era.[3] Thus, the soft, mellow characterization of this era is accurate. Some of this sound was surely driven by advances in studio technology. Expanded multitrack recording, for example, allowed engineers and producers to isolate and polish sounds more easily. I don't think that tells the full story, though.

---

[3] Another interesting comparison between the first era and this one is the return of the lyrical narrative, or song lyrics that tell a story with a distinct beginning, middle, and end. About 19 percent of songs in the first era have lyrical narratives, 13 percent in the second, 4 percent in the third, and 16 percent in the fourth. The death narrative also makes a small resurgence with songs like Vicki Lawrence's "The Night the Lights Went Out in Georgia" (April 7, 1973).

# A Grand Theory of Early 1970s Musical Softness

In Chapter 2, we looked at the changing demographic composition of artists, focusing on the increasing share of artists topping the charts in the early 1960s who were Black or women. These shifts had tangible effects on popular music. People from different backgrounds brought new experiences to the creative process. My first thought was that another demographic shift might have led to the rise in softness.

That doesn't seem to be the case, though. No matter the gender or race of the artist, the acousticness and loudness measures of their number one hits were pretty much the same in this era: 45 percent and −11 decibels, respectively.[4] I do think another piece of demographic information holds the key to understanding this sonic shift, though: age.

If you're in the business of topping the charts, it's a good idea to drink from the fountain of youth. In Figure 4.2, we see that the average age an artist tops the charts is consistently around 25 from 1958 to 1971. Additionally, in that period, 85 percent of chart-topping songs were by artists younger than 30. In his memoir *A Dream About Lightning Bugs*, musician Ben Folds posits that pop musicians are so young because pop music is music for the mating age:

[Pop music is] a soundtrack for that yearning, that youthful anger, those ideals and inside jokes of the teenagers and young adults as they experience the rough ride together . . . Good pop music, truly of its moment, should throw older adults off its scent. It should clear the room of boring adults and give the kids some space.

If you're post-mating age, you might enjoy new pop music to a degree, but it's not really for you. Post-mating-age adults have a whole other heap of problems, the likes of which the sickest beat and saddest rhyme are woefully unequipped to solve. You don't need an earful of sexy when navigating your

---

[4] In Chapter 1, I noted how the initial popularity of rock 'n' roll crossed racial barriers. We'll talk more about this in Chapter 6, but, despite its origins, rock music had become segregated by the 1970s, the most popular acts composed only of White men. Interestingly, some of those groups sang openly about race and racism on the number ones of this era, including Three Dog Night's "Black and White" (September 16, 1972), Stories' "Brother Louie" (August 25, 1973), and The Rolling Stones' "Brown Sugar" (May 29, 1971).

aging parents into an old folks' home or when you're worried your kids might be trying drugs at their delinquent friend's house.

In describing the youth of chart-topping artists from 1958 to 1971, I'm clearly burying the lede in Figure 4.2. Pop stars in this era got much older. From 1958 to 1971, only 15 percent of number ones were performed by artists at least 30 years old. From 1972 to the end of this era, 63 percent of number ones were by artists in that age cohort. That is a dramatic shift.[5]

Before we connect this to musical softness, there is one more piece of the puzzle to address: the dissolution of musical groups. From 1958 to 1971, 40 percent of number ones were performed by solo artists, meaning 60 percent were performed by duos or groups. Compare that to the period from 1972 to the end of this era. In that timeframe, 70 percent of number ones were performed by solo artists. Again, this is a dramatic shift. But why did it happen?

First, some popular groups fell apart. Diana Ross left The Supremes and topped the charts with "Ain't No Mountain High Enough" (September 19,

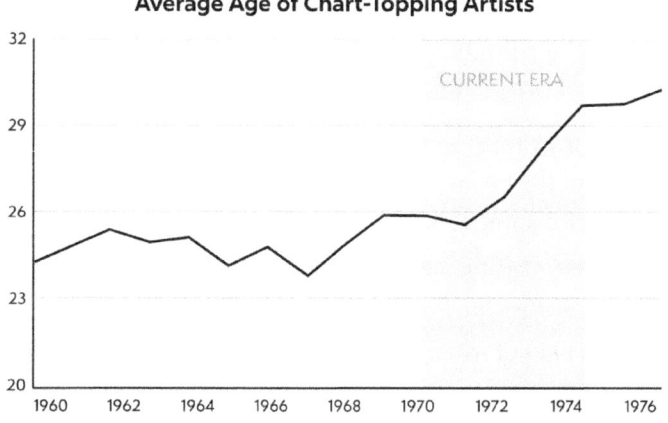

**Figure 4.2**

---

[5] In the keynote address at the 2012 South by Southwest music festival, Bruce Springsteen joked about how he was called the "new Dylan" in his early career: "The old Dylan was only 30, so I don't even know why they needed a fucking new Dylan."

1970) and "Touch Me in the Morning" (August 18, 1973). Eddie Kendricks did the same with "Keep on Truckin'" (November 10, 1973) after parting ways with The Temptations. Still a member of the British group Faces, Rod Stewart saw his solo career take off with old-woman-takes-your-virginity anthems like "Maggie May" (October 2, 1971). Neil Young—of Buffalo Springfield and Crosby, Stills, Nash, and Young fame—saw his solo star rise too. Even child stars like Donny Osmond and Michael Jackson moonlighted as solo performers on top of their successes with their respective family bands. Oh, yeah, and The Beatles broke up.

Secondly, some songwriters took the stage themselves. Carole King, who had written four number ones throughout the 1960s, topped the charts with her jazzy "It's Too Late" (June 19, 1971). Mac Davis, who penned some late-era songs for Elvis Presley, like "In the Ghetto" and "A Little Less Conversation," got to number one with a countrified warning to his lover, "Baby, Don't Get Hooked on Me" (September 23, 1972). Neil Diamond and John Denver, both of whom had already written number ones for other artists, also found themselves with their own chart-toppers in this era, namely "Cracklin' Rosie" (October 10, 1970) and "Sunshine on My Shoulders" (March 30, 1974), respectively.

With these facts about changes in acousticness, loudness, age, and artist structure in mind, we can finally put together my grand theory of musical softness.

- **Music is softer when made by the young and the old**: Spotify's acousticness score is 24 percent higher on average for number ones thus far by artists younger than 18 or older than 30 as compared to those between the ages of 19 and 29. Likewise, those hits by the young and the old were 24 percent quieter.

- **Music is softer when made alone**: Spotify's acousticness score is about 30 percent higher on average for number ones thus far by solo artists as compared to duos and groups. Similarly, those solo hits were 24 percent quieter.

Since we see chart-topping artists not only getting older in the early 1970s but also releasing music outside of duos and groups more regularly, we naturally see a rise in musical softness. This phenomenon also makes sense given my musical experiences.

There are probably two times in your life when you are likely to pick up an acoustic instrument and start making music by yourself. First, when you're young and just learning how to write and record. Second, when you're getting older, fed up with your collaborators, and decide to strike out on your own. This latter scenario was not only common in this era but had a notable impact on the music that was made.

# This Is the Law of All the Land

I was recently listening to Vampire Weekend's album *Modern Vampires of the City* with my friend Monica. Since we were listening on vinyl, I decided to leaf through the album's liner notes. While most of the songs were written by the two most visible members of the band—Rostam Batmanglij and Ezra Koenig—there were a few exceptions, one of which caught my eye: "['Step'] contains elements from 'Aubrey' (Gates) . . . Used by permission . . . Thanks to YZ's 'Who's that girl' for our hook 'Everytime I see you in the world you always step to my girl.'"

I found this confusing. I thought the hook on "Step" came from "Step to My Girl" by the hip-hop troupe Souls of Mischief. Additionally, I had no idea why David Gates got a songwriting credit. Gates was the frontman of Bread, a group that topped the charts in this era with the acoustic baby-maker "Make it With You" (August 22, 1970). Some internet sleuthing cleared up my confusion.

The Souls of Mischief's "Step to My Girl" sampled the hook from YZ's "Who's that Girl." YZ's song, in turn, sampled saxophonist Grover Washington's instrumental cover of Bread's "Aubrey." That's why Gates was credited.

Given this musical lineage, I could maybe see YZ getting a credit, but I was shocked that it warranted crediting Gates. While his composition may have borne an indirect influence, it felt wrong to think he was central to the compositional process. This also stood in sharp contrast to number ones we've seen thus far that have blatantly used bits from other songs without crediting anybody, like "Venus" by Shocking Blue (February 7, 1970).

Shocking Blue was formed in 1967 in the Netherlands and didn't have much success until they released "Venus," a rock song with some influence from both the folk and psychedelic veins of the genre. It ended up being a worldwide hit and the first Hot 100 number one performed by a Dutch act. Its only credited songwriter is Robbie van Leeuwen, Shocking Blue's guitarist. That makes it sound like Leeuwen created this song in isolation. That's not the case.

"Venus" is identical in all but lyrics to a 1963 folk song by The Big Three called "The Banjo Song." Additionally, the acoustic guitar in the introduction bears a great deal of resemblance to the rhythm and texture of The Who's "Pinball Wizard." If the Vampire Weekend standard had been the standard here, then van Leeuwen would have credited Tim Rose of The Big Three and Pete Townsend of The Who. But there's more. "The Banjo Song" is the lyrics of "Oh! Susanna" set to new music. "Oh! Susanna" was written in 1848 by Stephen Foster, often dubbed the "father of American music." Though it wouldn't be necessary because "Oh! Susanna" is in the public domain, if we wanted to be complete, we might also list Foster as a writer of "Venus" too.

Why did Vampire Weekend need to credit others while Shocking Blue didn't? The answer is tied to two different lawsuits involving songs from this era: "My Sweet Lord" by George Harrison (December 26, 1970) and "Alone Again (Naturally)" by Gilbert O'Sullivan (July 29, 1972). Let's first understand the facts of these cases and then turn to their implications.

## When the Courts Changed Songwriting

During 1970, there were a surprising number of chart-toppers with a spiritual undertone. "Bridge Over Troubled Water" by Simon and Garfunkel (February 28, 1970). "Let It Be" by The Beatles (April 11, 1970). "Everything is Beautiful" by Ray Stevens (May 30, 1970). "The Long and Winding Road" by The Beatles (June 13, 1970). "I'll Be There" by The Jackson 5 (October 17, 1970). It's hard to say why. My dad suggested that it might have been a reaction to the turmoil caused by the Vietnam War. If that were the case, I would have expected to see more songs mention the conflict beyond Edwin Starr's earth-shakingly intense "War" (August 29, 1970).

Regardless, George Harrison's "My Sweet Lord" (December 26, 1970) also fits into this spiritual category. Built around a wall of acoustic guitars, Harrison laments the difficulty of wanting to see the Lord but knowing that "it takes so long" to do such. This "Lord" doesn't belong to a specific religion, the background singers blending the eastern "Hare Krishna" with the western "Hallelujah" throughout. This religious mixture turns the warm song into a plea to see the humanity in every person.

While a member of The Beatles, Harrison lived in the shadow of John Lennon and Paul McCartney. "My Sweet Lord" was vindication that he was a musician and songwriter of the same caliber of his former bandmates. That must have been validating. But Harrison didn't have much time to enjoy that validation. A few months after the song came out, he was sued by Bright Tunes Music Corporation. They claimed that "My Sweet Lord" infringed on a song in their catalog: The Chiffons' "He's So Fine" (1963).

To summarize what resulted in decades of complex litigation, Harrison lost the case, meaning that he plagiarized pieces of "He's So Fine" on "My Sweet Lord." Throw on both songs and you'll understand why. "My Sweet Lord" and "He's So Fine" have melodic patterns close enough that the two choruses fit together like lost puzzle pieces. In his ruling, here's what Judge Richard Owen wrote on the matter:

> Did Harrison deliberately use the music of "He's So Fine"? I do not believe he did so deliberately. Nevertheless, it is clear that "My Sweet Lord" is the very same song as "He's So Fine" with different words, and Harrison had access to "He's So Fine." This is, under the law, infringement of copyright, and is no less so even though subconsciously accomplished.

In a musical copyright infringement case, the plaintiff must show not only that the two songs are similar but that the infringing composer had access to the song that they allegedly stole. This makes sense. You can't steal an idea you're not aware of. Since "He's So Fine" topped the charts in 1963, not long before The Beatles crossed the Atlantic, it's almost certain that Harrison was aware of the song. And if he wasn't, the production of the song also involved

Phil Spector, Eric Clapton, Peter Frampton, and Ringo Starr.[6] Someone in the studio must have known there were similarities between the songs.

Judge Owen wasn't concerned with that, though. He alleged that the copyright infringement was "subconsciously accomplished." This set up the precedent that you could be liable for infringing on the copyright of a song you had no recollection of hearing.

The case involving Gilbert O'Sullivan's depressing ballad "Alone Again (Naturally)" stands in contrast to the Harrison suit because it was about the deliberate use of another person's work.[7] Rapper Biz Markie sampled "Alone Again (Naturally)" on his 1991 song "Alone Again." Like his most famous work, "Just a Friend," "Alone Again" is a humorous song that sees Markie singing the hook of an older song off-key. O'Sullivan sued Markie for infringing on his original composition. This legal drama was not the first to involve hip-hop sampling, but it was unique because (a) it was settled in court and (b) Markie and his label had tried to clear the sample but, after O'Sullivan refused, released the song anyway.

Given this second fact, you probably won't be surprised that Markie lost. He had to pay damages and stop selling the song. Though parts of the opinion have been criticized, it reshaped how sampling worked. Now, there was precedent that each sample had to be cleared with the copyright holders. But taken with the Harrison ruling, it goes further: Even if you didn't draw from another song, you should probably credit that song's creators if it's close enough. This explains the songwriting credits on Vampire Weekend's "Step." But it also suggests some further implications.

---

[6] Though some of the relationships between former Beatles were rocky at this time, Harrison remained friends with Ringo Starr. In fact, he wrote some songs with Starr, including the drummer's number one "Photograph" (November 24, 1973).

[7] Along with Terry Jacks' dismal "Seasons in the Sun" (March 2, 1974), "Alone Again (Naturally)" is one of two songs in this era that mentions suicide.

# The Copylight-Copymight Dichotomy

If you're thinking about going to school for intellectual property law, I'll save you some money and give you a crash course on the history of federal musical copyright in the United States.[8]

- **1789**: The newly ratified Constitution grants Congress the power "to promote the Progress of Science and useful Arts, by securing for limited Times to Authors and Inventors the exclusive Right to their respective Writings and Discoveries."

- **1790**: Congress passes the first copyright law, setting the term to 14 years with an option to renew for an additional 14 years. Musical compositions are not explicitly protected by this law.

- **1831**: Copyright protections are granted for musical compositions. The initial copyright term is extended to 28 years.

- **1897**: Songwriters are granted the right to stop people from performing their work publicly.

- **1909**: Copyright terms are extended to 28 years with the option to renew for an additional 28 years. Protections are also added for mechanical reproductions of songs.

- **1917**: The Supreme Court upholds the right for copyright owners to be compensated for the public performance of their work, even if there was no charge to hear it.

- **1972**: Protections are granted for sound recordings.

- **1976**: Copyright terms are extended to the life of the author plus 50 years.

- **1995**: Protections are granted for the digital performance of sound recordings.

- **1998**: Copyright terms are extended to the life of the author plus 70 years.

- **2018**: Mechanical reproduction rights are updated for the digital age.

---

[8] If you promised your parents that you'd go to law school, please don't let this convince you otherwise.

The evolution of musical copyright since 1789 has enabled songwriters and artists to get paid when their work is performed in a concert, sold on CD, heard on streaming services, and so much more. In fact, these laws have enabled the music industry to exist. But there is one piece of copyright's evolution that gives me pause: the current term length, namely the life of the author plus 70 years. Here's what that means in practice. If a 20-year-old wrote and released a hit song in the year 2000 and lived to be 85, that person's heirs would control that song's copyright until 2135. That's a *really* long time. Long enough that it can lead to perversive incentives and problematic outcomes.

In his book *Copyrights and Copywrongs*, Siva Vaidhyanathan argues that when copyright is not properly limited in both scope and time, it amounts to censorship because the only people that have the willingness and ability to enforce these copyrights (i.e., file infringement lawsuits) are those that have been lucky enough to find extreme success.

> Copyright has developed as a way to reward the haves: the successful composer, the widely read author, the multinational film company. Copyright should not be meant for Rupert Murdoch, Michael Eisner, and Bill Gates at the expense of the rest of us. Copyright should be for students, teachers, readers, library patrons, researchers, freelance writers, emerging musicians, and experimental artists.

While I don't agree with Vaidhyanathan completely—I believe copyright should work for everyone—he is getting at an idea that I have dubbed "The Copylight-Copymight Dichotomy." The "copylight" piece of this phrase is in reference to how musicians, especially early in their career, benefit from light copyright enforcement. You lift riffs and pilfer lyrics while learning your craft. Even if your sources are more obscured as you refine your skills, the process never goes away completely.

Through this era, there are two ways that artists directly use other people's intellectual property to make new songs. The first is covering previously released songs in full, like Three Dog Night making a zonked-out rendition of Randy Newman's "Mama Told Me (Not to Come)" (July 11, 1970) and Ringo

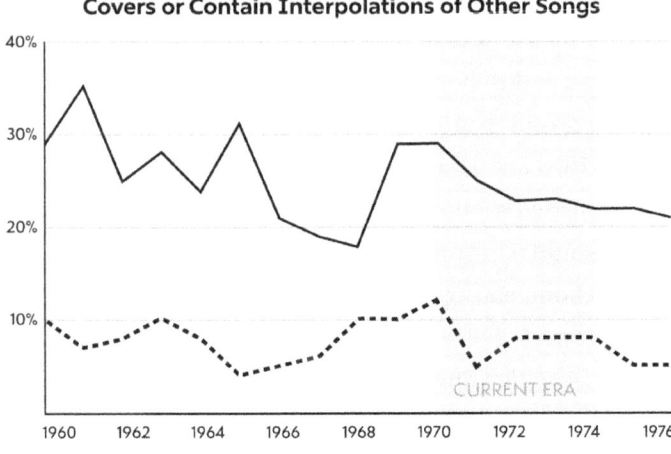

**Figure 4.3**

Starr taking a stab at the early 1960s hit "You're Sixteen" (January 26, 1974). The second way, often dubbed "interpolation," involves re-recording bits of older songs and putting them in new songs. Interpolations can be anywhere from subtle to overt.

- Steve Miller's "The Joker" (January 12, 1974) quotes the lyric "You're the cutest thing that I ever did see / Really love your peaches, wanna shake your tree / Lovey dovey, lovey dovey, lovey dovey all the time" from The Clovers' 1954 hit "Lovey Dovey."

- With a title inspired by Daddy Cool's Australian smash "Eagle Rock," the iconic falsetto in Elton John's "Crocodile Rock" (February 3, 1973) was drawn from the soaring vocal heard at the beginning of Pat Boone's "Speedy Gonzalez."

- Neil Diamond's "Song Sung Blue" (July 1, 1972) is the melody from Mozart's Piano Concerto No. 21 set to lyrics.

- The arrangement in The Staple Singers' "I'll Take You There" (June 3, 1972) bears a strong resemblance to a 1969 reggae instrumental called "The Liquidator."

Both covers and interpolations illustrate copylight, artists taking someone else's copyrighted material and turning it into something new. And there's no controversy around covers. Because of the establishment of the compulsory mechanical license in 1909, nobody can stop you from recording a cover of a previously released song so long as you pay the original songwriter at the government-mandated royalty rate. Interpolation isn't only where things get fuzzy but where copymight rears its ugly head. Let's turn back to "The Joker" and "I'll Take You There" to see how.

"The Joker" pairs a simple guitar riff with lyrics that are both captivating and humorous (e.g., "Some people call me the space cowboy / Some call me the gangster of love"). It was written by Steve Miller but later credited to Eddie Curtis, Ahmet Ertegün, and Miller after an out-of-court settlement over Miller's use of the previously mentioned Clovers' lyrics. Ertegün was the founder of Atlantic Records. When he started his famed label, did he and his songwriters lift music from a variety of sources and traditions? Of course. Did they always credit them? No. The fact that he sued Miller over the use of a short lyric is the perfect expression of copymight. It denies the truth about how creativity works. It also overstates the importance of "Lovey Dovey" on the creation of Miller's work. Part of the reason that Ertegün got to claim ownership was because he was a powerful man.

Compare that to "I'll Take You There." As noted, an obscure instrumental called "The Liquidator" provides the backbone to this loose, soulful jam helmed by Mavis Staples on the microphone. Whereas "The Joker" could exist without "Lovey Dovey," "I'll Take You There" *couldn't* exist without "The Liquidator." But the writer of "The Liquidator," a Jamaican man named Harry J, isn't credited on The Staple Singers' classic. Why? Unlike Ahmet Ertegün, Harry J didn't have the time, money, or resources to enforce his copyright. *Billboard* noted as much in his obituary: "[Harry J] was shocked to hear the song used in the Staple Singers' hit and took aggressive steps to collect royalties from Stax but made little progress."

The copylight-copymight dichotomy demonstrates how in practice copyright can be about power rather than the equal protection of intellectual property. In the post-Harrison-O'Sullivan world, we see people try to flex that power constantly. According to a 2019 *Wall Street Journal* report, the

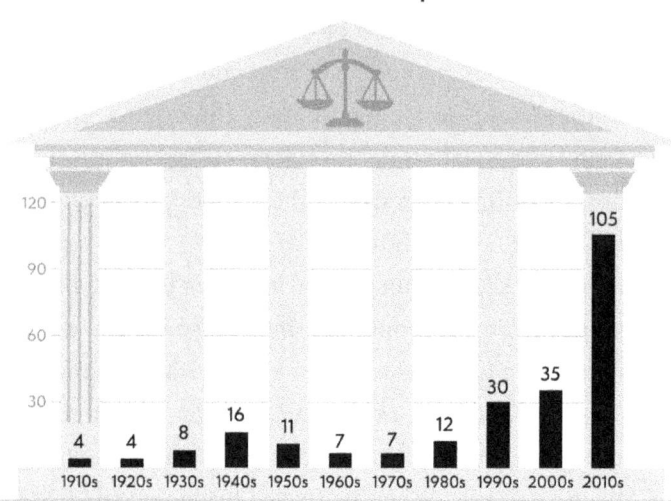

**U.S. Federal Musical Copyright Cases That Recieved a Judicial Opinion**

Figure 4.4

number of musical copyright infringement cases rose 31 percent between 2015 and 2018. While most of those suits never got very far, the number of cases that were litigated and received a judicial opinion in the United States also rose. In the information sourced from George Washington University in Figure 4.4, we see that cases of that ilk have risen 250 percent between the 1990s and 2010s.

While some of these cases involve two contemporary songs, others focus on songs released decades apart. For example, in 2014, Ed Sheeran released a soulful song called "Thinking Out Loud." Two years later, the family of Ed Townsend sued Sheeran, claiming the song infringed on Marvin Gaye's "Let's Get It On" (September 8, 1973), a song which Townsend cowrote. Though the case was eventually thrown out, the fun wasn't over for Sheeran.

In 2018, a company named Structured Asset Sales sued him again after purchasing partial rights to "Let's Get it On." This case went to trial, and Sheeran won, but that doesn't negate the fact that this entire legal drama should never have occurred. Part of the reason that it could was because copyright terms last a long time, long enough that faceless corporations and the heirs of long-dead artists can accuse people of infringement for decades.

Earlier, I mentioned that excessive copyright terms lead to perverse incentives. And this is one of them. But the problems don't end there. Exorbitant terms motivate labels to repackage and remonetize the past at the expense of the present. They prevent libraries and educational institutions from making works from long-dead artists available to the public. I would go so far as to argue that they even discourage creation. If I were one of Ed Townsend's heirs, why would I try to make new music when I could milk the royalties of "Let's Get It On" until 2074?

It's unlikely any of this will change. Though copyright is typically enforced within specific countries, there are international treaties that create uniformity in how it works across borders. My only hope is that artists, labels, and investors can be more realistic about what copyright infringement entails and how creativity works before filing their next bevy of lawsuits.

# Oh, Baby, Give Me One More Chance

You could make the case that Stephen Foster, a man who was only mentioned in passing in this chapter, is the patron saint of this era. That's kind of weird. Foster was born in 1826. But with the soft, sweet melodies he wrote on songs like "Oh! Susanna," "Hard Times Come Again No More," and "Old Folks at Home (Swanee River)," he could very well have found success in the early 1970s. But that's only part of Foster's story. An alcoholic, he died penniless at the age of 37. His life is a lesson in many things, one of which is the necessity of copyright.

Copyright protections in the 1800s were very weak. Had they been stronger, Foster wouldn't only have been a wealthy man, but his life might have turned out differently. Artists deserve protection for their work. While I think the term of that protection should be shorter than life plus 70 years, protections should be strong during that term. Music, we need to remember, has value.

# Highlights

1. **"I Want You Back" by The Jackson 5 (January 31, 1970)**[9]—From the opening glide down the piano, it's impossible not to feel the urge to get on your feet when this song starts roaring through your stereo. Every detail is impressive. The funky rhythm guitar. The tumbling melody on the chorus. The thick bass tone. Even the lyrics. You could spend years as a lyricist and not write anything as cutting as the first verse in this song. I went into this project thinking that this was the greatest pop song ever, and 321 songs later, I remain convinced.

2. **"Just My Imagination (Running Away with Me)" by The Temptations (April 3, 1971)**—The first three lines of this song feel pretty standard, a man appreciating his lover over a relaxing groove: "Each day through my window I watch her as she passes by / I say to myself you're such a lucky guy / To have a girl like her is truly a dream come true." Then the fourth line punches you in the gut: "Out of all the fellas in the world she belongs to you."

   The first three lines are the dream, the narrator thankful for the woman in his life. The fourth is reality reminding him that that life belongs to someone else. When the chorus arrives, The Temptations whisper the title as the strings swirl in the background, a mental fog. You can feel his pain because you've been there before.

3. **"Superstition" by Stevie Wonder (January 27, 1973)**—This is a masterclass in how to build a song, and Stevie does it for the listener in live time. He starts off with a drum groove. Then the bass and clavinet enter. Then more clavinet. Then the vocal. Then the horns. He never gives you too much at once. If he did, it would overwhelm you. But by the time you get to the end of this funky number, you're surrounded by so many different sounds that it's hard to remember how you got there.

---

[9] Both "Bridge Over Troubled Water" and "Me and Bobby McGee" were rated high enough to be included here. I mentioned them earlier.

# Lowlights

1. **"Go Away Little Girl" by Donny Osmond (September 11, 1971)—** How this was the first song to top the charts by two separate artists is beyond me. I thought with 13-year-old Donny Osmond behind the microphone it might make the song less weird than the 1963 Steve Lawrence version. If anything, paired with the palm-muted guitar, it sounds creepier. Please go away, "Go Away Little Girl."

2. **"My Ding-a-Ling" by Chuck Berry (October 21, 1972)—**We've seen this before: a legendary old-timer tops the charts with a lesser work later in their career. Dean Martin. Frank Sinatra. Louis Armstrong. Sammy Davis, Jr.[10] Their chart-topping swansongs were just sappy, though. Chuck Berry's isn't. It's a four-minute masturbation joke.

3. **"Tie a Yellow Ribbon 'Round the Ole Oak Tree" by Tony Orlando and Dawn (April 21, 1973)—**Tony Orlando could never just have a woman tell him they were into him. He always needed to find out in some strange way. In "Knock Three Times" (January 23, 1971) it involved banging on the ceiling three times. In "Tie a Yellow Ribbon 'Round the Ole Oak Tree" it involved an elaborate scheme of tying ribbons around trees. While I would advise Mr. Orlando and his lovers be more direct, he's got bigger problems on his hands. From the guitar masquerading as a ukulele to the hammy strings and whimpering harmonica, "Tie a Yellow Ribbon 'Round the Ole Oak Tree" might be the cheesiest song you ever hear.[11]

---

[10] Sammy Davis finally got to the top of the pops in this era with the syrupy song "The Candy Man" (June 10, 1972).

[11] Despite my aversion to the song, there is some interesting history baked into the lyrics. For at least a century, yellow ribbons symbolized that when an absent loved one returned home, maybe because they were in jail or serving in the military, that they would be welcomed with open arms. At the height of the Vietnam War, this likely led to some of the song's appeal.

## Argument Starters

"Ben" (October 14, 1972), Michael Jackson's first solo number one, is proof that even the King of Pop sometimes missed. And while I could commend Jackson's vocal, while also criticizing the fact that the song drags on a bit too long, the strangest thing about "Ben" is the movie that it was written for.

*Ben* is a horror film about a lonely boy named Danny that befriends a rat named "Ben." As they get closer, Danny must deal with the fact that Ben and his rat cronies are terrorizing people. The police then attempt to kill the vermin against Danny's wishes. We may not agree on the song "Ben," but everyone who judged this song agreed that the movie was much worse.

## Odds and Ends

1.  **"Family Affair" by Sly and the Family Stone (December 4, 1971)**— When "Family Affair" came out in 1971, it sounded out of place. Sly Stone built his cryptic song around a drum machine, the first number one to feature that rhythmic technology. Decades since, that technology has become so common that "Family Affair" feels like it could have been released last week. We'll talk more about the drum machine's meteoric ascent in Chapter 8.

2.  **"Want Ads" by Honey Cone (June 12, 1971)**—Pound for pound, this might be the most underrated number one thus far. It's a groovy, soulful song with a killer vocal and lyrics about looking for love in the newspaper that live at the intersection of playful and dead serious: "Wanted: young man, single, and free / Experience in love preferred but will accept a young trainee." Despite that, the song has left almost no cultural footprint. It's seldom covered or sampled. The Wikipedia page gets fewer than 50 views per day. The studio version hasn't even reached a million plays on Spotify or YouTube. Somebody help me turn this song into a classic.

3.  **"Papa was a Rolling Stone" by The Temptations (December 2, 1972)**— In his book *Mystery Train*, critic Greil Marcus describes how this song was so entrancing that he knew more than one person who "pulled

off the road and sat waiting, shivering" when they first heard it on the radio. While that sounds hyperbolic, I know exactly what he means.

"Papa was a Rolling Stone" is a mystery, a family prying their mother for information about their itinerant father who is now dead. But mama doesn't have much to add. She just hangs her head and tells her boys again and again, "Papa was a rolling stone / Wherever he laid his hat was his home." Sometimes the truth is simple. Sometimes it's complicated. Sometimes both scenarios leave us wanting more.

## Everything Else

"Thank You (Falettinme Be Mice Elf Agin)" by Sly and the Family Stone. "ABC" by The Jackson 5. "The Love You Save" by The Jackson 5. "(They Long to Be) Close to You" by The Carpenters. "I Think I Love You" by The Partridge Family. "The Tears of a Clown" by Smokey Robinson and the Miracles. "One Bad Apple" by The Osmonds. "Uncle Albert/Admiral Halsey" by Paul McCartney and Linda McCartney. "Joy to the World" by Three Dog Night. "Indian Reservation (The Lament of the Cherokee Reservation Indian)" by The Raiders. "Gypsys, Tramps and Thieves" by Cher. "Brand New Key" by Melanie. "American Pie" by Don McLean. "Let's Stay Together" by Al Green. "Oh Girl" by The Chi-Lites. "Lean on Me" by Bill Withers. "Brandy" by Looking Glass. "I Can See Clearly Now" by Johnny Nash. "I am Woman" by Helen Reddy. "Me and Mrs. Jones" by Billy Paul. "You're So Vain" by Carly Simon. "Killing Me Softly with His Song" by Roberta Flack. "Love Train" by The O'Jays. "Bad, Bad Leroy Brown" by Jim Croce. "The Morning After" by Maureen McGovern. "Delta Dawn" by Helen Reddy. "Half-Breed" by Cher. "Midnight Train to Georgia" by Gladys Knight and the Pips. "The Most Beautiful Girl" by Charlie Rich. "Show and Tell" by Al Wilson. "The Way We Were" by Barbra Streisand. "Dark Lady" by Cher.

# *When You're Hooked on Feeling with a Dancing Queen*

## April 6, 1974—April 9, 1977

### Play That Funky Music

When Prince was looking for help to write his autobiography, he asked potential collaborators to submit a short essay about their relationship with his music. Journalist Dan Piepenbring wrote about how Prince's music made him feel like he was breaking the law. Prince must have liked what he read. He gave Piepenbring the job. At the same time, when the two met, the pop star seemed to have some reservations. "The music I make," he told his new collaborator, "isn't breaking the law to me."

This confused me. Prince sings about sex (e.g., "Jack U Off"), incest (e.g., "Sister"), cunnilingus (e.g., "Head"), and basically anything not fit to talk about at a family dinner. What could he possibly mean? Luckily, he explained himself.

"I write in harmony. I've always lived in harmony—like this." He gestured at the room. "The candles." He asked if I'd [Piepenbring] ever heard of the devil's interval, or the tritone: a combination of notes that created a brooding, menacing dissonance. It reminded him of Led Zeppelin. Their kind of rock music, bluesy and harsh, broke the rules of harmony. Robert Plant's keening voice—*that* sounded law-breaking to him as a kid. Not any of the music that he and his friends made.

I saw what Prince meant. If you were twelve years old and heard the masturbatory opening line to his song "Darling Nikki" on the radio with your parents in the room, you'd probably be uncomfortable (i.e., "I knew a girl named Nikki I guess you could say she was a sex fiend / I met her in a hotel lobby masturbating with a magazine"). At the same time, you could mistake the bouncy melody underneath those words for something out of the 1940s. "Darling Nikki," in other words, was lyrically subversive but melodically and harmonically within the bounds of what we expect from popular songs.

While music of this era still followed those pop rules, the most powerful figure was one known to break them: the disc jockey, more commonly known as the DJ. DJs were so mighty during the middle of the 1970s because they dominated two places that could turn songs into hits: the radio airwaves and the dance club. Neither of these things was new. Radio had been around for decades, and people have been congregating to dance since the beginning of time. Nevertheless, FM radio not only began to supplant AM radio in popularity during this era, but there was an explosion in the depth and variety of radio program formats like never before.

At the same time, dance clubs, often referred to as "discos," proliferated across the United States. According to Peter Shapiro's book *Turn the Beat Around: The Secret History of Disco*, "By the end of 1975 there were an estimated five hundred discos in New York City alone and some ten thousand nationwide."

In many ways, it's misleading to use the term "DJ" to describe both people working at radio stations and discos. These are very different environments. Still, DJs in every space did have something in common beyond curating and mixing music. They broke rules. But this rule-breaking had very different consequences in each case.

## And Then She Turned on the Radio

When Casey Kasem died in 2014, almost every major news outlet published a laudatory obituary. The *Los Angeles Times* named him "among the nation's best known—and ubiquitous—radio personalities." *Time* wrote that he was "one of the most important disc-jockeys in the history of radio." *The New York*

*Times* said he was known for "creating and hosting one of radio's most popular syndicated pop music shows."

None of these assertions were exaggerations. Kasem's program—*American Top 40*, often shortened to *AT40*—began broadcasting on fewer than ten stations on July 4, 1970, but then swelled in popularity over the next few years. At its height, it was broadcast by hundreds of stations to millions of listeners. Coupled with the fact that Kasem also provided the voice for Shaggy on the TV series *Scooby-Doo*, he had one of the most recognizable voices in America in the second half of the twentieth century.

His show's premise was simple: Each week he would count down *Billboard*'s top 40 songs. This was not the first show to exclusively play the most popular records in the land. Top 40 radio allegedly goes back to a man named Todd Storz. Around 1950, Storz was at a diner and noticed that the patrons kept playing the same songs on the jukebox. "Why not just program a radio station to play a short selection of songs on loop?" he pondered. Noting that a jukebox held about 40 songs, he dubbed his new programming format "Top 40." It caught on fast. Kasem was part of the Storz lineage.

Because *AT40* used *Billboard* to seed its playlist, between 1974 and 1983, Kasem's show was controlled by a man named Bill Wardlow. During that time, Wardlow oversaw the compilation of *Billboard*'s charts. I have no proof that these two men ever met, but during this era, they symbiotically fed off one another, Kasem's popular show building Wardlow's industry clout and Wardlow's chart doing the same for Kasem.

Nevertheless, there wasn't much fanfare when Wardlow died in 2001. Here's what *Billboard*, his ex-employer, had to say upon his passing: "Willis 'Bill' Wardlow, former associate publisher and director of charts for *Billboard*, died Dec. 29, 2001, in Los Angeles at age 80. Known as the 'father of disco,' Wardlow worked in the music industry for 55 years, including stints at Columbia and Capitol Records."

There's a bit to unpack here. Primarily, this obituary is short. I'm not expecting *Billboard* to dedicate the cover to him, but 44 words feels curt, especially for someone who ran their charts during the magazine's expansion and pushed them to cover the burgeoning dance music scene. This brings us to the second oddity: Wardlow is referred to as the "father of disco."

Disco was created in nightclubs of New York City that largely catered to a Black and gay audience. In the wake of the 1969 Stonewall riots, the gay population was looking for safe spaces where they were free to be themselves and listen to the music they wanted. The spaces that emerged—like The Loft, Sanctuary, and Gallery—were socially and musically radical.

In the decades leading up to the 1970s, if you went out to hear live music, there were two things that were true. You were seeing a band, and that band was performing for you. Though it's commonplace now, at the time the idea of going somewhere to listen to someone play records was strange. If you wanted to listen to records, you could do that at home. DJs turned record-selecting into performance art.

But that wasn't the only radical thing they were doing. Their choice of records allowed them to create an open space where club-goers could focus on one another rather than a performer. This turned the historical audience-performer relationship on its head. It almost goes without saying that a middle-aged White man like Bill Wardlow had little to do with this revolution.

Still, Wardlow and *Billboard* brought more legitimacy to the disco scene by documenting it. And disco was tremendously popular during this era. The shortness of his obituary just made it seem like his ex-employer had a problem with him. According to Frederic Dannen's book *Hit Men: Power Brokers and Fast Money Inside the Music Business*, they did: Bill Wardlow was fired from *Billboard* in April 1983 over his mishandling of the charts.

## The Case for Fixing the Charts

From labels run by the mob to shady artist contracts, there has always been a degree of corruption lurking in the music business. Of course, corruption lurks in every industry, but music industry corruption is partially driven by the fact that it's a hits-driven business.

Say you're Hugh Hefner, and you want to start a record label that shares the name with your titillating magazine, *Playboy*. Most of your releases are flops, but then Hamilton, Joe Frank and Reynolds top the charts with their meandering ballad "Fallin' in Love" (August 23, 1975).[1] That one big single will likely compensate for most of your losses. Because of that, there are strong incentives to do whatever you can to get people to listen to your record, even if that means paying radio DJs to play your songs.

This practice of artists and labels paying DJs to play specific songs, commonly referred to as "payola," came to a head in the late 1950s and early 1960s when Congress hauled hundreds of radio DJs to Washington, D.C., for a hearing about the practice. After multiple radio personalities admitted to taking thousands of dollars in exchange for song placements, Congress amended the Federal Communications Act to force broadcasters to disclose if they were paid to play something. Payola, it seemed, was dead.

Not really. The law was never really enforced. Plus, independent promoters cropped up in the wake of the scandal who would shower DJs with drugs, money, sex, and whatever else they wanted to get songs on the air. Nobody would crack down on this evolved payola until the 1980s. Nevertheless, when something corrupt is going on, fraudsters usually leave a data trail.

In Figure 5.1, you can see that between 1958 and 1970, number ones typically spent two to three weeks atop the charts. There was variation, but one-week chart-toppers were not common, only occurring about 27 percent of the time. Then things changed. By the middle of the 1970s, the average time atop the charts fell close to 1.5 weeks with nearly 50 percent of number ones in the last two eras only leading the chart for a single week.

This does not technically mean something illegal was going on. But it's suspect. If you wanted to maximize your revenue for selling placements at number one, you'd probably want a ton of turnover. The oddities don't stop there, though.

Besides *Billboard*, other magazines ranked popular songs at the time. Take *Cashbox* as an example. From 1958 to 1972, *Billboard* and *Cashbox* listed the same number one in 64 percent of weeks. Between 1973 and 1978, the match

---

[1] Hugh Hefner did indeed found a record label. And Hamilton, Joe Frank and Reynolds were indeed signed to it. I get wanting to see your name in lights, but if that name sounds more like a law firm than a band, then you should probably go with something else.

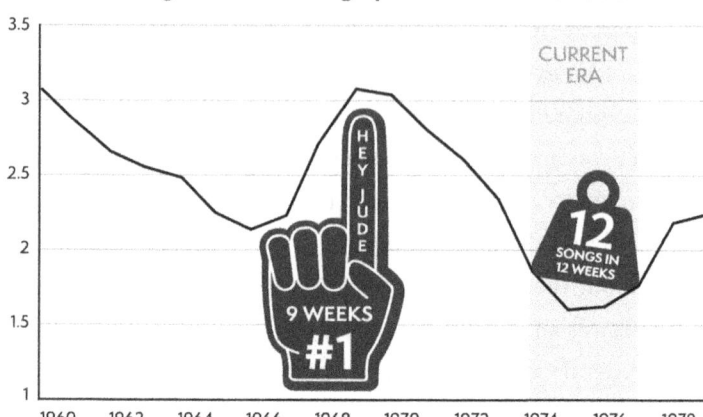

Figure 5.1

rate fell to 48 percent before returning to 71 percent in the period from 1979 to 1984.

At the same time, when songs were losing the top spot, they were falling farther down the charts than ever before. For example, Andy Kim's "Rock Me Gently" (September 28, 1974), a joyous record that you could mistake for the best of Neil Diamond, and Stevie Wonder's "You Haven't Done Nothin'" (November 2, 1974), a Richard-Nixon-protest-track, each fell from number one to number 12 in a single week. Similarly, Billy Preston's soulful jam "Nothing From Nothing" (October 19, 1974) and Dionne Warwick and The Spinners duet "Then Came You" (October 26, 1974) fell from number one to number 15 in a single week. When you look at the average fall from number one, it becomes clear that these weren't aberrations.

In Figure 5.2, you can see that from 1958 through most of 1974, when your average song lost the top spot, it was falling one to two slots. In this era, it was falling close to four slots before returning to the old rate of decline by the end of the decade. Something fishy was going on. And that something was Bill Wardlow.

In the book *And Party Everyday: The Inside Story of Casablanca Records*, here's how Larry Harris, a cofounder of the famed label, describes *Billboard* chart creation during the Wardlow era: "For the past two years, I had had

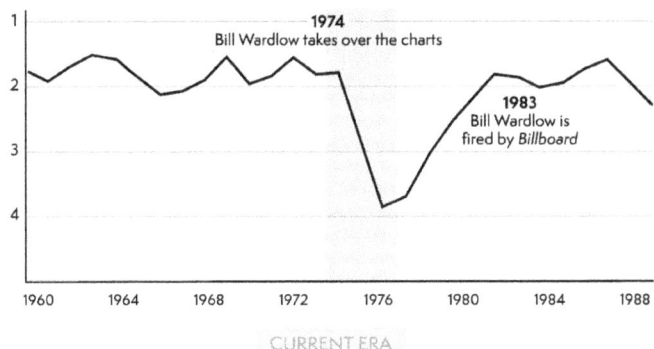

**Figure 5.2**

control over the *Billboard* charts and was able to significantly affect the positions of our records to help establish a perception that our company, Casablanca Records, and our artists . . . were the hottest in the music industry." Later on, he goes so far as to say, "Eventually, I could walk into Bill's office, tell him the position on the charts I felt a given album should have, and, lo and behold, there it would be." If we can take Harris at his word—and the statistical anomalies we've discussed suggest that we can—why would Wardlow do this?

"Bill loved disco," Harris wrote in his book. "Casablanca *was* disco . . . Bill wanted very much to be part of our scene, even going so far as to create a separate disco chart called National Disco Action Top 40." In an interview with the *AV Club* about the book, Harris also claimed there was a sexual component. Wardlow, he says, was gay and wanted to ingratiate himself with the gay disco scene.

Of course, Harris was not the only person involved in this behavior. Quid pro quo arrangements remained common in the radio world.[2] Did any involve Casey Kasem, the behemoth of the airwaves that we talked about at the beginning of this section? I haven't found any evidence that Kasem and

---

[2] When David Bowie's funky John Lennon-cowrite "Fame" (September 20, 1975) topped the charts, Bowie and his team allegedly sent Bill Wardlow a signed copy of the single as a thank you.

*Billboard* were in cahoots, but there was an incentive for the charts to shake out a certain way to make for better radio.

For example, when Carl Douglas's "Kung Fu Fighting" (December 7, 1974) ranked number one during the week of December 14, 1974, John Lennon's chart-topping "Whatever Gets You Thru the Night" (November 16, 1974) held onto the fortieth position for a second week on its way down the charts. Because Paul McCartney's "Junior's Farm," Ringo Starr's "Only You," and George Harrison's "Dark Horse" were also in the top 40 that week, it marked the only time each ex-Beatle had a simultaneous solo hit. Maybe *Billboard* did Kasem a favor for a good story. Anything is possible in the sketchy world of popular music.

## Move It In, Move It Around, Disco Lady

Here is a short scene that I've experienced at far too many band practices.

FADE IN:

INT. SUBURBAN GARAGE—DAY

CHRIS, a burgeoning rockstar, and his band are practicing in his parents' garage when the current song falls apart.

> CHRIS
>
> Stop! Can we go back to the second verse?
>
> DRUMMER
>
> Which part is that?
>
> CHRIS
>
> (Annoyed)
>
> The part we just played.

          BASS PLAYER

I thought that was the bridge?

          CHRIS

No. The bridge is after the third chorus.

          TRUMPET PLAYER

This song has a bridge?

          CHRIS

Just take it from the top.

                                    FADE OUT:

              THE END

In summary, sections of pop songs are hard to define. What you might think of as a chorus, another might call a verse. There are also certain songs in this era, like Paul McCartney's "Band on the Run" (June 8, 1974), to which our typical notions of verses, choruses, and bridges don't apply to. "Band on the Run" is three different songs smashed into one glorious pop 'n' roll epic.

Even songs that feel typical are often tricky to characterize. Take John Denver's "Annie's Song" (July 27, 1974) as an example. Like other Denver numbers, "Annie's Song" is an ethereal ode to a lover that evokes naturalistic images (e.g., "You fill up my senses like a night in the forest"). He sings three stanzas with a clear, evocative tone backed by an acoustic guitar, strings, and mandolin. Melodically, each stanza is identical, and lyrically, the first and third stanzas are identical. Does that mean the first and third stanzas are a chorus and there's one verse in the middle with the same melody? That doesn't make much sense.

Sadly for those who like tidy categorizations, musicians love breaking and stretching song structure. So, you've got to be a little fast and loose with definitions if you want to understand how those structures have changed. I'm not really the fast-and-loose type, but I tried to be so we could see how renegade DJs helped change the way songs were written without writing any themselves.

But first, we need to define each song type. And since it's the Christmas season as I write this, I'll identify each of these song types with a classic Christmas tune. If you want some additional fun, try to guess the sections of each Christmas song after reading the description. I'll drop a footnote identifying such at the end of each blurb, so you can see if you're correct.

## Verse: Songs Like "Silent Night"

These are songs that have one distinct musical section, usually called a "verse," that is repeated with different lyrics. Often, these verses will start or end with the same lyrical phrase, sometimes called a "refrain." The aforementioned "Annie's Song" follows the refrain-less form of this structure while songs like Simon and Garfunkel's "The Sound of Silence" (1966), Freddie Fender's "Before the Next Teardrop Falls" (May 31, 1975), Pink Floyd's "Another Brick in the Wall, Pt. 2" (1980), The Bangles' "Walk Like an Egyptian" (1986), and Sinéad O'Connor's "Nothing Compares 2 U" (1990) share the same structure but contain a refrain. In each of these cases, the refrain is the title.[3]

## Verse-Chorus: Songs Like "Last Christmas"

If verses up through this era are sections that share a melody but have different lyrics, then a chorus is a repeated section that shares both melody and lyrics. In a way, a chorus is a refrain that is long enough to be declared a distinct part of the song. Examples include Blue Swede's ooga-chaka-ing "Hooked on a Feeling" (April 6, 1974), LaBelle's half-gibberish, half-French "Lady Marmalade" (March 29, 1975), the Hues Corporation's soulful "Rock the Boat" (July 6, 1974), and Bachman-Turner Overdrive's stammering rocker "You Ain't Seen Nothing Yet" (November 9, 1974). "You Ain't Seen Nothing Yet" highlights another important quality of the Verse-Chorus form. Though verse and chorus are distinct, they can't work without one another.

During the first verse of "You Ain't Seen Nothing Yet," Randy Bachman sings about a "devil woman" who has wronged him. In the last line of said verse, he describes how this woman looked at him with her "big brown eyes" and said, "You ain't seen nothing yet." Technically, the words "She looked at

---

[3] Verse: "Silent Night" has three or four verses depending on the version you are looking at. Each of those verses begins with the refrain "Silent night, holy night," or "Stille nacht, heilige nacht" in the original German.

me with big brown eyes and said" are the last line of the verse, and "You ain't seen nothing yet" is the first line of the chorus. But they naturally lead from one to the other.[4]

## Verse-Mid: Songs Like "Winter Wonderland"

Like the Verse structure, verses in the Verse-Mid form repeat the same melody with different lyrics and often contain a refrain. What differentiates these songs is that they also have a second section, which I've chosen to call the "Mid."[5] This mid-section is usually repeated with the same music and lyrics. "But wait, Chris!" you might interject. "It sounds like you're describing a chorus." I'm not.

Though the mid-section often repeats the same melody and lyrics like a chorus, it has a very different relationship to the verses. While the two sections of the Verse-Chorus form are intimately connected, those in the Verse-Mid form show musical and lyrical independence. The cinematic classic "Over the Rainbow," as made famous in *The Wizard of* Oz, illustrates this well.

Each verse in the song opens with the somber, octave-leaping refrain "Somewhere over the rainbow," the narrator longing to get to a place far away. The mid-section, which starts with the line "Someday I'll wish upon a star," expresses much the same. That said, each represents a complete musical and lyrical idea.

If I were to sing you the first verse of "Over the Rainbow," I could stop at the line "Once in a lullaby" and things would feel relatively complete. Whereas the chorus in the Verse-Chorus form feels like a continuation of an idea, the mid-section of the Verse-Mid form feels distinct enough where even if you were to repeat it over-and-over, it wouldn't feel like the repeated section of a song in

---

[4] Verse-Chorus: Wham!'s original version of "Last Christmas" begins with the chorus (i.e., "Last Christmas I gave you my heart") before proceeding through three verses, the first of which starts with "Once bitten and twice shy."

[5] This song structure is sometimes referred to as Verse-Bridge, AABA, or 32-Bar form. I created this new name because we will use the word "Bridge" in another song structure and the second section in songs of this type was usually eight bars long and referred to as the "middle eight." Since these sections aren't always the same length, I shortened the term to be more inclusive but also make it similar enough to suggest its origin.

the Verse-Chorus form, like Barry White's baby-making "Can't Get Enough of Your Love, Babe" (September 21, 1974).[6]

## Verse-Chorus-Bridge: Songs Like "Santa Tell Me"

This form is identical to the Verse-Chorus form, except there is a third section usually called a "bridge" stuck somewhere near the end of the song. Some bridges are short, like the "Please be waiting for me, baby, when I come around / We could make a lot of loving before the sun goes down" part of the Starland Vocal Band's painfully unsexy sex song "Afternoon Delight" (July 10, 1976) or the equally brief "Yesterday's a dream, I face the morning / Crying on a breeze the pain is calling" part of Barry Manilow's melodramatic ballad "Mandy" (January 18, 1975).

Others can be longer and weirder, like The Doobie Brother's acapella breakdown in their drifting number "Black Water" (March 15, 1975). In any case, the goal of a bridge is to generate intrigue by contrasting with the monotony of the simple Verse-Chorus form.[7]

## Instrumental: Songs Like "Christmas Eve/Sarajevo 12/24"

Given that most of these song structures are built around lyrical ideas, I decided to partition instrumentals off by themselves. And by "instrumental" I mean anything that has no words or very few words, like Silver Connection's "Fly, Robin, Fly" (November 9, 1975), a song that only contains the title repeated three times followed by "Up, up to the sky."

As we spoke about in Chapter 2, the instrumental has never been that popular during the Hot 100 era. Nevertheless, it did make a bit of comeback in the mid-1970s with funky jams, like Average White Band's "Pick Up the

---

[6] Verse-Mid: Each verse of "Winter Wonderland" ends with the refrain "Walking in a winter wonderland." The mid-section is the part that begins, "In the meadow we can build a snowman."

[7] Verse-Chorus-Bridge: Ariana Grande's original version of this song opens with the chorus (i.e., "Santa, tell me if you're really there") before proceeding through two verses, the first of which begins, "Feeling Christmas all around." The bridge occurs between the third and fourth choruses and starts with "Oh, I wanna have him beside me."

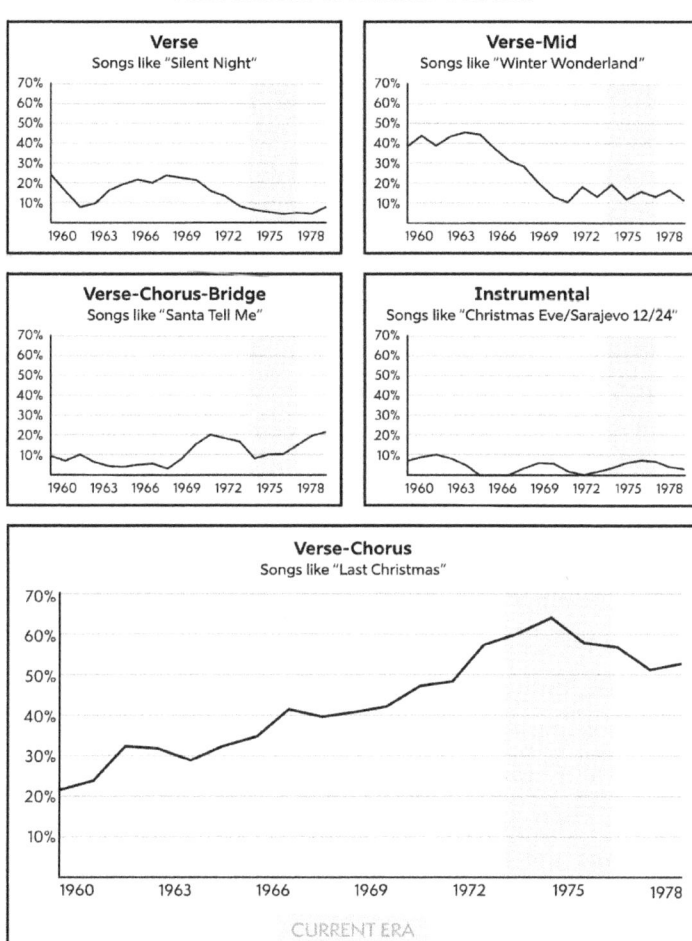

Figure 5.3

Pieces" (February 22, 1975), and rhythmic orchestral works, like MFSB's "TSOP (The Sound of Philadelphia)" (April 20, 1974).[8]

Okay. That was a lot of words to say that chart-topping songs typically fall into one of five structural categories: Verse, Verse-Mid, Verse-Chorus, Verse-

---

[8] Instrumental: Not sure what else to say here. It's an instrumental. It has no words.

Chorus-Bridge, or Instrumental.[9] And while the use of each of these has changed quite a bit between 1958 and the end of this era, the most important change is that the Verse-Chorus form has supplanted the Verse-Mid form as the most common structure used to write a pop song.

In Figure 5.3, you can see that at the beginning of the first era, 38 percent of songs were of the Verse-Mid form, while only 21 percent were of the Verse-Chorus form. At 24 percent, even the simple Verse form was more popular than the Verse-Chorus form. In less than 20 years, the Verse-Mid fell to 11 percent while the Verse-Chorus ballooned to 53 percent. That's an insane reversal. What happened?

Though the Verse-Mid and Verse-Chorus song forms are both quite old, the Verse-Mid form came to dominate popular song during the first half of the twentieth century. By 1960, it had been the main song form for at least 50 years. Not long after, it began to lose its hegemony. When you consider the rise of rock music and the fact that artists began writing their own songs more regularly as discussed in Chapter 3, it's not shocking that song structure began to change around then, too.

But during the mid-1970s, the Verse-Chorus form had become even more popular. It was used on country-inspired tunes, like Glen Campbell's "Rhinestone Cowboy" (September 6, 1975) and The Bellamy Brothers' "Let Your Love Flow" (May 1, 1976). It was used on spacey rockers, like Elton John's "Bennie and the Jets" (April 13, 1974) and Manfred Mann's Earth Band's "Blinded by the Light" (February 19, 1977).[10] It was also used on disco numbers, like KC and the Sunshine Band's "(Shake, Shake, Shake) Shake Your Booty" (September 11, 1976) and The Miracles' "Love Machine" (March 6, 1976). And though the Verse-Chorus form was used across genres, the key to understanding its reign in this era and the decades after comes back to the same maverick figure that started this chapter: the DJ.

---

[9] There is also a sixth category that captures structurally atypical songs, like Diana Ross's "Love Hangover" (May 29, 1976). These are so infrequent that they aren't worth discussing at length.

[10] In Chapter 1, I noted that Bruce Springsteen never performed a number one hit. He did write this wordy chart-topper, though.

# The Magic of the Mix

Francis Grasso didn't want the party to end. Could you blame him? One of the great human impulses is to buy yourself another drink when you're having a good time even though you know you should probably head home. But Grasso stayed up late. And he made sure that if he was up late, others would be there with him.

Grasso's secret was the mix. When a band played a popular song, people might rush to the dance floor. But when that song ended, there was always a pause before the next tune. Even if that pause was brief, it gave people enough time to head back to their seats. Grasso realized that with two turntables, you could turn the night into an endless groove, one record fading directly into the next. "Now," to quote Peter Shapiro's book *Turn the Beat Around*, "there was no abrupt ending, no jarring halt to your favorite song, no excuse, other than physical exhaustion, to stop dancing."

Francis Grasso was not the first club DJ. He was also not the first person to seamlessly mix records. But according to *Last Night a DJ Saved My Life*, Bill Brewster and Frank Broughton's comprehensive history of the disc jockey, "Before him, people had played records as if they were discrete little performances, Francis treated them like movements in a symphony." This was a revolutionary idea. As noted earlier, it's not obvious that listening to someone else play records should be entertaining. But given the right person behind the turntables, it was.

The way this worked was that Grasso and his DJing compatriots would "beat-match," meaning they'd find records with similar rhythmic qualities and either play them over each other or transition from one to the other. For example, maybe you notice that the Ohio Players' "Love Rollercoaster" (January 31, 1976) and Rose Royce's "Car Wash" (January 29, 1977) are both in 4/4 time and played at 115 beats per minute.[11] If you've got "Love Rollercoaster" playing

---

[11] 4/4 is your standard four-beat count that describes the rhythm of most popular songs, like "Beat It" by Michael Jackson (1983) and "Rich Girl" by Daryl Hall and John Oates (March 26, 1977). You can contrast 4/4 with 3/4, or the three-beat count, sometimes called "waltz time." The difference between these counts is made clear on Elton John's cover of The Beatles' "Lucy in the Sky with Diamonds" (January 4, 1975). The verses are in 3/4 and the chorus is in 4/4.

on one turntable and queue up "Car Wash" on the other, you can seamlessly transition between the two if you catch them on the right beat.

Similarly, maybe you think Paul McCartney and Wings' wistful "Listen to What the Man Said" (July 19, 1975) would sound great if it were played right into KC and the Sunshine Band's propulsive "Get Down Tonight" (August 30, 1975). If you've got two turntables, you can give it a try. Both are played at 113 beats per minute.

Of course, DJs aren't completely constrained by time signatures and beats per minute. They can manipulate their turntables to make two records work together that otherwise seem quite foreign. And the greatest DJs make non-obvious connections between songs. Francis Grasso, for example, was known to mash-up Robert Plant's orgasmic screams on Led Zeppelin's "Whole Lotta Love" over the percussion breakdown of Chicago Transit Authority's "I'm a Man."

While DJs could mix and match whatever music they wanted as long as it got people on the dance floor, the music that tended to go over well was what became known as disco. The most important thing about disco was the pulse. The record had to have a steady, four-on-the-floor beat. Though popular music in the Hot 100 era has always been obsessed with 4/4, disco made you think no other time signatures existed. In fact, in the first era, 75 percent of number ones were completely in 4/4. In this era, 95 percent were. The reason? It's harder to seamlessly mix songs in different time signatures.

There was also a funkiness to this rhythmic pulse. But there wasn't a hardness to that funk. It had a pretty, Motown-ish quality, often arranged with ornate strings. As James Brown's trombonist Fred Wesley allegedly put it: "[Disco] put a bowtie on the funk." That bowtie-funk is exemplified by Van McCoy's "The Hustle" (July 26, 1975), a lush instrumental with a driving rhythm and playful flute riff that took over dance floors during the summer of 1975.

And those dance floors could turn songs into unexpected hits. An independent company like TK Records could put out slinky, drum machine-driven track with a soaring falsetto, like George McCrae's euphoric "Rock Your Baby" (July 13, 1974), and have it top the charts without getting much radio play. All that mattered was that the right DJs liked the track, and dance floor patrons bought it after a night out.

Larger labels soon became hip to this fact that they could sell millions of records by releasing music that fit the disco mold. For example, ABC Records, the musical arm of the television behemoth, put out a disco-fied version of the theme song to their police procedural *S.W.A.T.* Performed by Rhythm Heritage, the song moseyed to the top of the charts in February 1976. Once bigger companies were in the game, they tried to get disco DJs to play the songs just as they had been doing with radio DJs for decades.

But what does this have to do with the Verse-Chorus song form? It goes back to the radical idea of DJs mixing songs, manipulating recorded music into new creations. The goal of a great mix is to keep patrons on the dance floor for hours on end. The Verse-Chorus structure is uniquely suited for this because songs of this form build up to a big, resplendent chorus rather than a short refrain.

Could disco DJs work with a song not of the Verse-Chorus form? Sure. Frankie Valli and the Four Seasons' "December, 1963 (Oh What a Night!)" (March 13, 1976) lives in the disco universe but adheres to the Verse-Mid form.[12] But DJs in this era preferred the Verse-Chorus to anything else. Disco was such massive phenomenon that the preferred tastes of DJs and dancers bled into every other genre. Even when the backlash against disco ensued, the preferences of those that made it and loved it lived on for decades. But we'll talk about that in the next chapter.

## Friday Night and the Lights Are Low

If you're ever going to make music, you need to trust your gut. There are just so many decisions that crop up during the recording process that you'll never get anything done if you're waffling at every turn. Since I've been playing in bands

---

[12] I need someone to figure out why 12 percent of number ones in this era had parenthetical titles. Either include the word in the name or don't. If you can't decide, you end up with something insanely long, like B. J. Thomas's "(Hey Won't You Play) Another Somebody Done Somebody Wrong Song" (April 26, 1975).

and recording music for a long time, I think I have a pretty good musical gut. And if my gut tells me that a song is good, I'll believe it. But if you ever want to doubt everything your musical gut tells you, look up songs that you think are horrible on YouTube. You're bound to find people gushing about them in the comments.

- "Billy Don't Be a Hero" by Bo Donaldson and the Heywoods (June 15, 1974)—"This sounds like such a sweet song!! I love the instrumental in the beginning, especially"

- "I Honestly Love You" by Olivia Newton-John (October 5, 1974)— "2:20. . . the pause, then spoken 'I love you', then they drop that minor chord in there . . . that always blew me away . . . even when I was 9 years old and first heard this song in 1974."

- "Convoy" by C.W. McCall (January 10, 1976)—"52 years old; this has always been and will continue to be my all-time favorite song, hands down"[13]

These comments are gut-humbling. I would never choose to listen to any of these songs again, yet there are people out there that are moved by them beyond comprehension. And while I do believe that the songs I list at the end of each chapter are genuinely good or bad, knowing that there are others out there who would angrily disagree with me is sort of beautiful.

## Highlights

1. **"Dancing Queen" by ABBA (April 9, 1977)**[14]—I wasn't comfortable enough with myself to start dancing until I went to college. I'm not a good dancer by any stretch. But with the help of peer pressure and cheap vodka, I learned to give in to the music. This stood in contrast to the

---

[13] At the beginning of Chapter 1, I lamented how no song has ever topped the charts with my home state New Jersey in the title. Given that near the end of this ridiculous record a convoy of truckers "laid a strip for the Jersey Shore" this is sadly the closest we have come to New Jersey number one glory up to this point. The second closest is when New Jersey native Frankie Valli mentions Ocean County, New Jersey's "Barnegat Bridge and Bay" in his beautiful schmaltz, "My Eyes Adored You" (March 22, 1975).

[14] David Bowie's "Fame" also ranked high enough to be included in this section. It was mentioned earlier.

dances that I went to in middle school. I still have visceral memories of the awkwardness, leaning against the wall, wishing I would disappear.

"Dancing Queen" is a trance-inducing song. Its arrangement is miles deep. When you think you've picked apart the entire thing, reach deeper and you'll come upon some percolating synth or melodic counterpoint that you missed. But the thing most mystifying about it is that it captures both the euphoria and sadness that we experience on the dance floor.

"Dancing Queen" involves two people, the titular queen and a narrator. When you surrender to "the beat from the tambourine," you are the dancing queen, "young and sweet, only seventeen," forgetting about your troubles for a few hours. But if you don't surrender, if you maintain the distance of the narrator watching the scene, you're the lonely middle schooler, holding up the wall, wondering how people could be so cheerful. Don't be that person. Always surrender to the groove.

2. **"Shining Star" by Earth, Wind and Fire (May 24, 1975)**—If you look up "Shining Star" on Wikipedia, there are three genres listed for the song: progressive soul, funk, and disco. And these are all fair characterizations. The verses are built around a hard funk, horn stabs filling out the background. On the chorus, some of that hardness is peeled back to reveal a disco-driven underbelly. But no matter how many genres you attach to "Shining Star," you still haven't captured the full breadth of the song.

   The guitar, mostly funking it up on the verses, plays a short solo that seems more indebted to the rock tradition than anything else. The vocal, seamlessly shifting from a deep baritone to a light falsetto, seems to exist outside of genre itself. "Shining Star" can't be boxed in.

3. **"I Wish" by Stevie Wonder (January 22, 1977)**—I imagine getting struck by lightning gives you the same feeling that Stevie Wonder conveys on "I Wish." The opening bass riff gives you a jolt just before a stack of synths leave your body shaking. And this shake is confusing. Should you be scared? Should you be dancing? Maybe both. Over a jittering groove, Wonder highlights the complexity of nostalgia, singing about how he longs to get back to the days of his youth even though not every moment was the brightest.

## Lowlights

1. **"The Streak" by Ray Stevens (May 18, 1974)**—In December 1973, *Time* wrote about a new fad: streaking. "Streakers generally race nude between two unpredictable points," the publication described, "and the idea is catching on among college students and other groups." Was this driven by the sexual revolution? The women's rights movement? In my case, it doesn't matter. What matters is that it led to the creation of Ray Stevens' ridiculous, half-spoken, half-sung tune about the practice.

2. **"Please Mr. Postman" by The Carpenters (January 25, 1975)**— Previously a number one by The Marvelettes (1961), something about the cleanness of this recording makes it feel lifeless, Karen Carpenter singing with an inexplicable smile while longing for a letter from her "boyfriend so far away."

3. **"Disco Duck" by Rick Dees and His Cast of Idiots (October 16, 1976)**—A common refrain during the late-1970s was that despite its massive appeal, disco sucked. Though we'll talk about why that wasn't true in the next chapter, if there were one song that might convince you otherwise, it's "Disco Duck."

   Though it has the typical disco pulse, "Disco Duck" doesn't beckon you to dance. It beckons you to gag, a nauseating, Donald-Duck-esque voice quacking catchphrases about an inane dance throughout the song. The best thing about "Disco Duck" is the name of frontman Rick Dees' backing band name: The Cast of Idiots. I felt like a member of that group after wasting my time listening to this.

## Argument Starters

You'll never catch me slandering "One of These Nights" by the Eagles (August 2, 1975). From the crisp falsetto to the smooth guitar solo and driving groove, it's an exemplar of some of the defining musical elements of this era. But it's that groove that caused the divisiveness. The other listeners thought that drummer Don Henley's hi-hat work was stilted. And I get it. Maybe if you had Dennis Bryon laying down a fat groove on "One of These Nights" like he did on the Bee Gees' "Jive Talkin'" (August 9, 1975), then the song would rise to another level. But Dennis Bryon wasn't on call. Don Henley had to play the drums. And I think he did a fine job.

## Odds and Ends

1. **"Silly Love Songs" by Paul McCartney and Wings (May 22, 1976)**— I'm going to lose any punk cred I have by saying this—and believe me there isn't much—but "Silly Love Songs" is one of the most punk songs you'll ever hear. This might confuse you. With its wildly melodic bassline, strong groove, and ornamental strings, "Silly Love Songs" seems like it has more to do with disco than punk. Sonically it does. But "Silly Love Songs" isn't punk in sound. It's punk in attitude.

   During his time in the spotlight, and especially after he left The Beatles, Paul McCartney was criticized for making songs that were overly sentimental. "Silly Love Songs" was his response to those critics, a song so saccharine that the chorus just features him singing "I love you." Yes, it's dripping in syrupy goo, but it's so sweet that it's defiant.

2. **"(You're) Having My Baby" by Paul Anka and Odia Coates (August 24, 1974)**—With lines like "The seed inside you / Baby, do you feel it growing?", Paul Anka managed to make the miracle of life sound as creepy as possible on this song. But the even bigger miracle of "(You're) Having My Baby" is that it upset everyone. Feminists derided Anka for referring to the child only as his baby, while the anti-abortion camp took offense to the line "Didn't have to keep it." Making groups that are often at odds come together in anger is something only a popular song can do.

3. **"I Write the Songs" by Barry Manilow (January 17, 1976)**—This is a sappy ballad that Barry Manilow ironically didn't write. I don't have much to say about it other than the fact than while researching it, I came upon an unbelievable anecdote from a 1990 *Rolling Stone* profile of Manilow: "[Manilow] suspects compliments . . . Bob Dylan stopped him at a party, embraced him warmly, told him: 'Don't stop doing what

you're doing, man. We're all inspired by you.' This actually occurred. He knew not what to make of the encounter. Nearly two years hence, it haunts him still."

## Everything Else

"The Loco-Motion" by Grand Funk. "Sundown" by Gordon Lightfoot. "Feel Like Makin' Love" by Roberta Flack. "The Night Chicago Died" by Paper Lace. "I Shot the Sheriff" by Eric Clapton. "I Can Help" by Billy Swan. "Cat's in the Cradle" by Harry Chapin. "Angie Baby" by Helen Reddy. "Laughter in the Rain" by Neil Sedaka. "Fire" by Ohio Players. "You're No Good" by Linda Ronstadt. "Best of My Love" by Eagles. "Have You Never Been Mellow" by Olivia Newton-John. "Lovin' You" by Minnie Riperton. "Philadelphia Freedom" by Elton John. "He Don't Love You (Like I Love You)" by Tony Orlando and Dawn. "Thank God I'm a Country Boy" by John Denver. "Sister Golden Hair" by America. "Love Will Keep Us Together" by Captain and Tenille. "I'm Sorry" by John Denver. "Bad Blood" by Neil Sedaka. "Island Girl" by Elton John. "That's the Way (I Like It)" by KC and the Sunshine Band. "Let's Do It Again" by The Staple Singers. "Saturday Night" by Bay City Rollers. "Theme from *Mahogany* (Do You Know Where You're Going To)" by Diana Ross. "50 Ways to Leave Your Lover" by Paul Simon. "Disco Lady" by Johnnie Taylor. "Welcome Back" by John Sebastian. "Boogie Fever" by The Sylvers. "Kiss and Say Goodbye" by The Manhattans. "Don't Go Breaking My Heart" by Elton John and Kiki Dee. "You Should Be Dancing" by the Bee Gees. "Play that Funky Music" by Wild Cherry. "A Fifth of Beethoven" by Walter Murphy and the Big Apple Band. "If You Leave Me Now" by Chicago. "Rock 'n Me" by Steve Miller Band. "Tonight's the Night (Gonna Be Alright)" by Rod Stewart. "You Don't Have to Be a Star (To Be in My Show)" by Marilyn McCoo and Billy Davis, Jr. "You Make Me Feel Like Dancing" by Leo Sayer. "Torn Between Two Lovers" by Mary MacGregor. "New Kid in Town" by Eagles. "Evergreen (Love Theme from *A Star is Born*)" by Barbra Streisand.

# *Don't Give Up on Us Just as It's Time for a Celebration*

## April 16, 1977—February 7, 1981

### Boogie No More, Listen to the Music

At some point in 2017, a Dutch record producer named YoungKio uploaded a beat to his online store that sampled the Nine Inch Nails' record "34 Ghosts IV." Many twenty-first century producers run stores like these. They exist so other artists can purchase samples and beats for their own use.

During the next year, an aspiring artist named Montero Lamar Hill purchased said beat and recorded a song. He released it in December 2018 under the name Lil Nas X. That song was "Old Town Road" (2019), and it took over the world for a few months, inspiring countless remixes on its way to breaking the record for weeks spent at number one on the Hot 100.

The popularity of "Old Town Road" was a product of the internet. A 2019 report by *New York* magazine unearthed that Lil Nas X first gained traction online by running popular Nicki Minaj fan accounts on Twitter that used dubious strategies to create viral posts. He converted one of those accounts into his personal Twitter while retaining his old followers. "Old Town Road" also benefited from widespread use on the short-form video app TikTok, along with a popular music video made up of shots from the video game *Red Dead Redemption 2*. The success of "Old Town Road" was a case study in how to market music in the 2010s. But some old-fashioned controversy also helped launch the song into the stratosphere.

## A Country Music Controversy

While country and rap began to interact in the 1990s, the two genres cross-pollinated more than ever during the twenty-first century. There were huge country songs with rappers, like 2012's "Cruise" by Florida Georgia Line featuring Nelly. There were popular country songs with hip-hop beats, like 2014's "Burnin' It Down" by Jason Aldean. There were even well-known hip-hop records that took cues from country, like Young Thug's 2017 mixtape *Beautiful Thugger Girls*.

Given this, it's not surprising that when Lil Nas X uploaded "Old Town Road" to SoundCloud, he listed it with tags like "Country Rap," "Trap Country," and "Hick Hop." He is rapping over a trap beat, but the song's sample is built around a banjo, his voice suggests a drawl, and the lyrics include country-ish imagery (e.g., "I got the horses in the back"). Looks like country. Acts like country. If I didn't think twice about calling Glen Campbell's "Southern Nights" (April 30, 1977) a country record even though it's largely pop music in overalls, then I shouldn't take issue with calling "Old Town Road" a country record.[1] And I didn't. But *Billboard* did.

During its ascent up the country charts, *Billboard* quietly removed the song. In a statement to *Rolling Stone*, *Billboard* said, "Upon further review, it was determined that 'Old Town Road' . . . does not currently merit inclusion on *Billboard*'s country charts . . . While 'Old Town Road' incorporates references to country and cowboy imagery, it does not embrace enough elements of today's country music to chart in its current version." The merits of this decision aside, *Billboard*'s removal ended up being one of the best things to happen to "Old Town Road." It inspired Billy Ray Cyrus to hop on the remix, which brought

---

[1] Campbell's hits often don't show it, but he was a guitar wizard. In a 2017 *Rolling Stone* article, rocker Alice Cooper—who formed an unlikely bond with Campbell over their respective sobriety journeys—recounted how Eddie Van Halen asked Cooper if he could set up some guitar lessons for him with Campbell.

the song to a new audience. It also led countless people to weigh in on the genre controversy.

Big and Rich's John Rich, most famous for the 2004 country record "Save a Horse (Ride a Cowboy)," was asked his opinion on the matter during a segment on Fox's *Brian Kilmeade Show*: "I think if you really want to be a country artist, then be one. Come to Nashville, write your music, really come up with something that's fitting somewhere around country music." Rich is equating country music to a place rather than a sound. True country can only emerge from Nashville.

We talked about the problems of authenticity and rock music in Chapter 3, but there may be no genre that's dealt with that problem more often than country music. The main issue is that the authenticity standard is in constant flux. A 2018 article in *Drum!* magazine, for example, described how all percussion was controversial in early twentieth-century country. "In backwoods venues throughout the South and onstage at the Grand Ole Opry," Bob Doerschuk wrote for the magazine, "drums weren't just absent—they were considered anathema to what [country] music was all about."

"Even so," you might be muttering, "Who cares? Jazz great Duke Ellington allegedly said there are two kinds of music, good and bad. Does it matter what we call 'Old Town Road'?"[2] It does. Though genre may seem like a neutral descriptor, it can also be a weapon. As noted in Chapter 2, *Billboard*'s current R&B chart descends from their Race Records chart. R&B charts are often catchalls not just for music that sounds a certain way but for artists that look a certain way.

Black musicians through the decades have derided these monikers for boxing them in. For example, in the early 1900s, pianist Little Brother Montgomery lamented, "If I could record whatever I want to play, I would have recorded some great numbers. Ballads and things like that. But they had us in a bracket. If you wasn't no great blues player . . . they wasn't gonna let us record no ways." Eight decades later, singer Frank Ocean expressed similar frustrations to *The Quietus*: "If you're a singer and you're Black, you're an R&B artist. Period." Because of

---

[2] Stevie Wonder's masterful ode to Ellington, "Sir Duke" (May 21, 1977), topped the charts in this era.

this, it's not surprising that the term "disco," a genre that was largely associated with Black and gay communities, was weaponized at the end of the 1970s.

Genre has come up in passing throughout this book. I've called certain songs "soulful" and others "country-inspired," along with a slew of other genre-related adjectives. But now I want to get a bit more precise, so we can pinpoint what we really mean when we describe something as a certain genre. A good place to start is July 12, 1979: Disco Demolition Night, the night disco apparently died.

# Did You Think I'd Lay Down and Die?

According to ESPN's Jeremy Schaap, Bill Veeck was Major League Baseball's P. T. Barnum. Elected to the Hall of Fame in 1991 and owning various teams throughout his life, Veeck was known for his strange gambits, some of which caught on, others of which were nothing more than publicity stunts.

- In 1947, Veeck's Indians signed Larry Doby, the first African American in the American League.

- In 1951, Veeck sent 3-foot, 7-inch Eddie Gaedel to the plate wearing the uniform number "1/8."

- In 1960, Veeck added last names to the backs of jerseys, now adopted by most sports teams.

- In the 1970s, he had announcer Harry Caray sing "Take Me Out to the Ball Game" during the seventh inning stretch, now a pastime at most ballparks.

Veeck's most infamous stunt occurred at the end of his tenure with the White Sox: Disco Demolition Night. The promotion was simple. If you brought a disco record to the ballpark that could be destroyed on field in between games of a double header, then you would be admitted for $0.98, a nod to the night's sponsor, 97.9 WLUP.

This was the brainchild of Steve Dahl, a WLUP DJ and avowed disco hater. Dahl's hatred was personal: He was fired in 1978 when his station moved from a rock to a disco format. It was also sort of his life's work. Along with his White

Sox promotion, Dahl snapped disco records in half on air, started an anti-disco organization, and released "Do You Think I'm Disco?", a parody of Rod Stewart's cartoonish but catchy "Do Ya Think I'm Sexy?" (February 10, 1979).

The White Sox hoped the promotion would draw 20,000 people. The official attendance for the double header was tallied at 47,795, a few thousand more than the stadium's official capacity. Eyewitnesses claim that when capacity was met, people started scaling the walls to get in. There were boxes set up for those people to deposit records, but as those filled up, fans proceeded to their seats with their vinyl in hand.

After the Sox lost the first game, Dahl, clad in military regalia, lapped the field in a Jeep and then declared the evening "the world's largest anti-disco rally." Soon after, a large box of records in center field was detonated. Vinyl rained down throughout the outfield. Those who couldn't fit their records in that box joined in on the fun by frisbeeing their records toward the destruction. Dahl then returned to his Jeep and was applauded as he left the field.

Though the festivities had ended, the pandemonium was only beginning. Some fans stormed the field while others headed for the exits. The latter found that all but one entranceway had been padlocked in an effort to hinder trespassers. The former found that nobody was stopping them. As Veeck tried to control the crowd, disco demolitioners wreaked havoc, sliding down the foul poles from the upper deck and starting a bonfire in center field. One eyewitness alleged to ESPN that he saw people having sex behind third base. In a last-ditch effort, Veeck and Harry Caray broke into song, trying to quell the crowd with "Take Me Out to the Ballgame." This did not work.[3]

At 9 p.m. the Chicago police took the field, finally disbanding the crowd. The grounds crew then tried to restore the diamond for game two, but it was in shambles, the outfield grass riddled with pockmarks and covered in beer. 39 people were arrested. Though there were no major injuries, the White Sox were forced to forfeit the second game as the field was deemed unplayable.

In the years since, Disco Demolition Night has been hailed as one of the worst promotions of all time. It has also been described as disco's death knell.

---

[3] Obviously.

This suggests two questions. First, given the slippery definition of genre, what were these protesters really trying to kill? Second, did Dahl's promotion work?

## What Was the Target on Disco Demolition Night?

House music pioneer Vince Lawrence was an usher at the ballpark during Disco Demolition Night. He recounted to NPR how people were showing up with "Records that were clearly not disco." He asked his boss if he should turn these people away but was told it was fine. As long as they had a record in hand, they got the discount. Years later, Lawrence quipped, "I want to say maybe the person bringing the record just made a mistake. But . . . it was just disco records and Black records in the dumpster."

While Dahl has denied such, various artists and critics have described Disco Demolition Night not just as an act of violence against disco but against Black and gay artists generally.

- Nile Rogers, whose group Chic got to number one with the groovy disco tracks "Le Freak" (December 9, 1978) and "Good Times" (August 18, 1979), likened the event to a Nazi book burning.

- Gloria Gaynor, the woman behind the resilient chart-topper "I Will Survive" (March 10, 1979), deemed the promotion "an idea created by someone whose economic bottom line was being adversely affected by the popularity of disco music."

- In a December 1979 *Rolling Stone* article where he mentions Steve Dahl, music critic Dave Marsh noted, "White males . . . are the most likely to see disco as the product of homosexuals, blacks and Latins, and therefore they're most likely to respond to appeals to wipe out such threats to their security. It goes almost without saying that such appeals are racist and sexist."

Though the chaos and violence of Disco Demolition Night were unique, the backlash against disco wasn't. To understand such, you first need to understand how ubiquitous the genre had become. During the time between Andy Gibb's "I Just Want to Be Your Everything" (July 30, 1977) and the Bee Gee's "Love

You Inside Out" (June 9, 1979) topping the charts, the number one song was a disco song in 67 percent of weeks. Half of those disco songs were written by members of the Bee Gees.[4] The group topped the charts six times themselves. Songs they wrote for their little brother Andy Gibb topped the charts three times. Respective songs written for Yvonne Elliman and Frankie Valli also topped the charts. That pair, Elliman's "If I Can't Have You" (May 13, 1978) and Valli's "Grease" (August 26, 1978), further highlight disco's reach.

Elliman's track was featured on the Gibb-penned soundtrack for *Saturday Night Fever*, a disco-centric movie that grossed hundreds of millions in 1977. The soundtrack spent 120 weeks on *Billboard*'s album chart and was an international sensation. Valli's number one was from *Grease*, the highest-grossing movie of 1978.[5] Though the film was a love story set in the 1950s, Valli's title track was a disco song. Plus, since the film starred *Saturday Night Fever*'s John Travolta, it also contributed to disco's cultural entrenchment.

On top of this, it felt like every artist was making disco. Marvin Gaye released the groovy "Got to Give It Up" (June 25, 1977). Donna Summer and Giorgio Moroder disco-fied "MacArthur Park" (November 11, 1978), Richard Harris's endless orchestral pop tune from 1968. Herb Alpert brought disco production to his sleepy instrumental "Rise" (October 20, 1979). Pink Floyd and Queen rocked the disco beat on "Another Brick in the Wall, Pt. 2" (March 22, 1980) and "Another One Bites the Dust" (October 4, 1980), respectively. Frank Sinatra and the Grateful Dead, two acts whose only overlap is their unrelatedness to disco, also recorded disco songs. After *Star Wars* came out, its theme song was given a disco makeover by Meco (October 1, 1977). "Gonna Fly Now" (July 2, 1977), the theme from *Rocky*, was given the same treatment by two separate groups: Current and Rhythm Heritage.

While the backlash against disco was partly fueled by racism and homophobia, it would be unfair not to acknowledge that some of it was also driven by resentment for an omnipresent cultural force that had become increasingly

---

[4] Only acknowledging the Bee Gees as a disco act distorts their long, varied career. "How Deep Is Your Love" (December 24, 1977) harkens back to their time as a folksy 1960s' group. Additionally, the intensity of "Tragedy" (March 24, 1979) could make for a great hard rock record.

[5] One of disco's great mysteries is how a song written by Barry Gibb for Frankie Valli contained no falsetto.

monetized and commodified. And the monetization and commodification often put the genre at odds with the scene that it emerged from.

As an example, take The Loft, an early dance party from which disco emerged. Loft sound engineer Alex Rosner noted that while the patrons were "probably about sixty percent black and seventy percent gay . . . There was a mix of sexual orientation, there was a mix of races, mix of economic groups . . . where the common denominator was music." Compare that to the scene at Studio 54, the posh disco club that opened in the late 1970s. While there was always an undercurrent of drug-fueled sexual liberation at disco clubs, Studio 54 helped take that to new heights with a focus on giving celebrities and the well-to-do priority admission. This was leagues away from the egalitarianism of The Loft. And almost any movement that grows so big so fast is destined to face some criticism.

## Did Disco Die on Disco Demolition Night?

Nearly everybody agrees that disco died at some point near the end of the 1970s. But we need to pinpoint when that death was to see if it was connected to Disco Demolition Night. One way to get at this is to use a similar strategy to what we used in Chapter 2 to track the rise and fall of surf rock: song titles.

To refresh your memory, many surf rock songs have the word "surf" in the title. By scanning the Hot 100 for any song containing that word, you can proxy when surf rock reached its commercial peak. Sure, you'll miss some stuff, but you capture enough to spot trends. Disco is similar because many disco song titles contain dance-related lingo, like Andy Gibb's "Shadow Dancing" (June 17, 1978) and A Taste of Honey's "Boogie Oogie Oogie" (September 9, 1978). If we count the percentage of songs that debuted on the Hot 100 in any given year that contain variants of the words "boogie," "dance," "disco," "groove," or "shake" in the title, then we can get a sense of disco's lifespan.

All the songs captured in Figure 6.1 are not strictly disco songs. Nobody was making disco music in 1959. But we can see the impact of the genre given the sharp rise in the percentage of songs with dance-related titles between 1976 and 1979. In fact, outside of that period, you almost never see more than 2 percent of Hot 100 debuts use titles of this nature. By 1978, 7 percent of songs that debuted on the Hot 100 had "boogie," "dance," "disco," "groove," or "shake" in the title. That's shockingly high for a set of five words. Two years later, that rate had fallen near 1 percent, never to rise again.

So, maybe Steve Dahl's destructive promotion did hand the genre its death blow. The event took place on July 12, 1979. By 1980, there were significantly fewer songs charting with dance-related titles. We don't have to guess, though. We can zoom in and look at the weekly title data.

In Figure 6.2, we can see that at the beginning of 1979, 8 percent to 12 percent of songs in any given week on the Hot 100 had a dance-related title, with the rate peaking at 15 percent during the week of May 12, 1979. Again, that is an absurdly high percentage. During that same week, only 12 percent of songs on the Hot 100 contained the word "the," the most used word in the English language. But then this dance-title rate starts falling. By the time Disco Demolition Night occurred, it was around 5 percent on its unimpeded descent to 0 percent by early 1980. In other words, Steve Dahl's destructive ballpark promotion just happened to occur when the genre was already losing its prominence.

At the same time, it's also inaccurate to say that disco was suddenly dead by the end of 1979. In the early 1980s, you still had joyous disco records topping the charts, like Michael Jackson's "Rock with You" (January 19, 1980), Lipps

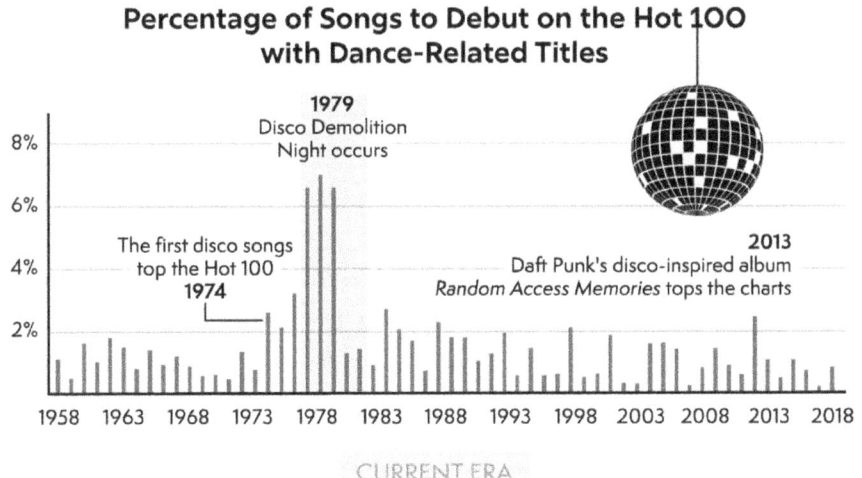

Figure 6.1

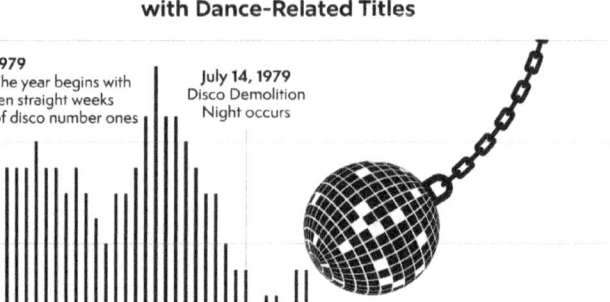

Figure 6.2


Inc.'s "Funkytown" (May 31, 1980), Diana Ross's "Upside Down" (September 6, 1980), and Kool and the Gang's "Celebration" (February 7, 1981). Similarly, Barry Gibb of the Bee Gees, the most prominent group of the late-disco era, continued to find success as the genre declined. In 1980, Gibb not only wrote and produced the chart-topping single "Woman in Love" (October 25, 1980) from Barbra Streisand's multi-platinum album *Guilty*, but he was pictured on the cover. The backlash against disco was real, but if the genre was dead, you wouldn't want one of its most prominent faces on the cover of your newest record.

In truth, disco never really died. Like rock music, its elements were incorporated into different styles, with artists like Madonna, Justin Timberlake, Daft Punk, and Dua Lipa, making disco projects in all but name in the decades since the insanity of Disco Demolition Night. Still, Disco Demolition Night highlights how genre can be a bit more sinister than a simple classification. With that in mind, let's define what people mean when they talk about genre.

# I Spent the Evening with the Radio

Genre is confusing. This confusion arises because when people talk about it, they are usually talking about one of three things.

1. Grouping artists by the musical and lyrical qualities of their work

2. Grouping artists by when, where, and with whom their work was created

3. Grouping artists by when, where, and which people are listening to their work

Definition (1) is the easiest to understand. This is when we group songs by use of melody, harmony, vocal style, and instrumentation, among other things. In its platonic form, it is devoid of any information about the artist. It allows us to say that The Knack's "My Sharona" (August 25, 1979) and Nick Gilder's "Hot Child in the City" (October 28, 1978) are the same genre because they are upbeat songs built around guitar riffs, big melodic hooks, and a stack of vocals on the chorus. It also allows us to put Blondie's "Heart of Glass" (April 28, 1979) and M's "Pop Muzik" (November 3, 1979) in the same genre bucket because they are built around percolating synths and disco-y rhythms. It even allows us to note the similarities between songs by artists who are known for making unrelated music, like "Three Times a Lady" by the Commodores (August 12, 1979) and "Babe" by Styx (December 8, 1979).

Though definition (1) makes the most intuitive sense, definition (2) is what people often use when they think they are using definition (1). (2) is a tool used to describe music scenes. It's the definition that John Rich is using when he says that if Lil Nas X wants to be a country artist he should "come to Nashville." While country has sonic qualities, it is also defined by where it is made and who it is made by.

Kenny Rogers' "Lady" (November 15, 1980) proves a good example of this. By the time "Lady" came out, Rogers was considered a country musician. Thus, "Lady" was considered a country record. In fact, it also topped *Billboard*'s Hot Country chart. But outside of Rogers, there is very little about "Lady" that would indicate it were a country song.

"Lady" was written by Commodore-soon-to-be-solo-star Lionel Richie. Had the Commodores recorded "Lady," there is no chance it would have been labeled country. I know this because they recorded "Still" (November 17, 1979), a stylistically similar ballad also composed by Richie. "Still" didn't appear on the country chart. Along with topping the Hot 100, it went to number one on *Billboard*'s R&B chart. Given that the Commodores were Black and Kenny Rogers was White, it's clear that genre in this situation had less to do with the music itself than who was making it.

## What Radio Stations Teach Us About Genre and Race

To get a better sense of how genre, race, and gender are entangled, I want to look at three popular radio formats: classic rock, oldies, and R&B. "Classic rock" is generally guitar-based music from the 1960s through the 1990s. "Oldies," sometimes called "classic hits," is generally top 40 hits from the 1960s through the 1990s. "R&B," sometimes called "urban," is generally lush, rhythmic music that combines pop, soul, funk, and smoother styles of hip-hop from the 1980s to the 2000s. While each of these formats overlaps in time frame, I'm always surprised which artists are played on each.

For example, while writing, I tuned into my oldies station and heard both "Purple Rain" by Prince and "Crazy Little Thing Called Love" by Queen (February 23, 1980). This makes sense. "Crazy Little Thing Called Love" topped the charts in 1980, and "Purple Rain" peaked at number two in 1984. Both classics. Both hits. They are also both guitar songs and thus could be considered classic rock. And when I go look at my classic rock station's recently played songs, they have indeed played "Crazy Little Thing Called Love" in the last few hours. But they haven't played "Purple Rain." For that matter, in all my years listening to my classic rock station, I don't think I've ever heard a Prince song. That's kind of strange given that his music is filled with great guitar work.

Because of this, I gathered data on these formats. I tracked the 119,504 most recently played songs on 104 classic rock, oldies, and R&B stations in the United States. Then I noted if the artist was a solo act, White, and a man. The results were startling. 90.6 percent of songs on classic rock stations were by White men. Oldies stations skew in the same direction, although the songs-

*Table 6.1  Demographics of Artists Heard on Classic Rock, Oldies, and R&B Radio Stations*

| Act Characteristic | Classic Rock (%) | Oldies (%) | R&B (%) |
|---|---|---|---|
| Solo Artist | 10.7 | 37.4 | 53.2 |
| All Members Men | 94.6 | 77.1 | 63.1 |
| All Members White | 95.9 | 83.1 | 1.5 |
| All Members White Men | 90.6 | 64.5 | 1.1 |

by-White-men rate clocks in at 64.5 percent. The demographic composition of artists whose songs are broadcast on R&B stations couldn't be more different, though. Only 1.1 percent of songs are by White guys.

So, why is this the case? Did more White dudes just make classic rock music than oldies or R&B? That's a piece to this puzzle. Another piece is that for decades, women were impeded from pursuing certain roles in the music industry (see Chapter 11). Because of that, 72 percent of number ones from 1958 to 1980 were performed by men.

Still, a vital piece to understanding the demographic groups that are lumped into a certain genre is the second way that I defined genre, namely as a way to group artists by when, where, and with whom their work was created. That's part of the reason why I heard Led Zeppelin's reggae-inspired "D'yer Mak'er" on eight classic rock stations in my sample, but not Blondie's equally reggae "The Tide Is High" (January 31, 1981). It's also why I heard The Rolling Stones' disco crossover "Miss You" (August 5, 1978) on 16 classic rock stations, but not Donna Summer's "Hot Stuff" (June 2, 1979).[6] While these pairs of songs have similar sonic qualities, Donna Summer is a woman and Blondie is fronted by a woman. Furthermore, Donna Summer is a Black woman. By definition (2), women, especially Black women, are barred from the classic rock boys' club.

The final rub is that it's not some guy sitting in an ivory tower deciding that Zeppelin's reggae is classic rock but Blondie's isn't. It's you and me. In his article "Why Classic Rock Isn't What It Used To Be," journalist Walt Hickey

---

[6] My friend Ken says that "Hot Stuff" rocks harder than a lot of songs you'll hear on classic rock stations. Honestly, Donna Summer's "Bad Girls" (July 14, 1979) does too.

interviews Eric Wellman, the programming director at WAXQ 104.3, a New York-based classic rock station. Here's how that article describes the creation of radio playlists:

> "The standard in the industry these days is an online music test or an auditorium music test where you just gather a sample and have [fans] rate songs based on the hooks—the most familiar parts of the song—and you just get back a whole slew of data," Wellman said. The stations find a cluster of people who like the music that makes up the core of classic rock, and then finds out what else they like. They like R.E.M.? Well, R.E.M. is now classic rock. "It's really that simple," Wellman said.

And this is where my third definition of genre emerges. Radio stations make money via advertising. If you are going to sell space to advertisers, it's easier if you can tell them things about your audience. If you have college students listening, maybe a cheap vodka brand will want to advertise. If you have middle-aged guys in the suburbs tuning in, maybe a lawnmower manufacturer will.

So, classic rock is classic rock, oldies is oldies, and R&B is R&B because of (1) how the music sounds, (2) who the artists are, and (3) who the listeners are. In fact, any place you are listening to music where there is also advertising, definition (3) is playing a critical role in how that music's genre is defined. In truth, all the radio formats are amorphous, ever-changing beings that move with listener demographics to service advertisers. Your favorites of today will be the oldies of tomorrow, soon to be relegated to footnotes in books on popular music as time marches by.[7]

When you dig into the history of genre, you'd be surprised to learn that our current conception of how we categorize music isn't really that old. Long ago, music was often organized by form and function. For example, in the 1600s and

---

[7] I was legally obligated to put a footnote here. But while you're here, I guess I'll give you a random fact. Because John Lennon's "(Just Like) Starting Over" (December 27, 1980) topped the charts after he was murdered, Lennon joined Otis Redding, Janis Joplin, and Jim Croce as the fourth artist to land a posthumous number one.

the 1700s, composers often wrote fugues. The actual details of what constitutes a fugue don't matter as much as the fact that you could group compositions of that form into a genre. Similarly, in the 1800s and early 1900s, you might see songs marketed as "parlor music," meaning songs specifically composed for amateurs to be performed in their homes.

Things began to change with the advent of recorded music. As talent scouts scoured the United States for musicians to record, there was always a keen focus on how those musicians should be presented and marketed. Often, as outlined throughout Karl Hagstrom Miller's book *Segregating Sound*, the default was to force Black artists to record certain types of songs and then market those records to Black people. This became known as "race music." The same thing happened with Whites in the southern United States, except the music was referred to as "hillbilly music."

Miller notes how this did not reflect the music that people actually made and listened to. "Black and white southerners," he writes, "listened to many of the same songs and styles, often performed by the same artists." As recorded music proliferated, listeners came to expect people who looked a certain way to perform a certain way too. Decades later, the names have changed, but we continue to live in this paradigm.

There are legitimate reasons for genres to be organized around people of certain demographic groups. Maybe, for example, groups are excluded from certain places and choose to make a music of their own. As noted throughout the last two chapters, that is partially how disco was born in the gay communities of New York City.

That said, we often apply gendered and racialized categories in ways that are both unhelpful and discriminatory. For example, when Tyler, the Creator—a Black man—won Best Rap Album at the Grammys in 2019, his reaction was mixed: "I'm very grateful that what I made could be acknowledged in a world like this, but also, it sucks that whenever we—and I mean guys that look like me—do anything that's genre-bending . . . they always put it in a rap or urban category, which is—I don't like that "urban" word. That's just a politically correct way to say the n-word to me." In saying this, Tyler, the Creator is expressing a frustration that Black artists have held for a long time.

But we don't have to live in this world. We can acknowledge the racism and sexism that have shaped popular music and still not call the explosive "Best of My Love" by The Emotions (August 20, 1977) an R&B record just because it was performed by Black women. Similarly, we also don't have to call the devout "You Light Up My Life" by Debby Boone (October 15, 1977) a country record just because it was performed by a White Christian woman. Maybe those records really are those things. But we can listen to the music and make an assessment rather than looking at a picture of the performer.

# Thunder Only Happens When It's Raining

During the writing of this chapter, I've been trapped in my house because of the coronavirus pandemic. I have a feeling that whenever this wretched thing ends, nobody is going to want to read anything about it. But I've got to tell you, it's been strange listening to so much 1970s dance music at a time when I'm not supposed to listen to music in public with anyone else. This experience has been a good reminder that as much as fancy headphones have tried to convince us that listening to music is a solo endeavor, the most powerful musical moments we have are those shared with others. And those shared musical moments have been rushing back to me as I've been cooped up in my basement.

Like in ninth grade when my friend Tom and I became buddies over a shared love of AC/DC's *Back in Black*. Or in tenth grade when my dad showed me an acoustic demo of Bruce Springsteen's "Growin' Up" while driving to buy some plants, and I felt like I'd seen the face of God. Or senior year of high school, when my friends and I missed a Passion Pit concert because of a snowstorm, so we snuck vodka into water bottles and went sledding while blasting their album *Gossamer*. Or the next year, when I was a freshman in college, and the head of my college's radio station lent me a copy of The Replacements' *Let it Be* like it was a sacred text. Or just a few months ago, when I was playing video games with my cousin John, and he shocked me by singing along to Sammy Davis, Jr.'s "I've Gotta Be Me." Nobody my age, I'd previously thought, was listening to Sammy Davis, Jr.

Though I've spent countless hours in my life listening to music by myself, when you find someone who likes the same thing as you, it's like you are speaking a secret language. Right now, all I can hope is that I get to speak that mysterious tongue sometime soon.

## Highlights

1. **"Dreams" by Fleetwood Mac (June 18, 1977)**[8]—Your typical number one hit features its title so prominently that you could probably guess it correctly 98 percent of the time. "Dreams" isn't your typical number one hit, though. It buries the title at the end of the second verse, Stevie Nicks asking, "And have you any dreams you'd like to sell?" That's the trick of this song. Nothing calls attention to itself. All you can do is look inward and try to answer Nicks's query as the song washes over you.

2. **"Stayin' Alive" by Bee Gees (February 4, 1978)**—As John Travolta struts down the street during the opening of the film *Saturday Night Fever*, "Stayin' Alive" plays in the background. It's a perfect audio-visual pairing. Kind of. The song is so visceral, Barry Gibb wailing over an incessant groove, that the visual not only feels redundant but lacking. There is sweat, fear, and triumph pulsating through "Stayin' Alive" in such a way that any attempt to render it in moving image falls short.[9]

3. **"Don't Stop 'Til You Get Enough" by Michael Jackson (October 13, 1979)**—Jackson is mumbling at the beginning of this record—"You know, I was, I was wondering, you know, if you could keep on / Because the force, it, it's got a lot of power / And it make me feel like, it, it make me feel like"—but when words prove futile, the song's dizzying strings set in behind a ticklish rhythm, capturing what he can't linguistically. Sometimes a good groove says more than words ever will.

---

[8] Gloria Gaynor's "I Will Survive" was also rated high enough to be included here. It was mentioned earlier.

[9] During the recording of this track, drummer Dennis Bryon had to attend to a family emergency. To continue working, the group looped a few bars from their "Night Fever" (March 18, 1978) and used it as the drum track on "Stayin' Alive." They credited it to a fictional drummer and received inquiries on how to contact him.

# Lowlights

1. **"Da Doo Ron Ron" by Shaun Cassidy (July 16, 1977)**—Every time I see that this record had the lowest rating, I think to myself, "That can't be right." Then I go back and listen. It's definitely right. And to understand why, you need to compare it to the original recording as done by The Crystals in 1963.

   While both versions tell of falling in love hard and fast (i.e., "I met him on a Monday and my heart stood still"), the "da doo ron ron" refrain comes across very different in each. The Crystals use it to stand in where words fail, your mind moving too fast to cobble together a coherent sentence. Shaun Cassidy, by comparison, renders that refrain true nonsense, unclear if he really understands the passion of the lyrics. On top of this, Cassidy's version falls victim to when it was recorded. The more primitive 1960s technology gives The Crystals' version a warmth that the sleeker, 1970s production lacks.

2. **"Do That To Me One More Time" by Captain and Tennille (February 16, 1980)**—Usually a song ends up in this section because it fails spectacularly on multiple fronts. "Do That To Me One More Time" doesn't suffer from that cross-board failure. In fact, certain pieces succeed, like Tennille's sultry vocals. But then this electronic wind-instrument called a lyricon rips a solo that ratchets the song's cheesiness up to levels unimaginable. If you don't feel like you're watching the credits to a bad 1980s porno by the end of this song, you've lucked out.

3. **"Knock on Wood" by Amii Stewart (April 21, 1979)**—If Amii Stewart happens to be reading this, I want to submit my sincerest apology. This song really isn't that bad. There were just a ton of great number ones in this era, and something had to end up in the bottom three. If anything, its greatest flaw is falling short of the two earlier versions done by Eddie Floyd and Otis Redding, respectively.

# Argument Starters

If you told the average person that the Eagles released the most divisive number one in two consecutive chapters of this book, they wouldn't believe you. The Eagles are one of the most popular groups of all time. And while I remain incredulous at the fact that "One of These Nights" (1975) was last era's most divisive song, I can at least understand why "Hotel California" (May 7, 1977) wore the crown in this era. And I say that as someone who thinks it's a perfect song, the introductory music is so vivid that when the vocal starts, it proves the opening "On a dark desert highway / Cool wind in my hair" unnecessary. And that's crazy given how compelling the song's lyrics are.

Still, "Hotel California" is so ingrained in the American consciousness that whether it's your favorite or least favorite song, you likely never need to hear it again. I'd go so far as to say that asking people to rate "Hotel California" on a scale from one to ten is akin to asking them to rate "Happy Birthday." It's just too ubiquitous to formulate a real opinion on.[10]

# Odds and Ends

1. **"Escape (The Piña Colada Song)" by Rupert Holmes (December 22, 1979)**—In a *Songfacts* interview, Rupert Holmes said, "I have a feeling that if I saved an entire orphanage from a fire and carried the last child out on my shoulders, as I stood there charred and smoking, they'd say, 'Aren't you the guy who wrote 'The Piña Colada Song'?'" Though he's had a varied career that included two Tony Awards, Holmes needs to understand why this fictional person would ask about "The Piña Colada Song." Beyond the fact that it's tremendously catchy, it has one of the strangest lyrical narratives of all time.

   The song features a man in an unhappy relationship who decides to meet up with a woman who put an intriguing personal ad in the newspaper. When the man gets to that "bar called O'Malley's" to see her,

---

[10] "Happy Birthday" stinks. Next time we write a song that we force people to sing in groups many times a year, let's not put an octave leap in the melody.

he finds that it's his current lover! In an attempt to cheat on one another, they both find that they have more in common than they thought. I'm sorry, Rupert. If you pull me out of a burning building, I'm asking about this song too.

2. **"Don't Leave Me This Way" by Thelma Houston (April 23, 1977)**— Should you come across someone who still believes that all disco sucks, put on this Thelma Houston song for them. If they don't change their mind by the second verse, please give them my contact information because I'd like to have a word with them.

3. **"You Don't Bring Me Flowers" by Barbra Streisand and Neil Diamond (December 2, 1978)**—Both Streisand and Diamond put out solo versions of this tune around the same time. Louisville-area DJ Gary Guthrie realized that each version was in the same key, so he spliced them together. It was a local hit. Somebody at Columbia Records caught wind and got Diamond and Streisand to record a definitive version with Four Seasons' hitmaker Bob Gaudio.

    Streisand's vocal histrionics generally irk me, but her silky voice pairs oddly well with Diamond's near-spoken performance on this song. The song is further elevated by some fine pop music poetry: "It used to be so natural to talk about forever / But used to be's don't count anymore / They just lay on the floor until we sweep them away."

## Everything Else

"Don't Give Up on Us" by David Soul. "When I Need You" by Leo Sayer. "I'm Your Boogie Man" by KC and the Sunshine Band. "Undercover Angel" by Alan O'Day. "Looks Like We Made It" by Barry Manilow. "Baby Come Back" by Player. "(Love Is) Thicker Than Water" by Andy Gibb. "With a Little Luck" by Paul McCartney. "Too Much, Too Little, Too Late" by Johnny Mathis and Deniece Williams. "You're the One that I Want" by John Travolta and Olivia Newton-John. "Kiss You All Over" by Exile. "You Needed Me" by Anne Murray. "Too Much Heaven" by Bee Gees. "What a Fool Believes" by The Doobie Brothers. "Reunited" by Peaches and Herb. "Ring My Bell" by Anita

Ward. "Sad Eyes" by Robert John. "Heartache Tonight" by Eagles. "No More Tears (Enough is Enough)" by Barbra Streisand and Donna Summer. "Please Don't Go" by KC and the Sunshine Band. "Call Me" by Blondie. "Coming Up" by Paul McCartney. "It's Still Rock and Roll to Me" by Billy Joel. "Magic" by Olivia Newton-John. "Sailing" by Christopher Cross.

# Rocking from 9 to 5 with My Buddy Amadeus

## February 21, 1981— March 29, 1986

### I Want to See You Clearly

At the 2009 Video Music Awards (VMAs), Taylor Swift won Best Female Video for her country crossover "You Belong with Me." When the 19-year-old Swift started thanking the crowd, she was cut off by Kanye West, the outspoken rapper who had stormed the stage. "Yo Taylor," he began, "I'm really happy for you. I'm gonna let you finish. But Beyoncé had one of the best videos of all time."

The backlash against West was, well, swift. Multiple media outlets lambasted his antics and President Barack Obama even referred to him as a "jackass" in leaked remarks. In response, West issued an apology on *The Jay Leno Show* and then retreated to Oahu, Hawaii, to work on music. When he released "Power" in June of the next year—the lead single from his magnum opus *My Beautiful Dark Twisted Fantasy*—he addressed the controversy (i.e., "They say I was the abomination of Obama's nation") and rescinded any of his previous repentance (i.e., "Screams from the haters, got a nice ring to it / I guess every superhero need his theme music").

Swift responded with "Innocent," a cut from her much-lauded 2010 album *Speak Now*, which she performed at the next VMAs. Things then simmered, the two allegedly becoming friendly, until West released "Famous," the lead single from his 2016 album *The Life of Pablo*. Swift took umbrage at West rapping, "I feel like me and Taylor might still have sex / Why? I made that bitch famous." West responded by saying that Swift had approved the lyric. In turn, Swift said that she approved "I feel like me and Taylor might still have sex" but not being referred to as a "bitch" or West taking credit for her career. While this saga would continue for years, let's return to the scene where it began: the VMAs.

When Kanye West stormed the stage at the ceremony, Taylor Swift was holding an MTV Moonman, a statuette given to every performer who wins a VMA. While both Swift and West are musicians, this award wasn't strictly about music. It was about the visuals that are paired with their music.

The importance of visuals was clear by looking at the two artists. They were both dressed to the nines. Their outfits were works of art. Their faces were works of art. Even their heads of hair were works of art. Before the proliferation of television and the internet, recorded music was a nonvisual medium. While today we know what most pop stars look like, listeners in the late 1950s might realistically not have been able to identify some. In fact, MTV cofounder Bob Pittman suggested in the book *I Want My MTV: The Uncensored Story of the Music Video Revolution* that "Before MTV, if you were a big act, no one knew what you looked like." Of course, there were outliers like The Beatles and Elvis Presley, but realistically, if you missed an artist perform on a handful of variety shows and didn't own one of their releases, you wouldn't have had an easy way to know what they looked like.

It was during this era—between Dolly Parton's jittery "9 to 5" (February 21, 1981) and Falco's Mozartian ode "Rock Me Amadeus" (March 29, 1986)[1]—that a musician's image began to matter as much as their music. While there were a variety of technological and economic forces underpinning this change, let's talk about its connection to MTV and growing record label concentration.

---

[1] During the chorus of "Rock Me Amadeus," my sister Emily thought Falco was saying, "Hot potatoes, hot potatoes" rather than "Amadeus, Amadeus." I can't unhear it.

**Percentage of Number One Hits with a Music Video**

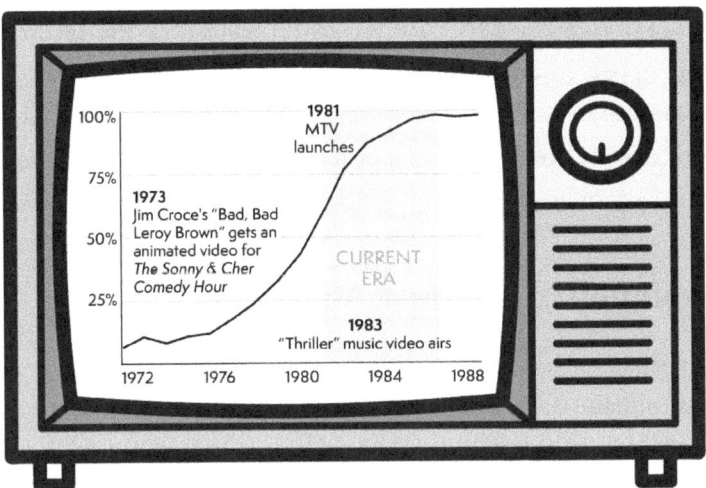

Figure 7.1

# I Want My MTV

When MTV launched at midnight on August 1, 1981, aptly airing The Buggles' "Video Killed the Radio Star," they weren't inventing the music video.[2] For that matter, beyond the declining costs to install cable, especially in rural areas, the primary reason that a music video television network could flourish was that there were videos in existence that they could use.

In Figure 7.1, we see a growing interest in the medium a few years before MTV's 1981 launch. In fact, Blondie—who unexpectedly has the honor of performing the first number one with a rapped verse because of their genre-bending "Rapture" (March 28, 1981)—released *Eat to the Beat*, a music video album, almost a year before the launch of MTV. So, music videos were a thing before MTV took to the air. But if there were few reliable places to show them, why were artists making them?

---

[2] I always thought that The Buggles were a fictional group concocted for MTV's debut. They were actually a short-lived British band formed by Trevor Horn and Geoffrey Downes. Both Horn and Downes were briefly members of the progressive rock band Yes. In fact, Horn cowrote and produced Yes's only number one: "Owner of a Lonely Heart" (January 21, 1984).

Video and music have a long, deep connection. From the 1950s onward, there were popular variety shows featuring musical performances, including *Soul Train, Saturday Night Live,* and *American Bandstand.* Pre-recorded videos sometimes appeared on these programs. Labels also realized that instead of flying a band to Britain to play on, say, *Top of the Pops,* they could create a video and have the program air that instead. Still, MTV-era videos represented a dramatic shift in how music and visuals would interact forever after.

## The Evolution of the Music Video

When artists first started creating videos, labels didn't have personnel dedicated to make them nor did they realize their power. Because there was little oversight and few rules, early videos were simple and sometimes strange. As MTV's influence grew and labels began to realize the ability of a video to make a hit, they morphed into big-budget affairs. Six-time chart-toppers Daryl Hall and John Oates demonstrate this progression.

There was no video made for Hall and Oates' first number one, "Rich Girl" (1977), but their next smash, the chipper "Kiss on My List" (April 11, 1981), had a video that appeared on MTV's first day of programming. Calling it a music video isn't totally accurate, though. It was a recording of the band playing the song live.

Soon after, "Private Eyes" (November 7, 1981) and "I Can't Go for That (No Can Do)" (January 30, 1982) got more legitimate videos. Albeit mostly lip-synched performances, some simple costumes and visual effects were used in these productions. Furthermore, they stood in contrast to a live performance video based on how they were edited. MTV-era music videos seldom linger on a single shot. For example, the video for Duran Duran's "The Reflex" (June 23, 1984) cuts to 30 different shots in the first minute. This dizzying editing style is one of the differentiating factors between videos of this era and their ancestors.

"Maneater" (December 18, 1982), Hall and Oates' next chart-topper, upped the ante a bit more. Again, there's a lot of band footage, but there are also shots of a tiger and a woman interspersed throughout. Though subtle, these two elements foreshadow the big-budget, sex-driven concepts that are to come.

By the time the duo released their final number one, "Out of Touch" (December 8, 1984), that new world had arrived. The video opens with a giant clapboard taking up the entirety of the screen. It falls to the ground, and we see both Hall and Oates trapped in a humongous kick drum. The video then cuts to their bandmates playing the drums with comically large sticks before the duo breaks free, soon crushed into two dimensions by the tumbling drum. Over the next four minutes, there are expansive sets, artistic lighting, and some basic choreography.

While many artists followed this progression from live concert footage to mini-movie, Michael Jackson is credited with inciting the change. The videos for his number ones from 1979's *Off the Wall* are elementary affairs, Jackson singing and dancing in front of a green screen. By the time he released his 1982 blockbuster *Thriller*, he had grander ambitions.

"Billie Jean" (March 5, 1983), the lead single from the album, allegedly tells the story of an obsessed fan making outrageous claims about him and his personal life. Though not explicitly capturing this unhealthy fanaticism, the video evokes some mystery while the dancing Jackson roams around an extensive set with sidewalk panels that light up when he steps on them.[3]

Jackson went even bigger for his next single "Beat It" (April 30, 1983).[4] The video opens in a diner where it becomes clear that two enemy gangs are spoiling for a fight. As the rivals approach one another, we find Jackson in his bedroom lamenting the needless violence. He then emerges, the two gangs locked in a knife fight, and joins the rumble, unifying them in a choreographed dance.

This video was reportedly so expensive that Jackson had to pay for it because his label refused to front him money. He also insisted that genuine

---

[3] Throughout its infanthood, MTV was dogged by accusations of racism. In fact, they refused to play "Billie Jean" until after it had topped the charts and Walter Yetnikoff, president of CBS Records, the parent of Jackson's label, told them, "I'm pulling everything we have off the air, all our product. I'm not going to give you any more videos. And I'm going to go public and fucking tell them about the fact you don't want to play music by a Black guy." The video subsequently was a huge hit and moved into heavy rotation.

[4] The guitar solo on this hard rock crossover was played by Eddie Van Halen, whose band topped the charts in this era with "Jump" (February 25, 1984). Quincy Jones reached out to Van Halen to play the solo, but the guitarist assumed it was a prank call. When they finally got him in studio, the speakers allegedly erupted in flames as he shredded.

gang rivals be cast in the video to foster goodwill between the groups. While Jackson wasn't awarded a Nobel Peace Prize, the video furthered his international stardom and highlighted the lengths he would go to for his visuals.

About a year later, Jackson released a video for "Thriller," his album's title track. In an effort to go bigger, he conceived of a thirteen-and-a-half-minute horror film with long sequences of dialogue that culminated in him leading the undead in a dance. This video turbocharged sales of his album, on its way to becoming one of the best-known videos of all time. It also convinced labels to pour money into videos and established MTV as a cultural juggernaut that could make or break careers. In the post-*Thriller* era, videos became grander than ever before.

- After double-doors swing open to reveal Prince in the bathtub, the video for the star's "When Doves Cry" (July 7, 1984) sees him riding his motorcycle to a variety of locations before arriving at a studio where a mirrored effect captures him dancing as the song fades out.

- In Madonna's video for "Like a Virgin" (December 22, 1984), she lives out a *Beauty and the Beast*-style fantasy as she's followed by a tiger through the streets of Venice.

- Dire Straits and a-Ha took the medium into the future with their respective videos for "Money for Nothing" (September 21, 1985) and "Take on Me" (October 19, 1985). The former was made with 3D computer animation over a decade before a feature film would be released in that style. The latter combined hand-drawn animation with live action footage of the band.

Labels were willing to spend millions on these elaborate videos because if MTV moved them into heavy rotation, they would almost certainly become huge hits, making the label their money back and then some. But the importance of MTV wasn't only how it created a new medium through which hits could be made. It also had a notable effect on who was popular, how their music sounded, how it was used in films, and how those films were shot.

# The British Are Coming . . . Again

If I told you to name a British band that was popular in the United States, your mind would probably dart to groups that first splashed on American shores in the 1960s. The Beatles. The Rolling Stones. Led Zeppelin. The Who. That would make sense. All those bands cast a large shadow on American popular music. Nevertheless, the British might have had an even wider impact during this era.

In November 1983, *Rolling Stone* observed, "On July 16th, 1983 . . . no fewer than eighteen singles of British origin charted in the American Top Forty, [topping] the previous high of fourteen, set on June 18th, 1965. There are now more British records on the US charts than at any other time in pop history." If we zoom in on the number ones, we see further proof of this second, larger invasion.

While Figure 7.2 makes the Brits' first chart invasion apparent, it also highlights how the second was more expansive. Between 1964 and 1966, 35 percent of number ones were by British artists. From 1983 to 1985, that number rose to 43 percent. Though these invasions originated in the same place, they couldn't have been more different musically. While the first focused on guitar music, the second helped bring synthesizers into vogue.

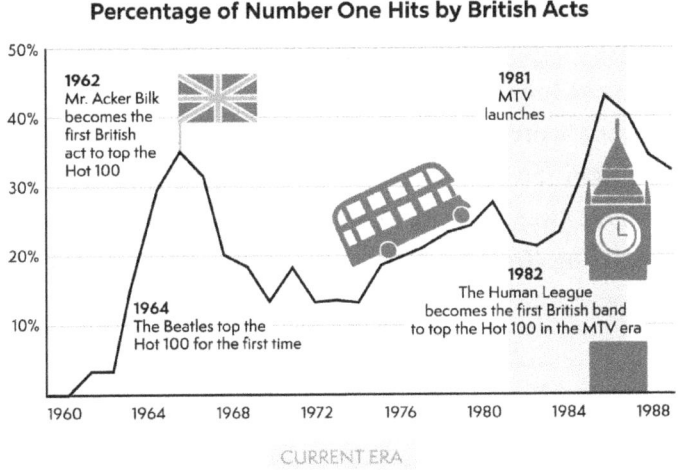

**Percentage of Number One Hits by British Acts**

**1962** Mr. Acker Bilk becomes the first British act to top the Hot 100

**1981** MTV launches

**1964** The Beatles top the Hot 100 for the first time

**1982** The Human League becomes the first British band to top the Hot 100 in the MTV era

CURRENT ERA

Figure 7.2

The Human League's "Don't You Want Me" (July 3, 1982) proves a good example of this synthy sound. "Don't You Want Me" kicks off with a percolating synth over a drum machine groove. More synths are piled on before Philip Oakey and Susan Ann Sulley begin their painful tale of failing love. From what I can hear, there are no guitars on this track. In fact, The Human League's lineup often lacked a guitar player, a mortal sin for groups of the first invasion.

Many other British groups fit this sonic palette. The Eurythmics, for example, took their brooding synths to number one on "Sweet Dreams (Are Made of This)" (September 3, 1983). Tears for Fears did the same on their momentous records "Everybody Wants to Rule the World" (June 8, 1985) and "Shout" (August 3, 1985), albeit also combining those synths with tasteful guitar work.

The extent of British success in this era went beyond groups of this ilk, though. For example, artists like Bonnie Tyler, Phil Collins, and Air Supply took their respective power ballads "Total Eclipse of the Heart" (October 1, 1983), "Against All Odds (Take a Look at Me Now)" (April 21, 1984), and "The One That You Love" (July 25, 1981) to the top of the charts in this era, while Wham!, the duo that would soon launch the career of George Michael, bucked both the synth and ballad trends with chipper hits like "Wake Me Up Before You Go-Go" (November 17, 1984).

So, what incited this invasion? Early MTV was simply putting British artists in heavy rotation. On the surface, this seems odd. MTV was an American network broadcasting to American households. Some people argue that the eccentric haircuts, outfits, and makeup seen in videos like A Flock of Seagulls' "I Ran (So Far Away)" and Culture Club's "Karma Chameleon" (February 4, 1984) were more interesting to look at than anything American artists were offering. That's probably part of it. But the main reason was a bit more mundane.

There happened to be more music videos made by British artists. In the previously mentioned *I Want My MTV*, MTV cofounder Bob Pittman recounts, "I think there were 250 videos in existence [at the start of MTV] . . . Because we didn't have enough videos, we'd play unknown British acts: U2, Madness, A Flock of Seagulls, Duran Duran." In other words, MTV's hand in this second invasion was driven by necessity rather than some deliberate programming choice.

## The Marriage of Music and Movies

When Bill Haley and the Comets released "Rock Around the Clock" in May 1954, few thought it was destined to be rock canon. No, it didn't flop, but it also wasn't a huge success. Things changed when the song was used during the opening credits of the Academy Award-nominated film *Blackboard Jungle* a year later. Within months, "Rock Around the Clock" had topped all three of *Billboard*'s pre-Hot 100 charts. Thus, in the same way that MTV didn't invent the music video, it also wasn't the first to inspire the symbiotic relationship between popular song and film. It did alter that relationship, though.

It's important to note that I'm not talking about scores. I'm talking about non-orchestral songs used in movies or television shows that aren't musicals. We'll henceforth refer to these as "soundtrack songs." For example, "Maria" from *West Side Story* wouldn't be part of this group because it's from a musical. Nor would the theme from *Mission: Impossible* because it's orchestral. But Simon and Garfunkel's "Mrs. Robinson" (1968) from *The Graduate* would. So would B.J. Thomas's "Raindrops Keep Falling on My Head" (1970) from *Butch Cassidy and the Sundance Kid* and Joe Cocker and Jennifer Warnes' "Up Where We Belong" (November 6, 1982) from *An Officer and a Gentleman*.

Additionally, these don't have to be songs that were written for a movie or television show. Like "Rock Around the Clock" in *Blackboard Jungle*, their popularity just needs to have been boosted by their inclusion in such. For example, Herb Alpert's "Rise" (1979) and Patti Austin and James Ingram's "Baby, Come to Me" (February 19, 1983) both began their move up the charts after being featured on the soap opera *General Hospital*. With this definition in mind, Figure 7.3 shows a notable increase in soundtrack songs topping the charts during this era. In fact, between 1983 and 1985, 31 percent of number ones were soundtrack songs, much higher than the 5 percent to 10 percent we see in most other periods.

Though you can trace the soundtrack song back decades, those in this era tend to have a different relationship with film than their forebears. We can see

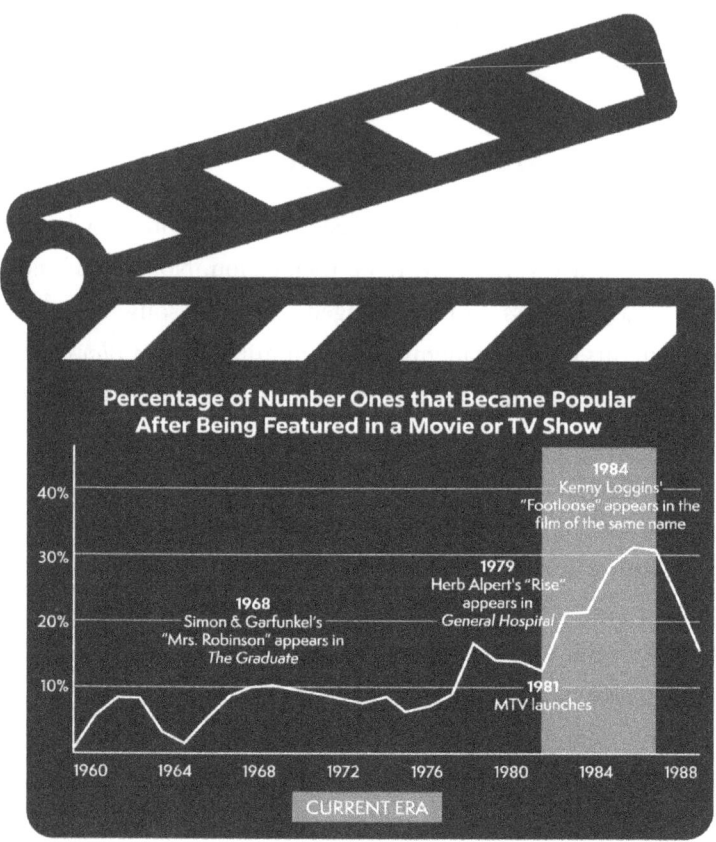

**Figure 7.3**

this by comparing the use of music in the 1977 film *Saturday Night Fever* with that of the 1983 film *Flashdance*.

On the surface, these films have a lot in common. Both were made on small budgets and grossed hundreds of millions of dollars at the box office. Additionally, each of their soundtracks sold millions of copies and spawned multiple number-one singles. The *Saturday Night Fever* soundtrack had four, and the *Flashdance* soundtrack had two, namely Michael Sembello's "Maniac" (September 10, 1983) and Irene Cara's "Flashdance . . . What a Feeling" (May 28, 1983).[5] Nevertheless, the way the music scenes in these movies are edited is wildly different.

---

[5] Joan Jett's pounding "I Love Rock 'n' Roll" (March 20, 1982) was also featured on this soundtrack, but it topped the charts a year before its inclusion, therefore disqualifying it from being called a soundtrack song.

Toward the beginning of *Saturday Night Fever*, there is an iconic sequence where John Travolta struts around his local disco to the Bee Gees' "You Should Be Dancing" (1976). Over the two-and-a-quarter minutes that he dances, there are 13 cuts to different camera angles, with an average of 9.6 seconds between cuts.

Compare this to the final scene in *Flashdance* where Jennifer Beals dances to the title track. During the three-minute-and-twenty-second scene, there are 44 cuts with an average of 4.4 seconds between cuts, half the length of the time between cuts as in Travolta's number.

The *Saturday Night Fever* dance routines come from an older tradition. Longer takes focused on the dancers are more akin to a live stage performance. *Flashdance* is steeped in the MTV-era music video tradition where excitement is created not by what is taking place on the screen but by how the scene is spliced together.

This goes beyond the use of dance routines, though. When "Don't You (Forget About Me)" by Simple Minds (March 18, 1985) plays at the end of *The Breakfast Club* and "The Power of Love" by Huey Lewis and the News (August 24, 1985) plays as Michael J. Fox skateboards in *Back to the Future* and "Eye of the Tiger" by Survivor (July 24, 1982) plays over the opening montage in *Rocky III* and "A View to a Kill" by Duran Duran (July 13, 1985) plays during the title sequence of the James Bond film of the same name, these movies are taking cues from MTV because (a) these sequences play like small music videos and (b) the sequences are built for the songs as much as the songs are built for the sequences.

This influence was also felt on television. The hit show *Miami Vice*—whose instrumental theme by Jan Hammer (November 9, 1985) topped the charts—was allegedly conceived by Brandon Tartikoff, the head of NBC's Entertainment Division, with two words: "MTV cops." Each episode of the show featured multiple then-contemporary songs. The show increased exposure for many of those tracks, including chart-toppers like John Waite's smoldering "Missing You" (September 22, 1984) and Mr. Mister's worshipful "Kyrie" (March 1, 1986).

While it's outside of my domain to assess if the proliferation of music videos was good for movies and television, I can try to weigh their impact on popular music itself. First, it's undeniable that you had some lackluster songs hit big because they had engaging visual concepts, like Toni Basil's "Mickey" (December 11, 1982). In a video with Basil dressed as a high school cheerleader, it's clear that she's more of a dancer than a singer. That's not to say that every song before MTV was a sonic masterwork. But there was now a very clear non-musical way to have a music career.

At the same time, videos made it possible for artists with interesting music to catch on that otherwise might not have. Take Men at Work as an example. The Australian rock band made a big splash in the United States with songs like "Who Can It Be Now?" (October 30, 1982) and "Down Under" (January 15, 1983). Part of the reason that was able to happen was because they made zany yet compelling videos that MTV put in heavy rotation. This is the price we must pay, though. For every artist that might have slipped through the cracks had they not caught your attention with a video, there are probably at least two dozen video-first artists with music severely lacking.

# Dig, If You Will, the Picture

Business historian Alfred D. Chandler, Jr. described industry maturation in the United States as "ten years of competition and 90 years of oligopoly." While I appreciate that aphorism, the evolution of the music industry has been more like 70 years of oligopoly, 20 years of competition, and then a lot more oligopoly. We can see this general pattern by looking at the unique number of labels to send a song to number one between 1940 and the end of this era.

In the first half of the twentieth century, the music industry was dominated by three labels: RCA, Columbia, and Decca. Some of their power came from the fact that they had created technology that was required to record and manufacture music. Then around 1950, there was an explosion of independent labels. As noted in Chapter 3, this explosion was driven by the economic boom after the Second World War, along with the emergence of the teenage demographic. You can see this in Figure 7.4. Between 1943 to 1945, every number one was released by one of four labels. From 1961 to 1963, that

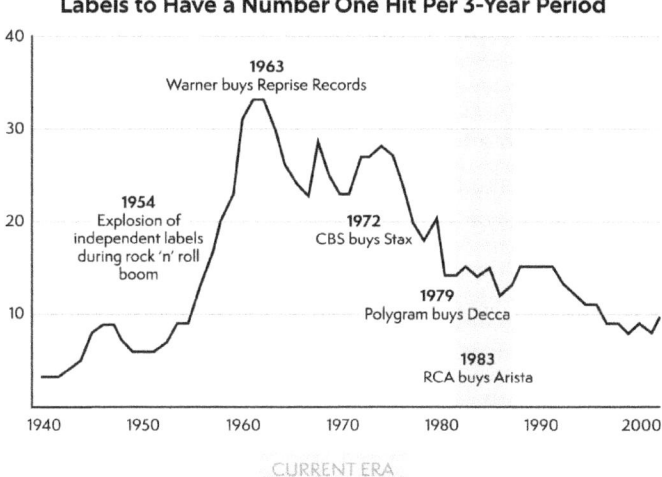

Figure 7.4

number had jumped to 33. By the end of that decade, the reconsolidation began, though.[6]

According to economic historian Gerben Bakker, there were three medium-to-large-sized mergers and acquisitions in the music industry in the 1950s. Between 1967 and 1977, there were 13. Between 1978 and 1988, there were 15. In the next decade, there were 34. By 2000, nearly every notable independent label of the twentieth century, from Atlantic to Def Jam and Motown to Virgin, had been gobbled up by international conglomerates like Sony, Universal, and Warner.

Before we talk about one of the most under-discussed effects of this conglomeration, we should answer a question we've been circling around in a couple parts of this book: What is a record label? In broad strokes, a record label is a company that does the following:

- Identifies musical talent
- Pays for that talent to record songs

---

[6] For clarity, I am talking about parent labels, meaning that since Atlantic Records also owned Bang and Atco in the 1960s, hits by any of those sublabels all counted toward the same label, namely Atlantic.

- Manufactures and distributes those recordings in a variety of formats

- Promotes those recordings to listeners

Though we'll talk about this a bit more in Chapter 10, when an artist signs a recording contract with a label, the agreement is usually that the label fronts the artist money to make a specified number of albums. Once an album is manufactured, distributed, and promoted by the label, the artist won't make anything until the label recoups what they spent out of the artist's royalties.

While that deal structure and the function of labels were the same for a long time, the music industry looked very different in 1985 compared to 1965. There were now fewer labels operating outside the purview of the corporatized and financialized media conglomerates chasing ever-higher profit margins. And the independence of small labels would continue to dwindle as these larger companies monopolized distribution.

Distribution was a notoriously hard problem. You could make a song as good as Cyndi Lauper's "Time After Time" (June 9, 1984), but nobody was going to be able to buy it if you couldn't get it to record shops across the globe. Though some big labels in the first half of the twentieth century ran distribution networks, there were many independent companies that offered those services. This gave small labels a bunch of options when they needed a distributor. Throughout the 1960s and 1970s, bigger labels devoted more resources to distribution. One way to make sure your distribution plants were operating efficiently was to assure they weren't waiting around for more music. Purchasing smaller labels was a great way to have an endless flow of records coming through the pipeline.

As big labels started to distribute more music—even those records they didn't technically own—it became increasingly difficult for small labels to compete. You might expect that this conglomeration would lead to musical homogeneity. That seemed to be the case with the major labels in the 1940s. They weren't nimble enough to keep up with the changing desires of their listeners. But the conglomerates of the 1980s were very different.

Sure, Madonna's "Crazy for You" (May 11, 1985) and Phil Collins' "Sussudio" (July 6, 1985) were both released by the giant Warner Music conglomerate. But "Crazy for You" was promoted on the Warner subsidiary Geffen, while

"Sussudio" came out on Atlantic, another Warner property. Yes, the respective success of those songs was benefiting the same corporate balance sheet, but these subsidiaries were in such fierce competition that many of the label heads hated each other. In short, though oligopoly reigned in the 1940s and 1980s, the 1980s' version of that oligopoly was much less centralized than that of the 1940s.

While this corporate concentration has generated enough repercussions to fill up a book by itself, including many related to the proliferation of the music video, it also led to a less-discussed change: the still image revolution.

## The Still Image Revolution

Before Columbia Records hired Alex Steinweiss as its art director in 1938, albums did not have cover art.[7] They were sold in generic packaging that labels could mass produce. Steinweiss realized that if an album were packaged with engaging art, it sold more copies. Other labels followed suit, and most albums since have been released with a front-facing image. The singles market was slower to adopt this visual counterpart, though.

As you can see in Figure 7.5, there was a growing interest in single cover art before this era, but its use became commonplace as the importance of MTV and image grew. I spoke to both Joel Whitburn and Fred Bronson, two leading authorities on the *Billboard* charts, and they concurred that this finding goes beyond the number ones. Single cover art wasn't prevalent until the 1980s.

While the relationship between single cover art and videos feels obvious, its connection to label conglomeration is a bit more subtle. To understand that connection, I first need to note how most singles before this era, like albums pre-1938, were sold in generic packaging.

The two sleeves pictured in Figure 7.6 are respectively from Decca and ABC-Paramount releases in 1958 and 1959. The Decca packaging is plain, mostly highlighting the name of the label, while the ABC-Paramount packaging stresses both the name of the label and other notable artists on their roster.

---

[7] Collections of recordings are referred to as "albums" because they were originally sold on sets of small discs packaged in photo albums.

**Percentage of Number One Hits with Cover Art**

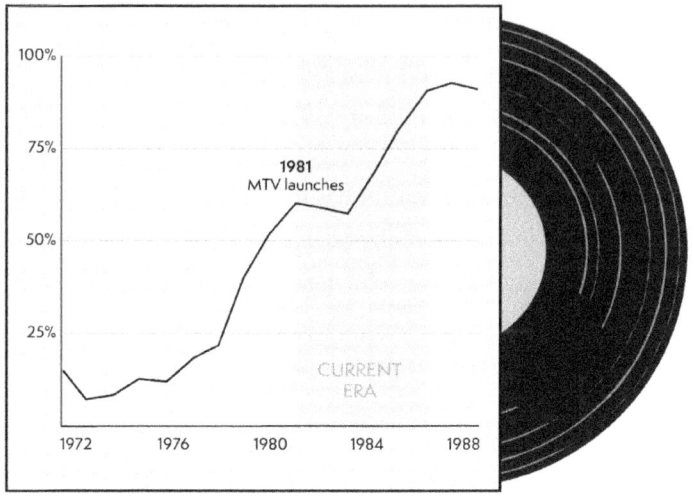

Figure 7.5

**Figure 7.6** *Record Sleeves from Number One Hits Released in 1958 and 1959.*

Most singles up to 1980 were packaged like this. If anything was promoted on the sleeve, it was for the label rather than the artist. This was for two reasons. First, it was cheaper to produce generic sleeves for all of a label's singles, which was important given that the financial return was smaller for singles than for albums. Second, independent labels had a stronger incentive to promote affinity for themselves rather than for a specific artist.

Motown proves a good example of this. Because there was sonic cohesion among Motown records, if you bought a Mary Wells song and saw the Four Tops advertised on the sleeve, you might go out and buy their record. This was even true of Motown through this era. If you liked Lionel Richie's ballad "Hello" (May 12, 1984), there was a good chance you'd also like Stevie Wonder's ballad "I Just Called to Say I Love You" (October 13, 1984). Nearly every other label started out like this. Atlantic focused on rhythm and blues. Casablanca focused on disco. Def Jam focused on hip-hop.

But as these labels were subsumed into larger companies, their distinctness was erased. Nobody, for example, was buying Billy Joel's "Tell Her About It" (September 24, 1983) because it was released on Columbia Records. In 2000, *New York Times* critic Jon Pareles made this exact point: "While a small label . . . can build insider cachet . . . The bigger the company, the less it means to people who care about a certain performer. The majors are so large that, paradoxically, they seem invisible." Because of this effect, it no longer made sense to advertise a label on a single sleeve. It made sense to advertise the artist, especially as music videos and images were ascendent.

While certain pieces of album artwork have become iconic—the opening monologue of Prince's "Let's Go Crazy" (September 29, 1984) almost involuntarily conjuring the image of the singer sitting on the motorcycle found on the cover of *Purple Rain*—single art is often more generic. As with Kenny Loggins' sprightly "Footloose" (March 31, 1984) and Whitney Houston's aching "How Will I Know" (February 15, 1986), it usually features a picture of the artist that was likely produced cheaply.

And if that wasn't cheap enough, sometimes the label would repurpose the artwork they were using for the album the song belonged to. For example, Phil Collins' droning "One More Night" (March 30, 1985) and The Police's sultry, stalker-anthem "Every Breath You Take" (July 9, 1983) are modified artwork from the former's *No Jacket Required* and the latter's *Synchronicity*.

While music videos can often generate polarizing opinions—in fact, Billy Squier has claimed that his awkward dancing in the video for his song "Rock Me Tonite" abruptly ended his career—single cover artwork seldom receives a comment, especially since it was relegated to a small thumbnail on the computer in the 2000s. That said, it's a good example of how seemingly innocuous things in the music business can signify deeper changes.

# Sucking on Chili Dogs Outside the Tastee-Freez

In an interview with *Rolling Stone*, Daryl Hall noted, "Most artists try to avoid clichés, but it's pretty hard to avoid them if you, yourself, end up being one." While Hall was lamenting a personal issue, he was incidentally highlighting something that all artists who have long careers encounter. Listeners come to expect certain things from continued hitmakers. After a certain point, almost anything an artist does will either come off as stale or as trying too hard to remain relevant.

That's why Paul McCartney, Stevie Wonder, and Diana Ross are all so incredible. All three had chart-topping careers for over 15 years as lead artists. Having a successful career for that long is hard. Topping the charts for that long is nearly impossible. All three also happened to end their chart-topping runs in this era while collaborating with other artists.

Ross's swan song was "Endless Love" (August 15, 1981), a meandering ballad with Lionel Richie for a film of the same name. McCartney's was "Say Say Say" (December 10, 1983), a toe-tapping duet with Michael Jackson. Wonder's was "That's What Friends Are For" (January 18, 1986), a benefit single for AIDS research with Elton John, Gladys Knight, and Dionne Warwick. Even though I wouldn't hold up any of these songs as examples of these legends' respective musical skills, I tip my cap to each of them.

## Highlights

1. **"Jack and Diane" by John Cougar (October 2, 1982)**[8]—John Cougar's tale of young love is memorable for its big moments—a huge hook, a brief drum solo, and memorable lyrical imagery—but it's close to perfect for its smaller ones: ticklish guitar notes at the end of the hook,

---

[8] Michael Jackson's "Beat It" was also rated high enough to be included here. It was mentioned earlier.

the entrance of the piano at the beginning of verse two, and the bass transitioning to its upper register at the start of the second chorus. While a song will fail if its fundamental pieces don't work, it will never reach perfection if its details don't keep you coming back.[9]

2. **"Saving All My Love For You" by Whitney Houston (October 26, 1985)**—In many senses, "Saving All My Love For You" is a throwback. 97 percent of chart-toppers in this era were in 4/4 time. "Saving All My Love For You" is in 12/8. 81 percent followed the Verse-Chorus or Verse-Chorus-Bridge song form. "Saving All My Love For You" follows the Verse-Mid form. Even the heart-warming lyrics were penned by 1960s hitmaker Gerry Goffin. But you won't notice any of these oddities when the song starts playing. All you'll notice is the vocal, Whitney Houston making it painfully obvious that nobody else can hold a candle to her vocal cords.

3. **"*Arthur's* Theme (The Best That You Can Do)" by Christopher Cross (October 17, 1981)**—In a 2022 post on Instagram, songwriter Dan Wilson—the man behind such songs as Semisonic's "Closing Time" and Adele's "Someone Like You" (2011)—recalled a review that "seemed to chide [Tom] Petty for writing songs so simple that they would stand or fall on the greatness of one simple unifying line." Wilson didn't think this was a criticism. It seemed like a mythic skill to "distill your song down to the simplest elements and still tell a tale."

I think about this each time I listen to "*Arthur's* Theme." From the opening chords to Christopher Cross's crystalline vocal, there's no denying that it's a beautiful song. But, for me, the success of the whole thing hinges on two lines at the end of the chorus: "When you get caught between the moon and New York City / The best that you can do is fall in love." Entire albums have been written without having been able to get to the heart of the matter as succinctly as those 21 words.

---

[9] "Jack and Diane" was released on a short-lived label called Riva Records, which, given my last name, makes me wonder if I have a distant music mogul relative who I should be ingratiating myself with.

# Lowlights

1. **"Ghostbusters" by Ray Parker Jr. (August 11, 1984)**[10]—Poor Ray Parker Jr. He was given the impossible task of working the word "Ghostbusters" into a song for a film of the same name. Under that constraint, I don't think you're going to find a better song than this. But given the clunkiness of the word, there are limits to how well you can do.

2. **"We Built This City" by Starship (November 16, 1985)**—Sometimes cited as the worst song of all time, these lyrics penned by longtime Elton John collaborator Bernie Taupin flit between ridiculous (e.g., "Marconi plays the mambo") and anti-corporate (e.g., "Someone's always playing corporation games / Who cares, they're always changing corporation names"). Those words feel like they should be relevant during this merger-heavy era, but the sleek production makes the song sound like the work of the corporations the lyrics claim to detest.

3. **"St. Elmo's Fire (Man in Motion)" by John Parr (September 7, 1985)**— I know my dad likes this song. And he's never specified why, but I'm pretty sure I know the reason: pace. He loves songs with a propulsive energy. Driven by a gurgling synth and a snare that won't quit, this song does have that propulsive pace that he's after. But—and I'm sorry, Dad— John Parr's vocal is a bit too melodramatic for me to give this one my stamp of approval. I hope you can forgive me. At least we can both agree that Bryan Adams' "Heaven" (June 22, 1985) is an all-time power ballad.

# Argument Starters

While "Africa" (February 5, 1985) is technically Toto's only number one, the members of Toto played on a lot of huge hits. Steve Lukather and Jeff Porcaro both played on Michael Jackson's aforementioned "Beat It." Lukather also played Olivia Newton-John's "Physical" (November 21, 1981), Lionel Richie's "Say You, Say Me" (December 21, 1985), and Chicago's "Hard to Say I'm Sorry" (September 11, 1982) in this era alone.

---

[10] Falco's "Rock Me Amadeus" was rated low enough to be included here. I mentioned it earlier.

While I respect the members of Toto for their musical skills, I am an avowed hater of the song "Africa." Yes, the chorus is monstrous. Yes, the vocal harmonies are tight. Yes, the synth riff will get stuck in your head for days. But for me, the song is lifeless, a zombie lumbering along. The only moment I truly love is the fade out. You might think that's weird, especially since I spent paragraphs bemoaning the fade out in Chapter 2. But in this case, the fade out is great. It means that my pain and suffering are about to end.

## Odds and Ends

1. **"Bette Davis Eyes" by Kim Carnes (May 16, 1981)**—I've spent too much time trying to figure out why the opening keyboard riff on "Bette Davis Eyes" is so hypnotic. Part of it is the tone. Musicians spend years chasing a sound like that. But it's also the chords. Though the song is in the key of C major, the verses loop through F major, A minor, and G major over and over. By never settling on C major, there's an undercurrent of tension that will "tease you" and "unease you" as Kim Carnes rasps along. As far as I can tell, that's why I'm catatonic when "Bette Davis Eyes" starts whispering through my speakers.

2. **"Stars on 45" by Stars on 45 (June 20, 1981)**—This song is a medley of Beatles' songs and assorted 1960s hits smashed together over a disco beat. While the renditions are faithful, the two vocalists approximating John Lennon and Paul McCartney well, the recording is most notable for being the longest-titled number one hit.

   Though it's commonly referred to as "Stars on 45," for legal reasons the actual title needed to include every song that was performed in the mash-up, thus making the title "Medley: Intro / Venus / Sugar Sugar / No Reply / I'll Be Back / Drive My Car / Do You Want to Know a Secret / We Can Work It Out / I Should Have Known Better / Nowhere Man / You're Going to Lose That Girl / Stars on 45."

3. **"Ebony & Ivory" by Paul McCartney and Stevie Wonder (May 15, 1982)**—Bring together three geniuses and the results should be great. That's what happened when David Bowie made "Let's Dance" (May 21, 1983). The

iconoclastic singer tapped Stevie Ray Vaughan to play lead guitar and Nile Rodgers to produce, and the results were unbelievable. "Ebony & Ivory" sadly had a different fate.

With a message worth celebrating—namely, a declaration for racial harmony like the black and white keys coexisting on the piano—it's one of pop music's great mysteries how Paul McCartney, Stevie Wonder, and producer George Martin got together, and this saccharine sing-along was the best they could come up. I'm still upset about it.

## Everything Else

"I Love a Rainy Night" by Eddie Rabbit. "Keep on Loving You" by REO Speedwagon. "Morning Train (Nine to Five)" by Sheena Easton. "Jessie's Girl" by Rick Springfield. "Centerfold" by J. Geils Band. "Chariots of Fire" by Vangelis. "Abracadabra" by Steve Miller Band. "Truly" by Lionel Richie. "Come on Eileen" by Dexys Midnight Runners. "Islands in the Stream" by Kenny Rogers and Dolly Parton. "All Night Long (All Night)" by Lionel Richie. "Let's Hear It for the Boy" by Deniece Williams. "What's Love Got to Do with It" by Tina Turner. "Caribbean Queen (No More Love on the Run)" by Billy Ocean. "I Want to Know What Love Is" by Foreigner. "Careless Whisper" by Wham! "Can't Fight This Feeling" by REO Speedwagon. "We Are the World" by USA for Africa. "Everything She Wants" by Wham! "Everytime You Go Away" by Paul Young. "Oh Sheila" by Ready for the World. "Part-Time Lover" by Stevie Wonder. "Separate Lives" by Phil Collins and Marilyn Martin. "Broken Wings" by Mr. Mister. "Sara" by Starship. "These Dreams" by Heart.

# You Already Got My Kiss, So Don't Forget My Number

## April 19, 1986—July 1, 1989

### Things You Do Don't Seem Real

Milli Vanilli was one of the hottest new groups at the end of the 1980s. Along with winning Best New Artist at the 1990 Grammy Awards, their American debut album *Girl You Know It's True* went six times platinum and spawned three number-one hits. But that wild success wouldn't last.

When they first made a trip to the United States, employees at MTV noted that the German-French duo had little mastery of English despite their music suggesting otherwise. The oddities kept growing from there. While performing the title track from their debut album on a tour sponsored by the television show *Club MTV*, it seemed like they got stuck singing the first line of the chorus on loop. What was even stranger was that it looked like neither Fab Morvan nor Rob Pilatus, the two members of the group, had the mic near their mouths. Pilatus then fled the stage as the loop continued before being ushered back to finish the performance. At the time, nobody made much of it, but it was becoming clear that Milli Vanilli wasn't performing live.

This wasn't unusual though, especially for acts whose performances included vigorous choreography. Paula Abdul, who was part of the same tour to promote her smashes "Straight Up" (February 11, 1989) and "Forever Your

Girl" (May 20, 1989), recounted, "Of course, we knew [Milli Vanilli] used backing tracks, but lots of acts, myself included, sang along to backing tracks during parts of their shows." It went further than that, though.

In December 1989, an unknown musician named Charles Shaw claimed that Morvan and Pilatus didn't sing on their debut album. It was Shaw and some other vocalists. Though he retracted his statement shortly afterward, rumors of musical fraud continued to circulate. In November 1990, the group's producer Frank Farian confirmed people's suspicions: Morvan and Pilatus didn't sing anything on the record or the tour.

The duo soon sat down for an interview with Chuck Philips of the *Los Angeles Times* and came clean. "We lied to our families and our friends," Pilatus admitted. "We let down our fans. We realize exactly what we did to achieve our success." Within a week, Milli Vanilli was stripped of their Best New Artist Grammy and all but banished from the music industry. Was this punishment fit for their musical crimes?

## The Vilification of Milli Vanilli

When German music producer Frank Farian assembled Milli Vanilli, it wasn't his first time creating a group where those musicians heard on the album were different from those you saw in concert. In 1976, Farian released "Baby Do You Wanna Bump" under the pseudonym Boney M. The song became successful, but Farian had no desire to front the band publicly. To further capitalize on the song, he hired a quartet of Caribbean singers to perform it live.

This feels similar to Milli Vanilli. The difference is that Milli Vanilli didn't sing on tour or in the studio. When you saw Boney M. in concert, the vocals you heard were actually from the people on stage. But was the Milli Vanilli deception that much worse?

In their tell-all with the *Los Angeles Times*, Morvan alleged that Farian was a con man: "Our producer tricked us. We signed contracts as singers but were never allowed to contribute. It was a nightmare." Pilatus continued, "We were just dumb little kids . . . After Frank released the album, he told us that it was too late to stop.'" When Morvan and Pilatus pressured Farian to let them sing on their follow-up, he went to the press and admitted the fakery.

I do believe that Morvan and Pilatus bear some guilt. Even if they were misled, they went along with Farian's ploy. Still, their fates have never felt fair to me. Here's Morvan in an interview decades later:

> To this day, I'm the poster boy for lip-syncing. But we didn't invent it. And what I did back then is no different from what people are doing today. With the audio tools we have . . . you can take anybody off the street and make him sound like a beautiful bird. We can enhance someone's performance, enhance someone's looks, we can enhance everything, and create something that appears to be, but is not.
>
> For years, everyone tried to crucify me and make me suffer for "not being authentic," and I'm like, "You're making me laugh now." There's so many people that came before me, and that came after me, and that will come after and after and after. Authenticity? No, it's about entertainment.

Last week, when my mom heard me listening to Milli Vanilli's chipper dance tune "Baby Don't Forget My Number" (July 1, 1989), she said, "You know they were frauds!" But when I described the situation to my younger coworker, she didn't bat an eye. She's spent her life idolizing artists like Young Thug, whose vocals are heavily manipulated in the studio and on stage. I'm not saying this to disparage Young Thug. But the road from Milli Vanilli to Young Thug isn't that long.

With these disparate takes in mind, I grew fascinated with understanding how society remembers popular music and how those remembrances can change. It made me want to understand how things that were once controversial can become commonplace.

## Would You Still Remember Me?

My freshman year of college, I met this kid named Dan who lived with three other guys at the end of the hall. Like me, Dan was also from New Jersey, and we became good friends over a shared love of beer, mathematics, and music.[1] I'll spare you the discussion about the first two and jump to our musical bond.

Typically, when I develop a musical friendship with somebody, we experience some external event that makes us realize we like the same artists. Maybe something like this:

FADE IN:

INT. APARTMENT HALLWAY—DAY

CHRIS, a clean-cut young professional, walks down the hallway of his drab apartment building when he hears music coming from behind his neighbor's door. He knocks thrice and the NEIGHBOR answers.

        CHRIS

Howdy, neighbor! I was walking by and heard you bumping "Walk Like an Egyptian" (December 20, 1986) by The Bangles. I love The Bangles! Do you prefer their peppier work or their slower stuff, like "Eternal Flame" (April 1, 1989)?

        NEIGHBOR

I love both. Let's be best friends!

                        FADE OUT:
            THE END

But Dan and I didn't have one of these eureka moments where we realized that we liked the same music. In fact, at the beginning of our friendship, Dan and I had little overlap in taste. I came up on pop and rock music. Dan, on the other hand, was raised on classical music, an area I knew little about. Because of this, I might mention a song that I assumed everybody knew, like Michael

---

[1] "Beer" has not appeared in any number one thus far. The most popular alcohol to sing about up to this era was wine. 15 number ones thus far have mentioned it, including this era's UB40-performed, Neil Diamond-penned "Red Red Wine" (October 15, 1988).

Jackson's glorious "Man in the Mirror" (March 26, 1988), and Dan would give me a blank stare. In the same way, he might mention a piece that he thought was common knowledge, like Chopin's Revolutionary Étude, and I would give him the same confused look.

While this may seem strange, it made for a powerful musical friendship because we both had to remain open to new sounds and ideas. It also taught me a valuable lesson: Things that we consider common knowledge may be obscure to other people.

I was thinking about this as I listened to the music of this era. It felt like all of the biggest number ones of the 1980s occurred at the beginning of the decade. There were some huge songs in this one that have remained popular, like Bon Jovi's "You Give Love a Bad Name" (November 29, 1986)[2] and Cutting Crew's "(I Just) Died in Your Arms" (May 2, 1987), but it felt like most failed to stand the test of time. Because of my experience with Dan, I wondered if I was biased. Maybe the weeks from April 16, 1986, to July 1, 1989, were my "classical music" of the number ones. Then I realized that I could test this.

## Wikipedia, Cultural Memory, and Popular Music

Just as our individual memories can be different, multiple groups can collectively remember things differently. "When asked to remember World War II," *Scientific American* noted, "Americans report numerous events, but the majority of people report the attack on Pearl Harbor, D-Day and the bombings of Hiroshima and Nagasaki. When Russians are asked . . . they mostly list a different set of events, such as the Battle of Stalingrad."

Also, while younger and older Americans listed the bombings of Hiroshima and Nagasaki as critical events in the war, the two groups had different thoughts about them. Older people rated them positively for sparing American lives, while younger ones rated them negatively for killing civilians. Similarly, it was

---

[2] "You Give Love a Bad Name" came from Bon Jovi's album *Slippery When Wet*, which also spawned the number one "Livin' On a Prayer" (February 24, 1987). Not long after, the hard rockers would top the charts with "Bad Medicine" (November 19, 1988) and "I'll Be There For You" (May 13, 1989), two songs from their record *New Jersey*, another example of my home state circling the top of the Hot 100 but never being mentioned in a song title.

possible that my perception of this era was biased by my age. Using Wikipedia, I could check.

Wikipedia is an online encyclopedia written and maintained collaboratively by its readers. Because anybody can edit it, and it's one of the most popular websites in the world, it sometimes functions like humanity's collective memory. Does something have an article written about it? If so, how long is it? How many people have read it? All these things clue us in on how well remembered something is.

Since every number one has a Wikipedia page, I pulled the page views in the last 30 days and the page length for each. If my hunch was correct, I would expect the songs of this era would have shorter pages and less views. That's exactly what I found.

As you can see in Figure 8.1, both page views and page size tell the same story. From the beginning of the Hot 100 to sometime near the end of the 1960s, we see songs becoming better remembered as we get closer to the present. This type of relationship is what researchers find when they look at, say, the cultural memory of US presidents. Other than a few outliers, the more recent presidents are better remembered than the older ones. But with the

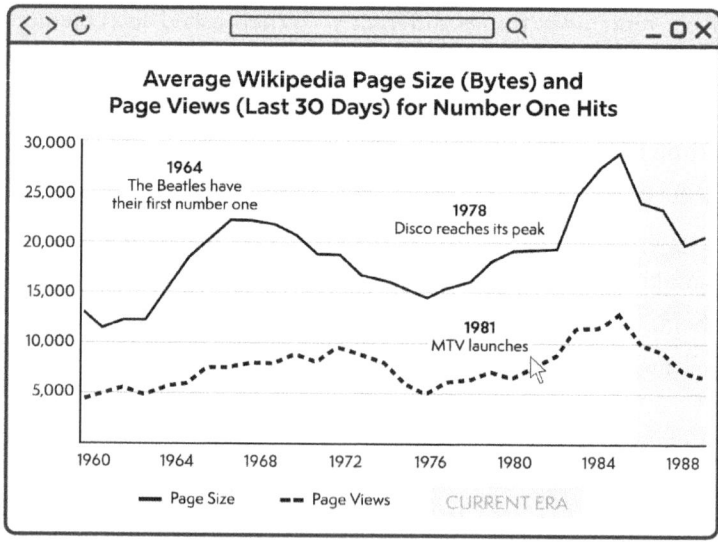

Figure 8.1

number ones, that relationship breaks down around 1969. There is a sharp decline in both stats in the early 1970s before we see an uptick during the disco era. From there, things skyrocket at the beginning of the 1980s before falling off a cliff during this era, thus giving credence to my hypothesis.

Is this the perfect way to measure cultural memory? No. But it's a decent way in the American context. A 2011 Pew Research survey found that 53 percent of adult American internet users consult Wikipedia. They also found that younger, more educated people are more likely to consult it. Because of this, we should expect recency bias, meaning newer songs would have more views and longer pages. So, that makes the decline at the end of the 1980s even more compelling. It's closer to the present but more on par with the mid-1960s or late-1970s in terms of page views and size.

With those trends in mind, let's look at the top ten and bottom ten number one hits between the start of the Hot 100 and the end of this era, ordered by Wikipedia views and page size, respectively. Though it's a small sample, it provides some insight into what we can glean from this data, along with its shortcomings.

Most of the data in Table 8.1 isn't that shocking. "American Pie" (1972), "Hotel California" (1977), and "Good Vibrations" (1966)—top ten in either page length or views—are all bona fide classics. But how did the "Monster Mash" (1962) come in at number four in page views? Initially befuddled, I soon realized why so many people were looking for this spooky song.

I generated this report a few days after Halloween, and the page views metric looked over the 30-day period immediately prior. If I had pulled this a month earlier, I'm certain the "Monster Mash" wouldn't appear. But its inclusion demonstrates one fault in this metric: It's affected by recent external events. Page size, on the other hand, doesn't seem to be as affected by things like this because it takes more effort to edit a page. But even size has some quirks.

Notice that six of the top ten songs by page size are from the 1980s. This is driven by the fact that these songs have music videos. Thus, there's more to say about them. The rise of music videos and soundtrack songs that we discussed in the last chapter explains the huge spike we see in the early-to-mid-1980s' page lengths. But when you consider this bias, along with recency

*Table 8.1  Top Ten and Bottom Ten Number One Hits by Wikipedia Page Views and Size*

| Top Songs | | Bottom Songs | |
|---|---|---|---|
| Views | Size | Views | Size |
| "American Pie" by Don McLean (1972) | "Like a Prayer" by Madonna (April 22, 1989) | "Don't Break the Heart that Loves You" by Connie Francis (1962) | "Mother-in-Law" by Ernie K-Doe (1961) |
| "We Are the World" by USA for Africa (1985) | "Good Vibrations" by The Beach Boys (1966) | "I Want to Be Wanted" by Brenda Lee (1960) | "I Want to Be Wanted" by Brenda Lee (1960) |
| "House of the Rising Sun" by The Animals (1964) | "My Sweet Lord" by George Harrison (1970) | "My Heart Has A Mind Of Its Own" by Connie Francis (1960) | "Pony Time" by Chubby Checker (1961) |
| "Monster Mash" Bobby Pickett and the Crypt-Kickers (1962) | "Hey Jude" by The Beatles (1968) | "Pony Time" by Chubby Checker (1961) | "If You Wanna Be Happy" by Jimmy Soul (1963) |
| "The Sound of Silence" by Simon and Garfunkel (1966) | "We Are the World" by USA for Africa (1985) | "The Happy Organ" by Dave "Baby" Cortez (1959) | "Mr. Custer" by Larry Verne (1960) |
| "Hotel California" by Eagles (1977) | "Billie Jean" by Michael Jackson (1983) | "There! I've Said It Again" by Bobby Vinton (1964) | "Lonely Boy" by Paul Anka (1959) |
| "Rapture" by Blondie (1981) | "Beat It" by Michael Jackson (1983) | "Moody River" by Pat Boone (1961) | "Let's Do It Again" by The Staple Singers (1975) |
| "Dreams" by Fleetwood Mac (1977) | "Like a Virgin" by Madonna (1984) | "Satisfied" by Richard Marx (June 24, 1989) | "Little Star" by The Elegants (1958) |
| "Lady Marmalade" by LaBelle (1975) | "All You Need is Love" by The Beatles (1967) | "Little Star" by The Elegants (1958) | "Moody River" by Pat Boone (1961) |
| "Never Gonna Give You Up" by Rick Astley (March 12, 1988) | "I Wanna Dance With Somebody" by Whitney Houston (July 27, 1987) | "I'm Telling You Now" by Freddie and the Dreamers (1965) | "Wonderland by Night" by Bert Kaempfert (1961) |

bias of page views, it really seems like the latter half of the 1980s has left a smaller cultural footprint.

And that lack of footprint becomes even clearer when you look at the bottom ten songs by page length or views, respectively. These songs are what you'd expect: old songs that have been largely forgotten by the public. The outlier is "Satisfied" (June 24, 1989), a vamping rocker by Richard Marx. Better remembered for his ballads, like "Hold on to the Nights" (July 23, 1988), Marx's "Satisfied" is not just the only song from this era in either Bottom Songs list, it's the only song released after 1965 with that honor.

I should nevertheless note that cultural memory evolves, forgotten songs of today becoming the classics of tomorrow. For example, Steve Winwood released two number ones in this era: "Higher Love" (August 30, 1986) and "Roll with It" (July 30, 1988). On most days, each of those songs would respectively receive 30 to 300 Wikipedia page views. Then, in 2019, electronic producer Kygo remixed Whitney Houston's cover of "Higher Love." While page views for "Roll With It" haven't really changed, views for "Higher Love" jumped into the few thousands per day up through the end of 2020, maxing out at 15,061 on August 26, 2019.

In other words, even though hits like "Head to Toe" (June 20, 1987) and "Lost in Emotion" (October 17, 1987) by Lisa Lisa and Cult Jam are both currently relics of the late 1980s, it's possible that they will be hailed as masterpieces in a few decades. Time shall tell.

## Forty-Seven Heartbeats Beating Like a Drum

When Don Lewis showed up for work at the Hyatt Convention Center in Oakland, California, in 1984, he was surprised to find picketers outside. Lewis was an engineer and musician who made a name for himself playing a self-constructed instrument called the Live Electronic Orchestra. Often shortened to LEO, the instrument united a Hammond organ with a variety of synths to create a futuristic sound and lively show. As he approached the convention center, Lewis assumed the workers were protesting the Hyatt. But then he saw their signs: "Non-Union Musician. Don Lewis, Unfair to Musicians Union,

Local 6." It was the American Federation of Musicians (AFM). They weren't picketing the Hyatt. They were picketing him.

You might remember the AFM from Chapter 2. They orchestrated huge strikes in the 1940s that halted all recording. Lewis had had problems with the union for some time. It had previously admonished him for performing as a solo artist at the Claremont Hotel, a room that was supposed to adhere to a six-musician minimum. Lewis, a onetime member of the union, jumped ship for the National Association of Orchestra Leaders (NAOL), an organization more supportive of his endeavors.

Though the AFM has gone to great lengths to make sure working musicians get paid a fair wage, they have also been sluggish to adapt to new styles and technologies. Musician minimums, for example, were a relic of the idea that recordings damage those who perform live. The AFM viewed Lewis as a threat because his mastery of synths and drum machines made other bandmates unnecessary.

With the help of the NAOL, Lewis filed an unfair labor practice charge against the AFM, alleging that they were illegally trying to coerce him to rejoin their union. An administrative law judge dismissed the complaint in 1985. With his options exhausted, Lewis put LEO in storage and supported his family by other means. In 1992, the Ninth Circuit overturned the earlier decision, but it was too late to revive his live act.

Lewis's story is an illustration of many things, one of which is how technological advancement can evoke apocalyptic fear. At every turn, from the invention of radio to the rise of digital sound to the proliferation of pitch correction, people have equated technological progress with musical destruction. But like our relationship with the past, our relationship with technology also changes.

Drum machines prove a good example of this. Though they initially faced backlash, they went on to be one of history's most popular pieces of musical technology. Let's get a sense of how this change happened.

## The Rise of the Drum Machine

In case it wasn't clear, a drum machine is an electronic device that simulates the sounds of acoustic drums and other percussive instruments. In Figure 8.2, you

**Figure 8.2** *Author's Korg Volca Beats Drum Machine. Credit: Evan P. Raftes*

can see my Korg Volca Beats drum machine. Though it's more contemporary, it has similar functionality to those drum machines from this era.

Along the bottom panel of the device, there are 16 buttons, the first ten of which are labeled with the different sounds that the machine can produce: kick, snare, low tom, high tom, closed hi-hat, open hi-hat, clap, claves, agogo, and crash. I can program a beat by selecting one of those sounds and placing them on one of 16 beats. Using the knobs at the top, I can then adjust the overall tempo and volume, along with the tone of each drum.

And that's sort of it. But with those basic tools, you can make everything from the straightforward beat you hear on Janet Jackson's flirty "When I Think of You" (October 11, 1986) to the alien rhythmic noises on Bananarama's "Venus" (September 6, 1986). Drum machines didn't always have this flexibility, though.

Drum machines of this era evolved from products often marketed to amateur organists. These devices came with presets like "samba" and "bossa nova" that made it easy for soloists to perform accompanied by rudimentary rhythms. Descendants of these presets are what appear on the first hits to use drum machines in the late 1960s and early 1970s, like Timmy Thomas's "Why Can't We Live Together" and Sly Stone's "Family Affair" (1971).

Everything changed in 1978, though. That's when the Roland Corporation released the CR-78, one of the first drum machines that allowed people to program and save beats. The CR-78 colored some hits of the last two eras, including "I Can't Go For That (No Can Do)" by Daryl Hall and John Oates (1982), "In the Air Tonight" by Phil Collins, "Heart of Glass" by Blondie (1979), and "Eminence Front" by The Who. Roland soon replaced the CR-78 with the TR-808.

Released in 1980, the TR-808 is the most famous drum machine of all time. Its influence on hip-hop is often compared to the influence of the Fender Stratocaster and Gibson Les Paul electric guitars on rock music. But like the electric guitar, the 808 has touched most genres. You can hear it on everything from Whitney Houston's "I Wanna Dance with Somebody (Who Loves Me)" (July 27, 1987) to Usher's "Yeah!" (2004) and Marvin Gaye's "Sexual Healing" to Drake's "God's Plan" (2018).

For many artists, the appeal of the 808 was that it didn't sound like the traditional drum kit you'd hear on a sweaty rock record, like Robert Palmer's "Addicted to Love" (May 3, 1986). It sounded different, or, as percussionist Remi Kabaka, Jr. said in the documentary *808*, "larger than life . . . like it had come from Mars or something." Those sounds had an otherworldly quality because they were produced through a process known as "analog synthesis," meaning they were generated by electrical hardware.

The 808 stood in contrast to the LinnDrum, a more human competitor that was also popular in the 1980s. I say it was "more human" because the LinnDrum's sounds were samples, meaning that when you clicked, say, the snare button on the device, you actually heard a recording of a snare drum. From Pet Shop Boys' "West End Girls" (May 10, 1986) to George Michael's "Faith" (December 12, 1987) and Bruce Hornsby's "The Way It Is" (December 13, 1986) to Tiffany's "I Think We're Alone Now" (November 7, 1987), these LinnDrum samples were everywhere in this era.

While understanding the evolution of drum machines is important because they are featured on so many hits of this era, it's doubly important because their proliferation had subtle effects on popular music. First, the drum machine continued to entrench our obsession with 4/4 time. Again, 4/4 is your standard four-beat count that you hear on everything from Los Lobos' "La

Bamba" (August 29, 1987) to Poison's "Every Rose Has Its Thorn" (December 24, 1988). And while that count has been so prevalent for so long that it's often called "common time," two things pushed it from common to ubiquitous.

First, the disco DJ. We talked about this extensively in Chapter 5, but the proliferation of disco and DJs mixing music made common time even more common. The drum machine pushed it further. The LinnDrum and the TR-808, and even my drum machine pictured in Figure 8.2, are all built around beats of four. Though you can make rhythms in other time signatures, the design doesn't suggest so.

When I asked LinnDrum creator Roger Linn about this via email, he concurred: "Technology tends to influence art, so people tend to make the kind of music that the machines want to make. My early drum machines came with preset beats that reflected the music of the day, which was nearly all 4/4 . . . So, lots of people simply used the 4/4 beats that came with the drum machines." In this drum machine-heavy era there were so few songs not in 4/4 that I can list them all for you: Tiffany's piano ballad "Could've Been" (February 6, 1988), George Michael's endless "One More Try" (May 28, 1988), and Billy Vera and the Beaters' smoldering "At This Moment" (January 24, 1987).[3]

The drum machine didn't only influence the types of rhythms that were played, though. It influenced how those rhythms were played. Drum machines are naturally perfect. By that, I mean when the drum machine on Billy Ocean's "Get Outta My Dreams, Get Into My Car" (April 9, 1988) was programmed to play a beat at 117 beats per minute, it was going to play that beat perfectly until the end of time. As listeners and artists became used to that machine precision, human drummers began to play as rigidly. We can see this with some data.

For every song on Spotify, they not only provide an estimate of the tempo but also an estimate of how confident they are in that tempo. For example, they're 67 percent confident that Madonna's "Live to Tell" (June 7, 1986) is 110 beats per minute, but 96 percent confident that her "Papa Don't Preach"

---

[3] Vera first put this song out in 1981 but had it rereleased when he found out it was going to be in the TV show *Family Ties*. Years later, Vera's voice became associated with another show when he sang the theme song on the CBS sitcom *The King of Queens*. This is my favorite non-instrumental sitcom theme, followed by *Cheers*, *The Golden Girls*, *The Mary Tyler Moore Show*, and *The Addams Family*.

**Figure 8.3**

(August 16, 1986) is 122 beats per minute. This makes sense. "Live to Tell" has a swirling synth introduction that is almost shapeless. "Papa Don't Preach," on the other hand, has rhythmic structure all the way through.

If we look at the songs on Spotify's decade-based "All Out" playlist series (e.g., "All Out 50s," "All Out 70s"), we can see how average tempo confidence has increased over the years. In Figure 8.3, we can see that with the looser arrangements of the 1950s, average tempo confidence sits at 30 percent. By the 1980s, it's more than doubled to 70 percent.

While part of this increase was driven by the proliferation of the mechanized rhythms of drum machines in the 1980s, it was also driven by human drummers trying to match that mechanized precision. If you compare Def Leppard's hits from this era, like "Love Bites" (October 8, 1988) and "Pour Some Sugar on Me," to their music from the early 1980s, you can hear this. Rick Allen played drums throughout this entire period, but there is more looseness to his earlier beats.[4] The same goes for Bob Seger. The troubadour's hits from the 1960s and

---

[4] Though Allen lost his left arm after a car crash in 1984, he continued to drum with Def Leppard by using a specially constructed drum set that allowed him to trigger certain sounds with a system of foot pedals.

1970s are much looser rhythmically than a late 1980s hit like "Shakedown" (August 1, 1987).

This change represented a fundamental shift in how popular music sounded. Given that it involved machines that could theoretically replace humans, it won't shock you that the change also came with some controversy.

## Why You Shouldn't Fear the Drum Machine

In 1984, the CBS Evening News produced a segment on synthesizers and drum machines. Here's how anchor Bob Schieffer introduced the story: "The next time you hear a drum beating or a violin playing, it may not be a real instrument at all. You might be listening to computer generated sounds from a synthesizer."

Schieffer then passes the report to Sam Ford. The camera pans over an orchestra as Ford narrates: "Much of the music was coming from a machine called a synthesizer and that has many musicians worried . . . Many professional musicians are so concerned these musical robots are taking jobs, unions are negotiating labor contracts prohibiting synthesizers from displacing traditional instruments."

The camera then cuts to Victor Fuentealba, the president of the AFM. Fuentealba's tone is apocalyptic: "They keep refining these devices to the point you can't tell the difference between the electronic device playing the instrumental part and the instrumental part being played by the live musician."

Fuentealba is expressing the same sentiment that James C. Petrillo expressed during the AFM strike that we discussed in Chapter 2. New musical technologies will destroy the lives of working musicians. In Petrillo's case, that technology was radio, records, and jukeboxes. In Fuentealba's case, it was synthesizers and drum machines. To a degree, both men were correct. These technologies did put musicians out of work. But that doesn't account for the fact that these technologies also transformed music.

The music industry of the 1980s was much bigger than that of the 1940s. Part of the reason for that was because artists embraced technologies that made it easier and cheaper to make music. You can get a sense of this by talking to some of the people who pioneered drum machine technology.

Roger Linn, the aforementioned creator of the LinnDrum, told me that part of his motivation was to help with the songwriting process: "When writing songs or simply jamming, it's helpful to have a drumbeat playing . . . [Producer] Giorgio Moroder once told me that before my drum machine, he would record a drummer playing a simple beat continuously for about 20 minutes, then play it back to write to." Clearly, Moroder put this technology to good use. Along with producing a handful of hits for Donna Summer, he cowrote and produced Blondie's "Call Me" (1980), Irene Cara's "Flashdance . . . What a Feeling" (1983), and Berlin's "Take My Breath Away" (September 13, 1986).

And what about Don Lewis? He told me that he started his career playing the organ at a bar in Denver. Because there wasn't enough space for a percussionist, Lewis used the organ's built-in drum machine as accompaniment. An engineer, Lewis rewired the machine to play beats beyond the presets.

Later, while working as a salesman for the Hammond organ company, Lewis continued to utilize drum machines to improve his sales pitch. It was through this job that he met Ikutaro Kakehashi, the head of Ace Tone, a company that made drum machines for organs. Kakehashi was impressed by the modifications that Lewis made to his machines, and the two became fast friends. In 1972, Kakehashi formed Roland and hired Lewis to help work on the first programmable drum machines.[5]

So, while artists worried that drum machines were destroying jobs, Lewis's interest in drum machines grew out of necessity to do his job. He continued to use them because he loved the sounds they made. To quote producer Quincy Jones in a documentary about Lewis's life, "[We] kind of rode technology all the way. These things changed music. To me, it was never an attempt to displace a musician or replace a musician. It was just another instrument and color in the orchestration."

---

[5] Kakehashi may have influenced popular music more than any other figure in the twentieth century. Along with his work at Roland, he founded Boss, a firm that produces guitar effects pedals, and was a key player in creating MIDI, a technical standard that allows electronic instruments to communicate with each other and recording software.

Many of Jones's productions with Michael Jackson in this era, including "Bad" (October 24, 1987)[6] and "The Way You Make Me Feel" (January 23, 1988), utilize a traditional drummer and a drum machine. U2's "With or Without You" (May 16, 1987) does the same thing. It starts with a dreamy, programmed beat before drummer Larry Mullen, Jr. arrives during the song's climax.

These examples illustrate not only how programmed beats can be complementary to traditional percussion, but how technology can grow rather than shrink the music industry. That doesn't mean that every programmed beat makes for good music. Kim Wilde's cover of The Supremes' "You Keep Me Hangin' On" (June 6, 1987) isn't as powerful as the original because the drum machine sucks the life out of it. But bad songs aren't enough to deny the fact that drum machines and synthesizers helped the music industry grow to new heights. And that growth would continue until a massive collapse around 2000. But we'll have to wait for Chapter 10 to talk about that.

# I Have Held the Hand of the Devil

In August 1999, Douglas Adams, the writer of the acclaimed sci-fi series *The Hitchhiker's Guide to the Galaxy*, wrote a piece for *The Sunday Times* about how people were reacting to this new-fangled technology called the "internet." In that piece, Adams captures how our relationship with technology changes throughout our lives:

1. Everything that's already in the world when you're born is just normal;

2. Anything that gets invented between then and before you turn thirty is incredibly exciting and creative and with any luck you can make a career out of it;

---

[6] In a 1997 interview with VH1, Prince claimed that Jackson offered him to duet on "Bad." Prince rejected him as follows: "The first line in that song is 'your butt is mine' so I was saying, 'Who's gonna sing that to whom? Because you sure ain't singing it to me, and I sure ain't singing it to you.' So right there we got a problem."

3. Anything that gets invented after you're thirty is against the natural order of things and the beginning of the end of civilisation as we know it until it's been around for about ten years when it gradually turns out to be alright really.

I try to think about this list anytime I have a knee-jerk reaction that a new technology is either scary or stupid, especially in the realm of music. Spotify's former data alchemist Glenn McDonald once explained to me how, in the abstract, technology is neither good nor bad. "Tools have no moral stature on their own," he said. "They're good if they increase our ability to do interesting, humane things. They're bad if they don't do that." What's important is that we try to make sure that new musical technology is used for things that are good, for things that bring us together. We'll touch on more controversial technology in Chapter 13, but all these years later, I think we can celebrate the drum machine for all of the music it's been used to create, good and bad songs included.

## Highlights

1. **"I Still Haven't Found What I'm Looking For" by U2 (August 8, 1987)**[7]—In 1895, American writer Stephen Crane published a short piece of verse:

> I saw a man pursuing the horizon;
> Round and round they sped.
> I was disturbed at this;
> I accosted the man.
> "It is futile," I said,
> "You can never —"
>
> "You lie," he cried,
> And ran on.

---

[7] U2's "With or Without You" was also rated high enough to be included here. It was mentioned earlier.

The man pursuing the horizon in this poem could well be the same man narrating this song: "I believe in the Kingdom come / Then all the colors will bleed into one / But yes, I'm still running." The arrangement is ethereal, a reverb-soaked guitar meandering over a staggering drum beat. By the time you get to the third verse, Bono is speaking in tongues, his voice on the cusp of breaking. He's still searching, but that's okay. The answer is in the endlessness of the journey rather than the destination.

2. **"Like a Prayer" by Madonna (April 22, 1989)**—When most people combine the sacred and the profane, they do so in such a way that the sacred is a thinly veiled metaphor for the profane. Madonna doesn't do that. She uses both the profane and the sacred in this song (e.g., "It's like a little prayer / I'm down on my knees / I wanna take you there"), but one is not a metaphor for the other. She is equating the two. When the gospel choir enters on the third chorus, you don't know which she's talking about. That's because she's talking about both.

3. **"Sweet Child O' Mine" by Guns N' Roses (September 10, 1988)**—If someone read you the lyrics "Now and then when I see her face / It takes me away to that special place," you'd probably assume they came from a ballad. And, frankly, despite the warm distortion of the introductory guitar riff, you could make a case that the beginning of "Sweet Child O' Mine" is a ballad. At least for a bit. Axl Rose's quasi-balladeering soon slips into the gnarly world of hard rock, culminating in Slash's cathartic guitar solo. But even as the guitar wails, it never undercuts that sweet lyrical sentiment. The two live in a dissonant harmony.

# Lowlights

1. **"Rock On" by Michael Damian (June 3, 1989)**—It feels like soap opera star Michael Damian wanted to deliver a grand message on this song. But all he does is paint vague, nostalgic images of the 1950s and then intone, "Rock on!" There's nothing wrong with that on the surface. But Damian's seriousness makes it feel like a parody gone wrong.

2. **"Who's That Girl" by Madonna (August 22, 1987)**—Madonna has the rare honor of being the only artist thus far to have one of the top three and bottom three rated records in the same era. And I respect her for that. Even when she misses, like she does on this faux-island track, she gives it her all.

3. **"Baby, I Love Your Way / Freebird Medley" by Will to Power (December 3, 1988)**—A karaoke song has never topped the charts. But this song gets as close as possible. It's a mash-up of Peter Frampton's "Baby, I Love Your Way" with Lynyrd Skynyrd's "Freebird" that removes every element that makes each of those songs interesting.

## Argument Starters

When one of the fellow judges told me that he hated Prince's "Kiss" (April 19, 1986), I was dumbfounded. For me, "Kiss" is a massive achievement, a sparse funk with lyrics that sound like they could have been written by a bluesman in the 1930s (e.g., "Ain't no particular sign I'm more compatible with / I just want you extra time and your kiss"). But none of that mattered to this judge. He found Prince's pinched falsetto off-putting. If you're looking for bad falsetto, you don't have to go far, though. This era featured New Kids on the Block's whispery ballad "I'll Be Loving You (Forever)" (June 17, 1989) that features falsetto that should never be imitated.

## Odds and Ends

1. **"Anything for You" by Gloria Estefan and Miami Sound Machine (May 14, 1988)**—In every era, there's one song I've never heard before that I quickly become addicted to. "Come Softly to Me" (1959). "He's a Rebel" (1962). "Wedding Bell Blues" (1969). "Want Ads" (1971). "Kiss and Say Goodbye" (1976). "You Don't Bring Me Flowers" (1978). "Against All Odds (Take a Look at Me Now)" (1984). In this era, it was "Anything for You." If all I learned from writing this book was how beautiful this song was, it would be enough.

2. **"When I'm With You" by Sheriff (February 4, 1989)**—Though "When I'm With You" seems like a straightforward power ballad, I'd argue that it's one of the strangest chart-toppers thus far. That strangeness has nothing to do with the music, though. The song was first released in 1983 to so little fanfare that Sheriff broke up two years later. Then in late 1988, a Las Vegas DJ started spinning the song as if it were new. Because listeners liked it, Capitol Records rereleased the song as a single. Despite the band never reforming and the song never getting a proper music video, it still made it to number one. I would have assumed that was an impossibility at the height of MTV's powers.

3. **"Sledgehammer" by Peter Gabriel (July 26, 1986)**—Long before his sole soulful chart-topper with one of the most insane music videos you will ever see, Peter Gabriel was the lead singer of Genesis. In this era, Gabriel's former band not only topped the charts (i.e., "Invisible Touch" (July 19, 1986)), but his former bandmates Phil Collins (i.e., "A Groovy Kind of Love" (October 22, 1988), "Two Hearts" (January 21, 1989)) and Mike Rutherford (i.e., "The Living Years" (March 25, 1989)) did too. The only band to spawn more chart-topping artists than Genesis is The Beatles, where all four members independently did it at least twice. This era witnessed the final number one by a Beatle, namely George Harrison's jubilant "Got My Mind Set On You" (January 16, 1988).

## Everything Else

"Greatest Love of All" by Whitney Houston. "On My Own" by Patti LaBelle and Michael McDonald. "There'll Be Sad Songs (To Make You Cry)" by Billy Ocean. "Holding Back the Years" by Simply Red. "Glory of Love" by Peter Cetera. "Stuck with You" by Huey Lewis and the News. "True Colors" by Cyndi Lauper. "Amanda" by Boston. "Human" by The Human League. "The Next Time I Fall" by Peter Cetera and Amy Grant. "Shake You Down" by Gregory Abbott. "Open Your Heart" by Madonna. "Jacob's Ladder" by Huey Lewis and the News. "Lean on Me" by Club Nouveau. "Nothing's Gonna Stop Us Now" by Starship. "I Knew You Were Waiting (For Me)" by Aretha Franklin and George Michael. "Always" by Atlantic Starr. "Alone" by Heart. "I Just Can't Stop

Loving You" by Michael Jackson and Siedah Garrett. "Didn't We Almost Have It All" by Whitney Houston. "Here I Go Again" by Whitesnake. "Mony Mony" by Billy Idol. "(I've Had) The Time of My Life" by Bill Medley and Jennifer Warnes. "Heaven Is a Place on Earth" by Belinda Carlisle. "So Emotional" by Whitney Houston. "Need You Tonight" by INXS. "Seasons Change" by Exposé. "Father Figure" by George Michael. "Where Do Broken Hearts Go" by Whitney Houston. "Wishing Well" by Terence Trent D'Arby. "Together Forever" by Rick Astley. "Foolish Beat" by Debbie Gibson. "Dirty Diana" by Michael Jackson. "The Flame" by Cheap Trick. "Monkey" by George Michael. "Don't Worry, Be Happy" by Bobby McFerrin. "Kokomo" by The Beach Boys. "Wild Wild West" by The Escape Club. "Look Away" by Chicago. "Lost in Your Eyes" by Debbie Gibson. "The Look" by Roxette. "She Drives Me Crazy" by Fine Young Cannibals. "My Prerogative" by Bobby Brown. "Wind Beneath My Wings" by Bette Midler.

# It's a Damn Good Thing We Danced the Macarena

## July 8, 1989—August 3, 1996

## And I Wonder If Tomorrow Will Be Like Yesterday

When P.M. Dawn's "Set Adrift on Memory Bliss" (November 30, 1991) got to the top of the charts, they were plumbing the depths of the past. The song—a nostalgia-soaked haze built around a sample of Spandau Ballet's 1983 hit "True" and rife with lyrical allusions to the music of Joni Mitchell, George Michael, The Pointer Sisters, and A Tribe Called Quest—captures the aching memory of a failed relationship.

Though P.M. Dawn was a hip-hop act, their musical creations stood apart from their contemporaries. To generalize, much of hip-hop at the time was either light-hearted party music—like MC Hammer's "U Can't Touch This" and DJ Jazzy Jeff and The Fresh Prince's "Parents Just Don't Understand"—or vivid, sometimes violent, socio-political commentary, like N.W.A's "Fuck Tha Police" and Public Enemy's "Fight the Power." P.M. Dawn was neither of those things. *People* magazine described their debut album as "something new, hip-hop that ignored the streets and aimed for the heavens." Their music was contemplative, ethereal, almost psychedelic.

Prince Be and DJ Minutemix, the two members of the group, were born in Jersey City, the eldest of seven siblings. Their father died when they were young, and their mother married a percussionist from the chart-topping group Kool and the Gang. The boys' stepfather introduced them to a ton of music, but it was the music of the 1960s that they most connected with. "Maybe I was born too late," Prince Be suggested in a 1991 Los Angeles Times profile. "I love the '60s—the colors, the attitudes and the music."

The duo shopped around a demo in the late 1980s but struggled to land a record deal. The independent label Warlock eventually released their debut "Ode to a Forgetful Mind" in 1989, but it failed to make an impact. Warlock soon licensed the record to the British hip-hop label Gee Street. After being purchased by Island Records, Gee Street would release the duo's debut album *Of the Heart, of the Soul, and of the Cross: the Utopian Experience* in August 1991. The romantically titled disc would go on to receive near-universal praise from critics.

Despite being deeply entrenched in the past, P.M. Dawn's music was symbolic of the future. Part of that symbolism was how it got to number one: "Set Adrift on Memory Bliss" was the first number one under SoundScan, *Billboard*'s new accounting system. But the other part was tied to what the song was: a hip-hop song by a Black duo who rapped the word "damn." Though both statements feel humdrum, they were harbingers of seismic shifts in American popular music.

# Let Me Reassure You That You Can Count On Me

Imagine you own a record store. It's late 1989, and Bad English's "When I See You Smile" (November 11, 1989) has been at number one for two weeks. You get a call from *Billboard*, and they ask what's been selling at your store. This isn't surprising. They call every week. It's how they compile the Hot 100. You're about to tell them that "When I See You Smile" remained the best-selling single. But you hesitate. You notice you have tons of copies of Milli Vanilli's newest record, "Blame It On the Rain" (November 25, 1989). It hasn't been selling as well as you were expecting. So, you decide to lie.

You tell *Billboard* that the European duo's tune is flying off the shelves. They thank you, and then you hang up the phone. You feel guilty, but your hope is that if you can inflate the sales of "Blame It On the Rain," then more people will buy it. Many of your customers shop that way. They dig through your display at the front of the store with *Billboard*'s most popular records when deciding what to purchase.[1]

In Chapter 5, we talked about chart impropriety from inside *Billboard*, but this imagined scenario illustrates how fraud wasn't only possible but incentivized on many sides of the business. And given that *Billboard* was aggregating their charts based on self-reported information, it wasn't even that difficult to do something shady. But this shadiness wasn't going to last.

In late 1991, *Billboard* started aggregating the Hot 100 via SoundScan rather than surveys. "Set Adrift on Memory Bliss" was the first song to get to number one under this new system. Derek Thompson described this change in his piece in *The Atlantic* titled "1991: The Most Important Year in Pop-Music History":

> So, for many years, *Billboard* wasn't a perfect mirror of American tastes. It was warped by label preferences and record-store inventories. It often over-counted songs that labels preferred . . . and under-counted genres they were indifferent toward . . .
>
> But in 1991, this changed. First, Nielsen ended the record-store charade by releasing SoundScan, which used point-of-sales data from cash registers in stores. Finally, Nielsen had timely information on which albums were really selling . . . The Hot 100 chart changed from a political document to a statistical register, honestly tracking the songs Americans were really buying and listening to.

When this change went into effect, it was clear that the old system had biases that benefited certain genres and artists. We'll talk about those genre biases in a bit, but on the artist side, Paula Abdul proves a good example. The cheerleader-turned-pop-star had her final number ones in this era: "Cold Hearted" (September 2, 1989), "Opposites Attract" (February 10, 1990), "Rush Rush" (June 15, 1991), and "The Promise of a New Day" (September 14, 1991). Each song summited the charts pre-SoundScan. None of her six singles released in the SoundScan era even cracked the top 10.

---

[1] Bad English would have been upset with your shenanigans, but Diane Warren, the woman who wrote the song, wouldn't. She penned both "When I See You Smile" and "Blame It On the Rain."

"Sure," you might contest, "but Abdul's creative output slowed to a near halt after 1991. Maybe she wasn't putting as much time into her music career." I'd agree that was part of it, but "The Promise of a New Day" provides additional evidence of the benefits she was reaping in the pre-SoundScan era. When "The Promise of a New Day" topped the Hot 100, it wasn't at the top of *Billboard's* sales or radio play charts, both of which had already switched to SoundScan. Thus, the future *American Idol* judge achieved the impossibility of having the most popular record in the country without having the most popular song on radio or in stores.

This isn't to say that Paula Abdul was unpopular. The human-reported, pre-SoundScan system just overstated that popularity. But beyond this specific example, there were more general changes that came about because of this improved data. One of the main things SoundScan taught us was that if pop songs were drugs, we'd all be hopelessly addicted.

## I Really, Really, Really Love This Song . . . Like Really

In 1960, Percy Faith sent his sprightly instrumental "Theme from *A Summer Place*" (1960) to number one for nine weeks, a new record. Beyond The Beatles matching that feat eight years later with "Hey Jude" (1968), this nine-week mark proved quite formidable. In fact, by the time Debby Boone's "You Light Up My Life" (1977) pushed the record to ten weeks in the late 1970s, Percy Faith had been dead for a year and a half.

This record also proved durable. Then *Billboard* switched to SoundScan, and everything changed. You can see in Table 9.1 that the record for weeks at number one only grew one week between 1958 and 1988. After SoundScan was introduced in 1991, the record was re-established three times in four years, eventually settling at 16 weeks. SoundScan, in effect, proved that our tastes were much stickier than the older, self-reported tracking system suggested.

This goes beyond number ones, though. In Figure 9.1, you can see the average percent of new entries in the top 40 and top ten over 52 weeks. Fewer songs entered the charts after *Billboard* made the switch to SoundScan.

*Table 9.1  Record for Consecutive Weeks atop the Hot 100 through 1996*

| Date | Song | Artist | Weeks |
|------|------|--------|-------|
| Aug-4-1958 | "Poor Little Fool" | Ricky Nelson | 2 |
| Aug-18-1958 | "Nel Blu Dipinto Di Blu" | Domenico Modugno | 5 |
| Sep-19-1958 | "It's All in the Game" | Tommy Edwards | 6 |
| Jun-1-1959 | "The Battle of New Orleans" | Johnny Horton | 6 |
| Feb-22-1960 | "Theme From *A Summer Place*" | Percy Faith | 9 |
| Sep-28-1968 | "Hey Jude" | The Beatles | 9 |
| Oct-15-1977 | "You Light Up My Life" | Debby Boone | 10 |
| Nov-21-1981 | "Physical" | Olivia Newton-John | 10 |
| Aug-15-1992 | "End of the Road" | Boyz II Men | 13 |
| Nov-28-1992 | "I Will Always Love You" | Whitney Houston | 14 |
| Aug-17-1994 | "I'll Make Love to You" | Boyz II Men | 14 |
| Dec-2-1995 | "One Sweet Day" | Mariah Carey and Boyz II Men | 16 |

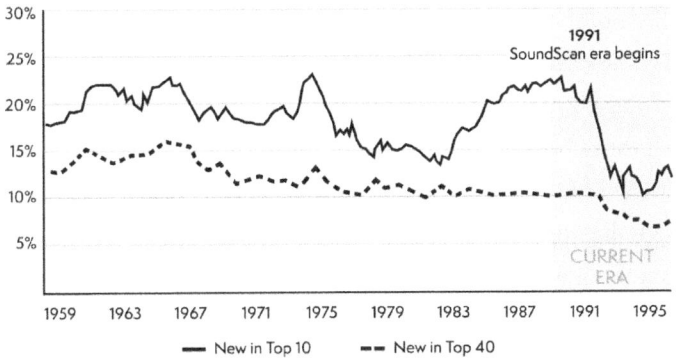

Figure 9.1

In short, when we like a song, we really *like* it. We want to keep hearing it until it drives us crazy. And then we'll listen a few more times. Take Los del Río's "Macarena" (August 3, 1996) as an example. If you've heard it once, you've heard it a thousand times. Yet it stayed at number one for 14 weeks and was so pervasive that politicians danced to it at the 1996 Democratic National Convention. But if SoundScan showed that we were disposed to pop song dependence, did it also show that we liked less variety than suggested by earlier number ones?

## The Musical Variety Paradox

A couple years ago, I was in the car with my dad when he put on the song "Tonight Is What It Means To Be Young" by Fire Inc. from the 1984 box office flop *Streets of Fire*. About 30 seconds in, he posed a question: "Who do you think wrote this?" Peeling my eyes from my phone, I listened more intently.

The song was grand, almost bombastic, with a woman wailing over a piano and a propellant drumbeat, automobile sounds coloring the background. I had a guess about a minute later: Jim Steinman. My hunch was correct, and my dad was proud.

Jim Steinman was a songwriter and producer most well-known for his collaborations with Meat Loaf. His compositions—including his number ones "Total Eclipse of the Heart" (1983) and "I'd Do Anything For Love (But I Won't Do That)" (November 6, 1993)—are usually built around a piano, contain romantic imagery, and clock in over five minutes. The song my dad put on checked all those boxes.

Even if it's a bit less specific than guessing who wrote a song, we do stuff like this all the time. Recently, my friend Annie texted me, "I swear this sounds exactly like another song," while listening to Mariah Carey's exultant "Emotions" (October 12, 1991). After some back-and-forth, we realized it bore a resemblance to The Emotions' disco-era hit "Best of My Love" (1975). Our discussion to arrive at this conclusion wasn't technical, but there's a more quantitative way we can make these comparisons.

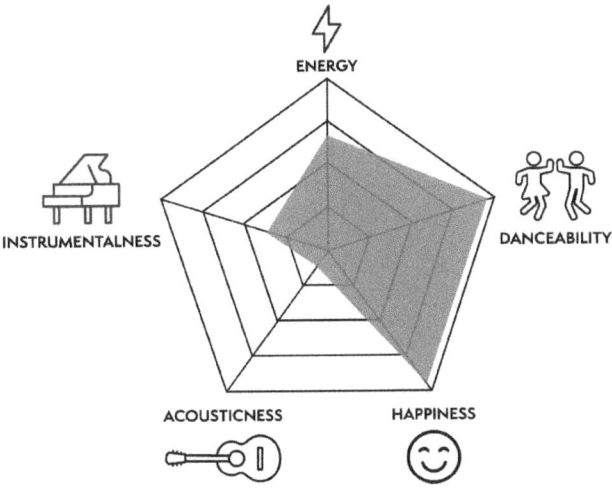

Figure 9.2

Let's pick a song, like Prince's "Cream" (November 9, 1991), and plot Spotify's energy, danceability, happiness, and acousticness metrics for it, along with the percent of the song that contains no lyrics (i.e., "Instrumentalness"). We'll call this the song's "sonic profile." You can see it visualized in Figure 9.2.

This data suggests that "Cream" is a moderately energetic and danceable song built around non-acoustic instruments and a good deal of vocals. If you listen, this checks out. It's laid-back, Prince's guitar snaking between his sensual lyrics. We can take this a step further and find the number ones that are most and least similar to "Cream."[2]

In Figure 9.3, we can see that "Cream" is most like The Staple Singers' loose groove "I'll Take You There" (1972) and least like Barbra Streisand and Neil Diamond's depressing duet "You Don't Bring Me Flowers" (1978). This makes sense. You could put "Cream" on a playlist with "I'll Take You There," and nobody would bat an eye. But if you did the same with "You Don't Bring Me Flowers," your friends would permanently revoke your DJing privileges.

---

[2] Nerd alert: I'm calculating similarity via a measurement called "cosine similarity."

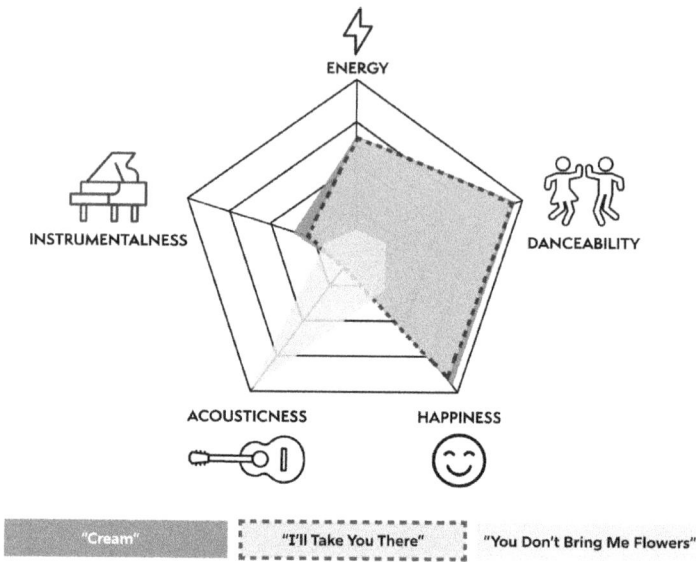

Figure 9.3

By expressing the similarity of number ones over a three-year period as a percentage between 0 percent and 100 percent, we can see if musical variety increased or decreased in the SoundScan era. For clarity, 0 percent indicates incredible variety and 100 percent indicates incredible similarity. In Figure 9.4, we see that this similarity measure sits consistently between 83 percent and 92 percent. What does this mean?

First, no matter the era, popular songs share many sonic qualities. In other words, if you want to find a really unique song, you're going to have to look somewhere other than the top of the charts. Second, you might recall that in Chapter 1 I wrote extensively about musical variety, making the case that the period from 1958 to 1963 is unfairly characterized as bland. The consistency of this similarity metric gives further credence to my point. You might like post-British Invasion music more than pre-British Invasion music, but you can't claim that there was less sonic variety before the British took over American charts in 1964.

Finally, though the charts became stickier in the SoundScan era, musical variety was about the same. This seems paradoxical. How could musical variety

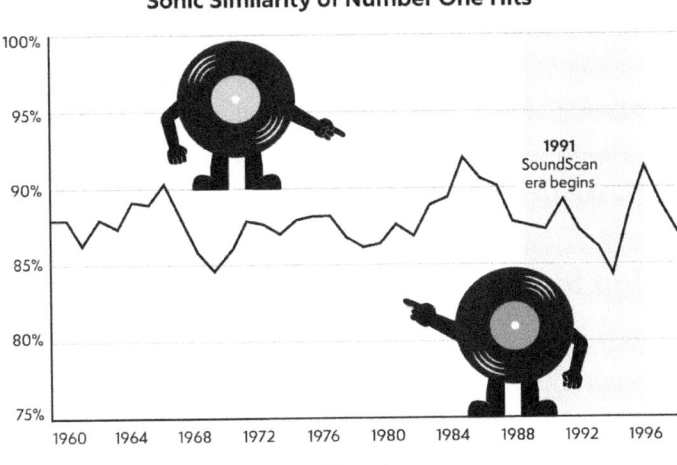

Figure 9.4

stay the same if there were fewer new songs charting? The reason is that when songs cycled on and off the charts more regularly in the pre-SoundScan era, you weren't getting more sonic diversity. You were getting a bunch of similar songs. You can see this by comparing the sonic similarity of number ones in 1977 and 1995.

In 1977, 29 unique songs topped the charts. In 1995, only 12 did. But the relative musical variety of those 12 songs in 1995 (i.e., 90 percent) was on par with the variety of the 29 songs in 1977 (i.e., 87 percent). Plus, we must remember that some of those earlier listening patterns were an illusion. It's unlikely that the way people engage with songs changed that much between the 1970s and 1990s. Charts were now a better reflection of reality.

## Take Heed 'Cause I'm a Lyrical Poet

If I stopped here, you would think that the intrigue around "Set Adrift on Memory Bliss" was only based on the fact that it was the first SoundScan number one. Whatever song happened to be number one when *Billboard* made the switch would have worn that symbolic crown. But, as I mentioned, its importance goes beyond historical happenstance because it was a hip-hop song by a Black duo who rapped the word "damn." Let's explore each part of that statement to understand how it relates to the most dramatic shift in lyricism since the 1960s.

# A Hip-Hop Song . . .

Earlier, we noted that before SoundScan, the Hot 100 was "warped by label preferences and record-store inventories. It often over-counted songs that labels preferred . . . and under-counted genres they were indifferent toward." In the same way that Paula Abdul's music was in the former category, the entire genre of hip-hop was in the latter.[3]

To be clear, hip-hop wasn't new in the 1990s. It had been growing in popularity for over a decade, and artists like Run-DMC and the Beastie Boys had already scored hits working within the genre. But its growth was accelerating during the final decade of the twentieth century.

In 1990, two songs featuring rappers got to number one: Paula Abdul and Wild Pair's "Opposites Attract" (February 10, 1990) and Glen Medeiros and Bobby Brown's "She Ain't Worth It" (July 21, 1990). But these weren't hip-hop songs. They were pop records with rap verses tacked on to appeal to a wider audience. Hip-hop wasn't to remain a chart-topping novelty, though. A few months later, Vanilla Ice scored the first full-fledged hip-hop number one with his inane "Ice Ice Baby" (November 3, 1990).

Over the next year, more hip-hop and hip-hop-adjacent music would top the charts. In early 1991, Freedom Williams rapped on C+C Music Factory's dance record "Gonna Make You Sweat (Everybody Dance Now)" (February 9, 1991). Six months later, a young Mark Wahlberg spit some verses on the Funky Bunch's groovy "Good Vibrations" (October 5, 1991). But after the

---

[3] The other undercounted genre was country. The style was wildly popular despite never topping the Hot 100 in this era. The closest it got was All-4-One taking an R&B cover of John Michael Montgomery's country ballad "I Swear" (May 21, 1994) to number one.

introduction of SoundScan, it was abundantly clear that hip-hop was being underrepresented on the charts.

Here's one way to see that. Five of the 50 number ones before SoundScan contained at least one rap verse. At most three of those 50 were true hip-hop songs, depending on how wide your definition of the genre is. Among the 50 after SoundScan's introduction, 11 contained someone rapping, 10 of which were bona fide hip-hop tracks.[4]

"Singers can hide their words . . . beneath a tune," critic Kelefa Sanneh wrote in his book *Major Labels*. "But rappers are more exposed than singers, because their form of expression is more similar to speech. And so rappers spend lots of time explaining who they are, what they're doing, and why they deserve your attention." This similarity to speech and, according to Sanneh, necessity to "say your name, make a claim, [and] emphasize the backbeat," led artists to pack more syllables in their songs.

As you can see in Figure 9.5, before P.M. Dawn kicked off the SoundScan era with their 136-word-per-minute chart-topper, number ones averaged around 67 words per minute. From "Set Adrift on Memory Bliss" through the end of this era, that average rose to 89. In fact, the top five songs measured by words per minute all occurred in this era. Four of them were hip-hop tracks. The outlier was "We Didn't Start the Fire" (December 9, 1989), Billy Joel's rapid-fire list of historical events.

## . . . By a Black Duo . . .

*Billboard* wasn't just undercounting hip-hop before implementing SoundScan, though. They were also undercounting songs by Black artists, like P.M. Dawn. This wasn't a big secret. In Gerald Posner's history of Motown, he recounts Marvin Gaye seething because "black artists like him . . . were at a disadvantage when it came to the pop chart since the people who compiled it [*Billboard*] tended to call only the large white record stores." The data seen in Figure 9.6 bears out this claim.

---

[4] The odd one out was Michael Jackson's pop rocker "Black or White" (December 7, 1991). It contains a cringey rap verse after the bridge.

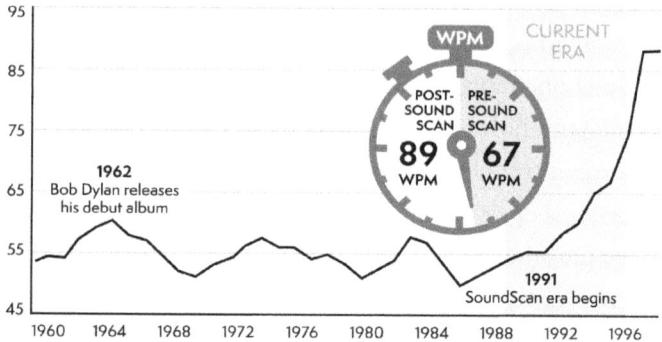

Figure 9.5

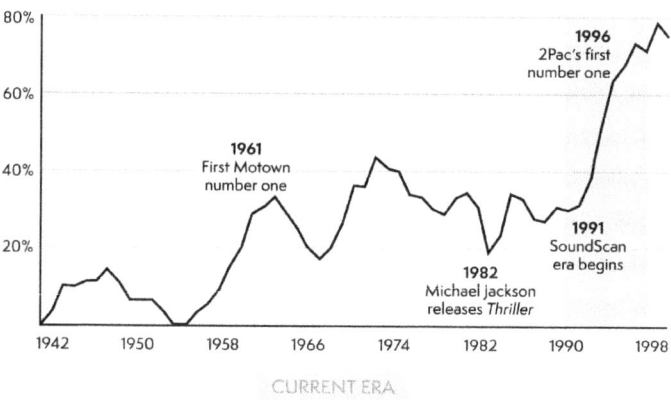

Figure 9.6

Pre-SoundScan, 31 percent of number-one songs were by Black artists or groups with at least one Black member. From the switch through the end of this era, 72 percent were. And this fact is independent of the rise of hip-hop. Among the first 50 non-hip-hop number ones in the SoundScan era, 76 percent were by Black artists.

The last time we talked about how songwriters were addressing new lyrical topics was Chapter 3. That's when artists were reacting to cultural and political events, including the Vietnam War, assassinations of prominent figures, and the civil rights movements for women and minority groups. While musicians continued to react to external events in this era, the change in lyrical topics was driven by the fact that people from different ethnic backgrounds were getting to the top of the charts.

- On "Gangsta's Paradise" (September 9, 1995), Coolio captures the needless violence of his environment: "Death ain't nothing but a heartbeat away / I'm living life do or die, what can I say."

- Both "Waterfalls" by TLC (July 8, 1995) and "Tha Crossroads" by Bone Thugs-N-Harmony (May 18, 1996) address addiction, death, and the plight of those suffering from HIV/AIDS

- Though Kriss Kross's "Jump" (April 25, 1992) and Montell Jordan's "This is How We Do It" (April 15, 1995) come across as straightforward party starters, they are also both laced with a boastful swagger that was a staple in the hip-hop world (e.g., "Don't try to compare us to another bad little fad / I'm the Mac and I'm bad, give you something that you never had").

We occasionally saw lyrical uniqueness from artists of other races in this era too. For example, Phil Collins preached about homelessness on "Another Day in Paradise" (December 23, 1989), Martika captured addiction on her droning "Toy Soldiers" (July 22, 1989), and Lisa Loeb brought a stream-of-consciousness approach to "Stay (I Missed You)" (August 6, 1994). Still, the lyrical changes were largely driven by Black artists.

## . . . Who Rapped the Word "Damn"

In the 1960s, appearing on *The Ed Sullivan Show* was a sign of success. But when you appeared on the program, you had to respect the wishes of the show's namesake. So, when The Doors were invited to perform "Light My Fire" (1967) on an episode of the show, they were asked to censor the lyric "Girl, we couldn't get much higher" because it might be interpreted as a drug reference. Though Doors' frontman Jim Morrison edited the lyric during the dress rehearsal, he sang the actual line during the taping. With Sullivan fuming, The Doors were never invited back to the program.

Jump forward to this era, and Morrison would be considered prude. Compare his quasi-poetry to the imagery on Janet Jackson's "That's the Way Love Goes" (May 15, 1993): "Oh, baby, don't stop, don't stop / Go deeper, baby, deeper / You feel so good I'm gonna cry." This slow jam would have made Ed Sullivan's head explode. And it was not unique in this era.

Madonna's steamy "Justify My Love" (January 5, 1991) was so lyrically and visually erotic that MTV refused to air the video. Sir Mix-a-Lot's "Baby Got Back" (July 4, 1992) was an earnest ode to the female derrière. And, among others, Toni Braxton's "You're Makin' Me High" (July 27, 1996) was a four-minute sexual fantasy (i.e., "Inside of my private thoughts / I can imagine you touching my private parts").

No, this wasn't the first time that popular music was engaging with controversial topics. In the 1950s, *Variety* decried the obscenity of rock 'n' roll "leer-ics." Two decades later, *Time* magazine lamented, "15% of [radio] air time is devoted to [sex songs]." A decade after that, the US Senate brought popular musicians to Washington, D.C. to discuss the effects of controversial lyrics, ultimately resulting in certain albums getting a "Parental Advisory" sticker. Nevertheless, in Figure 9.7 we see a much larger percentage of songs dealing with sex and other explicit topics in this era.

I define a song as explicit if Spotify labeled it as such or it was overly sexual, violent, drug-related, or profane for the time of its release. That definition sounds imprecise because it is. I'm using my discretion while keeping in mind that profanity changes over time. In a 2015 *Wall Street Journal* article, "How Dare You Say That! The Evolution of Profanity," linguist John McWhorter noted, "An anatomy book in the 1400s could casually refer to a part of the female anatomy with what we today call the C-word. But over time, referring to these things in common conversation came to be regarded with a kind of pearl-clutching horror."[5]

---

[5] While the "c-word" doesn't make an appearance in this era, the "f-word" does: 2Pac's "How Do U Want It" (July 13, 1996) was the first number one to feature the word "fuck."

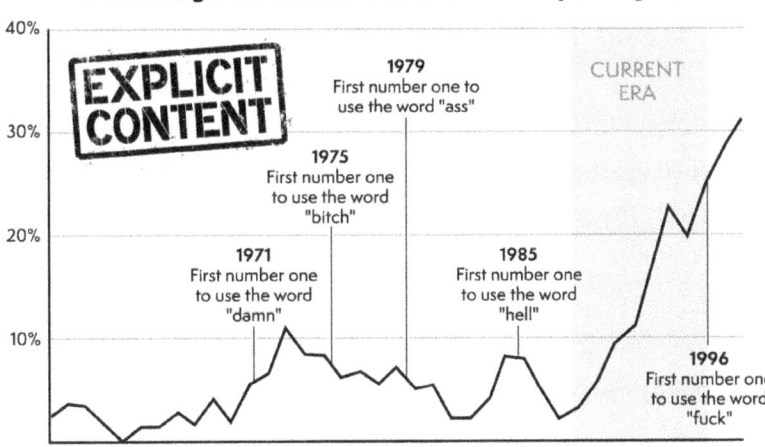

Figure 9.7

In his book *Nine Nasty Words*, McWhorter ruminates on this idea at length. He notes that over the last few hundred years, profanity has gone through three eras: profanity of religion (e.g., "damn," "hell"), profanity of the body (e.g., "shit," "fuck"), and profanity of people. The third group contains racial, sexual, and gender epithets and, given that I won't provide any examples, is obviously considered the most profane at the time of writing.

Because standards evolve, I wanted to acknowledge, for example, that though it wouldn't have been a big issue in this era, Johnny Horton's "The Battle of New Orleans" (1959) purposefully censored the word "hell" with a wink a few decades earlier: "We held our fire till we see'd their faces well / Then we opened up our squirrel guns and really gave 'em . . . Well, we fired our guns and the British kept a-coming." Even accounting for this, we see many more explicit songs in this era. Why?

It's not related to people becoming more profane. There are tons of examples of artists in the first half of the twentieth century not just releasing music that was considered profane in its day, but would be considered profane now.

- In 1931, Harry Roy released "My Girl's Pussy," a three-minute double entendre about cats and female genitalia (i.e., "There's one pet I like to pet / And every evening we get set / I stroke it every chance I get / It's my girl's pussy").

- In 1935, blues singer Lucille Bogan recorded a raunchy version of the song "Shave 'Em Dry" that wasn't released during her lifetime but may have been performed live (i.e., "I got nipples on my titties big as the end of my thumb / I got something between my legs'll make a dead man come").

- Bessie Smith, dubbed the Empress of the Blues, recorded the hedonistic classic "Gimme a Pigfoot" in the middle of the 1930s (i.e., "Give me a reefer and a gang of gin / Play me 'cause I'm in my sin").

- The Clovers, a 1950s doo-wop group best remembered for their song "Love Potion No. 9," recorded but never released "Rotten Cocksuckers' Ball," a song that can only make you laugh because the following lyrics are sung in earnest, four-part harmony: "We're going downtown to the cocksuckers' ball / Fuck, suck, and fight / Till the beginning of the broad daylight."

- In 1956, Johnny Cash almost got to the top of the charts with his sociopathic "Folsom Prison Blues" (i.e., "I shot a man in Reno / Just to watch him die").

Even though each of these records wasn't popular in its day, they illustrate how artists have always played with profanity. The important change in this era is that profanity wasn't only heard after hours in nightclubs or on studio throwaways. It was front and center on the most popular records in the land.

You could point to many reasons that explicit content moved from the shadows to the limelight. While linguistic scholar Melissa Mohr notes that "film production codes, radio and TV broadcast licensing, the baby boom and increasing numbers of people becoming middle class . . . dozens of court cases that eroded laws against obscenity . . . [and] declining church attendance" when discussing this change in her book *Holy Sh\*t: A Brief History of Swearing*, I think in the musical sense those changing legal standards around obscenity proved the most vital.

For most of the nineteenth and twentieth centuries, the US standard for obscenity was imported from Britain. It was known as the Hicklin Test. It established that a work of art was obscene if any part of it could "deprave and corrupt" those whose hands it fell into. This meant that if you wrote a 500-page book and there was a two-sentence sex scene at some point, your book could be considered obscene.

Judicial decisions in the middle of the twentieth century began to reshape this standard in the United States. In 1973, the Supreme Court established the Miller Test. This argued that something was only obscene if the work "taken as a whole, appeals to the prurient interest" and "lacks serious literary, artistic, political, or scientific value." This was a radical shift. While subjective, it's hard to argue that a work of art has zero value.[6]

That doesn't mean that songs in this era failed to stir controversy. When Silk sang, "Let me lick you up and down, till you say stop / Let me play with your body, baby, make you real hot" on "Freak Me" (May 1, 1993), for example, they felt the need to defend themselves to *The Washington Post*: "A lot of people blame us for opening the door to a lot of 'freaky' music . . . But it's really tame compared to a lot of things out there." A few years before Silk topped the charts, members of the hip-hop group 2 Live Crew were also arrested on charges of obscenity after performing tracks from their explicit album *As Nasty as They Wanna Be*. Nevertheless, the bar for what was obscene was much higher in this era.

So, would P.M. Dawn's use of the word damn (i.e., "Then you know I can't remember a damn thing") have been considered profane in 1991? No. By the 1990s, you weren't going to be saying words like "hell" or "damn" around your children, but among adults, those words weren't considered much more than spicy. Still, "damn" wasn't as common as you'd think at the top of the charts. It first showed up in the 1970s in Isaac Hayes's "Theme from *Shaft*" (1971) (i.e., "You're damn right"). In the intervening 20 years between Hayes's sole number one and P.M. Dawn's sole number one, the word only appeared in eight more chart-toppers. So, no, P.M. Dawn wasn't going to be criticized for obscenity,

---

[6] This has forced me to admit that even Michael Bolton's pointless cover of "When a Man Loves a Woman" (November 23, 1991) has some value.

but their work was indicative of the evolution of free speech, profanity, and popular lyrics.

Given the amount of time I've spent talking about P.M. Dawn, you might think that they were one of the most important hip-hop acts of all time. Though they presage some of the more melodic rap that we'll talk about in Chapter 12, I'd be lying if I said they were. For that matter, other than charting two top ten singles off their sophomore album, they were barely part of the future that their number one symbolized.

Part of their demise was based on perception. In their early years, P.M. Dawn was heaped with praise by White critics and largely ignored by Black critics. In the same review quoted at the beginning of this chapter, *People* wrote, "Embraced by the mainly white rock press as the second (non-threatening) coming of rap, the two Cordes brothers of Jersey City, NJ, were, not surprisingly, reviled by rappers for the sin of being soft."

But it wasn't just their perceived softness that put them at odds with the hip-hop community. It was their ideals. Prince Be opposed affirmative action (i.e., "It's too focused on race. It lets people who aren't qualified get jobs over people who are."), downplayed the continued effects of slavery (i.e., "Slavery was hundreds of years ago. It's time to forgive and forget."), and levied criticism at some of hip-hop's stars (i.e., "Public Enemy and people like that—they just make mountains out of molehills. KRS-One wants to be a teacher, but a teacher of what? N.W.A just don't do anything at all"). KRS-One took umbrage at that final comment. In 1992, he and his crew stormed the stage at a P.M. Dawn show in Manhattan and physically threw them off while MTV was filming.

The duo was also plagued by more existential issues. DJ Minutemix was charged with sexually assaulting an underaged cousin in 1995 a couple of weeks before the pair's third album dropped. As those legal troubles mounted, Prince Be was battling diabetes, which resulted in multiple health setbacks. He would die from renal failure in 2016. His *New York Times* obituary described the group he fronted succinctly: popular, maligned, underappreciated, and quietly influential.

# We Both Know I'm Not What You Need

Throughout my life, debates have raged about how we should treat problematic artists. Can I still enjoy "Christmas (Baby Please Come Home)" every holiday season even though it was written and produced by convicted murderer Phil Spector? Is it appropriate to listen to The Rolling Stones' "Start Me Up" even though their longtime bassist Bill Wyman had a relationship with a 13-year-old girl when he was in his fifties? What about listening to P.M. Dawn after the accusations against DJ Minutemix? I could make a long list of questions of this type. But no song highlights the complexity of these queries quite like Michael Jackson's final number one, "You Are Not Alone" (September 2, 1995).

Michael Jackson spent much of the latter half of his life dogged by allegations of sexual abuse and pedophilia. Even after he died in 2009, accusations continued to emerge. Because Jackson's songs remain ubiquitous, it seems that most people can enjoy art by a problematic artist.

But "You Are Not Alone" raises more questions. It was penned by R. Kelly, a man later convicted of sex crimes that make the words in his song "Bump n' Grind" (April 9, 1994) feel like a warning (i.e., "My mind's telling me, no / But my body, my body's telling me yes"). As accusations mounted in the years before his conviction, *The New York Times* noted that R. Kelly's songs were "all but erased from the radio and other commercial placements." As a point of comparison, they pointed out that Michael Jackson "remains steadily popular on air." Though Jackson was never convicted, R. Kelly's erasure was nearly complete before any guilty verdict was handed down. This dichotomy highlights how our standard is less precise: We can enjoy art by problematic artists if the art is good enough.

There are many complicating factors to these debates, though. Can you listen to a song if the artist was a saint, but the studio musician that played bass was later convicted of murder? Also, does it make a difference if you've spent years listening to an artist before finding out that they were a monster? If so, does the calculus change depending on how you are currently listening to them? After you've purchased a CD, for example, there is no monetary benefit to the artist each time you play it. But if you listen to that artist on a streaming service, they are likely making some money.

I tend to believe that people should listen to whomever they want. Beyond the fact that it's unrealistic to expect listeners to arbitrate the behavior of artists, those that do almost never apply a standard consistently. That doesn't excuse artist behavior. That behavior is just better litigated in our courtrooms and history books rather than by you and me each time we turn on the radio, songs great and horrendous about to meet our ears.

## Highlights

1. **"I Will Always Love You" by Whitney Houston (November 28, 1992)**[7]—Dolly Parton has claimed that she wrote "I Will Always Love You" and "Jolene" on the same day in the 1970s. If her memory serves her well, that would likely be the most productive day of songwriting in history. Parton also claims that Elvis Presley's team reached out about recording the song not long after she composed it. There was a problem, though. Presley's manager insisted that the King receive half of the songwriting royalties. Parton wouldn't agree to that. And she's lucky she didn't. Because when Whitney Houston released the song, she, in her own words, "made enough money to buy Graceland."

   I'm certain Elvis would have done "I Will Always Love You" justice. But I'm equally certain that he would not have held a candle to Houston's rendition. Houston's version stops you in your tracks. And while the power of her belting out the song's title is impressive, that's not what stops you. It's the control. The song begins with a whisper, Houston singing acapella, before launching into its full melodramatic glory. But it's that whisper, a whisper only someone of her caliber can control, that raises the song to new heights.

2. **"Always Be My Baby" by Mariah Carey (May 4, 1996)**—This song is all about groove. And for a vocalist that can sing circles around almost

---

[7] TLC's "Waterfalls" was rated high enough to be included here. It was mentioned earlier.

anybody else, Carey sits back and wades deep into that groove. She's in no rush. She knows her baby will be back again. She's able to capture that emotion so well by letting the song lead her rather than pulling it along with vocal flash.

3. **"More Than Words" by Extreme (June 9, 1991)**—As their name suggests, Extreme was a hard rock band. But you wouldn't know it from this track. It's a stunning ballad, Gary Cherone singing delicately over an acoustic guitar. But this doesn't sound like a heavy metal band recording a one-off acoustic love song. It sounds like it's coming from seasoned balladeers. When Cherone harmonizes with himself on the chorus, it's hard not to be entranced.

# Lowlights

1. **"Informer" by Snow (March 13, 1993)**—The early 1990s were filled with reggae-inspired crossovers, like "The Sign" by Ace of Base (March 12, 1994) and "(I Can't Help) Falling in Love With You" by UB40 (July 24, 1993). "Informer" falls into this category. And it's the worst of the lot. While you could criticize Snow, a Caucasian Canadian, for performing in a faux-Jamaican accent, his song's worst offense is that it is a cheap imitation of a rich genre.

2. **"Step by Step" by New Kids on the Block (June 30, 1990)**—This record can't decide what it wants to be. The rhythm is informed by hip-hop. The strings aim for disco. And the vocal gets lost somewhere in between. In trying to capture many different styles, "Step by Step" ends up capturing nothing.

3. **"One More Try" by Timmy T (March 23, 1991)**—I want to celebrate "One More Try" for being a rare number one released on an independent label. But it's hard for that celebration to last long when you hear the song, a ballad sung over a farting bassline and beat crafted on a TR-808, with one of the plainest vocals you'll ever hear.

## Argument Starters

Right Said Fred's "I'm Too Sexy" (February 8, 1992) is one of those records that burrows itself deep in your brain. The circular drum pattern. The half-sung lyrics. The synthetic horn line. It's an earworm. But like many earworms, it evokes a wide range of reactions. While I found it annoying, one of the other judges thought it was humorous (e.g., "I'm a model, you know what I mean / And I do my little turn on the catwalk").

## Odds and Ends

1. **"Dreamlover" by Mariah Carey (September 11, 1993)**—Despite scant mentions in this chapter, Mariah Carey was the queen of the 1990s. From her first number one—the soulful "Vision of Love" (August 4, 1990)—through the end of this era, she spent over 16 percent of weeks at the top of the charts. And those chart-toppers were diverse, ranging from moving piano ballads, like "Hero" (December 25, 1993), to hip-hop-infused tracks, like "Fantasy" (September 30, 1995). My favorite piece of hers is "Dreamlover." Like the aforementioned "Always Be My Baby," it sees the vocalist wade deep into a groove.

2. **"On Bended Knee" by Boyz II Men (December 3, 1994)**—With this clinic in vocal harmonies penned by Jimmy Jam and Terry Lewis, Boyz II Men became the second act since The Beatles to replace themselves at number one. The song before was the aforementioned "I'll Make Love to You."

    Jam and Lewis were dominant in this era, penning six additional number ones, five of which were with Michael Jackson's little sister, Janet. Their other was a sexy romp called "Romantic" (November 2, 1991) written for Karyn White, the future wife of Mr. Lewis.

3. **"Black Cat" by Janet Jackson (October 27, 1990)**—Speaking of Janet Jackson, like Mariah Carey, she too hopped across genres in this era. "Black Cat" is my favorite of her genre-bending experiments because it

sees the pop star attempt to make a hard rock record. The song rocked hard enough that the hard-living Lemmy Kilmister of Motörhead allegedly wanted to record a duet of the song with her.

# Everything Else

"Good Thing" by Fine Young Cannibals. "If You Don't Know Me By Now" by Simply Red. "Batdance" by Prince. "Right Here Waiting" by Richard Marx. "Hangin' Tough" by New Kids on the Block. "Don't Wanna Lose You" by Gloria Estefan. "Girl I'm Gonna Miss You" by Milli Vanilli. "Miss You Much" by Janet Jackson. "Listen to Your Heart" by Roxette. "How Am I Supposed to Live Without You" by Michael Bolton. "Escapade" by Janet Jackson. "Black Velvet" by Alannah Myles. "Love Will Lead You Back" by Taylor Dayne. "I'll Be Your Everything" by Tommy Page. "Nothing Compares 2 U" by Sinéad O'Connor. "Vogue" by Madonna. "Hold On" by Wilson Phillips. "It Must Have Been Love" by Roxette. "If Wishes Came True" by Sweet Sensation. "Blaze of Glory" by Jon Bon Jovi. "Release Me" by Wilson Phillips. "(Can't Live Without Your) Love and Affection" by Nelson. "Close to You" by Maxi Priest. "Praying for Time" by George Michael. "I Don't Have the Heart" by James Ingram. "Love Takes Time" by Mariah Carey. "I'm Your Baby Tonight" by Whitney Houston. "Because I Love You (The Postman Song)" by Stevie B. "Love Will Never Do (Without You)" by Janet Jackson. "The First Time" by Surface. "All the Man That I Need" by Whitney Houston. "Someday" by Mariah Carey. "Coming Out of the Dark" by Gloria Estefan. "I've Been Thinking About You" by Londonbeat. "You're in Love" by Wilson Phillips. "Baby Baby" by Amy Grant. "Joyride" by Roxette. "I Like The Way (Kissing Game)" by Hi-Five. "I Don't Wanna Cry" by Mariah Carey. "Unbelievable" by EMF. "(Everything I Do) I Do It For You" Bryan Adams. "I Adore Mi Amor" by Color Me Badd. "All 4 Love" by Color Me Badd. "Don't Let the Sun Go Down on Me" by George Michael and Elton John. "To Be With You" by Mr. Big. "Save the Best for Last" by Vanessa Williams. "I'll Be There" by Mariah Carey. "This Used to Be My Playground" by Madonna. "How Do You Talk to an Angel" by The Heights. "A Whole New World" by Peabo Bryson and

Regina Belle. "Weak" by SWV. "Again" by Janet Jackson. "All For Love" by Bryan Adams, Rod Stewart, and Sting. "The Power of Love" by Céline Dion. "Here Comes the Hotstepper" by Ini Kamoze. "Creep" by TLC. "Take a Bow" by Madonna. "Have You Ever Really Loved a Woman?" by Bryan Adams. "Kiss From a Rose" by Seal. "Exhale (Shoop Shoop)" by Whitney Houston. "Because You Loved Me" by Céline Dion.

# *I Mean It, No Diggity, I Like the Way You Move*

## November 9, 1996— February 14, 2004

### It Seems My Life Is Gonna Change

It's the fall of 2004, and I've recently started the fourth grade. I'm at my friend Jake's house. We're sitting in his TV room playing Nintendo 64. Jake's older brother is in the same room on the family computer. As Jake and I play *Super Smash Bros.*, I can hear his brother clacking away on AOL Instant Messenger. Then there's a pause. A few clicks. And a song is coming from the computer's tinny speakers.

It's an entrancing song. The artist is rapping, but there's a light bounce to his flow that makes it feel melodic. As I try to listen while focusing on our Nintendo battle royale, I know that I should really be trying to shut my ears off. My fourth-grade brain can't discern what the song's lyrics mean, but with references to sipping Bacardi, going to a party, doing X, and having sex, I know that this is a song that my parents wouldn't want me to hear.

I come to learn that it's called "In da Club" (March 8, 2003). It's by a popular rapper named 50 Cent. He's about to go on a tear with other hits, like "21 Questions" (May 31, 2003) and "P.I.M.P." Beyond hearing my friend's older brother play his music, 50 Cent is not really on my radar. I'm mostly into rockers from the 1960s and 1970s, some of whom would resurge in this era, like Elton John with a remake of his "Candle in the Wind" (October 11, 1997) and Santana with his Latin-infused crossovers "Smooth" (October 23, 1999) and "Maria Maria" (April 8, 2000). But 50 Cent stays with me because something about his music feels illicit to my elementary school ears.

This experience isn't unique. Most people can identify transgressive art from their youth that left them somewhere between disgusted and intrigued. If you grew up in the 1950s, maybe it was Link Wray's distorted guitar on "Rumble," an instrumental that was allegedly banned from the radio for inciting riots. In the 1960s, maybe Country Joe's live Woodstock recording of "I-Feel-Like-I'm-Fixin'-to-Die Rag," where he has the audience shout "Fuck" before launching into the song. In the 1970s, maybe Donna Summer's moans on "Love to Love You Baby." In the 1980s, maybe a shirtless Prince crawling across the floor in the "When Doves Cry" (1984) music video. In the 1990s, maybe Next singing about an erection on "Too Close" (April 25, 1998) (i.e., "I wonder if she could tell I'm hard right now") or Christina Aguilera telling her lover "You gotta rub me the right way" on "Genie in a Bottle" (July 31, 1999).

Despite the cross-generational ubiquity of these experiences, my specific experience was somewhat unique. Primarily, when I described my friend's brother playing "In da Club," he wasn't playing it via vinyl, cassette, or CD. He was playing it over the internet. For the first time in history, recordings were divorced from physical media. More specifically, we were listening to much of this music via MP3s downloaded illegally from file-sharing sites like LimeWire.

But technology wasn't only shifting how popular music was listened to. It also transformed how it was recorded. Since the 1980s, there was a slow shift from recording being done on tape to on computers, meaning recordings were now digital rather than analog. In 1999, Ricky Martin's "Livin' La Vida Loca" (May 8, 1999) became the first number one recorded, mixed, and mastered in Pro Tools, a digital audio workstation. By the end of this era, digital recording was the default. Let's talk about why this shift was so profound.

## A Primer on Digital and Analog Sound

Sound is a vibration that travels through the air as a wave. If you had a device to capture those vibrations, you could store them somewhere and then replay them. That's how a record player works. Somebody makes sound around a microphone, which captures the sonic vibrations. Those vibrations are then etched into something, say a piece of vinyl. When you run a record player's needle over the vinyl, it's recreating the sound by generating the same vibrations that the performer did.

But as we noted in Chapter 1, since the vibrations are also being pressed onto a physical object, there are limits to how much sound can be stored without degrading. Until the LP was introduced in 1948, there were few commercially available discs that held more than four minutes of sound. Because of that, artists had to work within those constraints.

In his 1936 autobiography, composer Igor Stravinsky recalled, "In America I had arranged with a gramophone firm to make records of some of my music . . . This suggested the idea that I should compose something whose length should be determined by the capacity of the record. And that is how my 'Sérénade En La Pour Piano' came to be written."

In his 1926 book *Jazz*, bandleader Paul Whiteman noted a similar phenomenon: "Previous to 1897 every song had to have six or seven verses and each verse had eight or ten lines. Now there are two verses of a scant four lines each . . . The whole story must be told in the first verse and chorus." When we look at the average length of number ones in Figure 10.1, we see the time constraints that musicians had to work within and when technological advancement unshackled them from those constraints.

From the invention of the phonograph until the middle of the 1960s, singles were stuck in the realm of two-and-a-half to three minutes. Once recording technology improved, we began to see longer songs climb the charts, like The Beatles' "Hey Jude" (1968). By 1980, the average number one sat around four minutes and remained there for decades. Thus, analog recording technology had a deep impact on popular music. We see the same thing with digital recording technology.

Digital sound is captured and produced by computers. Because computers are built on a binary system, they can't exactly recreate continuous analog sound waves. Computers approximate those sound waves by slicing them into tiny parts. This is why many people claim that analog sound is better than digital sound. Nevertheless, the more slices the computer makes, the closer it

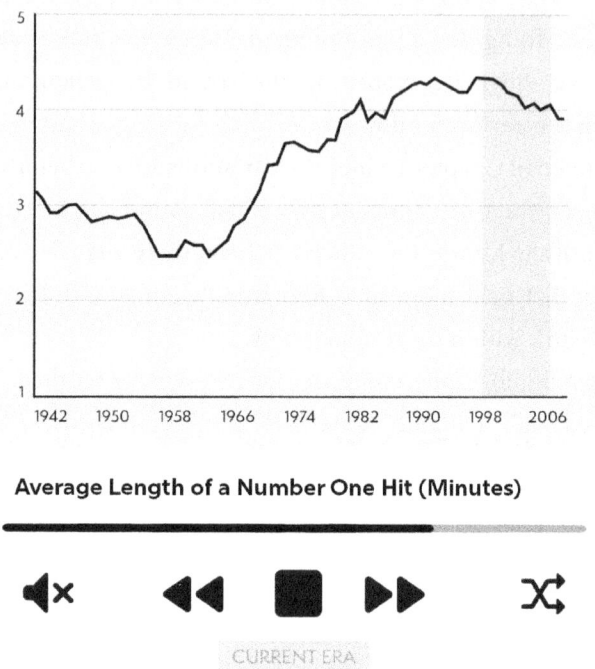

**Average Length of a Number One Hit (Minutes)**

Figure 10.1

will get to recreating the original sound wave. You can see a visualization of that in Figure 10.2.

The advent of digital technology led to more flexibility in the recording process, allowing producers to make new sounds via sampling. Additionally, it changed the way that people discover music. Instead of digging through the crates at your local record shop, you could find almost any song on the internet. Throughout this chapter, we are going to take a closer look at these changes and how they affected both artists and listeners.

## Couldn't Cut It as a Poor Man Stealing

In 1847, Ernest Bourget and his friends sat down to eat at the Café des Ambassadeurs in Paris. It was a nice day, so the group enjoyed some live music

**Digital Approximation of Sound Waves**

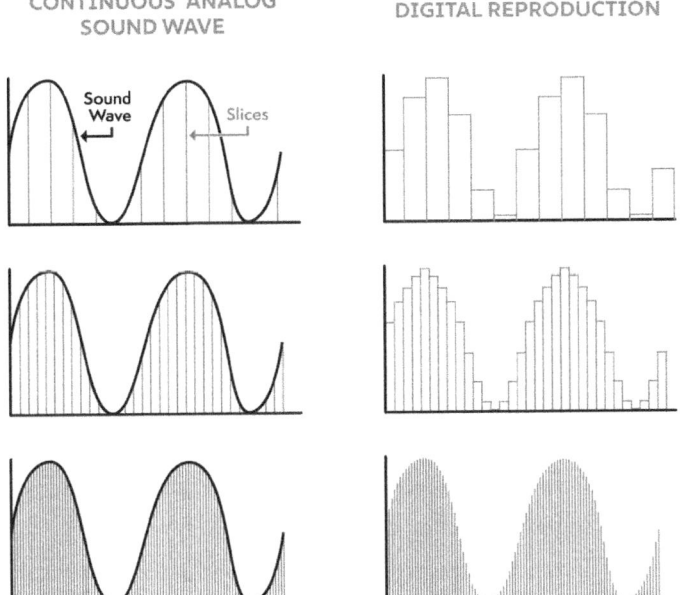

Figure 10.2

and drinks. But when the bill arrived, they refused to pay. The owner of the café came over to Bourget's table thinking he knew what the issue was. The prices were higher today, he explained, because there was live music. They increased the prices so they could pay the musicians.

Bourget wasn't satisfied. He was a playwright and lyricist, and the musicians at the café had played some of his songs. Why should he pay for food and drink if the café wasn't going to pay composers and authors for using their songs? The café's owner was incensed. The idea of paying a composer for musicians performing their work was ludicrous.

After a few years of legal back-and-forth, Bourget helped establish that composers deserved to be remunerated for the performance of their work. He then went on to found SACEM, the first performance rights organization, an entity whose goal was to collect and distribute payments to artists for the public performance of their work.

Despite being about 150 years earlier, Bourget's compensatory concerns bear a strong resemblance to concerns that arose in this era around how people were listening to and paying for music. In Bourget's age, music was primarily a service. Technology transformed music into a product during much of the twentieth century. Then different technology transformed it back into a service in this era.

## Music as a Product and Music as a Service

For most of history, musicians made money by (a) performing, (b) teaching, or (c) receiving support from a wealthy benefactor. This is what I mean when I say that music existed as a service. Musicians had to be actively engaged in making music to survive.

By the mid-1800s, sheet music publishing became big business in the United States. For the first time, music could be sold as a product to supplement music as a service. But copyright protection was weak, so most musicians continued to make their living by providing services.

The advent of recording toward the end of the nineteenth century changed all of this. Over the next hundred years, the music business itself wasn't only born, but it developed as a product business, selling music in many different formats to consumers. Looking at data from the Recording Industry Association of America (RIAA) in Figure 10.3, we can see some of the products that drove the music business during the last quarter of the twentieth century.

Vinyl was king in the 1970s. During its reign, revenues peaked at almost $16.5 billion. After that, the industry experienced a sharp decline as the popularity of disco waned before rising from the ashes on the back of the CD. Between 1980 and 2000, revenues increased 86 percent, peaking at $22.7 billion in 1998. Though technological innovation had enabled extravagant profits, it was also to be their downfall. This time it was due to two innovations: peer-to-peer file sharing and the MP3.

- **Peer-to-Peer File Sharing**: When you log onto your favorite video streaming service, you are interacting with a company's servers so that you can watch something. This is the client-server model. Peer-to-peer turns this relationship on its head. Peers on the network act as both a client and a server. As an example, a peer-to-peer video sharing network would mean that I can download videos from anybody on the

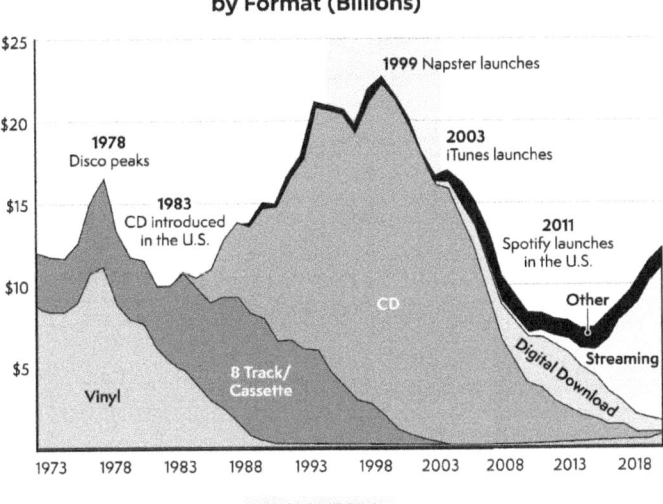

**Figure 10.3**  *Source: RIAA.*

network, and the videos on my device will be available to download by anybody else on the network.

- **MP3**: In the late 1970s, Professor Dieter Seitzer and his graduate student Karlheinz Brandenburg began researching how to send speech more efficiently over phone lines. The underlying idea was that you can throw out certain sonic frequencies that aren't vital for the human brain to understand the transmitted sound. After a decade of work, the MP3 was born. Because the MP3 was dramatically smaller than an uncompressed audio file, it was easier to transmit.

So, how did these technologies come together to erode the music industry's profits? Primarily, peer-to-peer networks made it easy to access the music collections from masses of people around the globe. Still, raw music files were large enough that transferring them over the low-bandwidth internet connections of the 1990s was impractical, or at least time-consuming enough that your mom would get mad because she had to make a phone call during

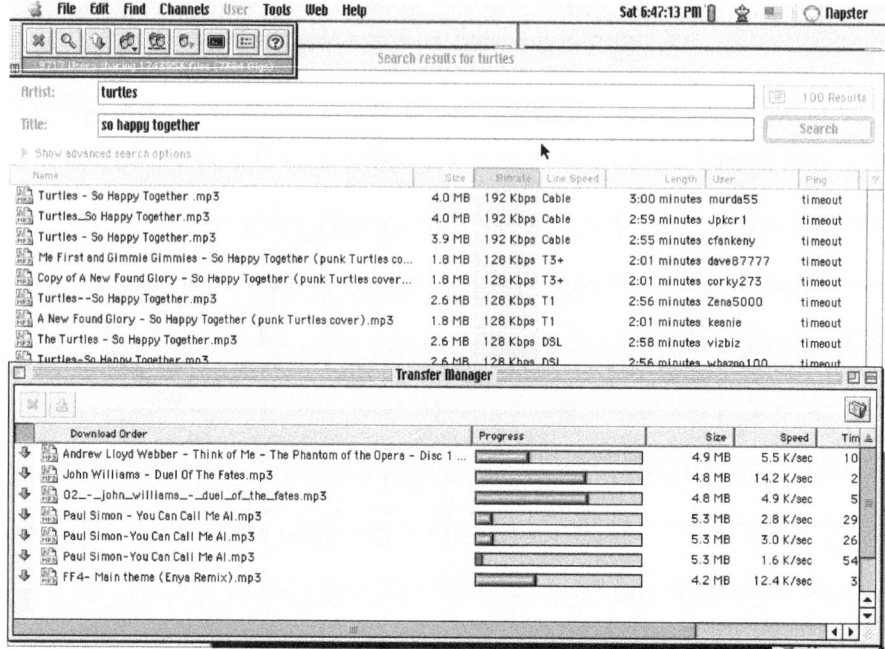

**Figure 10.4** *Napster Running on an iBook in March 2001. Credit: Njahnke.*

your download session.[1] The MP3 changed that. There was now a small, relatively quality music file that could be quickly shared and downloaded.

While there were many peer-to-peer services that popped up throughout the 1990s, the most influential was Napster, founded by Shawn Fanning and Sean Parker in 1999. Napster had tens of millions of users before being forced to shutter its doors in 2001.

In Figure 10.4, you can see a version of the Napster interface. The way the product worked was that it would return a list of files available from other users who were online that matched whatever you searched for. If one of those files was the one you wanted, Napster would connect you with that person's computer so you could download it.

There have been thousands of pages written in both popular and academic presses about the legal battles surrounding Napster, file sharing, and the music industry. I don't want to focus on the legality of these services as much as

---

[1] Known as "dial-up," early internet connections ran over telephone lines. Because of that, nobody could place a phone call while you were online.

(a) how the music industry reacted to file sharing and (b) how file sharing heralded a new era for listeners.

## Why Labels Hated Napster, But Some Artists Didn't

When Sony and Philips introduced the compact disc (CD) to label heads at a conference in 1981, their innovation wasn't well received. In journalist Steve Knopper's book *Appetite for Self-Destruction: The Spectacular Crash of the Record Industry in the Digital Age*, Jan Timmer, an industry executive, recalled the industry response: "Hostile. Very hostile. I am fortunate there weren't any rotten tomatoes in the room. Otherwise, they would have thrown them at me."

There were clear advantages to CDs over other popular formats available at the time. They didn't degrade like cassettes and vinyl. They were also very portable. Though some people, like Neil Young, claimed that the digital sound of CDs wasn't only inferior to the analog sound of vinyl but "an insult to the brain and heart and feelings," the record industry's initial opposition had little to do with sound quality. Switching over to a new format was expensive.

But the industry did an about-face when they realized something else: They could charge more for a CD than they charged for vinyl. And this wouldn't only apply to new releases. They could also re-release all their older material at this higher price point.

Though two decades before the rise of Napster, I mention this story for a few reasons. First, as a reminder that the industry was making more money than it ever had in the run-up to this era. Second, that the industry has always been resistant to change. And the CD change was only a format change. It was still a physical product. The transition in this era was much more radical. It was driven by computer wizards outside the industry's purview who were pushing music back to Bourget's time, where service rather than product was king.

So, what was the industry's response to this radical shift? Lots of litigation. First came lawsuits against Napster and other online music services. Courts were receptive to these lawsuits, and Napster was forced to shut down in 2001 for facilitating the distribution of copyrighted material. The next set of lawsuits came against consumers, meaning the industry was suing average Joes who had downloaded infringing music from peer-to-peer services. Though most defendants would end up settling for a few thousand dollars, those that refused could be pushed toward bankruptcy.

While the consumer lawsuits were unpopular, especially after the press caught wind that some were against children and single mothers, the reaction to suits against Napster and other peer-to-peer services varied.[2] Along with the RIAA and most major labels, the face of the Napster legal drama was Lars Ulrich, the outspoken drummer of the heavy metal band Metallica. Napster drew the ire of Ulrich when he found out that much of Metallica's catalog was circulating on the site. In 2000, he outlined his position on *Charlie Rose*:

> The core issue is sort of people's perception of the internet, people's perception of what their rights are as an internet user and how it relates to intellectual property . . . People take it for granted that because it comes through the computer . . . that they have a right to it.

Not every artist felt the same as Ulrich, though. Here is what some other prominent voices from that time had to say.

- In a 2001 interview with Dennis Miller, Nirvana drummer and Foo Fighters' frontman Dave Grohl said, "There should be no such thing as a price tag on music. Okay, maybe there's a price tag on the package that you buy . . . But I don't wanna turn on my fucking radio and have to put a nickel in it to hear Metallica."
- Rap-rockers Limp Bizkit went on a free tour sponsored by Napster.[3]
- Though Madonna's team threatened legal action after a demo of her electronic song "Music" (September 16, 2000) leaked on Napster, she later clarified her position to *Rolling Stone*: "I feel covetous about my work, and I don't want people to hear it until it's finished. At the same time . . . the trading of information is inevitable . . . Napster could be a great way for people to hear your music who wouldn't have the chance to hear it on the radio."

---

[2] You might assume that these lawsuits were largely against people ripping thousands of songs, but my friend Matt recently told me how his family got a threatening letter from their internet service provider after he tried to download a copy of Drake's 2011 album *Take Care* from some file-sharing site.

[3] Limp Bizkit was part of a movement that combined rap and rock in the 1990s, sometimes dubbed nu-metal. Despite its popularity, the only nu-metal-ish song to top the charts was Crazy Town's "Butterfly" (March 24, 2001).

- When Radiohead's *Kid A* leaked on Napster weeks before its release, frontman Thom Yorke celebrated: "The cool thing about Napster is it encourages bootlegging, it encourages enthusiasm for music in a way that the music industry has long forgotten to do."

Why would prominent artists take the side of people pirating their music rather than the organizations that put up money to produce and market it? To understand, you need a brief overview of how recording contracts work. Typically, when an artist signs a record deal, the label agrees to advance them cash. When the artist puts out music, they won't make any money until they recoup the advance for the label out of their share of royalties. On the surface, this doesn't seem horrible. They're getting access to the label's resources, along with being paid to make music. The details are often less rosy.

Let's say you signed a one-album deal with a $300,000 advance and a 20 percent royalty. Let's assume your album is going to sell for $10 and the retailer gets 10 percent. That leaves $9 left for you and the label. 20 percent of each $9 sale, or $1.80, belongs to you. Sort of. Until you sell enough copies for the label to recoup their $300,000, you won't collect anything.

If you do the math, that means that you'll start collecting royalties after the label sells 33,333 copies ($300,000 advance / $9 per album), right? Nope. Your advance is not recouped based on what your album grosses. It's only recouped out of your royalty share. In other words, you won't start making money until the label sells 166,667 copies ($300,000 advance / $1.80 royalty per album) even though at that point they would have already made $1.5 million (166,667 albums x $9 per album). If you never sell that many copies, you won't make anything beyond the advance.

Though this seems like a bad deal for most artists, labels take on tremendous risk when signing them. Most artists don't recoup their advance. Plus, the label provides a network of resources that would otherwise be inaccessible. That said, when you look at some clauses that were standard in recording contracts, it starts to feel like the label didn't really want artists to make any money.

The label, for example, might not count 10 percent of sales toward recoupment because of "breakage," a term that emerged when fragile shellac records would crack during shipment. Even as goods became more durable, a breakage clause was standard. At the same time, labels would charge artists to package all their CDs, cassettes, and vinyl.

These clauses made it very hard for artists to recoup their advances. Thus, you can probably understand why some artists weren't eager to back the labels, especially when their opponents were often fans. Plus, the internet wasn't going away. Rather than fighting an unwinnable battle against something that couldn't be killed, the industry needed to figure out how to embrace a service-centric world, the same way that Bourget did in the 1800s.

And there were proposals. In a July 2000 Congressional hearing on file sharing, Jim Griffin, the head of technology at Geffen Records from 1993 to 1998, said, "No one is here to defend free music, but music can and should be made to feel free, even when it is not free." Later, Griffin noted that in the "music world, like so many others, service is replacing product." The answer to the music industry's problems "lie in new business models, not technology-based solutions." He continued, "The best forms of copy protection . . . destroy the motive to copy, not its mechanism . . . We are transitioning . . . [to] an economy that emphasizes the wine, not the bottle."

Griffin, among others, suggested online music stores, running ads on file-sharing sites, subscription-based streaming services, and even a tax on all internet users to cover the illegal trading of content. Despite these suggestions, the industry at large was slow to do anything beyond filing lawsuits.

Though Napster was a peer-to-peer service, part of the reason it could be shut down was because its architecture still involved a central server that indexed users who were online. If that server was shut off, Napster wouldn't work. Many of the peer-to-peer services that came online in its wake were not just decentralized but also anonymous, making it harder to shut them down and sue their users.

BitTorrent, a new technology launched in July 2001, was the most sophisticated. If you were to download something, say, the gorgeous soul song "Fallin'" by Alicia Keys (August 18, 2001), you wouldn't be downloading it from any single person on the network. You would download a piece of it from, maybe, someone in Istanbul, and another piece from someone in Reykjavík, and maybe another from someone in your neighborhood. Then it would all be assembled for your listening pleasure. This made file transfers even faster than anything Napster-style systems could offer.

By the time the industry realized litigation wasn't the best way forward and that any of their efforts to sell music online weren't going to cut it, it was almost too late. The best they could do was join forces with Steve Jobs and his new iTunes Store. This was doubly ironic. Primarily, the only company that remained in the product part of the music business was Apple, selling millions of iPods. Secondly, those iPods were likely filled with songs from file-sharing sites. Despite the music industry's refusal to accept the death of physical product, why did consumers love these new ways of listening?

## Why Listeners Loved Napster

Many consumers adored Napster, file sharing, and digital music for four key factors that transformed the listening experience: affordability, flexibility, accessibility, and portability.

### *Listeners Love Affordability*

Music in this era became cheaper than it ever had been. And I don't mean when you were downloading it for free. I mean that once you remove the cost of a physical product, music becomes inexpensive. In 2020, most music streaming services charged under $15 per month for unlimited listening to their entire catalog. In the early 1980s, a new vinyl album would run you around $10, which would have been the equivalent to $25 in 2020 after adjusting for inflation. A new vinyl single was closer to $1.50, which comes to $3.75 after adjusting for inflation. And a new CD was about $16, or close to $40 adjusting for inflation. That's not cheap today. And it wasn't back then.

In the early 1980s, Tom Petty delayed releasing his album *Hard Promises* because his distributor MCA wanted to increase the price from $8.98 to $9.98. Petty voiced his objections to the press and allegedly considered naming the album *Eight Ninety-Eight* before MCA backed down. Furthermore, by the turn of the millennium, CDs had become illegally expensive. In 2000, Time Warner, BMG, Sony, EMI, and Universal settled with the FTC over price-fixing allegations, allegedly overcharging consumers by $500 million over a four-year period, or $2 to $5 per CD.

## *Listeners Love Flexibility*

When Steve Jobs introduced iTunes at the 2001 MacWorld conference, he demonstrated how to make a playlist: "I want a song from this album, a song from this album . . . Put it together in a playlist, rearrange the order, and listen to them in any order I want. The music compiled the way I want, not the way some record company wants." Sounds like the guy you want as your last resort to save the old-fashioned music business.

Regardless, Jobs' demonstration was prescient. iTunes made every listener a DJ. Want to hear Mariah Carey's "Heartbreaker" (October 9, 1999) and Beyoncé's "Crazy in Love" (July 12, 2003) back-to-back because both feature Jay-Z? No problem. Download them from LimeWire, put them on a playlist in your iTunes library, and then either rip the playlist to a CD or drop it on your MP3 player.

This change also unbundled the album. If you wanted to listen to "Honey" by Mariah Carey (September 13, 1997) when it came out in 1997, you'd likely have to buy her entire album *Butterfly* even if you disliked everything else on the record. That was no longer an issue in this era. You could pull an album apart and stitch it back together however you wanted.

## *Listeners Love Accessibility*

In 2000, critic Eric Weisbard noted, "Pop music has grown too diverse for listeners to feel comfortable deciding on purchases; radio can't keep up with all the styles and back catalog . . . Music fans needed to cut through the maze. Napster turned out to be the answer."

Weisbard was correct. But it goes beyond Napster. In general, digital online music allows listeners to access songs across space and time that might otherwise elude them. Imagine it's 1982 and your grandfather mentions some obscure record by the recently deceased big-band leader Bert Kaempfert.[4] If he didn't own it, it might take you months to track it down. That changed in

---

[4] Kaempfert, who was mentioned back in Chapter 1 for his chart-topper "Wonderland by Night" (1961), got an unexpected shout out in this era's "One Week" by the Barenaked Ladies (October 17, 1998): "Bert Kaempfert's got the mad hits."

this era. Now, punch the song name into your favorite online music service, and it would be there.

This search functionality eventually became more robust. Imagine you own Toni Braxton's "Un-Break My Heart" (December 7, 1996). You love the song and notice that it's written by Diane Warren. You search Warren's name on your favorite online music service and realize that she also wrote Aerosmith's "I Don't Want to Miss a Thing" (September 5, 1998) and Brandy's "Have You Ever?" (January 16, 1999), among many other hits. Search for "I Knew I Loved You" by Savage Garden (January 29, 2000) and you'll come to learn that they have other hits, like "Truly Madly Deeply" (January 17, 1998). Search for anything, and you'll find more music than you could ever listen to.

### *Listeners Love Portability*

The slogan for the original iPod was "1,000 songs in your pocket." Sure, there were portable CD and cassette players, but a CD held only 74 minutes of music. If we assume the average song is four minutes, that means a CD can hold about 19 songs. To match the capacity of the original iPod, you would have to carry around 53 CDs. Now, you can travel with entire discographies and not have to look like a lunatic with 53 CDs spilling out of your jacket.

It's easy to romanticize the technology of yore. And my growing collection of vinyl suggests that I'm as guilty of this as anybody else. But it's important to remember that though the technological changes in this era caused headaches for music industry executives, they were largely of benefit to listeners.

# Mix a Little Bit of Ah Ah

Clive Campbell was a fledgling DJ in the Bronx in the early 1970s when he made a simple but powerful observation. Campbell, known as DJ Kool Herc, noticed that there were certain parts of songs, usually the rhythmic breaks, that partygoers reacted to more energetically than others. He realized that if he had two copies of a record and two turntables, he could extend those parts as long as he wanted by starting one record at the beginning of the popular section as the other got to the end of it.

On August 11, 1973, Herc and his sister decided to throw a party at 1520 Sedgwick Avenue in the Bronx. Entry was $0.50 for men and $0.25 for women. Herc would be spinning tunes all night, and the profits would go toward his sister updating her wardrobe for the new school year.

The story handed down is that on that night DJ Kool Herc invented hip-hop. Is this lore true? According to research conducted by the PBS program *History Detectives*, the 1520 Sedgwick party did occur. But was hip-hop invented at the party? Not exactly. Like anything else, hip-hop developed over time. What can be said is that over the next few years, Herc and his crew established many key elements of hip-hop. They built new music by sampling older records. They delivered spoken word, sometimes in the form of rhyme, over those samples. They shaped a new culture.

We spoke about some of hip-hop's effects on lyrics in the last chapter. Now, I want to talk about how sampling inside and outside of hip-hop represented both a profound shift and continued history in music production and how it was impacted by the proliferation of digital sound.

## A History of Musical Quotation

Instruments were invented to create music. Record players were invented to replay recordings of music. This seems so obvious that it isn't worth stating, but it demonstrates how innovative the pioneers of sampling were. These people looked at a device meant to replay recorded music and decided that it could also be an instrument. This innovation didn't begin in the Bronx of the 1970s with DJ Kool Herc and the rise of hip-hop, though. It went back further.

Though composers and critics began to imagine using previously recorded sounds to create new music at the beginning of the twentieth century, it wasn't until the 1940s that French musician Pierre Schaeffer realized many of these ideas via "musique concrète." Schaeffer described the principles of musique concrète as follows: "Instead of notating musical ideas on paper . . . and entrusting their realization to well-known instruments, the question was to

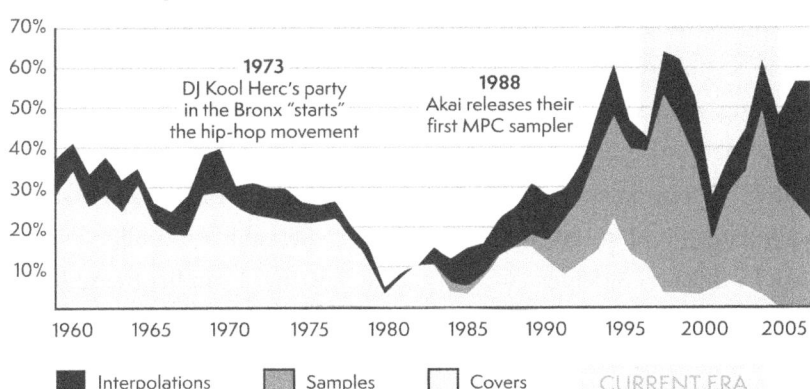

**Percentage of Number One Hits That Quote Other Songs**

**Figure 10.5**

collect concrete [recorded] sounds . . . and to abstract the musical values they were potentially containing." Schaeffer composed "Cinq études de bruits" in 1948, which was built by manipulating previously recorded sounds, just like hip-hop producers would do decades later.

This isn't to suggest that the pioneers of hip-hop were influenced by musique concrète. In fact, musique concrète has a more direct lineage with the experimental of works of The Beatles (e.g., "Revolution 9") and Frank Zappa (e.g., "The Return of the Son of Monster Magnet") than that of hip-hop's forefathers. It's to say that though they are of a distinct descent, the techniques emerging in the Bronx in the 1970s were also being explored by many others, including the disco DJs down-the-road in Manhattan that we discussed in Chapter 5.[5]

While repurposing existing recordings was an innovative, paradigm-shifting act, in a more abstract sense, it fits with the evolution of other genre traditions. From the blues to country to jazz, songs have always been composed by quoting older works. We can see the evolution of these quotations through the number ones in Figure 10.5.

Along with samples, there are two other ways that artists can (clearly) base their works on older pieces: covers and interpolations. We discussed some of

---

[5] The use of turntables and recorded sounds in disco and hip-hop are related but not the same. Disco DJs used a song-centered approach while hip-hop DJs focused on rhythmic breaks.

this in Chapter 4, but let me jog your memory. A sample is when an artist reuses part of another recording in a new song. An interpolation, sometimes called a "sample replay," is when an artist re-records part of an older work for a new song. And a cover is a recording of an entire song originally composed and recorded by others.

The cover saw a slow and steady decline at the top of the charts since the inception of the Hot 100. In the first era, 32 percent of number ones were covers. In this era, 3 percent were. That's so few that I can list them: Monica's "Angel of Mine" (February 13, 1999), Christina Aguilera's "What a Girl Wants" (January 15, 2000), and Christina Aguilera, Lil' Kim, Mýa, and Pink's "Lady Marmalade" (June 2, 2001).

The death of the cover is related to the proliferation of recorded music that we discussed in Chapter 1. As recordings became ubiquitous, listeners became used to specific productions of songs rather than the songs themselves. For example, though we associate the song "Hey Ya!" (December 13, 2003) with Outkast, the duo that recorded it, had it been released decades prior, there would have been other competing versions of the song out at the same time. Nevertheless, the death of the cover did not lead to the death of musical quotes. Those quotes just appeared in different ways.

- **Interpolation**: In the introduction of Aaliyah's "Try Again" (June 17, 2000), Timbaland, the song's producer, raps a piece of Eric B. and Rakim's "I Know You Got Soul."

- **Sampling**: The Notorious B.I.G. raps over Herb Alpert's instrumental "Rise" (1979) on "Hypnotize" (May 3, 1997).

- **Interpolation and Sampling**: Shaggy, who'd already interpolated War's "Smile Happy" on his licentious "It Wasn't Me" (February 3, 2001), teamed up with Ravon for "Angel" (March 31, 2001), a song that samples the guitar riff from the Steve Miller Band's "The Joker" (1974) and interpolates the chorus of "Angel of the Morning," a song that was recorded a few times in the 1960s and 1970s.

While interpolation remained common throughout this era—13 percent of number ones interpolated elements of other songs—it was the rise of sampling that represented the most notable way that artists were quoting older works. In total, 31 percent of number ones in this era contained a sample.

The rise of sampling was driven by the proliferation of affordable digital samplers. In the 2014 TED Talk "How Sampling Transformed Music," producer Mark Ronson said, "30 years ago you had the first digital samplers, and they changed everything overnight. All of a sudden, artists could sample from anything and everything that came before them, from a snare drum from The Funky Meters to a Ron Carter bassline [to] the theme to *The Price Is Right*."

When compared to the sampling that DJ Kool Herc was doing in the early 1970s, digital samplers made sampling much easier. Let's understand how digital samplers work and how their use is no less creative than writing songs on, say, a guitar or piano.

## A Sampling of Sampling

When an artist samples another song, they take a snippet of an existing recording, alter it in some way, and then make a new song from it. When sampling pioneers were doing this, it involved physically altering the tape that the music was recorded to.[6] So, if you wanted to chop up a song into a sample, you had to physically snip the tape where the desired sample was. If you wanted to reverse it, you had to flip the tape over and play it backward. If you wanted to splice it with another sample, you had to attach the tape that each was recorded on. As you'd imagine, this was a laborious, error-prone process.

Digital samplers changed this. Companies like Akai and Roland released devices that allowed artists to chop, edit, splice, process, and loop samples by clicking a few buttons. These devices thought of sampling a bit more generally than we've conceived of it thus far, though. In fact, they were descendants of the drum machines we discussed in Chapter 8. But they had more flexibility.

---

[6] I'm describing how early sampling was done in studio. If you wanted to do it live, like DJ Kool Herc, you had to manipulate your turntable and records like we described in Chapter 5.

Yes, you could sample, say, "The Glow of Love" by Change like Janet Jackson did with Jimmy Jam and Terry Lewis on "All for You" (April 14, 2001), but you could also sample things that weren't necessarily associated with another song, like individual drum hits or horn stabs.

In Figure 10.6, you can see my Akai MPC digital sampler. The MPC was created in 1988 by Roger Linn in conjunction with the Akai, and it was built off much of Linn's previous drum machine work that we discussed in Chapter 8. The MPC takes your samples and maps them to each of the 16 pads on the left. Then you can tap any of the pads to play the samples, sort of how you would play a traditional instrument. In fact, in the operator's manual for the MPC3000, Linn wrote, "I like to think of the MPC3000 as the piano or violin of our time, and you as an MPC3000ist." The MPC and its competitors helped artists create some fascinating work in this era.

Sometimes, an artist would take a tiny musical snippet of an older song and turn it into something wildly different. For example, Monica, with producer Jermaine Dupri, chopped up a piece of Diana Ross's sensual record "Love Hangover" (1976) and turned it into "The First Night" (October 3, 1998), a song about sexual uncertainty.

On "Doo Wop (That Thing)" (November 14, 1998), Lauryn Hill sampled the ascending horn line from The 5th Dimension's "Together Let's Find Love." In addition, BLACKstreet, with some help from Dr. Dre and Queen Pen, built

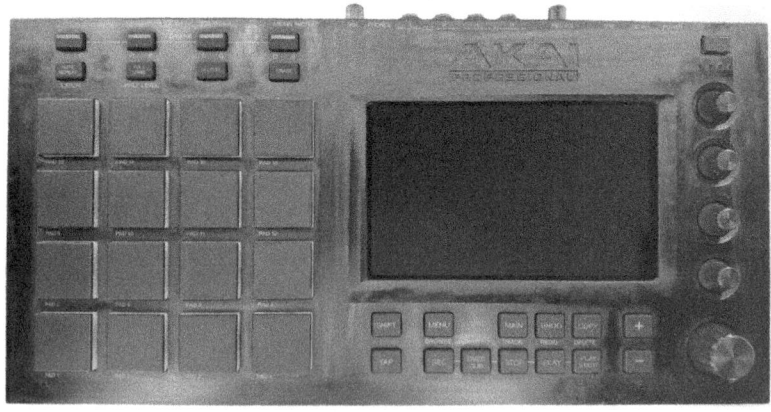

**Figure 10.6** *Author's Akai MPC Sampler. Credit: Evan P. Raftes.*

their swaggering record "No Diggity" (November 9, 1996) around a sample of Bill Withers' "Grandma's Hands."[7]

But artists wouldn't always sample the music from other tunes. Sometimes they'd cut up lyrical sections. "All I Have" by Jennifer Lopez and LL Cool J (February 8, 2003) uses a sped-up vocal sample from Debra Laws' song "Very Special."[8] "Mo Money Mo Problems" (August 30, 1997), released posthumously by The Notorious B.I.G., sampled the music and lyrics from Diana Ross's "I'm Coming Out."

"Mo Money Mo Problems" was produced by Sean Combs, sometimes known as Puff Daddy or Diddy. Bad Boy Records, founded by Combs, sent five records to number one in this era, almost all of which were produced by its founder. Despite the success, Combs was often criticized for liberally sampling from known hits. In 1999, Dr. Dre told *Newsweek*, "I respect Puffy as a businessman . . . But as a musician, he's really hurt the art form. Don't just throw something out there over somebody else's beat." The best example of Dre's criticism is "I'll Be Missing You" (June 14, 1997), a collaboration between Combs, Faith Evans, and 112.

"I'll Be Missing You," a song mourning the death of The Notorious B.I.G., samples the guitar riff from The Police's massive hit "Every Breath You Take" (1983), along with interpolating the chorus. Because of that, it feels like Combs is trying to cash in on nostalgia by making songs that quote hits from yesteryear.

Combs isn't the only culprit of this. On "Gettin' Jiggy Wit It" (March 14, 1998), Will Smith ditched his longtime collaborator DJ Jazzy Jeff and teamed up with producers Poke and Tone to create a party starter centered around samples from Sister Sledge's classic "He's the Greatest Dancer" and The Bar-Kays' deeper cut "Sang and Dance." The next year, he took the same

---

[7] Dre was a frequent user of the MPC and likely used it on two songs in this era: Mary J. Blige's "Family Affair" (November 3, 2001) and 50 Cent's aforementioned "In da Club."

[8] The technique of speeding up old soul samples, sometimes called "chipmunk soul," is closely associated with Kanye West. Before his rise as an artist, West was a celebrated producer. He got his first credit on a number one in this era, cowriting and producing Ludacris's aggressive record "Stand Up" (December 6, 2003).

approach with a new set of collaborators on "Wild Wild West" (July 24, 1999), a song built around Stevie Wonder's "I Wish" (1977).

Given the popularity of these records, it's clear that the public doesn't hate sampling of this type. My friend Monica once told me that she loves the few seconds of uncertainty when you're at a bar and can't tell if they're playing Stevie Nicks's "Edge of Seventeen" or Destiny's Child's "Bootylicious" (August 4, 2001). The latter samples the well-known guitar riff of the former. My friend adores both.

Still, tracks like these are the ones that people will bring up when they characterize sampling as uncreative. And in this case, I'd agree with them. But they're generalizing. Acclaimed sample-heavy albums—like *Fear of a Black Planet* by Public Enemy, *3 Feet High and Rising* by De La Soul, *Donuts* by J Dilla, *Since I Left You* by The Avalanches, and *Paul's Boutique* by the Beastie Boys—build their songs by manipulating snippets from unexpected, often obscure works to create something novel.

Big Boi, one-half of Outkast, vocalized this same sentiment in a 1998 interview: "We like to do creative sampling. We sample a horn riff or some kind of kick or snare . . . You never know where it came from cause we alter it so much to fit what we doing." And he wasn't exaggerating. Some online sleuths suggest that Outkast's "Ms. Jackson" (February 17, 2001) samples The Brothers Johnson's 1977 cover of Shuggie Otis's "Strawberry Letter 23." If it does, it's unrecognizable.

For Outkast, Dr. Dre, and many others, sampling isn't a cop-out. It's a creative act, as creative as picking up a guitar and writing a song. In fact, the way artists innovated with digital samplers in this era is akin to how guitar-slingers did the same in the 1960s. Both were using new technology to push their art further.

## If You had One Shot or One Opportunity

Debates raged throughout this era about what music's true value was. Some of this was related to file-sharing. The proliferation of Napster made it feel like individual songs were worth effectively nothing. iTunes pricing every recording in history at $0.99 did not assuage these fears. But it wasn't only music on the internet that sparked these conversations. It was also sampling. When Ashanti and her producers sampled DeBarge's "Stay With Me" on "Foolish" (April 20, 2002), they had to get permission from whoever owned the respective copyrights of both the DeBarge recording and song. That permission likely required an upfront payment and a share of the royalties.

You could run economic analyses in any of these scenarios to try to determine what the value of a specific song is or what the value of music is generally. I don't want to do that here. I just want you to remember that music has value. There's a reason that every human society has music. It's part of what makes us who we are. So, next time you're walking down the street and some street performer catches your ear, don't be scared to throw some money in their case. A world without music is not one anyone would want to live in.

## Highlights

1. **"Lose Yourself" by Eminem (November 9, 2002)**[9]—In 2016, my buddy Denny got a text from his father: "Just heard my first rap song." After we laughed about the improbability of his father having never heard a rap song, my friend asked what it was. "Lose Yourself," his dad responded. "I like it." Neither of us was shocked by his enjoyment.[10]

   "Lose Yourself" is one of the rare songs that has something for everybody. An eerie piano introduction. A lurching electric guitar. An intense, motivational chorus. Above all else, Eminem holds your attention with a complex internal rhyme scheme that sees him bend words to his will both within and across lines.

2. **" . . . Baby One More Time" by Britney Spears (January 30, 1999)**— This song wastes no time to announce itself, its opening three-note

---

[9] "Mo Money Mo Problems," "In da Club," and "Hey Ya!" were all rated high enough to be included here. They were mentioned earlier.

[10] It wasn't a total surprise that my friend's dad thought he'd never heard a rap song. He mostly listened to rock music that emerged in this era. A big fan of Creed, he told my friend that he listened to their "With Arms Wide Open" (November 11, 2000) on the way home from the hospital the day my friend was born. I had to bear the bad news that the song came out five years too late for that to happen. "Maybe it was your sister," his father quipped. Pop songs, it seems, are so visceral that they can affect our memories.

motif as dramatic as the opening of Beethoven's Fifth Symphony. That's the wizardry of the song's composer, Swedish pop maven Max Martin, who, along with his co-producer Rami, crafts a slow, funky burn.[11] But Spears is no slouch. 17 years old when the song topped the charts, her vocals exist at the crossroads of innocence and passion.

3. **"No Scrubs" by TLC (April 10, 1999)**—In case there was any confusion, TLC defined the word "scrub" in the first verse of their 1999 hit: "A scrub is a guy that thinks he's fly / Always talking about what he wants / And just sits on his broke ass." If that wasn't clear enough, they list some scrub-like behaviors during the bridge: not owning a car, living with your parents, not showing your girlfriend enough love, and being broke.

   You might think the trio was being harsh. And people agreed. According to a *Washington Post* article from not long after the song's release, the song "provoked heated radio debates, and prompted furiously penned answer songs in New York and Los Angeles." If "No Scrubs" is harsh, it isn't for lack of reason. In one sense, it's a response to decades of sexism in popular music, men declaring how women should look and act if they want to be desirable. That's why "No Scrubs" feels so urgent. There is urgency in the directness of the lyrics, but that urgency is also baked into the instrumental, an electronic guitar arpeggiating over a strong groove, synths rising and falling in the background like a slow, controlled breath.

## Lowlights

1. **"This is the Night" by Clay Aiken (June 28, 2003)**—After my friend David rated this song, he told me that he considered ending our friendship because without me he wouldn't have been forced to listen to this musical travesty. My friend was being a bit dramatic, like this vocal ballad.

---

[11] Martin also cowrote NSYNC's "It's Gonna Be Me" (July 29, 2000). We'll hear more about him in the next chapter.

Clay Aiken, the voice on this ballad, finished in second place on the second season of the popular television singing competition *American Idol*. He, nor that season's winner, Ruben Studdard, fared as well as Kelly Clarkson, the first season's victor. Clarkson got to number one in this era with a more powerful but thematically similar ballad, "A Moment Like This" (October 5, 2002).

2. **"I'm Your Angel" by R. Kelly and Céline Dion (December 5, 1998)**— There's no doubting that R. Kelly and Céline Dion can sing. The former's "Bump n' Grind" (1994) and the latter's "My Heart Will Go On" (February 28, 1998) are proof of that. But the thing that sticks with you on this song isn't the vocals. It's that it drags on forever.

Even so, the reason this ended up in the bottom three is that one of the judges gave it the lowest possible score given that she can't stomach anything R. Kelly has done after the decades of sexual abuse that we discussed in the last chapter. Regardless of what you think of this song, that reaction is a good example of how people try to grapple with the sins of pop stars.

3. **"Everything You Want" by Vertical Horizon (July 15, 2000)**—I also said this when writing about "Knock On Wood" (1979) in Chapter 6, but I have no idea how this song ended up in the bottom three. While it's not my favorite song, it's got an interesting, pulsating guitar and memorable chorus. Its inclusion here speaks to the fact that this era was packed with great music.

## Argument Starters

Andy Hildebrand was looking for a musical problem to solve when his friend's wife allegedly quipped, "Why don't you make a box that will let me sing in tune?" Looking at Hildebrand's career, this was a strange request. He spent the 1970s working on complex geophysical problems for Exxon before founding Landmark Graphics, a software company that revolutionized the mapping of the Earth's subsurface. Hildebrand was a musician at heart, though. In fact, he helped fund his college education by teaching flute lessons. After taking Landmark Graphics public and later selling it for $525 million, he dedicated his time to composition and musical software. That's when his friend's wife's request got stuck in his brain.

Digital pitch correction software was a highly sought-after piece of musical technology, but it was hard to build given that it required a tremendous amount of processing power to pick apart and adjust a sound wave. Hildebrand realized that many of the statistical and signal processing techniques that he'd used while working in the oil industry could be used to correct the pitch of a voice with limited computing power. Over a few months, he used those ideas to build Auto-Tune, the first product from his new company, Antares.

Auto-Tune was an immediate hit among producers when Hildebrand debuted it at the 1996 National Association of Music Merchants conference. Now, rather than spending hours stitching together vocals to get the perfect take, producers could make quick adjustments on the fly with Hildebrand's technology. Nevertheless, Auto-Tune was a bit of an industry secret for a few years, mostly used to nudge notes that were slightly off-key. Then Cher topped the charts with "Believe" (March 13, 1999). Producers Mark Taylor and Brian Rawling ratcheted up the settings on the Auto-Tune software so that instead of correcting the pitch of Cher's vocal, it transformed and distorted it in extraterrestrial ways. Auto-Tune was no longer a tool. It was somewhere between an effect and an instrument. And not every judge enjoyed it. While I think "Believe" is a powerful dance record, one judge found the use of Auto-Tune, the signature piece of the track, off-putting.

## Odds and Ends

1. **"Can't Nobody Hold Me Down" by Puff Daddy ft. Mase (March 22, 1997)**—If you've made it this far, you know that I dream of my home state New Jersey being mentioned in the title of a number one hit. "Can't Nobody Hold Me Down"—another song that sees Puff Daddy sample a popular song, namely Grandmaster Flash's "The Message"—obviously doesn't mention New Jersey in its title, but we do get a brief mention in the lyrics: "I be out in Jersey puffin' Hershey."

   Oh, yeah, Ja Rule and Ashanti's "Always on Time" (February 23, 2002), also mentions New Jersey, albeit as a descriptor for a place that's not New Jersey: "And I'm just outside of Jersey past the Palisades." If this book fails, maybe I can at least become the Chief Musical Historian of New Jersey, or something like that.

2. **"Stutter" by Joe ft. Mystikal (February 24, 2001)**—I'm not sure how a label let singer Joseph Lewis Thomas build a career around the super common name "Joe." With four top 40 hits, including the lightning-fast, chart-topper "Stutter," Joe has made that nominal genericness work. And he's clearly very proud of his name. Since 2000, he's released three albums specifically mentioning it: *My Name Is Joe*; *Joe Thomas, New Man*; and *My Name Is Joe Thomas*.

3. **"How You Remind Me" by Nickelback (December 22, 2001)**— This is a well-constructed rock crossover from one of Canada's most successful yet maligned acts. Millions of records sold later, Nickelback probably doesn't pay much mind to the criticism they've garnered, but their detractors would take pleasure in how frontman Chad Kroeger described the group to Fred Bronson in *The Billboard Book of Number One Hits*: "There are two types of bands that get signed. There's the kind that has a buzz and you've got fifteen different labels with deals on the table, or else you have to sell so many records on your own that it doesn't matter if you're four monkeys farting into a box . . . so we tried to be the four monkeys."

## Everything Else

"Wannabe" by Spice Girls. "MmmBop" by Hanson. "4 Seasons of Loneliness" by Boyz II Men. "Together Again" by Janet Jackson. "Nice & Slow" by Usher. "All My Life" by K-Ci and JoJo. "My All" by Mariah Carey. "The Boy is Mine" by Brandy and Monica. "Lately" by Divine. "If You Had My Love" by Jennifer Lopez. "Bills, Bills, Bills" by Destiny's Child. "Bailamos" by Enrique Iglesias. "Unpretty" by TLC. "Thank God I Found You" by Mariah Carey ft. Joe and 98 Degrees. "Amazed" by Lonestar. "Say My Name" by Destiny's Child. "Be with You" by Enrique Iglesias. "Bent" by Matchbox Twenty. "Incomplete" by Sisqó. "Doesn't Really Matter" by Janet Jackson. "Come On Over Baby (All I Want Is

You)" by Christina Aguilera. "Independent Woman, Part 1" by Destiny's Child. "U Remind Me" by Usher. "I'm Real (Murder Remix)" by Jennifer Lopez ft. Ja Rule. "U Got It Bad" by Usher. "Ain't it Funny (Murder Remix)" by Jennifer Lopez ft. Ja Rule and Caddillac Tah. "Hot in Herre" by Nelly. "Dilemma" by Nelly ft. Kelly Rowland. "Bump, Bump, Bump" by B2K ft. P. Diddy. "Get Busy" by Sean Paul. "Shake Ya Tailfeather" by Nelly, P. Diddy, and Murphy Lee. "Baby Boy" by Beyoncé ft. Sean Paul. "The Way You Move" by Outkast ft. Sleepy Brown.

# Slow Jamz Run Down to the Deepest Part of Me

## February 21, 2004— March 3, 2012

### Every Simple Song I Wrote to You

There's this meme I often see online that drives me nuts. On the left side, it shows a picture of Queen frontman Freddie Mercury above the text "Bohemian Rhapsody. 1 writer. 1 producer" followed by the lyrics to the song. On the right side, it shows a picture of Beyoncé above the text "Run the World (Girls). 6 writers. 4 producers" followed by the lyrics to the song. The point of this comparison is typically to demonstrate how degraded culture has become. It took a bunch of people to make a song like "Run the World (Girls)," which repeats the titular phrase 37 times, while a masterpiece like "Bohemian Rhapsody" was birthed from one mind.

Why does this meme make me mad? First, it's misleading. Sure, "Bohemian Rhapsody" only credits Freddie Mercury as a songwriter, but producer credits are typically granted to Roy Thomas Baker and Queen. Queen was composed of four members, thus bringing the producer total to five, one more than "Run the World (Girls)." Plus, even if there really were only one songwriter and one producer, there's no denying that Queen's other three members made vital contributions to the song.

Secondly, songs are not poems. Comparing lyrics discounts the importance of the relationship between music and lyrics. As an example, take the opening lines of Katy Perry's chart-topper "Firework" (December 18, 2010): "Do you ever feel like a plastic bag / Drifting through the wind wanting to start again?" This reads like it was written by someone who recently learned what a simile was. Luckily, those words are only part of the equation. Sung over a shimmering synth loop, it gets the point across. In fact, by the time you get to the monstrous chorus (i.e., "Cause baby you're a firework / Come on show them what you're worth"), the silliness of that opening line almost feels earnest.

Of course, these online memes and arguments mostly boil down to people wanting to claim that their generation created the best art. While you can make a strong case that some eras have stronger output than others, I hope one thing you take away from this book is that every generation also produces loads of musical crap. Still, I do have to give those online meme-lords credit for one thing. "Run This World (Girls)" does have a lot of credited songwriters. And that's not unique in this era.

## The Life, Death, and Myth of the Lone Musical Genius

People love the idea of the lone genius, the auteur sitting alone channeling the voice of God to create a masterpiece. But at the top of the charts, especially in the world of songwriting, that image is fantasy. In Figure 11.1, we see that solo songwriting was never that common. In fact, for the first few decades of the Hot 100, the most common way to write a number one was in a duo. Then around 1990, something changed. From there through the end of this era, the average number of songwriters per number one doubles.

This shocked me. But then I thought I cracked the code: sampling. As we discussed in Chapter 4, when you sample another recording, you must credit whoever wrote the sampled song. For example, Imogen Heap is listed as a songwriter on Jason Derulo's "Whatcha Say" (November 14, 2009) because Derulo's song samples her song "Hide and Seek." As discussed in Chapter 9, when SoundScan was introduced in 1991, hip-hop, a sample-heavy genre,

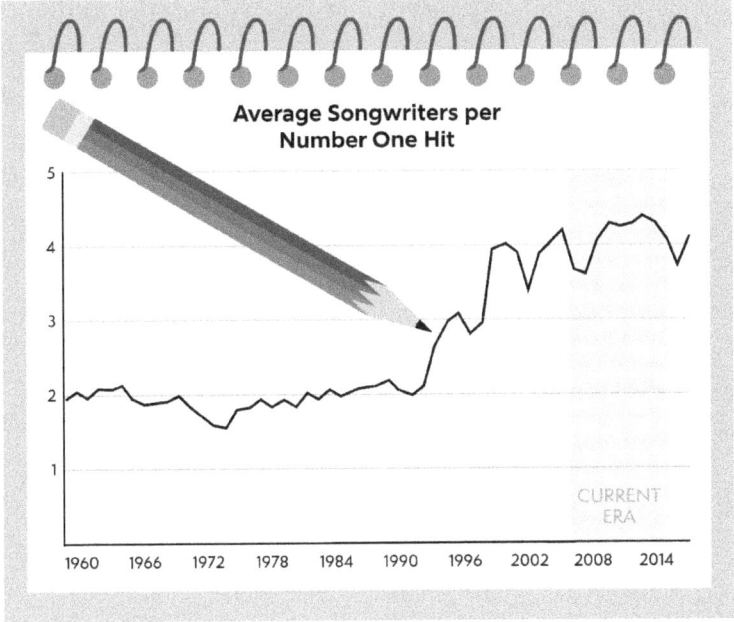

**Figure 11.1**

became much more prevalent on the Hot 100. Mystery solved, right? Sadly, it doesn't check out.

In Figure 11.2, you see two lines. The top line is identical to the line in Figure 11.1. It shows the average number of songwriters per number one. The bottom line is the average songwriters per number one, excluding those listed because their work was being sampled or interpolated. This allows us to disaggregate those who were and weren't actively working together to create a song. When we do that, we see that sample and interpolation credits account for some of the increase in songwriters per number one, but not the entire thing. If that were the case, the bottom line would look similar before and after 1990.

To understand this shift, we need to see how the songwriting process fundamentally changed. This change not only teaches us about the music of this era but will illustrate how women remained excluded from many roles in the music industry.

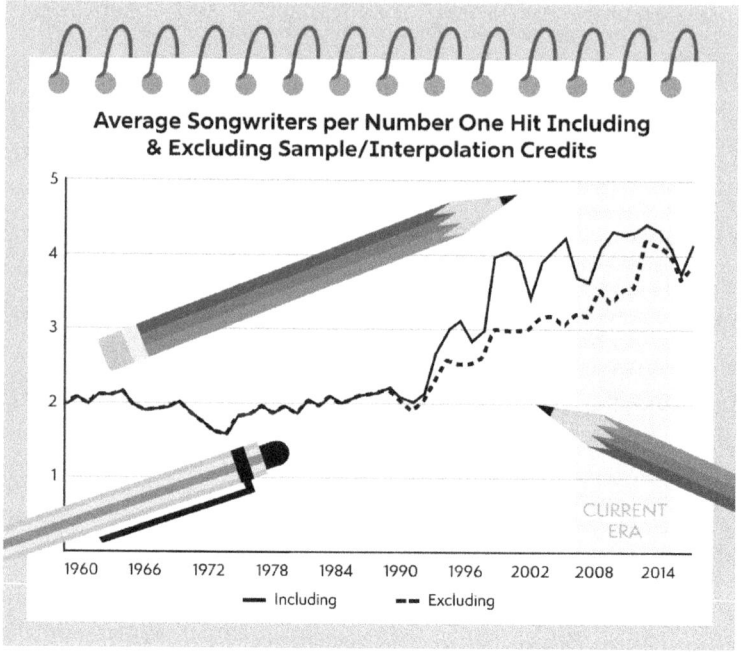

Figure 11.2

# That Digital Spit, Next Level Visual Shit

In 2016, Led Zeppelin went to court. They had been sued by Michael Skidmore, a trustee of the estate of Randy California. Led Zeppelin had allegedly lifted the opening of their magnum opus "Stairway to Heaven" from California's instrumental "Taurus," which he had written for his band Spirit.

These allegations were not new. Spirit released "Taurus" in 1968. Zeppelin put out "Stairway" three years later. And people have noted the similarities for decades, including California. In fact, he mentioned the resemblance in a 1997 interview not long before he died.

I'm not bringing this case up because of its outcome. I'm bringing it up because of a detail that emerged during the proceedings. According to Michael Einhorn, an expert on music royalties, "Stairway to Heaven" generated an eye-popping $60 million between May 2011 and May 2016 for composers Jimmy Page and Robert Plant.

In short, popular songs can be quite valuable, and as the music industry has become more concentrated, corporatized, and financialized (see Chapter 7), that potential value has only increased. This has made it possible for songs like "Stairway to Heaven" to generate millions of dollars decades after they came out.

Since hit songs are so valuable, there's been a two-pronged effect. Primarily, labels are keen to bring in outside help to assure an artist has a guaranteed hit. But artists aren't stupid. They also know how valuable a hit can be. So, it's important that they get a writing credit even if they didn't write anything. In fact, it's long been an open secret that popular artists can use their star power to get writing credits on songs they didn't contribute to because they know how valuable it will be to the actual songwriter if they release it. With that in mind, it's not a shock that the performing artist is listed as a cowriter on 86 percent of number ones in this era, up from 38 percent in the 1960s.

The increased financial viability of hit songs only explains a small piece of why there were so many songwriters credited on the hits of this era, though. To understand an even bigger piece, we need to head to Sweden.

## How the Swedes Altered the Songwriting Process

Dag Krister Volle loved pop music. And his colleagues clowned him for it. But Volle didn't care. As part of SweMix, a Swedish DJ collective that remixed American hits for European audiences in the 1980s, he defiantly assumed the name Denniz PoP. While working, PoP noticed there were two strains of music that people enjoyed. There was the rhythmic music that they danced to in nightclubs and the melodic music that they sang along to on the radio. Maybe, PoP posited, there was a way to combine them. John Seabrook described this in his 2015 book *The Song Machine: Inside the Hit Factory*:

> In the United States, melody was kept at arm's length by the DJs who were the producers of house music, because in the clubs, whenever a strong melody came over the speakers, the dancing stopped. But in Sweden, it was different. As Jan Gradvall observes, "In discos in small towns all over Sweden in the '80s, people danced to the biggest hit song rather than the funkiest songs or best mixes. When choruses came around, that's when the dance floor boiled."

After PoP and his colleagues sold SweMix, he set out to create his version of popular music. In 1992, he and Tom Talomaa opened Cheiron, a studio and label. Though the label foundered, the studio got work. In 1994, PoP produced the reggae-infused earworm "The Sign" for Ace of Base (1994), and it went on to be the biggest hit of the year. At the same time, he was assembling a team of songwriters and producers to work for him. This team would soon find wild success writing and producing some of the biggest hits of the 1990s.

That success wasn't a fluke. Over the years, PoP's protégés have continued to write smashes. Rami Yacoub, for example, worked on "Rain on Me" by Ariana Grande and Lady Gaga (2020), "Starships" by Nicki Minaj, and some songs by One Direction. Andreas Carlsson helped craft "Inside Your Heaven" for Carrie Underwood (July 2, 2005) and "Waking Up in Vegas" for Katy Perry. Jörgen Elofsson cowrote Kelly Clarkson's chart-toppers "A Moment Like This" (2002) and "Stronger (What Doesn't Kill You)" (February 18, 2012).[1] That said, all the Cheironites paled in comparison to Karl Martin Sandberg.

Sandberg was the onetime singer of a Cheiron Records rock band called It's Alive. After their album *Earthquake Visions* failed to make an impact, It's Alive was dropped from the label. PoP saw something in Sandberg, though, so he invited him to stick around to write and produce for others. It was during this time that PoP gave the young man a new name: Max Martin.

In the four years between his first credits on a Cheiron production and becoming the de facto leader of the studio after Denniz PoP's death from stomach cancer in 1998, Martin transformed into a pop music maven, writing and producing 12 top ten hits for everyone from teen stars—like Britney Spears (e.g., "Oops!... I Did It Again"), Robyn (e.g., "Show Me Love"), NSYNC (e.g., "It's Gonna Be Me" (2000)), and the Backstreet Boys (e.g., "I Want It That Way")—to established acts, like Céline Dion (e.g., "That's the Way It Is") and Bon Jovi (e.g., "It's My Life").

If the Max Martin story ended there, he would be known as a talented musician who made a very specific brand of pop music throughout the late

---

[1] This Clarkson tune was one of two number ones in this era built around philosopher Friedrich Nietzsche's adage "That which does not kill us makes us stronger." The other was Kanye West's "Stronger" (September 29, 2007).

1990s and early 2000s. And for a while, that's what it looked like. Between 2001 and 2004, Martin didn't write any top ten hits.

Years later, Martin reflected on this period: "We were doing so well . . . Then music changed. Pharrell came and ruined it all, crashed my party, and I found myself in a place where I actually thought everyone else was wrong and I was right."

Martin is referring to Pharrell Williams, one-half of the production duo The Neptunes that Williams founded with Chad Hugo in the 1990s. And he was correct. Pharrell's music was dramatically different than his. "Drop It Like It's Hot" (December 11, 2004), a song The Neptunes crafted with Snoop Dogg, is exemplary of this. It's a sparse hip-hop record whose rhythm is built around mouth pops and tongue clicks, not the drum machines and synths that Martin was familiar with.

But it wasn't only Pharrell. Martin also had to deal with the likes of Timbaland and Scott Storch. Timbaland brought off-kilter beats to songs like Missy Elliott's "Get Ur Freak On," Jay-Z's "Dirt Off Your Shoulder," and both Justin Timberlake's "SexyBack" (September 9, 2006) and "My Love" (November 11, 2006). Storch's rhythms were more traditional, but some of his tracks, like Terror Squad's "Lean Back" (August 21, 2004) and 50 Cent's "Candy Shop" (March 5, 2005), had Middle Eastern flair.

While most would double down on how they originally found success, Martin decided to change: "I remember clearly that I had [an] epiphany . . . Maybe I'm the one that's wrong. Maybe I'm the one that should start listening to some other music." And that's what he did.

The Swede headed to New York, where he befriended Lukasz Gottwald, an aspiring producer who paid the bills playing guitar in the *Saturday Night Live* studio band and DJing around the city under the name Dr. Luke. Luke and Martin's skills complemented one another. Whereas Martin could show Luke how to produce vocals and write a strong melody, Luke could introduce Martin to other genres, like hip-hop, and use his guitar to expand Martin's instrumental palate.

In late 2004, the two wrote and produced "Since U Been Gone" for Kelly Clarkson. It peaked at number two and was Martin's first hit since 2000. Since then, Martin's success has continued unimpeded. That success is partly due to the process that Deniz PoP created, and he carried on.

## PoP Principles: Melody and Rhythm Should Work Together

This was the key insight that inspired PoP's music. You could make music with a strong enough rhythm, so people could dance, and a strong enough melody that people could sing along. You can hear this idea on Katy Perry's Martin-cowritten "California Gurls" (June 19, 2010). The melody is deeply catchy, but you feel compelled to move while you hum along.

## PoP Principles: Keep Things Simple

PoP despised complex harmonies. His SweMix colleague StoneBridge recalled, "Whenever I would play . . . complicated jazzy chords, Denniz would make a face. That was the thing that drew him to pop—the simplicity of it." You can hear how Martin agreed with his mentor's sentiment on a four-chord romp, like Katy Perry's "Part of Me" (March 3, 2012).

## PoP Principles: Lyrics are Secondary

English wasn't PoP's first language. So, he grew up listening to American music without any idea what the lyrics meant, and he liked it all the same. Because of that, he wasn't willing to sacrifice a musical element for a clever lyric. This put Swedish-crafted pop in direct opposition to the wordplay-heavy hip-hop that was also popular at the time.

Martin continued this lyrics-serve-the-melody tradition. Bonnie McKee, a frequent collaborator, summed it up succinctly: "Max doesn't really care about lyrics because he's Swedish . . . I can write something I think is so clever . . . but if it doesn't hit the ear right then he doesn't like it. He's also really stubborn about syllables . . . If you add a syllable, or take it away, it's a completely different melody to him."

You can hear the syllabic stringency in many of his compositions. The verses on Pink's "So What" (September 27, 2008) are built around a 13-note guitar riff that the vocal melody follows. This leads to lines like "The waiter just took my table / And gave it to Jessica Simps." Whereas many composers would bend the melody to fit Jessica Simpson's entire name, Martin won't.

His Swedish origin has also led to some of his compositions being accidentally controversial. Whereas Martin's lyric "Hit me baby one more time" on Britney Spears' " . . . Baby One More Time" (1999) was an attempt to use hip American lingo to mean "hit me up on my phone," some took it to be sado-masochistic. Similarly, Martin was surprised when Katy Perry's "I Kissed a Girl" (July 5, 2008) sparked outrage. Growing up in the socially progressive Sweden, bi-curiosity wasn't a big deal.

## *PoP Principles: The Bigger the Chorus the Better*

PoP and Martin loved songs with massive choruses, like Def Leppard's "Pour Some Sugar on Me" and Europe's "The Final Countdown." Listening to Usher's "DJ Got Us Fallin' In Love," Pink's "Raise Your Glass" (December 11, 2010), or any other Cheiron-descended composition, you can hear how the chorus is always the focal point.

## *PoP Principles: Collaboration is King*

You will seldom find a Cheiron production written or produced by a single person. The Swedish artist E-Type compared Cheiron to an Italian painter's studio in the 1500s: "One assistant does the hands, another does the feet, and another does something else, and then Michelangelo walks in and says, 'That's really great, just turn it slightly. Now it's good, put it in a golden frame and out with it. Next.'"

After Cheiron closed, Martin continued collaborating. When he was inducted into the Songwriters Hall of Fame, he noted, "In my career . . . a lot of the songs there's two or three or four, sometimes maybe five, writers . . . I don't think I would have lasted this long if I had been stubborn sitting in my chamber alone writing."

It should thus come as no surprise that in the same way Denniz PoP took Max Martin under his wing, Martin has done the same for others, his two most famous protégés being Shellback and the aforementioned Dr. Luke.

Shellback (née Karl Johan Schuster), another long-haired, Swedish hardrocker-turned-pop-savant, has created his most well-known work with Martin but has also had some big hits without his mentor, like Maroon 5 and Christina Aguilera's "Moves Like Jagger" (September 10, 2011).

Dr. Luke has achieved even more success. Along with collaborating on most of Martin's number ones in this era, he worked on Miley Cyrus's "Party in the USA," Avril Lavigne's "Girlfriend" (May 5, 2007), and Kesha's "We R Who We R" (November 13, 2010), among many other hits. Like Martin, both Shellback and Dr. Luke never work alone.

Whether you like Martin's work or not, the Swedish-style collaboration model was exported all over the world as he and his colleagues found success both within and across genres. But, again, this isn't enough to explain the entirety of the rise in songwriters on hit songs in this era. There's one more piece to this puzzle, a piece that affected everybody, including Martin: the digital audio workstation.

## How the Computer Altered the Songwriting Process

Earlier, I noted that from the beginning of the Hot 100 (i.e., 1958) through 1990, your average number one was written by two people. This trend goes back further, though. If you look at the most beloved songs from 1900 and 1960, you'll notice that they were also often written by duos. Not only that, but the division of labor in those duos was clear. One person was the composer, meaning they wrote the music, which included the chords and melody, or tune. The other was the lyricist, meaning they set the composer's melody to words.

When it was time to turn a song into a recording, it was handed off to producers and arrangers to decide how that specific rendition was going to sound. Let's take "My Favorite Things" from the Broadway show *The Sound of Music* as an example. Richard Rogers composed the music. Oscar Hammerstein II wrote the lyrics. When it was turned into a film in 1965, Irwin Kostal arranged the music and lyrics for Julie Andrews to sing. Over the years, the song has been recorded in scores of styles. John Coltrane turned it into a 14-minute jazz masterpiece in 1961. Tony Bennett swung it on a 1968 holiday album. Kenny Rogers even gave it some countrypolitan flavor in 1981.

While this setup remained common as the twentieth century wore on, the division of labor became fuzzier. John Lennon and Paul McCartney, for example, wrote songs as a duo but neither was dedicated to music or lyrics. They each did a bit of both. And sometimes they'd even get involved with producing those songs. By this era, the entire writing and producing process was turned on its head, though. You can see that by looking at Ne-Yo's ballad "So Sick" (March 18, 2006).

"So Sick" started out as an idea from Mikkel Eriksen and Tor Hermansen, a Norwegian duo known as Stargate. They had recorded a looping four-chord progression backed by a kick drum and handclaps when they ran into Ne-Yo in New York City. Ne-Yo had already achieved success as a songwriter, cowriting Mario's "Let Me Love You" (January 1, 2005), but he had yet to do the same as an artist. Upon their chance meeting, Ne-Yo was surprised that these two bald Norwegians made R&B music. They decided to collaborate. With Ne-Yo improvising some lyrics and melodies over Stargate's sparse progression, "So Sick" quickly came to life. Though it feels mundane, this story is exemplary of a radical shift in how songs were written and recorded.

First, those two processes had merged. When Stargate showed Ne-Yo their sketch of "So Sick," one of the Norwegians didn't sit down at the piano and start tickling the ivories like Burt Bacharach might have done when showing Dionne Warwick a song in 1964. They went to the computer and clicked play on a basic track with simple percussion. In other words, Stargate wasn't showing Ne-Yo a completed song. They were showing him the beginnings of the recording of a song.

Max Martin summarized this change when accepting the Polar Music Prize in 2016: "Writing and producing . . . I don't really know what's what anymore. The old sort of way of here's a song and you record it and produce it, it doesn't really work like that anymore . . . It's kind of married together." Martin was correct. During the first era, 13 percent of number ones had at least one songwriter also listed as a producer. During this era, 91 percent of songs did.[2]

Because of this, the division of labor had also changed. The old model, as I established, saw one person—a composer—writing the chords and melody, or music, and another—a lyricist—writing the words to that melody. Now, you had someone, typically a producer, recording the chords and beat, or "track,"

---

[2] For clarity, the Black Eyed Peas' "Boom Boom Pow" (April 18, 2009) was written by will.i.am, Fergie, Taboo, and apl.de.ap. It was produced by will.i.am, John Baptiste, and Poet Name Life. will.i.am is common to both groups.

and another writing the melody and lyrics, often called the "hook" or "topline." In the example of "So Sick," Stargate produced the track and Ne-Yo wrote the hook, or topline.

This approach is sometimes referred to as "track-and-hook." It stands in contrast to the earlier "music-and-lyrics" approach. Stargate used the former on all their number ones. The duo teamed up with Ne-Yo again to help write toplines on Beyoncé's "Irreplaceable" (December 16, 2006) and Rihanna's "Take a Bow" (May 24, 2008). They then established a productive relationship with Ester Dean, the most prolific topliner of this era. Among other songs, Dean contributed toplines to many of Rihanna's number ones, including "Rude Boy" (March 27, 2010), "What's My Name?" (November 20, 2010), "Only Girl (In the World)" (December 4, 2010), and "S&M" (April 30, 2011).

This approach was first used in both hip-hop and dancehall music before it was industrialized by pop producers. In hip-hop, for example, somebody records a beat, maybe something like the sparse rhythm on D4L's snap-happy "Laffy Taffy" (January 14, 2006), and then somebody raps over it.[3] In dancehall, a Jamaican genre that originated decades earlier, there are popular "riddims" that every artist performs over. For example, the riddims on both Sean Paul's dancehall crossovers "Get Busy" (2003) and "Temperature" (April 1, 2006) can be heard on other popular songs.

But why did this approach become ubiquitous in popular music? The short answer is the proliferation of the digital audio workstation, or DAW. We talked about digital sound in the last chapter, but we need to understand the digital recording process to see how it led to the track-and-hook approach.

A DAW is a piece of software that allows you to record, edit, and process audio files. DAWs like Pro Tools, Logic Pro, and Ableton not only became the popular mode to record throughout the 1990s and 2000s, but they became incredibly cheap.

---

[3] "Laffy Taffy" is part of a short-lived hip-hop subgenre called "snap," characterized by—you guessed it—prominent snaps as part of the percussion. Along with "Laffy Taffy," the most famous snap songs are Lil Jon's "Snap Yo Fingers," T-Pain's "Buy U a Drank (Shawty Snappin')" (May 26, 2007), Dem Franchize Boys' "Lean wit It, Rock wit It," and Soulja Boy's "Crank That" (September 15, 2007). The success of these songs, and this style, is sometimes attributed to the fact that they sounded good when used as ringtones on cheap cell phones. Of note, ringtones were a big moneymaker for the music industry in this era.

Since recording was more expensive before the DAW, your song had to be fleshed out before you headed to the recording studio. If not, you'd be wasting money. Now, I can open Ableton in my bedroom and screw around with a half-baked idea at almost no cost. This is why Stargate could show Ne-Yo the seeds of a recording without a complete song. It's also the reason why track-and-hook could replace music-and-lyrics.

The DAW's effects have been even more far-reaching, though. In Figure 11.3, you can see a song that I recently recorded in my DAW, Logic Pro, to understand why.

Let's start by looking at the second pane from the left, the one that you see "Guitar—Arpeggio" at the top of. This pane displays each track you are recording. So, when I needed to record a bass, I created a new track, labeled it "Bass," and was able to capture the sound.

Now, look to the right of the bass track. You can see a visual representation of what I've recorded. But something interesting is going on here. I only recorded two bars of the bass. I then copy and pasted those same two bars throughout the entire song. I was able to do this because I built this song around a bunch of short loops. After that, I went back and wrote the melody

**Figure 11.3** *Logic Pro X File for Author's Song "My Whole Heartbeat".*

and lyrics over the recorded track. This is the track-and-hook approach in action. You can see it visually here, but you can also hear its effects on the popular music of this era.

Take "Break Your Heart" by Taio Cruz (March 20, 2010) as an example. A synthy pop song that sounds like it could have been written with the help of Max Martin, the verses of "Break Your Heart" are built around a repeated six-note phrase (e.g., "Listen to me, baby"). That phrase is so short that you can't really do anything interesting with it. But "Break Your Heart" was written with the track-and-hook approach. Brief, looping melodies that would bore listeners if they were just sung over an acoustic instrument can be made more interesting by adding different synthesizers and percussion elements, an option much more feasible if you were writing while recording directly into your DAW.

Compare "Break Your Heart," a song with short melodic phrases made interesting by adding and removing production elements, to something like "Hey There Delilah" (July 28, 2007) by the Plain White T's. Built around a solo acoustic guitar, "Hey There Delilah" was written using the older music-and-lyrics approach, albeit both elements were written by Plain White T's frontman Tom Higgenson. Given that Higgenson didn't have the tools of a DAW while writing, he had to build intrigue using the old-fashioned tools of melody and harmony. That's why the verses of "Hey There Delilah" have a much longer melodic arc than that of "Break Your Heart." While the latter has verses built around a repeated six-note phrase, the former has a long, 44-note phrase.

The differences between compositions built using these two approaches are stark once they've been pointed out to you. Part of the reason that "Down" by Jay Sean (October 17, 2009) and "Last Friday Night (T.G.I.F.)" by Katy Perry (August 27, 2011) are leagues apart from "Rolling in the Deep" by Adele (May 21, 2011) is that those first two songs—short melodic phrases and all—were built using the track-and-hook approach, while the final one was built, at least in part, using an older songwriter's toolkit.

But the length of melodic phrases isn't the only difference between these methods. The track-and-hook approach also helped kill the key change. In Figure 11.4, we can see that from the start of the Hot 100 through 2000, 23

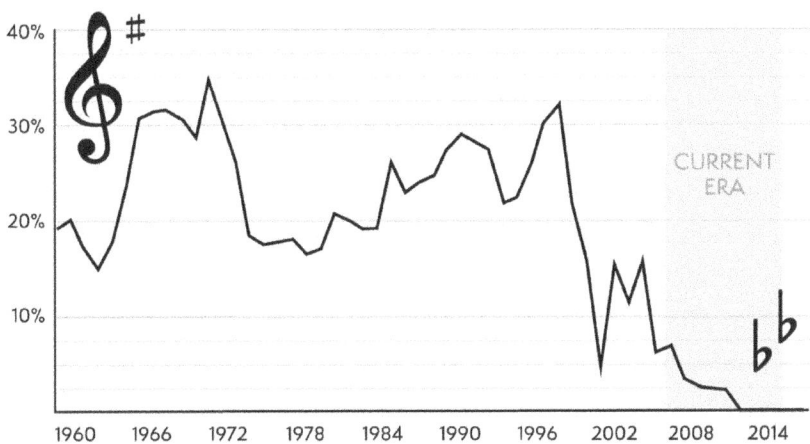

**Figure 11.4**

percent of number ones contained a key change.[4] By the end of this era, the key change was dead. Again, if I am sitting alone with an acoustic guitar writing a song and need to build intrigue, changing the key is a great tool that I have. If I'm sitting at my DAW, I might be less inclined. I can just pile on another weird synthesizer.[5]

In short, the DAW-centric, track-and-hook approach led to a shift in how songs were written. But there's one more thing it did, and it's the main reason that I'm writing about it. it led to more songwriters on hit songs. Usher's crunk smash "Yeah!" (February 28, 2004) is a good example as to how.

In the early 2000s, Jonathan Smith, the producer and DJ known as Lil Jon, was making beats for a new project by the rapper Mystikal. Since Mystikal only used a few, Lil Jon pitched the remaining beats to different artists. One of

---

[4] Don't assume that fewer key changes inherently imply musical degradation. 60 percent of key changes on number ones between 1958 and this era are the key moving up a half or whole step near the end of the song. As an example, Whitney Houston's "I Will Always Love You" (1992) shifts from A major to B major before the last chorus. Though effective, it's not the most sophisticated compositional move.

[5] Most DAWs come preloaded with audio loops, synth sounds, and processing tools, many of which can be heard on hit songs. Rihanna's "Umbrella" (June 9, 2007), for example, was built around the Vintage Funk Kit 03 drum loop that comes with GarageBand, the DAW preloaded on Macbooks. Usher and Young Jeezy's "Love in This Club" (March 15, 2008) is built around Euro Hero Synth 02 and 03, both found in a GarageBand loop expansion pack.

those artists was Usher, the R&B singer that had already scored multiple hits. Usher took one of those beats, wrote a topline, and turned it into "Yeah!"

There was one problem, though. Unbeknownst to Lil Jon, Jive Records had also been shopping his unused beats around. Rapper Petey Pablo had already taken the beat that Usher turned into "Yeah!" and made "Freek-a-Leek," which was being serviced to radio stations. Usher was in a bind.

Lil Jon had a solution, though. He'd make a similar-sounding beat. Usher liked it. "Yeah!" would go on to be the lead single from his fourth album *Confessions*. Along with "Yeah!", the album would also send "Burn" (May 22, 2004), "Confessions Part II" (July 24, 2004), and "My Boo" (October 30, 2004) to the top of the charts on its way to selling millions of copies.

While this particular scenario is sort of crazy, the idea of shopping a beat or a track around isn't. It's like how songwriters would shop their songs around during the twentieth century. The big difference is that when those songs were shopped, they were complete. When tracks are shopped, they are a work in progress. As different groups get their hands on them, the songwriter list begins to grow, especially because credits are doled out for things that didn't get credits decades ago, like adding rhythmic elements. This is why, even though they ostensibly came from the same beat, "Yeah!" has six songwriters and "Freek-a-Leek" has five, but only two are common between those groups.

So, why has the number of songwriters increased on hit records? For one, money. Whether you're a sampled artist or somebody who was tangentially involved in a song, everybody wants their cut, especially since hit songs are so valuable. Secondly, the success of Denniz PoP and his songwriting descendants has led to the collaborative Swedish process being used around the world. Finally, the rise of the DAW led to a shift in the compositional approach that also lends itself to collaboration and crediting songwriters for musical elements that used to not result in writing credits. Despite this profound shift, you might have noticed something odd. There are indeed more songwriters credited on hits than ever before, but few of them are women.

# Womanizer, Woman, Womanizer, You're a Womanizer

Sharon Sheeley thought she'd written a good song. But she needed the right person to record it. Maybe she could get her friend Ricky Nelson to do it. Nelson was a burgeoning singer and on the popular sitcom *The Adventures of Ozzie and Harriet*. It seemed like a good fit. Because she was an 18-year-old woman, Sheeley knew she'd have trouble convincing most any man to record one of her songs, even Nelson. So, she lied. She allegedly told him that her godfather had written it. Nelson believed her. He soon recorded Sheeley's song, "Poor Little Fool" (1958). It became the first number one on the Hot 100.

After surviving a serious car crash that took the life of Eddie Cochran, the early rocker whom she was dating, Sheeley went on to form one of the first all-women songwriting teams with Jackie DeShannon. Though she'd stepped away from the music business by the mid-1960s, Sheeley was a trailblazer.

When "Poor Little Fool" reached the top of the charts, it was shocking if a woman was involved with any non-singing part of the record-making process. In Figure 11.5, we can see that in this era, it's mundane, 50 percent of number one hits having at least one songwriter who's a woman. That's great, right? Totally. But that statistic doesn't tell the full story.

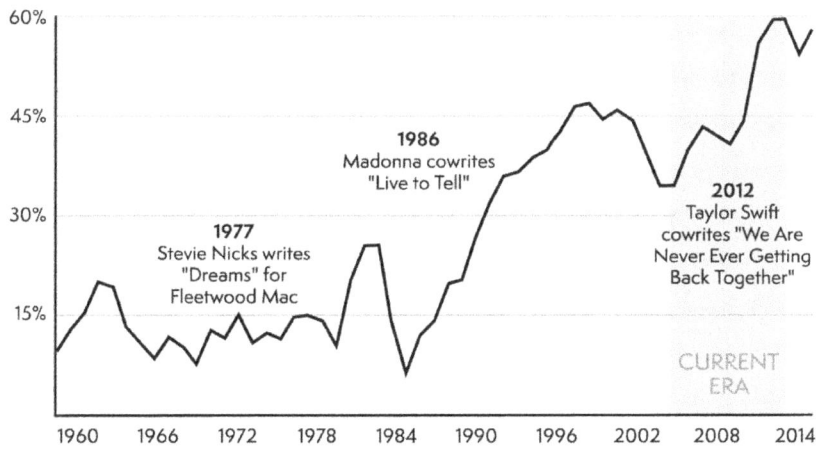

**Percentage of Number One Hits with at Least One Woman Songwriter**

Figure 11.5

As noted earlier, in this era, 86 percent of all number ones were cowritten by the performing artist. Simultaneously, more women were artists. Much of the rise in women getting writing credits is attributable to these dual factors. In Figure 11.6, we can see that the percent of number ones written or cowritten by a woman who is *not* the performing artist has remained largely unchanged since the start of the Hot 100.

Of course, there were women that found success in this era writing songs for others. The two biggest examples were mentioned earlier: Bonnie McKee and Ester Dean. The former worked closely with Katy Perry, while the latter did the same with Rihanna. But the respective success of these women highlights two other things. First, even when women are included in the hit-making process, they are often siloed to certain roles. On many of their number ones in this era, McKee and Dean worked on toplines. When you see a non-performing woman with a songwriting credit, they are usually topliners. They are rarely making the beats or producing. Among the 1,013 number ones between the start of the Hot 100 and this era, 76 (8 percent) had at least one producer who was a woman (e.g., Mariah Carey is one of three credited producers on her "We Belong Together" (June 4, 2005)). Only seven (1 percent) had producers

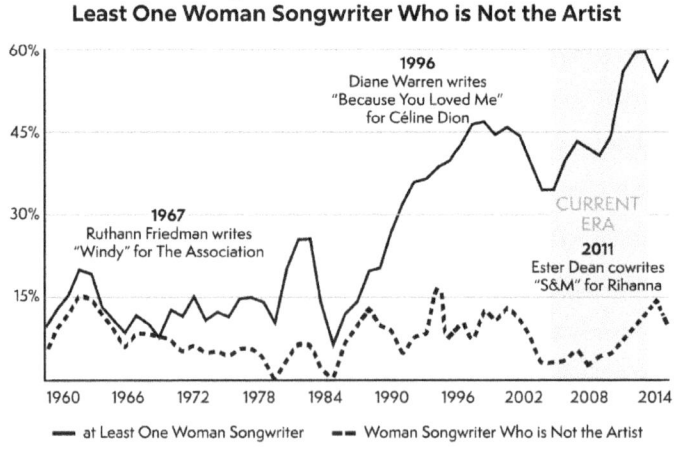

Figure 11.6

that were only women (e.g., Alicia Keys is the only credited producer on "Fallin'" (2001)).

Second, you rarely see male artists cowrite songs with non-performing women. Of the 633 number ones performed by men between the start of the Hot 100 and this era, only 51 (8 percent) had at least one songwriter who was a woman (e.g., Amanda Ghost is one of three credited songwriters on James Blunt's "You're Beautiful" (March 11, 2006)). Only nine (1 percent) had songwriters who were only women (e.g., Diane Warren is the sole credited writer on Aerosmith's "I Don't Want to Miss a Thing" (1998)).

On top of this, the contributions of women, songwriting or not, are often undervalued. One way you could read the last section of this chapter is that it didn't matter who Max Martin or Dr. Luke or Stargate were working with. They were the true talents. The women bringing their ideas to life were just lucky that they were given great songs.

This isn't true. Part of the reason that Kesha's "Tik Tok" (January 2, 2010) works is because of the production prowess of Dr. Luke. But Kesha's free-flowing vocal is of near equal importance. Furthermore, many of the women that initially achieved success with a specific producer have repeated that success working with others. Sure, songwriters and producers of the Cheiron universe helped launch the career of Britney Spears, but she found comparable success outside of that universe.

In 2004, Spears worked with Bloodshy and Avant on "Toxic," a top ten hit built around a sample from the Bollywood song "Tere Mere Beech Mein." In 2007, she cracked the top five with the Danja-produced "Gimme More." Then a year later, she was back at number one with "Womanizer" (October 25, 2008), a song put together by The Outsyders.

In summary, women are not only excluded from certain parts of the creative process, but when they are included, their contributions are downplayed. To understand why, we need to head back to school.

## Gender Bias in the Music-Making Process

Each September, my elementary school would have an assembly encouraging everyone to sign up to learn an instrument. Our teachers would file us down to the gymnasium to find all the music teachers in the district seated up front. They'd each play a short piece and then tell us why we should sign up for lessons. In September 2004, I signed up for trumpet lessons.[6] Some of my guy friends did too. In fact, our school band was divided along gender lines. Boys played brass and percussion. Girls played flute and violin. While it's possible that these gendered selections were innocuous, history tells us otherwise.

From the dawn of time, women have been discouraged from playing nearly every instrument, even those seen as feminine in this era. In the sixteenth century, for example, Italian courtier Baldassare Castiglione pondered, "Imagine how unlovely it would be to see a woman play drums, fifes or trumpets, or other like instruments." In 1860, an unknown author was dismayed at the thought of women cellists having to straddle their instruments: "Lady-fiddlers we are tolerably well accustomed to, but the attitude of a lady grasping with all her limbs a violoncello is one to the grotesqueness of which usage has not yet reconciled us." 44 years later, German-American composer Gustave Kerker took umbrage at how certain instruments distorted women's faces: "Women cannot possibly play brass instruments and look pretty, and why should they spoil their good looks?"

Despite tremendous progress since Kerker's comments, these historical biases have been hard to shake. A 2001 study from the University of Washington found that children as young as five believe that certain instruments are appropriate for boys, while others are appropriate for girls. Because of this, it shouldn't be shocking that these attitudes have implications far beyond elementary school bands.

An August 2018 survey of 2,438 full-time musicians in 22 of the world's top orchestras found that 69 percent of musicians were men, with the disparity skewing further by section. 95 percent of double bass players were men, along with 86 percent of bassoonists. Among brass players, there was one

---

[6] The only song to prominently feature a trumpet in this era was Shakira's "Hips Don't Lie" (June 17, 2006), a song infinitely more interesting than anything my elementary school forced us to play.

woman.[7] Similar forces explain the dearth of women in popular songwriting and production.

One of the most pernicious musical biases is that, though women are unfit for creative roles, they are great interpreters of songs, especially as vocalists. Critic George Upton espoused this belief in his 1880 essay "Woman in Music":

> Woman is emotional by nature . . . The emotion is a part of herself, and is as natural to her as breathing . . . She feels its influences, its control, and its power; but she does not see these results as man looks at them. He sees them in their full play, and can reproduce them in musical notation as a painter imitates the landscape before him. It is probably as difficult for her to express them as it would be to explain them . . . Man controls his emotions, and can give an outward expression of them . . . It does not seem that woman will ever originate music in its fullest and grandest harmonic forms. She will always be the recipient and interpreter, but there is little hope she will be the creator.

You might chalk Upton's perspective up to nineteenth-century sexism, but contemporary women continue to battle this bias. It's why Taylor Swift, who began her meteoric ascent in this era, has spent a large part of her career making it clear she writes her own music. It's why Sophia Somajo, a cowriter on Britney Spears's "3" (October 24, 2009) with Max Martin and Shellback, noted in a 2018 interview that "Being young and a woman I could only be a singer, and that was it." It's why women in this era were repeatedly siloed to toplining roles.

But discouragement and historical structures are not the sole reason women have struggled to break into the behind-the-scenes roles in the music industry. Women have also been victims of both physical and sexual violence with few repercussions for their abusers.

From 2007 to 2009, Rihanna dated Chris Brown. Brown, who topped the charts twice in this era with "Run It!" (November 26, 2005) and "Kiss Kiss" (November 10, 2007), would go on to cowrite her song "Disturbia"

---

[7] It would be remiss not to acknowledge the gendering of certain instruments is related to how some of those instruments were historically associated with war.

(August 23, 2008). Not long after, he pled guilty to assaulting her. Any backlash against Brown didn't last long. In the five years after the incident, he put out 12 top 40 records.

In 2014, Kesha sued Dr. Luke to break her contract with his record label, alleging that over a decade he had drugged and raped her, physically abused her, and verbally denigrated her to the point that she developed an eating disorder. The case dragged on for years with Dr. Luke countersuing for defamation before the two both agreed to drop their lawsuits. In the process, scores of artists came out in support of Kesha, while others detailed uncomfortable experiences working with Dr. Luke, albeit none as grisly as Kesha's allegations.

Kelly Clarkson alleged in an interview that despite her protests, her label forced her to continue to work with Dr. Luke. In anger, she refused a cowriting credit on "My Life Would Suck Without You" (February 17, 2009) because she didn't want to be associated with his name: "I don't want my name near his. I want to pretend this didn't happen in my life and I want to forget it." In a 2017 interview with *The New York Times*, Pink said, "I don't know what happened. But I know that regardless of whether or not Dr. Luke did that, this is his karma and he earned it because he's not a good person." Lady Gaga—who scored three number ones in this era with "Just Dance" (January 17, 2009), "Poker Face" (April 11, 2009), and "Born This Way" (February 26, 2011)—also defended Kesha's claims in a deposition.

To be clear, Dr. Luke wasn't convicted of anything. But you would at least think that in the wake of the lawsuits and statements from his past collaborators that he wouldn't be getting as much work until more information emerged. That wasn't the case. Despite using the pseudonyms "Made in China" and "Tyson Tracks" for a few years, he continued to work with and develop popular artists, including Ne-Yo, Doja Cat, Kim Petras, Young Thug, and The Kid LAROI.

I don't write this to say that nobody is worthy of redemption and that people can't be absolved of their past behavior. I write it to say that despite decades of wins, we are still in want of social progress. And that social progress is important in and of itself. People deserve to feel safe everywhere, including a music studio. But I think that progress is also important because if we discourage half of the population from writing and producing, we're missing out on a lot of great songs.

# Don't Forget Me, I Beg

The Velvet Underground booked their first paid gig on December 11, 1965. They were going to get $75 to open for The Myddle Class at a high school in Summit, New Jersey. They had one problem. Their percussionist Angus MacLise quit the band because he said they were selling out. MacLise was replaced by Maureen Tucker, thus rounding out The Velvet Underground's classic lineup with Lou Reed, Sterling Morrison, and John Cale.

People like Angus MacLise are few and far between. Not only would it be hard to find someone who considers getting paid $75 to open for a band at a high school "selling out," but it would be hard to find anyone who considers The Velvet Underground to have "sold out" at any point. By the standards of this book, The Velvet Underground were wildly unpopular.

That doesn't mean they weren't influential. In a review of their live record *The Quine Tapes*, famed critic Robert Christgau referred to them as the third best band of the 1960s after The Beatles and James Brown and His Famous Flames. Furthermore, influential producer Brian Eno joked that though their debut album sold only 30,000 copies in the first five years, every person who bought it started a band.[8]

It has never been, and never will be, cool to like pop music. It will never be cool to say you like Britney Spears more than The Velvet Underground. But after writing this much about the history of popular music, I've come to respect those that create it.

This respect was cemented when I was at my cousin Katie's wedding a few months ago, listening to the cover band rip through tons of hits. The interesting thing is that most of these songs weren't obscure in their day. They were songs that were both popular in their day and written by people who were trying to write popular songs. We heard a smattering of Motown songs composed by Holland-Dozier-Holland. We heard some soulful numbers by Kenny Gamble and Leon Huff. And, of course, we heard a handful of Max Martin's smashes.

---

[8] Eno has had a long-varied career, including founding Roxy Music, developing ambient music, designing the startup sound for Microsoft Windows 95, and producing popular acts like U2 and Coldplay. Coldplay's Eno-produced "Viva La Vida" (June 28, 2008) topped the charts in this era.

Though I respect Angus MacLise for his decision to not make music but for the sake of itself, while I was dancing that night, I was grateful for those that have shamelessly made music for the masses.

# Highlights

1. **"Someone Like You" by Adele (September 17, 2011)[9]**—Whenever I listen to this song, I want to thank Adele and her collaborator Dan Wilson for showing restraint. They could have dressed "Someone Like You" up with orchestral frills, maybe even a guitar and some horns. Instead, they opted for none of that. It's just a piano and a vocal, barely more than a demo. That sparseness allows you to focus on the song itself, its heart-wrenching lyrics and stunning contrast between the melody on the verse and chorus.

2. **"Gold Digger" by Kanye West ft. Jamie Foxx (September 17, 2005)**— In 1954, Ray Charles took the melody from "Must Be Jesus" by The Southern Tones and set it to secular lyrics. The new song was called "I Got a Woman." It married the music of a Saturday night with that of Sunday morning.

   50 years later, Kanye West would do a similar thing. He took a snippet of "I Got a Woman," a song about a faithful lover (i.e., "She gives me money when I'm in need / Yeah, she's a kind of friend indeed"), and turned it into a song about the opposite (i.e., "She take my money when I'm in need / Yeah, she's a trifling friend indeed"). To an extent, Kanye West is always rapping about Kanye West, but he's at his best when those monomaniacal raps are a musical conversation with the past.

3. **"Teenage Dream" by Katy Perry (September 18, 2010)**—This may be the quintessential Max Martin composition. It's a four-chord pop

---

[9] Adele's "Rolling in the Deep" and Usher's "Yeah!" were rated high enough to be included here. They were both mentioned earlier.

song with melody and rhythm working together for the payoff of a massive chorus that he wrote with four other people. And while Martin's compositions are not typically known for their lyrics, "Teenage Dream" stands above the rest because of them. Those words were handled by Katy Perry and Bonnie McKee. And it took them countless days to nail the euphoric feeling of being young and in love: "You think I'm pretty without any makeup on / You think I'm funny when I tell the punchline wrong / I know you get me, so I let my walls come down."

# Lowlights

1. **"Fireflies" by Owl City (November 7, 2009)**—I'm always surprised at the vitriol this song about insomnia evokes. But I think its most egregious affront is the lame lyrical imagery: "Cause I'd get a thousand hugs / From ten thousand lightning bugs / As they tried to teach me how to dance."

2. **"Crack a Bottle" by Eminem, Dr. Dre, and 50 Cent (February 21, 2009)**—Much of Eminem's career is built around shock, dropping songs filled with so much obscenity and violence that they could make you sick. At his best, maybe on something like "Love the Way You Lie" (July 31, 2010), that shock is a vehicle for his talents as a lyricist, spitting multisyllabic rhymes laden with wordplay.

   "Crack a Bottle" isn't one of those songs. Opening with the narrator bragging about his criminal history (i.e., "In this corner, weighing 175 pounds / With a record of 17 rapes, 400 assaults, and 4 murders"), it has no value beyond its shock value. Art made only for shock seldom has a long shelf life.

3. **"Do I Make You Proud" by Taylor Hicks (July 1, 2006)**—To say *American Idol* had a stranglehold on the American public would be an understatement. Not only did the debut songs of each of the first five

winners all crack the top two, but the song they played when someone was voted off during season four, Daniel Powter's "Bad Day" (April 8, 2006), also topped the charts. Taylor Hicks's problem—and it pains me to say this because I rooted for him when he was on the show—is that for the winner of a singing competition, he isn't a great singer. He's not a bad singer. But he doesn't have the power to carry a ballad like this.

## Argument Starters

Though it's an inane electronic record, "Party Rock Anthem" (July 16, 2011) delivers on its name. In fact, it delivers so dutifully that one of the judges gave it a ten. That judge wasn't me, but I appreciate that the song accomplishes what it set out to.

For me, the most interesting thing about this song is the artist: LMFAO. Primarily, LMFAO is comprised of an uncle and nephew. You've got to have an interesting family dynamic to write a song with the lyric "Yo, I'm running through these hoes like Drano" with your uncle. But it's not only the dynamic that's interesting. It's the family itself. RedFoo and SkyBlu, the stage names of said uncle and nephew, are the son and grandson of Berry Gordy, the founder of Motown. So, the same gene pool that gave us "I Want You Back" (1970) also gave us "Party Rock Anthem" and "Sexy and I Know It" (January 7, 2012).

## Odds and Ends

1. **"OMG" by Usher ft. will.i.am (May 15, 2010)**—The most ridiculous thing about this song isn't that it contains the lyric "Honey got a booty like pow, pow, pow / Honey got some boobies like wow, oh, wow," but that some people accused songwriter will.i.am of stealing it from Homer Simpson. On a 2003 episode of *The Simpsons*, Homer sings a song with a similar cadence: "Christmas in December: wow, wow, wow / Give me tons of presents: now, now, now."

2. **"Empire State of Mind" by Jay-Z and Alicia Keys (November 28, 2009)**—In Chapter 1, I said that California, Georgia, Kansas, and Texas

were the only US state names directly mentioned in the title of a number one. On "Empire State of Mind," Jay-Z and Alicia Keys come close to adding New York to that list.

3. **"Nothin' On You" by B.o.B. ft. Bruno Mars (May 1, 2010)**—Before he launched his successful solo career with songs like "Grenade" (January 8, 2011) and "Just the Way You Are" (October 2, 2010), Bruno Mars got his start as one third of the writing and production team called The Smeezingtons. This was his first number one where he was credited as an artist. While both Mars's hook and B.o.B.'s verses are well done, the thing to marvel at on this track is Brody Brown's bassline.

## Everything Else

"Slow Jamz" by Twista ft. Kanye West and Jamie Foxx. "I Believe" by Fantasia. "Slow Motion" by Juvenile ft. Soulja Slim. "Goodies" by Ciara ft. Petey Pablo. "Hollaback Girl" by Gwen Stefani. "Don't Forget About Us" by Mariah Carey. "Grillz" by Nelly ft. Paul Wall, Ali and Gipp. "Check on It" by Beyoncé ft. Bun B and Slim Thug. "SOS" by Rihanna. "Ridin'" by Chamillionaire ft. Krayzie Bone. "Promiscuous" by Nelly Furtado ft. Timbaland. "London Bridge" by Fergie. "Money Maker" by Ludacris ft. Pharrell Williams. "I Wanna Love You" by Akon ft. Snoop Dogg. "Say It Right" by Nelly Furtado. "This Is Why I'm Hot" by MiMS. "Glamorous" by Fergie ft. Ludacris. "Don't Matter" by Akon. "Give It To Me" by Timbaland ft. Nelly Furtado and Justin Timberlake. "What Goes Around . . . Comes Around" by Justin Timberlake. "Makes Me Wonder" by Maroon 5. "Big Girls Don't Cry" by Fergie. "Beautiful Girls" by Sean Kingston. "No One" by Alicia Keys. "Low" by Flo Rida ft. T-Pain. "Bleeding Love" by Leona Lewis. "Touch My Body" by Mariah Carey. "Lollipop" by Lil Wayne ft. Static Major. "Whatever You Like" by T.I. "Live Your Life" by T.I. ft. Rihanna. "Single Ladies (Put a Ring on It)" by Beyoncé. "Right Round" by Flo Rida. "I Gotta Feeling" by Black Eyed Peas. "Imma Be" by Black Eyed Peas. "Not Afraid" by Eminem. "Like a G6" by Far East Movement ft. The Cataracts and Dev. "Hold It Against Me" by Britney Spears. "Black and Yellow" by Wiz Khalifa. "E.T." by Katy Perry ft. Kanye West. "Give Me Everything" by Pitbull ft. Ne-Yo, Afrojack, and Nayer. "We Found Love" by Rihanna ft. Calvin Harris. "Set Fire to the Rain" by Adele.

# All I Know Is That We Are Young, Dumb Suckers

## March 17, 2012—March 16, 2019

### Had to Hit My Old Town to Duck the News

Drake puts his arm around Travis Scott as they walk toward the front of the stage. "I want you to take this shit in," the Canadian superstar tells Scott. "This is your city." Drake isn't lying. It's November 2021. They are performing for tens of thousands in Houston, Texas. Travis Scott is from Houston. And this is his music festival, Astroworld. Over the last decade, no rapper has had an ascent as rapid.

Calling Scott a rapper is a bit strange, though. He doesn't use dense, multisyllabic rhymes, like The Notorious B.I.G. or Rakim. He doesn't have rapid-fire verses, like Eminem or Busta Rhymes. He also doesn't deploy clever wordplay, like Lil Wayne or Jay-Z. Travis Scott is something different. He broods over brooding beats.

One of those brooding beats is about to start. Scott prepares the crowd. "If I know one thing," he begins, Drake still by his side, "it's from the front to the back, we better make this motherfucker earthquake." The warbling synths of "SICKO MODE" (December 8, 2018) begin blaring through the speakers. The crowd is quaking like Scott wanted.

What Travis Scott doesn't seem to know is that multiple people in attendance have been crushed to death by the surging crowd. And they've likely been dead for some time. There were signs that something was amiss. Scott paused the show at various points to try to control the crowd. But it never seemed like anyone considered bringing it to an early close. In fact, during one of those pauses, Scott shouted, "If everybody good, put a middle finger up in the sky." While people shouted for help, some middle fingers went up.

A comment like this is par for the course. Travis Scott shows are rowdy. In 2015, just after he was arrested for inciting a riot during his set at the music festival Lollapalooza, *GQ* described his live show as a combination of "crowd surfing, moshing, sweat, blood, [and] vomit." But this 2021 event crossed a new, tragic threshold that would lead to multiple deaths, dozens of injuries, and a bevy of lawsuits.

Of course, tragedy has struck concerts before. When The Rolling Stones played the Altamont Speedway Free Festival in December 1969, a security force led by the Hells Angels motorcycle club killed a Black attendee named Meredith Hunter. In 1979, a crowd crush at a Cincinnati, Ohio, concert for The Who left eleven dead. Two decades later, three people would die at a revival of Woodstock, while others would report rampant sexual assault.

Often, when these tragedies arise, they are taken to be symbolic of something larger. Altamont was evidence that the dreams of equality in the 1960s were no more. Woodstock 1999 suggested that the brash hard rock and hip-hop of the time had violent consequences. In the same way, Astroworld was framed as an indictment of music and culture of the 2010s, the logical result of nihilistic maximalism lurking in our most popular songs.

I'm not comfortable going that far. Single-day events are rarely notable enough to diagnose societal malaise. Still, each time I listen to Travis Scott's "SICKO MODE," I'm struck by how it *is* symbolic of both everything and nothing that went on in music between March 17, 2012, and March 16, 2019. In many ways, "SICKO MODE" stands alone. In an era of short songs with little harmonic experimentation, it smashes together three distinct compositions in three distinct keys with three distinct beats over five enthralling minutes.

At the same time, "SICKO MODE" is exemplary of everything that went on in this period. With its curt, all-caps title, it represents the apex of the moody hip-hop that turned fledgling performers on various internet platforms into global superstars. Many of those platforms, especially Spotify and YouTube, came to reshape not only how artists like Scott made music but how they became popular. Even if the events of Astroworld can't explain this era, the sound of "SICKO MODE" and the technology that made it possible just might.

# Getting on the Internet and Checking on Who Hit Me

Scores of music streaming services cropped up during the late 2000s and early 2010s. Apple Music. Deezer. Audiomack. SoundCloud. While you could slice-and-dice these platforms in many ways, we're going to put them into two broad categories: distributor platforms and direct platforms. To understand the power of the former, we need to look at the Swedish streaming giant Spotify. For the latter, we'll zero in on the video platform YouTube.

## Distributor Platforms: Sean Parker's Revenge

You would think nobody would let Sean Parker get near the music industry again. As mentioned in Chapter 10, Parker cofounded Napster, the file-sharing service that kicked off a 68 percent decline in United States recorded music revenues between 1999 and 2014. But Parker was an enterprising figure.

Not long after Napster was shut down, he became the first president of Facebook, a nascent social media platform founded by Mark Zuckerberg. He seemed to have the magic touch. In 2006, he took that touch to the Founders Fund, a venture capital firm that allowed him to invest in early-stage start-ups. *Vanity Fair* wrote about one of those start-ups in 2010: "[Parker's] current passion: a London-based music company called Spotify, which he thinks can finish the job that he and Fanning started with Napster—this time, legally."

Comparing Spotify to Napster was apt. Founded in 2006 by Daniel Ek and Martin Lorentzon, the original technology for Spotify was inspired by the same peer-to-peer technology that powered Napster and its imitators. Here's how Sven Carlsson and Jonas Leijonhufvud described the idea in their book *The Spotify Play*:

> The plan was to base the system on BitTorrent technology. The users would download the Spotify client and offload its own servers by storing parts of

the songs on their own hard drives, sharing them with other users in the network. The arrangement would speed up the system and outsource some of Spotify's broadband expenses . . . Spotify intended to share a part of its advertising revenue with artists and record companies. But the founders clearly felt their users shouldn't have to pay for music.

By 2014, Spotify would switch to a less sophisticated client-server model, meaning that when you clicked play on a song, the application would request the file from Spotify's servers. That said, their initial technology involved innovative use of peer-to-peer systems. Spotify's greatest innovation wasn't technological, though. It was cultural and political.

- **Cultural Innovation**: Aside from radio, the music industry spent over a century equating music listening with ownership. Even when disruptive services like Napster came online, the model revolved around the fact that you got to keep the music you were listening to, albeit illegally. Spotify needed to convince listeners that accessing music was at least as good, if not better, than owning it.

- **Political Innovation**: There were seeds of shadiness baked into even the most legitimate music products of the 2000s. By 2010, for example, you could buy an iPod that stored tens of thousands of songs. Sure, you were supposed to pack it with songs purchased from the iTunes store or ripped from CDs you owned, but many people were loading those devices with songs downloaded from illegal file-sharing services.

  Spotify was also built from the ashes of file-sharing technology. As noted, much of their early architecture was built around peer-to-peer technology that powered Napster, LimeWire, and the like. Spotify had to convince the major music rightsholders that (a) they wanted to make their service legitimate and (b) ad-supported and subscription-based models could be a cash cow for the industry.

After years of negotiation, Daniel Ek and his team, with some help from Sean Parker, managed to convince listeners and labels to buy into their vision. Any doubts were assuaged by the fact that streaming started to grow industry revenues. As you can see in Figure 12.1, in the decade after Spotify's 2011 launch in the United States, recorded music revenues had grown 74 percent. No, they hadn't reached the pre-Napster peak, but things were moving in the right direction.

Artists and labels quickly came to see how powerful Spotify was. Part of that power was Spotify's model. They didn't allow people to upload directly to their platform. You had to work with a distributor to make your music available for listeners. This allowed them to choose what was on the platform. But through human and algorithmic curation, they could also influence what people listened to.

On April 2, 2013, Sean Parker added "Royals" (October 12, 2013), a sparse record by a young New Zealand singer named Lorde, to his popular "Hipster International" playlist. Parker told *Forbes* that he added the song because it was "the antidote to disposable pop music." This was a common perspective at the time. Lorde's off-kilter pop music, laced with criticism of materialism (e.g., "But every song is like gold teeth, Grey Goose, tripping in the bathroom"), supposedly stood in contrast to lavish anthems that dominated the airwaves, like Katy Perry's "Roar" (September 14, 2013).

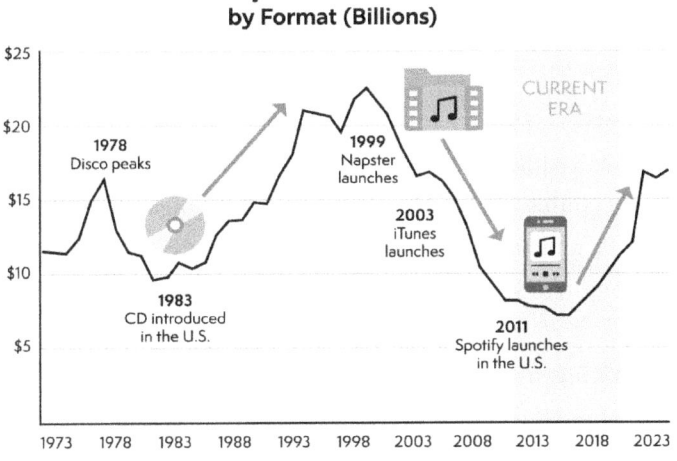

**Figure 12.1** *Source: RIAA.*

Not long after, Parker playlisted the song, it was going viral on Spotify. It soon hit number one. Like radio in the 1970s and MTV in the 1980s, getting added to the right Spotify playlist was your new ticket to the top of the charts.

Spotify also gave deeper insight into how people listened. In fact, as *Billboard* began to integrate streaming data into its charts, those charts became very different tools despite their names remaining the same. For decades, *Billboard* registered popularity by tracking sales and radio play. Streaming allowed people to see not what people were buying but what they were listening to. Maybe in 2012, you bought Bruno Mars's CD *Unorthodox Jukebox* to hear "Locked Out of Heaven" (September 22, 2012). You didn't care about anything else on the album, including his chart-topping ballad "When I Was Your Man" (April 20, 2013). From *Billboard*'s perspective, this didn't matter. A sale was a sale. Spotify was proof that listening and purchasing habits could be divergent.

In *Pivot*, a book by Spotify's former chief economist Will Page, he describes how when he joined the company in 2012, he aggregated a list of the biggest albums of the year. Gotye's *Making Mirrors* topped the chart. Then Page decided to build the list again but instead of using the total streams across all the songs on an album, he looked at the median streams across those songs. *Making Mirrors* tumbled down the list because most of the streams came from one eerie song: "Somebody That I Used to Know" (April 28, 2012). It was assumed that many album purchases in the past were driven by a handful of hits, but Spotify gave us proof that this supposition was true.

## Direct Platforms: Jawed Karim's Trip to the Zoo

In 19 seconds, Jawed Karim said something that set off a chain of events that would alter the course of the music industry: "Alright, so here we are in front of the elephants, and the cool thing about these guys is that they have really, really, really long trunks, and that's cool. And that's pretty much all there is to say."

I'm exaggerating a bit. This statement itself did not change the music industry. But where it was said made all the difference: YouTube. Those words come from "Me at the zoo," the first video uploaded to YouTube, the website that Karim cofounded in 2005. Of course, YouTube had a natural connection to the music video. As MTV moved away from music programming, YouTube became the hub for music videos. In fact, most of YouTube's top-viewed videos are music videos.

- Wiz Khalifa and Charlie Puth's "See You Again" (April 25, 2015), a tribute to actor Paul Walker, was briefly the most viewed video on the platform.

- Justin Bieber's twitchy dance party for "Sorry" (January 23, 2016) hit a billion views in just over four months. Adele's sepia-soaked video for "Hello" (November 14, 2015) did it in under 90 days.

- The nearly four billion views of Ed Sheeran's wintery visuals for "Perfect" (December 23, 2017) don't hold a candle to the six billion his boxing-inspired video for "Shape of You" (January 28, 2017) has racked up.

But YouTube's power was not just that it was a repository for music videos. Unlike Spotify, it allowed anyone to upload directly to the platform. Some of those uploaders, from Justin Bieber to The Weeknd, would turn their DIY videos into careers. At the same time, YouTube radically altered the barrier between artist and fan while also diminishing the ability of artists to control their work. Baauer's "Harlem Shake" (March 2, 2013) proves a good example of this.

Recorded in his bedroom, Baauer originally uploaded his goofy instrumental to his SoundCloud page. It caught the ear of the producer Diplo who then gave it a commercial release during the summer of 2012. Throughout the rest of the year, the song picked up some steam but was far from a hit.

Then in February 2013 everything changed. A YouTuber named Filthy Frank uploaded a video with the song playing in the background while a group of people flailed their limbs during the beat drop. Videos imitating the trend quickly racked up hundreds of millions of views. When *Billboard* began counting YouTube views toward the Hot 100, the first number one song was naturally Baauer's joyfully bizarre recording.

Months before, Baauer and his label put together a video for the song. It had no impact. It took an online personality who had no connection to the song to make that happen. In an Instagram post celebrating the tenth anniversary of his surprise hit, Baauer recalled, "I remember when it first became a meme it felt out of my control and I didn't like it." Though he acknowledged how he came around to it when he saw the song was bringing people together, this signaled a new era. You could have very little to do with your song becoming a smash. In fact, people might not even associate it with you. YouTube and other direct upload platforms made it so that the line between artist and fan was becoming blurred.

As the internet came to dominate people's lives, this effect only grew. But even in the immediate future, online trends could spark a song's popularity. Carly Rae Jepsen's ebullient earworm "Call Me Maybe" (June 23, 2012) caught fire when Justin Bieber and some friends uploaded a YouTube video dancing and singing along to it. In the coming months, scores of fans would upload their own versions. Four years later, Rae Sremmurd's "Black Beatles" (November 26, 2016) would ascend the charts after it became associated with the Mannequin Challenge, a viral trend that involved people standing as still as possible while the song played in the background. Again, Rae Sremmurd was not involved in the creation of this challenge. Power was now in the hands of the fans.

## The Effects of Online Music Platforms

The rise of distributor and direct platforms illustrated concurrent but oppositional shifts. Distributor platforms centralized power in new companies, like Spotify and Deezer. By contrast, direct platforms like YouTube, SoundCloud, Instagram, and Audiomack gave power to anyone who was willing to upload something. These platforms did inspire some similar shifts, though. And many of them focused on shrinking.

### Th!s $ecti0n's TitL3 is t0o long

In the early 1800s, Beethoven finished his haunting composition "Moonlight Sonata." Well, sort of. Beethoven didn't give the piece that name. It was denoted Piano Sonata No. 14. The more well-known title didn't become standard until after the composer died. This titling shift was significant, though.

As noted in Chapter 6, for a long time compositions were mostly named by form or function. Bach's Mass in B minor was written for the church. His Sonata No. 1 in G minor utilized the sonata compositional form. This would be like if "I'm the One" by DJ Khaled, Justin Bieber, Quavo, Chance the Rapper, and Lil Wayne (May 20, 2017) were called Posse Cut in G major. A "posse cut" is a hip-hop song where a different rapper is heard on each verse. As intellectual property rights became stronger throughout the nineteenth century and musical success became equivalent with celebrity, artists began to get more creative with how they referred to themselves and their songs. In this era, that involved using unexpected capitalization and punctuation.

- In 2008, Nate Ruess, Jack Antonoff, and Andrew Dost dubbed their new trio fun., purposefully all lowercase with a period at the end. Four years later, they'd take their anthem "We Are Young" (March 17, 2012) to the top of the charts.

- In 2012, four Canadians would start a reggae fusion band with the energetic name MAGIC!, capital letters and exclamation mark included. Not long after, they turned "Rude" (June 26, 2014), a failed plea with a father for his daughter's hand in marriage, into an irritating hit.

- On Justin Timberlake's disco pastiche "CAN'T STOP THE FEELING!" (May 28, 2016) and Kendrick Lamar's braggadocious "HUMBLE." (May 6, 2017) capitalized letters were used to convey energy.

- Ariana Grande's "thank u, next" (November 17, 2018), an ode to learning from ex-lovers, used all lowercase letters to suggest intimacy.

These examples were far from outliers. In the last week of this era, when the Jonas Brothers' "Sucker" (March 16, 2019) was at number one, 35 percent of songs in the top 40 either had titles with non-standard capitalization and punctuation or were by artists with names of the same type. Though artists had done some experimentation with typography and spelling in the past (e.g., The Beatles, k.d. lang), the prevalence in this era was due to a generation of people who grew up communicating in informal, online, text-based channels. Notably, many of these channels, including text messaging and most early social media platforms, did not allow you to stylize text. Inventive capitalization and punctuation were the only way to get your point across.

But song titles weren't just changing in how they were stylized. They were also changing in length. As you can see in Figure 12.2, between 1958 and 1999, chart-topping song titles were consistently between 15 and 20 characters. Around the millennium, titles started falling below 15 characters with some regularity before sinking down to 11 characters as streaming became more common in the 2010s.

When uploading music online, most platforms have character limits for names and titles. Although those limits are much greater than anything your average artist is going to use, long titles get truncated on digital displays, especially if those displays are on a tiny mobile phone. For example, Taylor Swift's "We Are Never Ever Getting Back Together" (September 1, 2012) gets cut off after the word "Getting" on my iPhone 15. And that iPhone has a much larger screen than those that were common in this era. I don't think it's a coincidence that artists started shortening their titles as listening became common on the computer, and then did so even more as that listening went mobile.

## *The Short Song/Long Album Paradox*

The most controversial thing about streaming is how recorded music royalties are paid. Throughout this era, this system was called "pro rata." Here's a simple

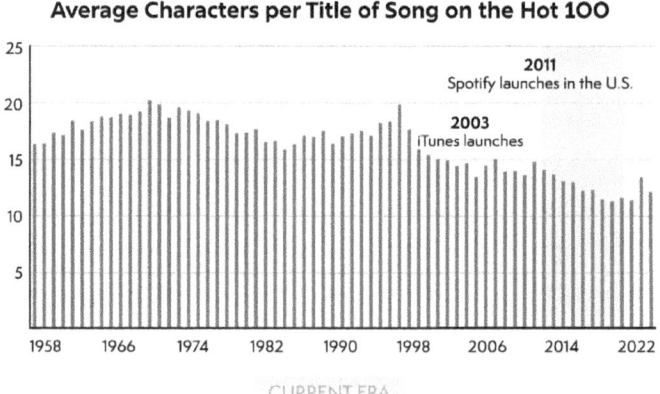

Figure 12.2

example of how it worked. Let's say you have a music streaming service that only has two songs: "Cheerleader" by OMI (July 25, 2015) and "Shake It Off" by Taylor Swift (September 6, 2014). Against all odds, you get people to subscribe to this service and generate $1,000 in revenue. For your efforts, you get to keep 25 percent, or $250. The remainder will get paid out to OMI and Taylor Swift. But how do we determine what each of them get?

Basically, you see what percentage of total streams each artist received and then pay them out that share of revenue. In this example, let's say there were 10,000 streams across the platform. 2,500 of those streams were for "Shake It Off." 7,500 were for "Cheerleader." With this data, we can calculate the final royalty payments.

- "Shake It Off" generated (2,500 streams / 10,000 streams) x ($750), or $187.50

- "Cheerleader" generated (7,500 streams / 10,000 streams) x ($750), or $562.50

Seems simple. And sort of fair. What's the problem? First, if you calculate a payout per stream, it's incredibly small. In my fictional example, that rate comes out to $0.01. In reality, it's much less than that.[1] Second, your subscription dollars are not paid directly to who you listen to. As illustrated in my example, they are put into a giant pool and paid out based on the share of streams that each song commands. In other words, if you spend the next month only listening to Macklemore's "Thrift Shop" (February 2, 2013) on Apple Music, your subscription dollars won't be going right into the Seattle rapper's pocket.[2]

Finally, this model disadvantages music that doesn't inspire repeat plays. That seems like an odd issue. Why should people nobody listens to make money? But there are harsh and difficult styles of music that people love but

---

[1] Again, royalties in this era were not paid out on a per stream basis, but if you wanted to increase the rate under this system, you could (a) increase subscription prices, (b) get more listeners to take out subscriptions, (c) decrease the platform's take, or (d) set a rate floor.

[2] I would say not to do this because the looping horn line in this song will damage your brain, but my cousin John swears listening to certain music can benefit you. He once spent a month only listening to 50 Cent. His goal was not to line the rapper's pockets but to motivate himself to train for a marathon. He did finish the race, so maybe he's onto something.

can't be listened to ad nauseam, the way cookie-cutter pop songs are designed to be.

Though alternate royalty schemes have been suggested and implemented in the years since, most notably SoundCloud's user-centric system that was pioneered by executive Michael Pelczynski, I want to focus on the two-pronged effect that the pro rata scheme had on artists. First, it led to shorter songs.

As we discussed in Chapter 10, from the 1940s through the mid-1960s, song length was constrained by how much sound a vinyl record could hold without degrading. By the end of the 1960s, improvements made it possible to store more high-fidelity sound. By 1980, single length had climbed to about four minutes, and it would stay there for almost 30 years. As you can see in Figure 12.3, when streaming took hold, song length fell 13 percent as compared to 1990.

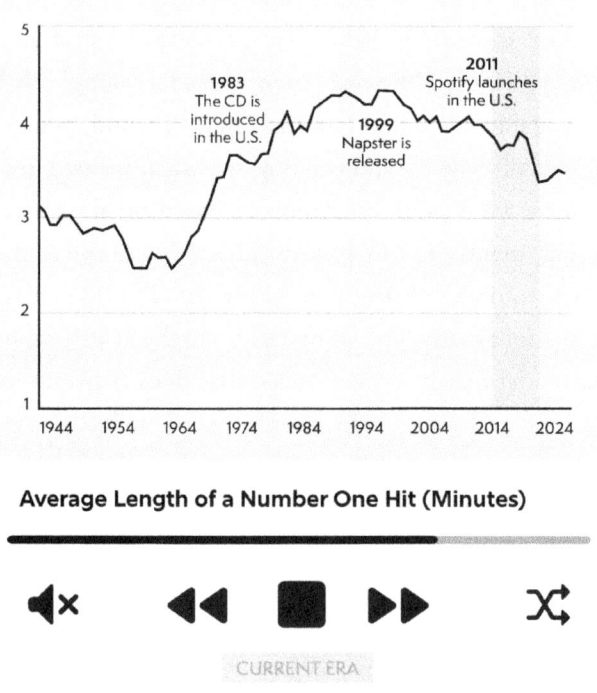

**Average Length of a Number One Hit (Minutes)**

Figure 12.3

Because you get paid more if you command a high portion of a platform's streams, it's potentially more lucrative if your songs are shorter. As an example, in an hour, you can listen to Post Malone and Swae Lee's two-minute-and-thirty-eight-second "Sunflower" (January 19, 2019) almost 23 times. Travis Scott's behemoth "SICKO MODE" could only be played half as many times. Of course, Travis Scott isn't hurting for cash, but it's clear that artists respond to changing incentives.

Interestingly, as songs have gotten shorter, albums have gotten longer. You can see this in Figure 12.4. From the 1960s to the 1980s, chart-topping albums were usually between 10 to 12 tracks. As the CD—which held more sound than most vinyl—reigned supreme in the 1990s and 2000s, track counts were closer to 14 or 15. While this was steady during the 2010s, the average jumped closer to 17 in the 2020s. Unshackled from the constraints of physical media, chart-topping albums in that decade had 58 percent more tracks than what you'd see on your average chart-topping album in the 1980s.

The seemingly contradictory trends of song-shortening and album-lengthening make sense in the streaming universe. For the largest royalty payouts, you want to command as many streams as possible. A good strategy to do that is to release a long album where every song is short. Even passive fans will listen through at least one time. Plus, more songs mean more chances to

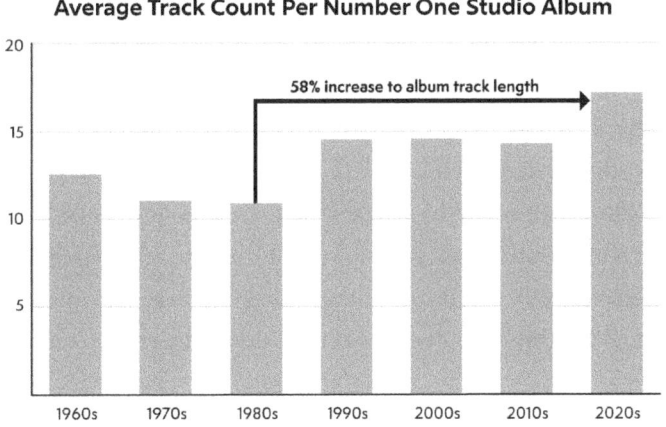

Figure 12.4

get added to playlists and various algorithmic systems to start recommending your music. You'll have to wait for the next chapter to hear if these incentives are good, but for the time being, we can be sure that despite its uncharacteristic length, there's a reason "SICKO MODE" comes from an album with 17 tracks that average under three-and-a-half minutes. Artists aren't dumb. They might be sad, though.

# It's So Sad to Think About the Good Times

In Chapter Two, when we spoke about the joyfulness of music in the early 1960s, I recalled a conversation that I had with George O'Har, one of my college professors. Here's what he said: "I find myself listening to mostly Latin music these days because American pop music is just so depressing. Pop music is supposed to bring people together and make you feel good."

My former professor made that statement during the height of the era covered in this chapter. And I remember nodding along in agreement. Many of the Latin-infused songs that topped the charts in this era—like Luis Fonsi, Daddy Yankee, and Justin Bieber's "Despacito" (May 27, 2017) and Cardi B, Bad Bunny, and J Balvin's "I Like It" (July 7, 2018)—were dripping with joy.

At the same time, if you tossed every other chart-topper into a bag and reached in to grab one, I felt certain you'd come out with a song that was wholly depressing.[3] But as with everything in this book, we trust our gut but make sure it isn't deceiving us. And in this case, there doesn't seem to be any deception. There are a few caveats, though.

During the 2010s, there was a slew of research conducted on sentiment expressed in popular songs. Nearly all of it showed a growing degree of sadness or anger. A May 2018 study by five mathematicians out of the University of California, Irvine found that across 500,000 songs released in the United Kingdom between 1985 and 2015, there was a "clear downward trend in 'happiness' and 'brightness,' as well as a slight upward trend in 'sadness.'" Seven

---

[3] I used a random number generator to select a song from this era, and it spit back Childish Gambino's "This Is America" (May 19, 2018), a song whose music video opens with a guy getting shot in the head.

months later, computer scientists Kathleen Napier and Lior Shamir published a paper in the *Journal of Popular Music Studies* that showed how between 1951 and 2016 lyrics expressing "anger, disgust, fear, sadness, and conscientiousness [had] increased significantly, while joy, confidence, and openness . . . [had] declined." A year later, a paper published in *Evolutionary Human Sciences* found a similar lyrical trend.

In short, beyond trusting your ears, quantitative evidence suggests that songs were sad in this era. The rub is that this sadness was not new. Most studies suggest that the trend began in the 1980s. If we look at the average happiness score of a number one hit as per Spotify in Figure 12.5, we see this general trend, albeit with significant ebbs and flows.

From 1960 to 1980, Spotify's happiness score regularly sits around 70. It begins to decline in the 1980s before reaching its nadir in 1994 as alternative rock and gangsta rap take over the charts. Though the score starts to recover during the early 2000s, those gains are wiped out over the next 15 years, falling to 50 by the end of this era. Of course, this doesn't mean that every song in this era was laced with sadness. Pharrell Williams' relentlessly happy "Happy"

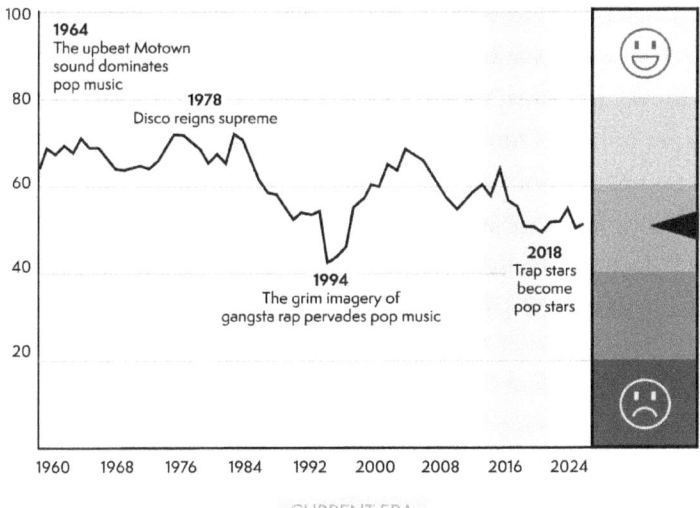

**Average Spotify Happiness Score per Number One Hit**

1964
The upbeat Motown
sound dominates
pop music

1978
Disco reigns supreme

1994
The grim imagery of
gangsta rap pervades pop music

2018
Trap stars
become
pop stars

CURRENT ERA

Figure 12.5

(March 8, 2014) spent ten weeks atop the charts in this era. But for every "Happy," there was at least one "SAD!" Literally. XXXTentacion's relentlessly sad "SAD!" (June 30, 2018) topped the charts almost four years after "Happy." But why did this music feel so sad?

## Sad Tempos

It's the fall of my senior year of college. I'm out at a bar. Sean Paul starts dictating that the women in the bar "rock with it," "bounce with it" and "dance with it" as "Cheap Thrills" (August 6, 2016), his collaboration with Sia, starts coming through the speakers. The ladies do indeed start rocking, bouncing, and dancing. I'm kind of a "Cheap Thrills" hater, so I head to the bathroom. When I return, a new song is on: "Blurred Lines" (June 22, 2013), a Marvin Gaye-inspired collaboration between Robin Thicke, T.I., and Pharrell Williams. I'm kind of a hater of this song too.[4] But that doesn't matter. The people love it, dancing until the bartenders make us go home.

"Cheap Thrills" and "Blurred Lines" are both dance records. But they are very different dance records. "Blurred Lines," clocking in at 120 beats per minute, is up-tempo and funky. "Cheap Thrills," with its dancehall-infused rhythm, is a more leisurely 90 beats per minute. From Drake's "In My Feelings" (July 21, 2018) to Iggy Azalea's "Fancy" (June 7, 2014), if people were dancing in this era, they were usually doing it to a tempo more like "Cheap Thrills" than "Blurred Lines." In fact, 43 percent of number ones in this era were less than 100 beats per minute. Compare that to the period from 1960 to 1989. Only 25 percent of number ones were below that tempo threshold. While "slow" isn't equivalent with "sad," musical psychologist Michael Bonshor told *Esquire* in 2023 that "The most obvious feature of a sad song is the tempo. It tends to be fairly slow . . . like a relaxed heartbeat."

## Sad Keys

In a 2017 paper "The Minor Fall, the Major Lift: Inferring Emotional Valence of Musical Chords Through Lyrics" researchers found that people associate

---

[4] It's okay to be a hater sometimes. Just don't be a hater all the time.

minor chords and minor keys with darker or sadder sounds. Those chords and keys were much more prominent in this era. In fact, from the start of the Hot 100 through 2000, 25 percent of songs were in minor keys. Between 2000 and the end of this era, 55 percent were.

Rihanna's "Diamonds" (December 1, 2012) proves a good example of minor key sadness. Though the song's first verse opens with the uplifting line "Find light in the beautiful sea, I choose to be happy," there is a tinge of somberness laced throughout. Of note, the song is in the key of B minor.

## Sad Genres

In the early 1900s, a dark, emotive style started to transform popular music: the blues. Emerging after the abolition of slavery in the United States, the music was characterized by a 12-bar chord progression, hypnotic rhythms, notes bent expressively, and call-and-response lyrics chronicling the anguish of everyday life. A century later, hip-hop's own form of the blues would come to dominate the charts: trap.

Though it's a stretch to compare these two genres, they are both good examples of how certain styles are sadder than others. Trap is a branch of hip-hop defined by hi-hats exploding in short bursts at inhuman speeds, booming 808 kick drums that double as bass lines, and dark lyrics focused on street life. "Bad and Boujee" (January 21, 2017), a song where Migos grunt and murmur about "Cooking up dope with a Uzi" over tittering hi-hats and bass drums that could register on the Richter scale, is a quintessential example of the genre. And I really can't stress how dark songs in this genre can be. Both Desiigner's "Panda" (May 7, 2016)[5] and Cardi B's "Bodak Yellow" (October 7, 2017) almost leave me shaking in fear. While scores of other trap songs were popular in this era, its importance was how it influenced other genres. To quote rapper 2 Chainz in a 2017 interview with *Rolling Stone*: "Trap rap is pop now."

---

[5] Coincidentally, Desiigner is the grandson of blues musician Sidney "Guitar Crusher" Selby.

Halsey injected twitchy trap hats on her moody pop song "Without Me" (January 12, 2019).[6] Taylor Swift did the same on "Look What You Made Me Do" (September 16, 2017). The Weeknd ratchets these elements up on "The Hills" (October 3, 2015), your speakers shaking from an overdriven trap bass line that sounds like it was written for a horror film that takes place in a strip club. These sounds became so prevalent that in 2018, *Complex* noted, "Now, it seems you can't find a song *without* trap hi-hats."

When you take elements of a grim genre and use them in other styles, that grimness remains. That's especially true when you consider a few of the more melodic styles of hip-hop that also co-opted trap elements in this era.

Often referred to as some combination of "emo rap," "mumble rap," or "cloud rap," these styles—which proliferated on online platforms like SoundCloud, Audiomack, and DatPiff—traded the wordiness that typically characterized hip-hop for hazy, dreamlike atmospheres. Both XXXTentacion's aforementioned "SAD!" and Post Malone's "Psycho" (June 16, 2018) illustrate this sound. With pittering hi-hats and woozy synths, they feel like hip-hop songs shot with a tranquilizer, MCs functioning more like lethargic singers than rappers. Like trap, songs in these genres are somewhere between ominous, dark, depressing, and angry.

If you've made it this far in this book, you'll know that sad songs are nothing new. In Chapter 1, we had a long discussion about teenage tragedy songs. In Chapter 4, two songs about suicide came up. A few chapters after that, we covered the grim imagery of certain hip-hop songs in the 1990s. Still, people often worry about the consequences of dark, depressing music. If my daughter starts listening to emo rappers, will she engage in self-harm? Could my son's obsession with trap lead to drug use?

I'm not really worried about these things. If you recall the The High-Tide/ Low-Tide Theory of Popular Music that I outlined in Chapter 2, musical styles usually come in waves. If one dark, depressing song tops the charts, you'll see scores of otherwise happy artists trying to imitate it. Furthermore, there's a

---

[6] In Chapter 4, I recounted an argument I had about the four greatest musicians from New Jersey. My girlfriend recently tried to make the claim that Halsey was in the top four. I remain at a loss for words.

long history of people worrying that music will lead to unhealthy or immoral behavior. Nearly all those panics amounted to thinly veiled racism or sexism.

This doesn't mean that music can't have negative consequences. But self-expression is usually healthy. If you want to scream along to a depressing song, you should. It's probably a better outlet for your anger or angst than anything else.

Nevertheless, when sad sounds characterize large swaths of popular music, we should consider if there is an underlying cause. These considerations shouldn't be used to condemn the music. They should be used to make sure that people are okay. During this era, there was a slew of worrying research about anti-social trends among young people. In fact, in an early 2025 article for *The Atlantic*, journalist Derek Thompson went so far as to call this period the beginning of "The Anti-Social Century."

While assessing these ideas falls outside the scope of this book, it's a good reminder to pay attention to the songs people listen to and how they sound. Sometimes, pop music is truly just that, a sugary confection to please your ears. Sometimes it's a bit more, though.

# Magic, Madness, Heaven, Sin

I've spent so long trying to get this book published that during the process, I had the time to meet my girlfriend Devin, date her for multiple years, move in together, and then get engaged. In fact, that last piece happened so recently that when I mentioned Devin in the last footnote, she was still my girlfriend. As I write this section, she's my fiancé. That relationship change was a nice reprieve from all the musical darkness in this era. Naturally, it also got me thinking about number ones that could be wedding songs.

Beyond John Legend's "All of Me" (May 17, 2014), the pickings are slim in this era. Frankly, if you're only looking at chart-toppers, there aren't many great options. Maybe the Bee Gees' "How Deep is Your Love" (1977), Al Green's "Let's Stay Together" (1972), or The Tymes' "So Much in Love" (1963). Given that I work in the music business and spend an ungodly amount of time both making and writing about music, I probably need to pick something obscure, though. All I can say for certain is that, independent of quality, I won't choose any of the musical highs and lows from this era.

# Highlights

1. **"Blank Space" by Taylor Swift (November 29, 2014)**[7]—In an era of big choruses, there might not be any bigger than this one by Taylor Swift. And that's surprising. There's not much going on in this song. It's got a circular keyboard riff. Some percussion. A thick synth bass. The occasional acoustic guitar. But by paring the song back to its essentials, Swift and her collaborators, Max Martin and Shellback, let each element feel bigger than if they'd layered more things on top. "Anybody can play weird," jazz legend Charles Mingus told *Mainliner Magazine* in 1977, "that's easy . . . Making the simple complicated is commonplace. Making the complicated simple . . . that's creativity."

2. **"Nice For What" by Drake (April 21, 2018)**—Drake was on one of those runs in this era that you can only compare to The Beatles in the 1960s, the Bee Gees in the 1970s, or Michael Jackson in the 1980s. Everything he touched not only sold millions of copies but was heaped with critical praise. "Nice For What" might be the best example of that dual success.

   Built around an infectious Lauryn Hill sample, "Nice For What" was described by Kevin Lozano at *Pitchfork* as "hip-hop spectacle at its very best: pure fun and star power." On the track, you not only get to see Drake's power as a rapper, weaving rhymes between Lauryn Hill's chopped vocal, but as a pop star, inspiring you to head to the club even if you haven't danced in years.

3. **"Uptown Funk" by Mark Ronson ft. Bruno Mars (January 17, 2015)**—When Jim Farber reviewed Mark Ronson's album *Uptown Special* for the *New York Daily News*, he was not pleased with the lead single: "['Uptown Funk'] isn't even a song. It's a vamp, a rush of 'hit me'

---

[7] Lorde's "Royals" was also rated high enough to be included here. It was mentioned earlier.

rhythms of the style patented, and made deep, by James Brown." Oddly, I think this complaint is what makes "Uptown Funk" work.

"Uptown Funk" is an amalgam of retro moments gloriously smashed together. The doh-doh-ing intro. The incessant horn stabs. A vocal that's equal parts braggadocious and humorous (e.g., "I'm too hot, hot damn / Make a dragon wanna retire, man). It's a miracle that Mark Ronson was able to pull it all together. And he almost didn't. The producer allegedly fainted while trying to nail the rhythm guitar. I get where he was coming from, though. When you know you've got something good, you can't stop until it's done.

# Lowlights

1. **"One More Night" by Maroon 5 (September 29, 2012)**—Built around a reggae-infused feel, my biggest problem with "One More Night" is its redundancy. The verses contain a 15-note melody repeated again and again. The pre-chorus and chorus do the same thing with phrases of different lengths. It would be one thing if these repeated phrases were catchy or moving. But they aren't. They're irritating.

2. **"7 rings" by Ariana Grande (February 2, 2019)**—Here's something that sounds bad in theory: Ariana Grande singing the melody of *The Sound of Music*'s "My Favorite Things" over a trap beat. Sadly, that's what "7 things" is. And I regret to report that it sounds as confused in practice as it does in theory.

3. **"Whistle" by Flo Rida (August 25, 2012)**—How long can you stretch out a metaphor about oral sex? Flo Rida's "Whistle" contends nearly four minutes. And despite that fact that the fellating hook is catchy, that catchiness is soon forgotten when you have to sit through line-after-line of eyeroll-inducing lyrics (e.g., "Girl, I'm the whistle man, my Bugatti the same notes / Show me your perfect pitch, you got it, my banjo / Talented with your lips like you blew out a candle").

## Argument Starters

Maroon 5 and Cardi B's pop rap concoction "Girls Like You" (September 29, 2018) is a rare argument starter where I've lived on both sides of the argument. The song is musically seductive, the looping guitar riff drawing you in as the sonic texture changes. But that riff is also redundant, played on repeat throughout the entire song. The only reprieve you get from that redundancy is Cardi B's brief verse where she injects some fun rhymes (e.g., "You don't want a girl like me, I'm too crazy / But every other girl you meet is fugazi"). Whether that fun compensates for the six-string redundancy is up to your taste.

## Odds and Ends

1. **"Shallow" by Lady Gaga and Bradley Cooper (March 9, 2019)**—As of the day I write this, the film *A Star is Born* has been made four times. First, in 1937. Then in 1954, 1976, and 2018. Two of those versions have had a song from the soundtrack top the charts. The first was Barbra Streisand's "Evergreen" (1977). The second was Lady Gaga and Bradley Cooper's "Shallow." Both songs are serviceable ballads that suggest a surefire way to top the charts is to remake *A Star is Born* and release a soundtrack for the film.

2. **"Love Yourself" by Justin Bieber (February 13, 2016)**—The lyrics that I wish that I'd written could fill a list that runs miles long. But on certain days, the Ed Sheeran-penned "My mama don't like you and she likes everyone" from Justin Bieber's "Love Yourself" is at the top of that list. In nine words, it manages to not only describe my mama but to convey more than most songwriters can in entire albums.

3. **"Closer" by The Chainsmokers ft. Halsey (September 3, 2016)**—Somehow Denny scored an invite. The popular girls were throwing a "Christmas in July" party during the summer of our junior year of college while we lived in Brighton, Massachusetts. He said we had to go. So, we grabbed some ratty Christmas sweaters, ripped off the sleeves to reveal our aspiringly muscular arms, and made the sweaty walk across town to the party.

That was the last I saw of my friends. Denny got caught up talking to whoever invited him. Our buddy Eddy got lost in the night. I was somehow cornered in a conversation with this annoying guy from my math class who actually wanted to talk about math over warm beer. I didn't stay long. Nevertheless, my most vivid memory of that party was this new song by Halsey and The Chainsmokers being played at least ten times: "Closer."

Throughout my senior year of college, you couldn't go anywhere without hearing "Closer." When I would stand back and listen to it, a budding songwriter, I knew that it was not a song that I wanted to emulate. The vocals were plain. The lyrics were filled with weird images about stolen mattresses and Blink-182 songs. But it didn't matter. I loved "Closer." To this day, it reminds me that the world is endless, and a pop song can save your life.

## Everything Else

"Just Give Me a Reason" by Pink ft. Nate Ruess. "Can't Hold Us" by Macklemore and Ryan Lewis. "Wrecking Ball" by Miley Cyrus. "The Monster" by Eminem ft. Rihanna. "Timber" by Pitbull ft. Kesha. "Dark Horse" by Katy Perry. "All About That Bass" by Meghan Trainor. "Bad Blood" by Taylor Swift ft. Kendrick Lamar. "Can't Feel My Face" by The Weeknd. "What Do You Mean?" by Justin Bieber. "PILLOWTALK" by Zayn. "Work" by Rihanna ft. Drake. "One Dance" by Drake ft. Wizkid and Kyla. "Starboy" by The Weeknd ft. Daft Punk. "That's What I Like" by Bruno Mars. "rockstar" by Post Malone ft. 21 Savage. "Havana" by Camila Cabello ft. Young Thug. "God's Plan" by Drake.

# On That Dusty Old Town Road, I Died with a Smile

## April 13, 2019—January 11, 2025

### Love When They Argue the Hardest MC

I've spent too much of my life debating the finer points of popular music. What's the first rock 'n' roll song? Are The Rolling Stones better than The Beatles? Is 2Pac better than Biggie? Do the Grammys matter? While many of these questions are fun because they are unresolved, there is one with an indisputable answer: What's the best year in jazz? And the answer is 1959.

First, Miles Davis's *Kind of Blue* was released that year. Not only is *Kind of Blue* regularly referred to as the greatest jazz record, but it's the best-selling instrumental jazz album of all time. And it's only the tip of the iceberg. Charles Mingus's *Mingus Ah Um*, Dave Brubeck's *Time Out*, John Coltrane's *Giant Steps*, and Ornette Coleman's *The Shape of Jazz to Come* were also released that year. Each of those records has cast a long shadow on the genre. In fact, NPR argued in 2019 that if you take a trip out to any jazz club, you're bound to hear people evoking ideas from those records.

Beyond quality, the most interesting thing about 1959 is that there weren't that many jazz albums released. In a 2023 edition of his popular newsletter *The Honest Broker*, music historian Ted Gioia noted, "Somebody once told me that *Downbeat*, the leading jazz magazine, only received around 500 jazz records to review during the entire year of 1959. It's hard to imagine somebody releasing a jazz record in 1959, and not submitting it for review."

Let's compare that to this era. By 2023, over 100,000 tracks were being added to Spotify each day. If you also consider direct upload platforms—like YouTube, SoundCloud, and Audiomack—that number is much larger. In fact, Will Page, Spotify's former chief economist, told the online publication MusicRadar that "More music is being released today (in a single day) than was released in the calendar year of 1989."

That is an eye-popping claim. And it's true. But how is it possible for that much music to be released? Also, why would we even want that much music to be released? And is it a good thing to have that much music being released? Answering those questions holds the key to understanding this era.

# I Just Ain't Release My New Shit

Of course, the reason that so many recordings can exist has to do with the proliferation of digital audio workstations that we discussed in Chapters 10 and 11. Home computing and the internet made recording so much cheaper that hit songs could be made in bedrooms for next to nothing. And some were. Billie Eilish and her brother Finneas famously recorded their spooky hit "bad guy" (August 24, 2019) in a bedroom of their family's house. By the 2010s, recording software had even made it onto mobile phones, so hits could be made on the go.

Still, breaking down the barriers to record music doesn't mean that the barriers to distribute and store your recordings would also come crashing down. But they did. Scores of platforms in this era were eager to host millions of recordings. We're going to talk about three platforms—Spotify, TikTok, and Suno—and why they wanted every recording, whether it was made in the dingiest of bedrooms or the flashiest of studios.

## Spotify: Millions of Recordings to Cut Costs

George Owen Squire wasn't someone you'd expect to change the music industry. Born in 1865 and eventually attaining the rank of major general in the US army, Squire was a polymath best known for the creation of multiplexing, a system that allowed multiple telephone conversations to be transmitted over the same wire. After selling his patent to AT&T and nearing retirement, Squire decided to use his knowledge of signal processing for one more venture: a music service.

With radio in its infancy, Squire thought it made sense to allow people to pay a monthly fee to get music and news piped into their houses via wire, kind of like a utility. That idea never caught on, but Squire and his business partners realized that the innovation had other applications. They began selling their service under a name that Squire coined right before his 1934 death: Muzak.

Over the next few decades, Muzak would succeed in getting their light background instrumentals into so many businesses and elevators that their name would become synonymous with any music of that kind. And it really was their music. To contain costs and avoid licensing issues, Muzak built up a library of over 7,500 original recordings during the 1930s. They would eventually claim that piping in the right music at the right time could influence the mood and behavior of listeners.

Though the ownership of Muzak would change a few times over the decades and the style of music they were known for would lose favor, it doesn't take much of a leap to see how the company is a distant ancestor of Spotify. Like Spotify, Muzak sold monthly subscriptions to a catalog of recordings that could soundtrack every moment. The similarities run deeper, though.

From the creation of the company through 2023, Spotify never turned an annual profit. Part of the reason for that was due to spending vast amounts of money acquiring users. But another part was that it's expensive to run a music streaming service. Most of Spotify's revenues had to be paid out in royalties to songwriters, artists, and labels. To keep shareholders happy, Spotify had to come up with ways to contain those costs. Some of those efforts were to push people toward cheaper content, like podcasts and audiobooks. But others were a bit shadier.

For years, rumors had circulated that Spotify was packing popular playlists with stock music they'd commissioned through third parties. These recordings were allegedly paid out at lower royalty rates. In her 2025 book *Mood Machine: The Rise of Spotify and the Costs of the Perfect Playlist*, journalist Liz Pelly confirmed these rumors:

So its music programming execs tried something new: they developed a scheme to lower royalty costs by populating the most-followed mood playlists with low-budget filler tracks; stock music from background music studios to fit certain moods and genres, licensed by Spotify under what former employees and a review of internal records confirmed were special, cheaper deal terms.

Here's how something like this might work in practice. Say Spotify added Taylor Swift's low-key record "cardigan" (August 8, 2020) to their *Chill Vibes* playlist. Of course, people love Taylor Swift's lyricism, but Spotify realizes that most people are listening to this playlist passively, throwing it on in the background while they cook dinner or bang around in a spreadsheet at work.[1] Will anyone notice if they contract someone to make music that sounds like "cardigan" but is paid out at a lower royalty rate? Probably not. Most people who put on *Chill Vibes* are looking for a mood rather than a specific song.

As I write, most of this modern Muzak is clustered on mood-based playlists focused on relaxing or sleeping. But what incentive would Spotify have to stop there? Why put Selena Gomez's "Lose You to Love Me" (November 9, 2019) and Lewis Capaldi's "Someone You Loved" (November 2, 2019) on their *Heartache* playlist when they know those songs are expensive? In fact, because they were released by major labels, they're going to be even more expensive. In *Mood Machine*, Pelly also reported that the biggest labels got better royalty rates than independent artists.

In short, Spotify has a strong incentive for the platform to be flooded with music by anonymous artists they commission through third parties, along with true independent artists, because it's favorable to their bottom line. And while they could never do this at scale because labels would eventually leave the platform if they lost prominent playlist placements, you don't want the world's biggest streaming platform prioritizing certain songs purely because they are cheaper. Interestingly, while their bigness made them a powerful force in determining what was popular, this era saw another platform flooded with just as many songs become even more powerful in making hits: TikTok.

---

[1] I swear I'm not talking about myself.

# TikTok: Millions of Recordings to Sell Goods and Services

While TikTok is technically a single application that exists both on mobile devices and desktop computers, it's helpful to think of it as four separate things:

- **TikTok is a Social Media Platform**: Users create accounts to connect with digital communities. Those communities can post publicly or privately and have other members of those communities share and reply to those posts. Unlike other forms of social media, TikTok is exclusively focused on video and, especially in its early days, videos shorter than a minute.

- **TikTok is a Search Engine**: Like every social platform, TikTok has a search function that you can use to find other users and posts. But it's a bit more generalized than that. Need to figure out where to take your boyfriend on a date? Turning to Google is so 2005. Punch "date ideas" into the TikTok search bar, and you will be met with scores of videos of people telling you where to woo your man.

- **TikTok is a Music Discovery Service**: Music had been integrated into social media sites for decades, but TikTok made that integration even more prominent. Part of this was its history. In 2017, TikTok bought Musical.ly, a popular platform that allowed users to create and share lip-sync videos. The TikTok interface not only allowed users to browse through recordings, but it prompted them to use those recordings in their posts. As other people scrolled through those posts, they could see the names of the songs they were hearing. As those posts grew popular, users would head to streaming services, like Spotify, to hear the full songs.

- **TikTok is a Digital Mall**: While music continued to play a prominent role on TikTok as time went on, it often was used to help sell goods through their shop. The TikTok Shop not only made it possible for users to make purchases directly within the app, but it also allowed those same people to post videos with those products and earn a commission if someone made a purchase via their post.

These ideas existed before TikTok was founded in 2016. But TikTok's innovation was combining them with a near-magical algorithm that was great at fostering trends among its more than one billion users. Throughout this era, those trends birthed so many hit songs that finding a number one in the 2020s that had no success on TikTok was like finding a number one in the 1980s that didn't have a music video.

As you might expect, many of these trends were focused on dancing. For example, on March 10, 2020, Keara Wilson posted a TikTok of herself dancing to Megan Thee Stallion's "Savage" (May 30, 2020). Her choreography quickly went viral on the platform, with celebrities and average joes copying her dance. 18 days later, the song broke into the Hot 100. Not long after, it was at number one. From The Weeknd's "Blinding Lights" (April 4, 2020) to DaBaby's "ROCKSTAR" (June 13, 2020), many other songs followed similar paths after spawning viral dances.

Not all hit-making TikTok trends were focused on dancing, though. Some focused on artful transitions. For example, Sabrina Carpenter's "Please Please Please" (June 29, 2024) was coupled with a trend where users would show themselves looking upset before something swiped in front of the camera as the lyric "And please, please, please / Don't bring me to tears when I just did my makeup so nice" played. When you saw the user again, they were dressed to the nines. SZA's murder fantasy "Kill Bill" (April 29, 2023) sparked a similar trend. As TikTok users dramatically mouthed the lyric "I just killed my ex," they would swing their arm past their face, faux weapon in hand, to reveal themselves in a completely new outfit.

Artists started playing into these trends too, putting lyrics in songs that were begging to be turned into TikToks. For example, when Drake released his song "Toosie Slide" (April 18, 2020) with lyrics telling people how to do a certain dance (i.e., "It go, right foot up, left foot slide"), it wasn't a shock when people started following the directions.

At the same time, artists also seemed to test songs out on the platform. For example, on August 18, 2022, Sam Smith and Kim Petras leaked a clip from their carnal song "Unholy" (October 29, 2022). It quickly went viral. The duo continued to tease the song before it was released a month later. I venture that

**Figure 13.1** *Author talking about ABBA's "Dancing Queen" (1977) on TikTok.*

if the initial response was more tepid, they would have reconsidered putting the song out.

Part of the reason TikTok was willing to host all this music was because they needed it to inspire viral trends. And everything from a major label masterpiece to a bedroom recording could do that. Popular trends led more people to the platform, which led to more advertising dollars being spent and more users promoting products through the TikTok Shop.

Still, the strangest thing about TikTok was that artists and labels couldn't figure out exactly how it worked. First, the TikTok algorithm didn't show a bias for the preferences of the artist. Take Steve Lacy as an example. After putting out his spacy song "Bad Habit" (October 8, 2022), a random person uploaded a sped-up version of the recording. That sped-up version ended up getting used more frequently on TikTok than the original.[2]

Doja Cat also experienced something similar. None of the first four singles from her 2019 album *Hot Pink* cracked the top 40. Then, a popular TikToker named Haley Sharpe posted a clip of herself dancing to "Say So" (May 16, 2020), a groovy cut from the album that wasn't set to be released as a single. As the song picked up traction on the platform, Doja Cat and her team rerouted, officially promoting the song.

TikTok also didn't show preference for the present over the past. In 2017, a flute-wielding, half-singing, half-rapping artist named Lizzo released a self-help anthem called "Truth Hurts" (September 7, 2019) to little attention. Two years later, people on TikTok started making humorous posts centered on the lyric "I just took a DNA test, turns out I'm a hundred percent that bitch." As the meme took off, so did the song. It eventually spent seven weeks at number one.

Decades-old songs could resurge too. Fleetwood Mac's "Dreams" (1977), for example, would climb all the way to number 12 on the charts in 2020 after a TikTok of a man skateboarding while drinking from a large jug of Ocean Spray cran-raspberry juice as the song played went mega-viral. The past

---

[2] Manipulating the speed of a popular song predates TikTok. Artists like DJ Screw, for example, grew followings in the 1990s by remixing songs in a slowed down style, often referred to as "chopped and screwed." Nevertheless, the speeding up and slowing down of songs grew so popular on TikTok that labels began releasing alternate versions of songs with different combinations of speed and effects.

wasn't only alive on TikTok, but it was competing with the present. This was a dramatic shift.

From music videos in the 1980s to ringtones in the 2000s, various forms of media have been used to promote songs. But these initiatives were always artist-led. A fan wasn't making the Madonna video that ended up on MTV. On TikTok, your fate could be in the hands of a random teenager who liked your song. Of course, labels and artists would try to seed trends. But it wasn't as easy as paying off the right radio DJ to play your song in the 1970s. And even if your song did spark a trend, it was possible that you would remain anonymous, like Jawsh 685.

In 2019, the 17-year-old producer uploaded a bouncy beat to YouTube. A year later, it sparked a viral dance on TikTok. Pop-star-turned-TikTok-star Jason Derulo reached out to the young producer to see if he could turn his beat into a song. Under the name "Savage Love (Laxed—Siren Beat)" (October 17, 2020) it topped the charts. To date, it's in a small class of songs that have surpassed one billion plays on Spotify. Nearly every other song in this elite club is by a superstar artist with name recognition. "My Girl" by The Temptations (1965). "Stayin' Alive" by the Bee Gees (1978). "Africa" by Toto (1983). "Wannabe" by the Spice Girls (1997). "Stronger" by Kanye West (2007). "Circles" by Post Malone (November 30, 2019). "Die with a Smile" by Bruno Mars and Lady Gaga (January 11, 2025).

Amid these superstars, you find Jawsh 685. I venture that most people who are familiar with "Savage Love (Laxed—Siren Beat)" would have no idea that he is listed as the lead artist on the track. They either associate it with a TikTok dance or Jason Derulo, a singer whose fame predates the platform. TikTok gave Jawsh 685 a huge hit but left him unknown.

As we talked about in the last chapter, this trend existed before TikTok. It first became prominent with direct upload platforms, like YouTube, and songs that went viral on those platforms, like Baauer's "Harlem Shake" (2013). But TikTok industrialized this anonymization. Platforms were stealing power from artists. But this anonymization was about to become worse with the rise of a new platform: Suno.

# Suno: Millions of Recordings to Make Artists Pay

Lee Sodel was somewhere between shocked and scared. The South Korean was a master of Go, a complex board game created in China over 2,000 years ago. His emotional distress was due to an opponent he'd recently played: AlphaGo. AlphaGo wasn't human. It was a computer program specifically built to play Go.

Computer programs had beaten humans at chess since the 1990s. But Go was more difficult than chess. Sodel thought he would beat the program handily. He was wrong. AlphaGo beat him in four of five contests. His world was so shaken that he retired from the game. "Losing to A.I., in a sense, meant my entire world was collapsing," he told *The New York Times* in 2024. "I could no longer enjoy the game, so I retired."

Though most people will never master a skill the way Lee Sodel mastered Go, most of us will have a moment where we interact with a piece of technology that affects how we see the world. For me, that technology was Suno.

Founded in Cambridge, Massachusetts, Suno was part of a wave of generative artificial intelligence tools that splashed on the scene in the 2020s. The interface, which you can see in Figure 13.2, was simple. You described a song in a text box—maybe something like "a dreamy industrial rock song about driving down the highway"—and in moments, you would have two recordings that met your specifications.

The first time I used Suno, I had a similar feeling to what Lee Sodel described when he was defeated by AlphaGo. I'm not the world's greatest musician, but I've spent years playing in bands and recording songs. What had I wasted all that time for? The Suno songs were not masterful, but some were on par with compositions by amateur musicians. Furthermore, at the pace the technology was evolving, I could see the output being indistinguishable from man-made music in a matter of years, with the right prompt creating a song that bangs as hard as Taylor Swift's "Cruel Summer" (October 28, 2023).

Of course, this didn't stop me from making music. Music isn't just a means to an end. It's an end in and of itself. Despite Suno CEO Mikey Shulman claiming on the *20VC* podcast in early 2025 that "the majority of people don't

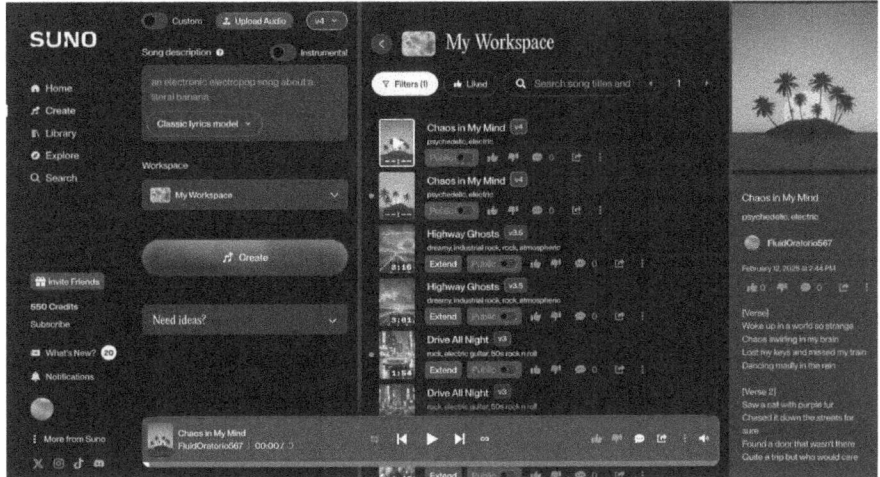

**Figure 13.2**  *Author making an AI-generated song on Suno.*

enjoy the majority of time they spend making music," working through the creative process is part of the fun. But Suno had a strong incentive to convince people that this was a better way to make music.

In one sense, you can view Suno as an artificial intelligence product. In another, you can view it as an artist services product. They charge a monthly fee to allow people to create recordings with their software. And they need a lot of people making a lot of songs if they want to make money. Shulman told *Rolling Stone* that he "envisions a billion people worldwide paying 10 bucks a month to create songs with Suno." That's a lofty goal. But there are a few hurdles that Shulman and his company must clear first.

When Suno was released publicly, people noticed that you could generate music very similar to well-known songs. Maybe you prompt the system for a laid-back melodic rap song with a ukulele about being a celebrity, and it returns something eerily like Polo G's "RAPSTAR" (April 24, 2024). Artists, labels, and industry organizations were soon thinking that the technology was built on millions of copyrighted songs. Suno demurred at first. But after they were sued, it was revealed that the product used nearly every piece of recorded music on the internet. Their claim was that their models were transformative and thus fair use. In other words, they could use the recordings without paying royalties.

While I'm skeptical of this notion, the artificial intelligence revolution began to rage during this era. Users started to upload covers using the technology to YouTube, like Céline Dion "singing" Cardi B and Megan Thee Stallion's raunchy rap "WAP" (August 22, 2020). Listeners also claimed to find scores of artist pages on Spotify with nothing but music generated by artificial intelligence. Spotify wasn't the only platform with this problem, though. In January 2025, Deezer revealed that over 10,000 tracks generated by artificial intelligence were being uploaded to their platform daily.

If Spotify was packing playlists with nameless artists and TikTok was creating viral moments for songs while leaving their artists in the shadows, then Suno was the anonymization of the musician at scale. Maybe a world was near where everybody had their own personal yet nonexistent pop star making music finely tuned to their ears. Maybe Lee Sodel's fears were justified.

# I Don't Wanna Argue, But I Don't Wanna Bite

It's been a very different experience writing the last few chapters of this book as opposed to the first few. I was born in 1995, so when I was writing about, say, radio in the 1970s, I had no skin in the game. But I'm pretty involved with everything we've discussed in this chapter. I not only release music on streaming services regularly, but I work for the streaming service Audiomack. I also have 100,000 followers on TikTok. Even though I was talking about many problematic trends in the last section of this chapter, I don't think these technologies are all bad. In fact, I think they've spawned many good things.

The rise of TikTok, digital distribution, and various streaming platforms have made it easier than ever to share your music with the world and grow an audience. As discussed in the last chapter, those streaming platforms have also reversed the trend of declining revenues that plagued the music industry since the rise of Napster. Sure, there are important questions about how those revenues are divvied up, but every month at Audiomack I see how independent musicians can make money from their art in a way that didn't exist a few years earlier and how listeners can discover more music than ever before.

There's also always been this fear that music streaming flattens culture, that algorithms amplify the biggest artists to be bigger than ever before. In a 2023 paper that I wrote with Will Page, Spotify's former chief economist, who I've mentioned a few times, we found this wasn't the case.

Decades before, if you looked at local music charts around the globe, they were filled with American and British acts. This was partially because of a logistical issue. In the 1980s, for example, economies of scale made it cheaper for a label to create millions of Michael Jackson records and distribute them around the world than to distribute different local artists to each market. "Streaming changed those economics," as we wrote in the paper, "slashing the costs of production and distribution, and making local music within global labels more profitable to invest in." According to our research, as streaming took hold in our sample of European markets, more local acts began to dominate their local charts (i.e., more Italian artists on the Italian charts).

In short, while there are issues with the musical technology of this era, there is also undoubted good that has come out of it. Though I could go on about that, I want to investigate two controversial claims that I felt like I persistently heard in his era. First, that all popular music was beginning to sound the same. Second, that musicians were becoming true pop stars much less frequently.

## Does All Pop Music Sound the Same?

Country music was arguably bigger than ever before in this era. In fact, when "Try That in a Small Town" by Jason Aldean (August 5, 2023), "Rich Men North of Richmond" by Oliver Anthony (August 26, 2023), and "I Remember Everything" by Zach Bryan and Kacey Musgraves (September 9, 2023) got to number one consecutively in 2023, it was the first time in Hot 100 history that three country songs topped the charts one after another.[3]

---

[3] Both Aldean and Anthony's respective chart-toppers were part of a trend where fans would do whatever they could to get a song to number one to prove a point. Both of those country songs were pushed to the top of the charts in support of conservative political ideals. The journey to number one for BTS's "Butter" (June 5, 2021) was similar, albeit unrelated to politics. *Billboard* noted that BTS superfans employed "tactics like bulk purchases of physical albums and coordinated digital buying to influence chart performance."

At the same time, artists from outside the country universe began releasing country songs. Beyoncé stomped and clapped her way to the top of the charts on "TEXAS HOLD 'EM" (March 2, 2024). Onetime rapper Post Malone sang about a toxic relationship on "I Had Some Help" (May 25, 2024). Everyone was doing country. And no one did it bigger than Morgan Wallen on "Last Night" (March 18, 2023).

"Last Night" not only topped the Hot 100 for 16 weeks and the country chart for 25 weeks, but it was the most popular song in 2023 according to *Billboard*. Country music was now pop music. But was "Last Night" even country? Sure, "Last Night" has some elements that we associate with the style. A pedal steel sobs throughout. The lyrics are filled with references to alcohol (e.g., "Last bottle of Jack, we split a fifth"). There's even a slight drawl to Wallen's vocal. But, to my ears, "Last Night" has as much in common with hip-hop as it does with country.

Throughout the entirety of the song, an acoustic guitar loops the same four bars. This is like how a sample might do the same throughout a hip-hop track. While Wallen is singing over that loop on the chorus (i.e., "Last night we let the liquor talk"), his cadence on the verses is akin a rapper's flow (i.e., "Last night I kissed your lips / Make you grip the sheets with your fingertips"). Furthermore, the rhythm section on this track takes more cues from hip-hop than country. The percussion is mostly programmed, built around snaps and a faint hi-hat on the chorus. The bass is a booming synth that doubles as a kick drum.[4]

The hip-hop influence on "Last Night" becomes clearer when you compare it to a bona fide hip-hop track, like Doja Cat's "Paint the Town Red" (September 16, 2023). Built around a sample of Dionne Warwick's 1964 hit "Walk On By" that loops through the entire song, the arrangement is fleshed out with pittering hi-hats, repeated snaps, and a thunderous synth bass that doubles as a kick drum. Additionally, Doja Cat both sings and raps on the track. No, "Paint the Town Red" isn't a country song. But if, as we spoke about in Chapter 6, there was controversy around Lil Nas X's "Old Town Road" (April 13,

---

[4] Maybe none of this should be a surprise. "Last Night" was created with Charlie Handsome, a producer known for his work on hip-hop songs, like Jack Harlow's "First Class" (April 23, 2022).

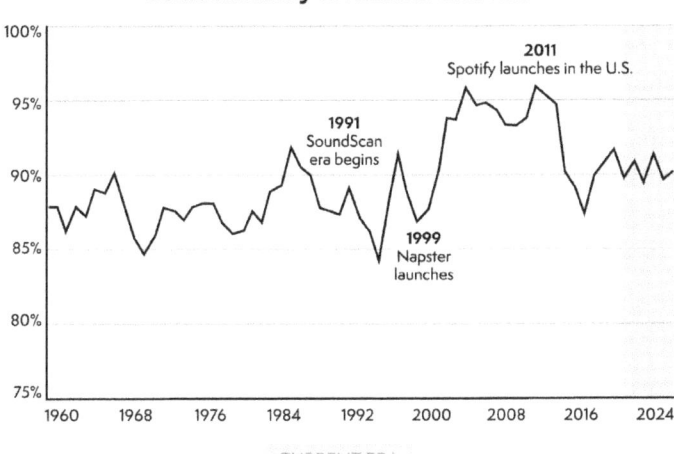

Figure 13.3

2019) being considered a country song, there should have been some around Wallen's massive hit.

But there wasn't. And though it's worthwhile to understand why, the importance here is the idea that the various platforms in this era incentivized genres to combine in one heap of blandness. Critics at *The New York Times* have disparagingly referred to music like this as "Spotifycore," a genre built to succeed on passive, algorithmically driven platforms from this era.[5] But are songs really being melded into a forgettable, genre-less goo?

In Chapter 9, we measured the sonic similarity of number ones by looking at four metrics from Spotify (i.e., danceability, happiness, energy, acousticness) and the percent of each song that contains no lyrics. That analysis—which you can see again in Figure 13.3—showed that up through 1996, (a) number one hits released around the same time have a good deal of sonic similarities and (b) while there was variation, no period's hits were that much more

---

[5] I've seen the term "Spotifycore" applied to a variety of songs, but I think "Peaches" by Justin Bieber (April 3, 2021) proves a good example. It's got a laid-back groove that could be enjoyed if you're barely paying attention. And while it's broadly R&B, some of the vocals allude to hip-hop, making it appropriate for a variety of vibey playlists.

similar than others. If we extend that analysis up through this era, we see something interesting.

During the first decade of the 2000s, the sonic similarity of number ones shot up. This aligns with related analyses published in *Scientific Reports* in 2012 and *The New York Times* in 2018. Pop music became more homogenous during that decade. The typical explanation is that, as we spoke about in Chapter 11, Max Martin and his compatriots found so much success during that period. Many artists were turning to the same stable of songwriters, resulting in similar sonic results.

Though Martin remained a powerhouse through this era, cowriting hits like "we can't be friends (wait for your love)" by Ariana Grande (March 23, 2024) and "My Universe" by Coldplay and BTS (October 9, 2021), we began to see a bit more sonic variety as streaming took hold in the 2010s. Again, this similarity rate was still high, but by the end of this era, it sat around the same level as it did between 1960 and 1999. Thus, while I do agree that this "Spotifycore" sound exists, it didn't homogenize the top of the charts as much as you'd expect.

Furthermore, my ears felt like there was a good deal of variety in this era. You had house-inspired tracks, like Beyoncé's "BREAK MY SOUL" (August 13, 2022). You had big ballads, like Adele's "Easy on Me" (October 30, 2021). You had the moody hip-hop we discussed in the last chapter, like Travis Scott's "HIGHEST IN THE ROOM" (October 19, 2019). You had more traditional hip-hop like Kendrick Lamar's "squabble up" (December 7, 2024). You even had burning soul tracks, like Teddy Swims' "Lose Control" (March 30, 2024). You might not have liked any of these songs, but the streaming era brought variety from nameless bedroom acts to the biggest pop stars.

## Are There No New Pop Stars?

In early August 2023, *Billboard* published an article that sounded an alarm for the music industry: "Pop Stars Aren't Popping Like They Used To—Do Labels Have a Plan?" In the piece, journalist Elias Leight discussed how industry professionals thought it was harder to create new superstars in this era. Some of the issues went back to ideas we discussed earlier in this chapter. Platforms like TikTok could make a song take off, but those platforms were unpredictable.

I didn't find this claim convincing. The song that was at the top of the charts when the article was published, Jungkook and Latto's "Seven" (July 29, 2023), was a good example as to why. Jungkook was a member of BTS, the Korean superstars that had been popular for over a decade. Latto, on the other hand, had scored her first top ten hit in 2021. One old star. One new star. And there were other examples of nascent pop success.

Along with the aforementioned "First Class," Jack Harlow scored two other chart-toppers with "Lovin On Me" (December 2, 2023) and "INDUSTRY BABY" (October 23, 2021), a collaboration with Lil Nas X, a mere three years after his first true hit. Olivia Rodrigo parlayed her role on a Disney Channel show into a string of smashes, including "drivers license" (January 23, 2021), "good 4 u" (May 29, 2021), and "vampire" (July 15, 2023). Shaboozey went from never having charted a song to turning the country crossover "A Bar Song (Tipsy)" (July 13, 2024) into one of the biggest hits of the decade. There were other examples, but those alone felt like enough to disprove the fears in the article. We can take a closer look, though.

On the surface, this seems like a simple thing to measure. Grab every artist in the history of the Hot 100, set a threshold for how many songs an artist must chart to qualify as a star, and count both the number of total stars and new stars by year. Sadly, it's not that easy.

Throughout this book, we've noted that even though its name has remained the same, the Hot 100 isn't a static document. In Chapter 9, for example, we saw how *Billboard*'s switch to SoundScan resulted in fewer artists charting. This didn't indicate that there were fewer superstars. It indicated a change in measurement.

Additionally, throughout the 2000s, hit songs regularly credited multiple artists. For example, Kanye West and Ty Dolla $ign were listed as the lead artists on "CARNIVAL" (March 16, 2024), but Rich the Kid and Playboi Carti were listed as featured artists. In other words, that's a hit for each of them. To measure the rate at which new stars emerged, we need to account for these things.

First, I went through the entire history of the Hot 100 and separated out each artist listed on a hit. "Señorita" (August 31, 2019), for example, was counted as a hit for Camila Cabello and Shawn Mendes because both were listed as artists on the track. Similarly, "Rain on Me" (June 6, 2020) counted for both Lady Gaga and Ariana Grande.

Second, because the Hot 100 has changed over the years, I had to create a fluid definition of how to define a star. What I elected to do was look at how many top 40 hits an artist had in rolling five-year increments. If they had more hits than 90 percent of artists who charted in the top 40 during that period, then they were considered a star. To count as a new star, it had to be the first time they met that threshold.

By this methodology, the new stars to emerge between 1972 and 1976 were ABBA, Bachman-Turner Overdrive, Barry Manilow, Seals and Crofts, Earth, Wind and Fire, and Marie Osmond. From 2002 to 2006, Chris Brown, Lil Wayne, John Mayer, Justin Timberlake, Pharrell Williams, and The Pussycat Dolls met the criteria. From 2020 to 2024, Jelly Roll, Karol G, Playboi Carti, Sabrina Carpenter, and Tyler, the Creator did the same. These results made enough sense to me that I was ready to crunch the numbers at scale.

In Figure 13.4, we see that in most five-year periods, between 1 percent and 3 percent of artists who chart a song in the top 40 are new pop stars. Furthermore, between 10 percent and 30 percent of pop stars are new pop stars.[6] Despite the ebbs and flows in this data, it gives some credence to the *Billboard* article that we discussed at the beginning of this section. Of the five periods with the lowest percentages of new pop stars, three occurred since 2010. That said, if there had been a decline, it wasn't new to this era. It's been going on since the turn of the millennium.

And this makes sense. As we've established over the last few chapters, the changes in how the music industry works between 2000 and 2020 have

---

[6] Nerd alert: I want to hammer home what each of these numbers represents. When I refer to "Percentage of Pop Stars Who are New Pop Stars," I am doing this calculation: (Count of artists who, for the first time ever, have more hits than 90 percent of artists that charted a top 40 song) / (Count of artists who have more hits than 90 percent of artists that charted a top 40 song). When I refer to "Percentage of Top 40 Artists Who are New Pop Stars," I am doing this calculation: (Count of artists who, for the first time ever, have more hits than 90 percent of artists that charted a top 40 song) / (Count of artists who charted a song in the top 40).

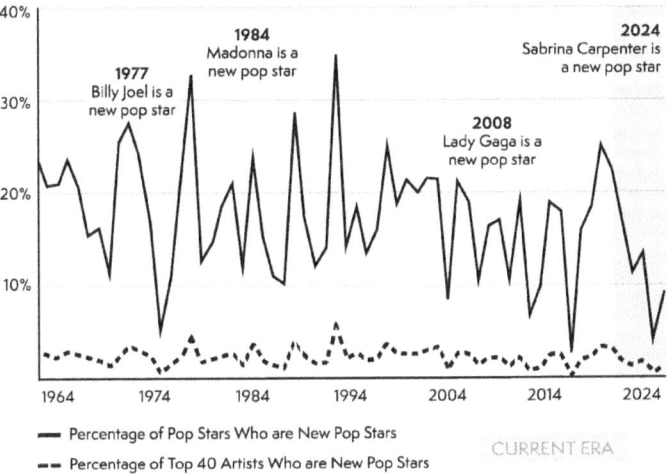

**Figure 13.4**

been dramatic. After file sharing almost broke the industry, the rise of digital production and online platforms has reshaped how artists are discovered and introduced to fans. TikTok and Spotify are the latest iteration of trends that emerged with Napster and YouTube, among other internet destinations.

In short, while there are worrying trends in popular music, some of which we've discussed in this chapter, there are still new artists finding stardom. Stardom in this era looks different than it did in, say, the 1980s, but I don't think the star is dead. The music industry is just adapting to new technologies, the same way it did when recording was invented in the 1870s, radio was ascendent in the 1920s, the LP was introduced in the 1940s, and the CD was dominant in the 1990s.

# It's Supposed to be Fun Turning 21

It's kind of strange writing the end of this book. Sure, there have been some themes that we've hit on repeatedly, but there is no end to popular music. The day this book comes out, there will already be number-one hits not included here. And that excites me. It excites me that there's always more music to discover. Plus, like I said in Chapter 2, I didn't set out to cover everything in this book. I set out to cover the topics that the data led me to. Hopefully, along the way, you've enjoyed some of those insights, seen popular music in a new way, and picked up a few songs you've come to love and hate.

Still, I wish there was a way to put a bow on this thing. It would have been cool if I discovered some secret to writing hit songs. While I do think my songwriting skills have improved by studying the number ones, I didn't discover some trick to writing a hit. If I did, you'd be listening to my words sung on the radio rather than reading them in print. Nevertheless, if I had to come up with some eternal musical truths that I gathered along the way, I'd go with these three:

1. Popular music is neither created nor destroyed. It evolves.

2. Let enough time pass, and musical ideas that are out of fashion will become fashionable again.

3. If somebody derides a musical element or tradition as "not real music," they inevitably like a song that utilizes that element or some variation of it.

When you listen to thousands of hits across many decades, you become a bit more open-minded. You become infatuated with songs that once disgusted you. You see the humanity in people that lived decades before you, along with those currently thriving in music scenes that leave you confused. And, most importantly, your faith in the power of music is constantly reaffirmed. To paraphrase one of the great songwriters of the twentieth century: I know it's only pop music, but I like it.

## Highlights

1. **"All Too Well (10 Minute Version)" by Taylor Swift (November 27, 2021)**[7]—When Bruce Springsteen gave the keynote address at the

---

[7] Kendrick Lamar's "squabble up" was also rated high enough to be included here. I mentioned it earlier.

2012 South by Southwest music festival, he noted how Bob Dylan had a unique skill: "He sings verse, after verse, after verse, and it doesn't get boring." Taylor Swift was able to tap into that ability on "All Too Well."

Whereas Dylan's longest compositions are filled with mysterious, surreal images, Swift sticks with the everyday on this song, chronicling the rise and fall of a relationship. But it's in her vivid honesty and attention to detail that she keeps you enthralled for ten minutes without playing more than four chords.

2. **"Not Like Us" by Kendrick Lamar (May 18, 2024)**—When J. Cole teamed up with Drake on "First Person Shooter" (October 21, 2023) and claimed that he, Drake, and Kendrick Lamar were hip-hop's "big three," he didn't realize that he was starting a war. Though Lamar rapping "Motherfuck the big three . . . it's just big me" on "Like That" (April 6, 2024) was technically a swipe at J. Cole and Drake, the former quickly bowed out of the feud, leaving only Drake to fend for himself against the Compton rapper.

   For weeks, this beef dominated pop culture, the two rappers firing off diss tracks at a moment's notice. Then Lamar released "Not Like Us," and it was clear that Drake had lost. While "Not Like Us" was interesting purely as a piece of celebrity gossip, it was a force to be reckoned with because, in the words of journalist Brian Hiatt, it combined "pop accessibility, virtuosity, lyrical density, and brutal attacks."

3. **"Leave the Door Open" by Silk Sonic (April 17, 2021)**—A super-duo consisting of Anderson .Paak and Bruno Mars, Silk Sonic's goal was to reimagine 1970s soul and R&B for the 2020s. While you might be inclined to criticize the group as a tribute act, when you hear the complex harmonies and smooth production on "Leave the Door Open," it's clear that they weren't mailing it in. They'd studied this sound and tried to push it further. Frankly, that is Bruno Mars's superpower. Even if you don't like his songs, you can't deny that they are crafted better than the output of most of his contemporaries.

# Lowlights

1. **"TROLLZ" by 6ix9ine and Nicki Minaj (June 27, 2020)**[8]—The career of rapper 6ix9ine is filled with so much legal controversy that his actual music feels like a footnote.[9] "TROLLZ" is a good example of that. After being sentenced to probation for pleading guilty to sex crimes against a child, the rapper got caught up in unrelated racketeering charges. Because he turned state's evidence, he was able to serve the rest of his term under house arrest. During that time, he released "TROLLZ." While there is a strong case that "TROLLZ" is the worst number one in history, 6ix9ine mumbling and screaming over a mind-numbing beat, you'll probably understand why that is overshadowed by a litany of horrendous crimes.

2. **"Slime You Out" by Drake ft. SZA (September 30, 2023)**—One of Drake's great skills is how prolific he is, rapping and singing across genres with great facility. But "Slime You Out" sounds like it was tossed together in moments, the rap star called in to croon some lines about a toxic relationship at the eleventh hour. Frankly, some of those lines could have used a second take (e.g., "You got my mind in a terrible place / Whipped and chained you like American slaves / Act like you not used to Sheraton stays").

3. **"FRANCHISE" by Travis Scott ft. Young Thug and M.I.A. (October 10, 2020)**—The great miracle of "FRANCHISE" is that despite featuring three different artists, there isn't one memorable lyric. Though some of that is due to the trio of performers—Travis Scott, Young Thug, and M.I.A.—I can't put all the blame on them. The track isn't much more than three distorted synth bass notes repeated ad nauseam.

---

[8] Jason Aldean's "Try That in a Small Town" was rated low enough to be included here. I mentioned it earlier.

[9] I made this same joke in Chapter 6, but how could I not put a footnote here? For your time, I'll give you another fun fact. In an episode of the podcast *Song Exploder*, Dave Bayley of Glass Animals related how the first person to hear their sleeper hit "Heat Waves" (March 12, 2022) was actor Johnny Depp. Depp was apparently working in the same recording complex and accidentally walked into Bayley's studio while he was finishing up the track.

## Argument Starters

In Chapter 10, I complained about lazy samples, artists cashing in on nostalgia by taking a hit from yesteryear and turning it into something new but lacking. Built around a sample of Rick James's 1981 hit "Super Freak," Nicki Minaj's "Super Freaky Girl" (August 27, 2022) is a prime example of this phenomenon. One of the judges didn't care, though. The "Super Freak" instrumental is too much fun to rap over. MC Hammer realized this when he made "U Can't Touch This" in the 1990s. And Nicki Minaj did the same with "Super Freaky Girl" in the 2020s.

## Odds and Ends

1. **"WAIT 4 U" by Future ft. Drake and Tems (May 14, 2022)**—Last chapter, I compared trap to the blues in that they are both dark, somber genres. Though "WAIT 4 U" lives a bit more in the R&B universe than the trap universe, given that it's helmed by Future, one of the great trap MCs, it's a good example of why I sometimes refer to trap as the hip-hop blues.

2. **"Anti-Hero" by Taylor Swift (November 5, 2022)**—One TikTok trend that I enjoyed in this era was artists taking popular songs and reimagining them in different styles. Occasionally, these reimaginations would make me realize that some hits were better than I originally thought. That's what happened when I heard Josiah and the Bonnevilles' countrified cover of Taylor Swift's "Anti-Hero" on TikTok.

   Though no stylistic changes could save clunky lyrics like "Sometimes I feel like everybody is a sexy baby" and "Did you hear my covert narcissism I disguise as altruism / Like some kind of congressman?", a little twang made me realize that there were stronger melodic ideas on this song than Swift's synthy original suggested.

3. **"Rockin' Around the Christmas Tree" by Brenda Lee (December 9, 2023)**—The past and the future are contained in "Rockin' Around the Christmas Tree." Originally released in 1958, it didn't top the charts until

2023. This was driven by the fact that because *Billboard* now tracked listening habits (i.e., streams) in addition to purchases, Christmas songs, like Lee's "Rockin' Around the Christmas Tree" and Mariah Carey's "All I Want for Christmas is You" (December 21, 2019), would dominate the charts each December.

But "Rockin' Around the Christmas Tree" doesn't only live in the future because of some change in chart accounting. It lives in the future because in 2024 Lee released a Spanish-language version of the classic. The oddity? The 79-year-old didn't perform the song in Spanish. The translated vocal was partially powered by artificial intelligence. I don't know where popular music is headed, but if "Rockin' Around the Christmas Tree" is any indication, it's going to be weirder than we expect.

## Everything Else

"Heartless" by The Weeknd. "The Box" by Roddy Ricch. "THE SCOTTS" by Travis Scott and Kid Cudi. "Stuck With U" by Ariana Grande and Justin Bieber. "Watermelon Sugar" by Harry Styles. "Dynamite" by BTS. "Mood" by 24kGoldn ft. iann dior. "positions" by Ariana Grande. "Life Goes On" by BTS. "willow" by Taylor Swift. "What's Next" by Drake. "Up" by Cardi B. "MONTERO (Call Me By Your Name)" by Lil Nas X. "Save Your Tears" by The Weeknd and Ariana Grande. "Permission to Dance" by BTS. "STAY" by The Kid LAROI and Justin Bieber. "Way 2 Sexy" by Drake ft. Future and Young Thug. "We Don't Talk About Bruno" by *Encanto* Cast. "As It Was" by Harry Styles. "Jimmy Cooks" by Drake ft. 21 Savage. "About Damn Time" by Lizzo. "Flowers" by Miley Cyrus. "Die for You" by The Weeknd and Ariana Grande. "Like Crazy" by Jimin. "Is It Over Now?" by Taylor Swift. "yes, and?" by Ariana Grande. "HISS" by Megan Thee Stallion. "Too Sweet" by Hozier. "Fortnight" by Taylor Swift ft. Post Malone. "Love Somebody" by Morgan Wallen.

# *Bibliography*

Nearly every claim made in this book is supported by one of the sources listed in this bibliography. I say "nearly" for two reasons. First, because Fred Bronson's *The Billboard Book of Number One Hits* is not listed, despite being consulted in almost every chapter. It felt redundant to list it 13 times. If you are looking for an obscure fact about a specific number one hit and can't locate it in any other sources, it almost certainly came from Bronson's book. Second, because many claims in this book are based on original research. You can access that data that powered that research at https://chrisdallariva.com/uncharted.

## That Poor Little Fool Fell into the Moody River

Anand, Narasimhan. "Charting the Music Business: Billboard Magazine and the Development of the Commercial Music Field." In *The Business of Culture: Strategic Perspectives on Entertainment and Media*, edited by Joseph Lampel, Jamal Shamsie, and Theresa Lant, 139–54. London: Lawrence Erlbaum Associates, 2008.

Beviglia, Jim. "Behind The Song: The Traditional 'Barbara Allen.'" *American Songwriter*, August 2, 2021.

Clayson, Alan. *Death Discs: An Account of Fatality in the Popular Song*. London: Sanctuary, 1998.

Dylan, Bob. *Chronicles, Volume One*. New York: Simon & Schuster, 2004.

"F.B.I. Chief Opposes Use of 'Delinquent.'" *The New York Times*, December 30, 1960.

Flanagan, Bill. "Q&A with Bill Flanagan." *BobDylan.com*, March 22, 2017.

Gioia, Ted. *Music: A Subversive History*. New York: Basic Books, 2019.

Holt, Marilyn Irvin. "White House Conferences Focused on Youths and Societal Changes in Postwar America." *Prologue Magazine* 42, no. 2 (Summer 2010). https://www.archives.gov/publications/prologue/2010/summer/youth.html

House, James. *American Masters*. Season 37, episode 5, "Little Richard: King and Queen of Rock 'n' Roll." Aired June 2, 2023, on PBS.

Huntemann, Nina. "Corporate Interference: The Commercialization and Concentration of Radio Post the 1996 Telecommunications Act." *Journal of Communication Inquiry* 23, no. 4 (October 1999): 390–407. https://doi.org/10.1177/0196859999023004006

"Jersey City Orders Rock-And-Roll Ban." *The New York Times*, July 10, 1956.

Johnson, David. "See How Americans' Belief in God Has Changed Over 70 Years." *Time*, April 7, 2016. https://time.com/4283975/god-belief-religion-americans/

"Juvenile Crime: Is Your Boy Safe?—All Our Children." *Newsweek*, November 9, 1953.

Levitin, Daniel J. "Cathy's Clown—The Everly Brothers (1960)." From the Library of Congress, National Recording Registry Titles with Descriptions and Expanded Essays. https://www.loc.gov/static/programs/national-recording-preservation-board/documents/CathysClown.pdf

O'Brien, Conan. "Elvis Costello." Produced by Team Coco. *Conan O'Brien Needs a Friend*. November 1, 2017. Podcast. https://teamcoco.com/podcasts/conan-obrien-needs-a-friend/episodes/elvis-costello

Plato. *Five Dialogues: Euthyphro, Apology, Crito, Meno, Phaedo*. Translated by G. M. A. Grube. Indianapolis: Hackett, 2002.

Polgreen, Lydia. "The Death of Local Radio." *Washington Monthly*, April 1, 1999.

Radel, Cliff. "Billboard Celebrates 100 Years of Hits." *The Seattle Times*, November 3, 1994.

Reynolds, Simon. *Retromania: Pop Culture's Addiction to Its Own Past*. New York: Faber and Faber, 2011.

"Rock-and-Roll Called 'Communicable Disease.'" *The New York Times*, March 28, 1956.

"Rock-and-Roll Gets Slowed to a Waltz." *The New York Times*, Jul 12, 1956.

Schrum, Kelly. *Some Wore Bobby Sox: The Emergence of Teenage Girls' Culture, 1920–1945*. London: Palgrave Macmillan, 2004.

"Segregationist Wants Ban on 'Rock and Roll.'" *The New York Times*, March 30, 1956.

Thompson, Derek. "A Brief History of Teenagers." *The Saturday Evening Post*, February 13, 2018.

Was, David. "Tracing the History of a Song: 'It's All in the Game.'" *NPR*, April 5, 2006.

Yagoda, Ben. *The B-Side: The Death of Tin Pan Alley and the Rebirth of the Great American Song*. New York: Riverhead Books, 2015.

Young, Brian. "Classic Tracks: Del Shannon's 'Runaway.'" *Mix*, October 1, 2008.

# Meet Me at Quarter to Three with Your Sugar Pie

"About the Topic of Race." United States Census Bureau. Last modified December 20, 2024. https://www.census.gov/topics/population/race/about.html

Bangs, Lester. "British Invasion." In *The Rolling Stones Illustrated History of Rock & Roll*, 2nd ed., 164–176, New York: Random House, 1980.

"Beach Boys' Dennis Wilson, Drummer, Drowns At Marina." *The New York Times*, December 29, 1983.

Beaumont, Mark. "Crazed Girls, Loose Bladders, and JFK: How The Beatles Defied the Odds to Break America." *The Independent*, February 7, 2024.

*Behind the Music*. Season 4, episode 11, "Brian Setzer." Aired November 12, 2000, on VH1.

Browne, David. "Big-Band Leader Glenn Miller Vanished 80 Years Ago. His Death Started the 'Legacy' Band Trend." *Rolling Stone*, December 15, 2024.

Chung, Evan, and Josh Levin. "The Day The Music Stopped." Produced by *Slate*. One Year: 1942. November 3, 2022. Podcast. https://slate.com/podcasts/one-year/s4/1942/e3/recording-ban-1942-james-c-petrillo-the-american-federation-of-musicians-and-the-creation-of-bebop

Coughlan, Robert. "Petrillo." *Life*, August 1942.

Flam, Laura, and Emily Sieu Liebowitz. *But Will You Love Me Tomorrow?: An Oral History of the '60s Girl Groups*. New York: Hachette, 2023.

Franklin, Andrew K. "A Day in the Life: The Beatles' First Appearance on American Television." *NBC News*, November 18, 2013. https://www.nbcnews.com/nightly-news/day-life-beatles-first-appearance-american-television-flna2d11612597

Gordy, Berry. *To Be Loved: The Music, the Magic, the Memories of Motown*. New York: Grand Central, 1994.

Gordy, Margaret. "The Singing Nun Makes Comeback with More Somber Melodies." *Youngstown Vindicator*, February 8, 1979.

Greenblatt, Mike. "Joey Dee of the Starliters remembers The Peppermint Lounge, The Beatles as Opening Act and a Young Hendrix." *Goldmine: The Music Collector's Magazine*, June 11, 2022.

Grimes, William. "Phil Spector, Famed Music Producer and Convicted Murderer, Dies at 81." *The New York Times*, January 17, 2021.

Hamilton, Jack. "Did JFK's Death Make Beatlemania Possible?" *Slate*, November 18, 2013.

Harris, Keith. "Phil Spector, Famed 'Wall of Sound' Producer Convicted of Murder, Dead at 81." *Rolling Stone*, January 17, 2021.

Hylton, J. Gordon. "The Link Between the Kennedy Assassination and the Onset of Beatlemania." *Marquette University Law School* (blog), February 10, 2014. https://law.marquette.edu/facultyblog/2014/02/the-link-between-the-kennedy-assassination-and-the-onset-of-beatlemania/

Kahn, Ashley. "Jerry Wexler: The Man Who Invented Rhythm & Blues." *Rolling Stone*, August 15, 2008.

Leadbetter, Russell. "How America fell for the Beatles in aftermath of JFK Assassination." *The Herald*, September 7, 2023.

Lewis, Randy. "The Beatles, JFK and Nov. 22, 1963." *Los Angeles Times*, November 22, 2013.

MacDonald, Ian. *Revolution in the Head: The Beatles' Records and the Sixties*. Chicago: Chicago Review Press, 2007.

"Maxine Powell, Motown Charm Coach, Dies at 98." *Billboard*, October 14, 2013.

Miller, Karl Hagstrom. *Segregating Sound: Inventing Folk and Pop Music in the Age of Jim Crow*. Durham: Duke University Press, 2010.

Milner, Greg. *Perfecting Sound Forever: An Aural History of Recorded Music*. New York: Farrar, Straus and Giroux, 2009.

"Motown: A Game-Changer For Black Americans." *NPR*, February 23, 2011.

"Research Starters: Worldwide Deaths in World War II." *The National WWII Museum*. https://www.nationalww2museum.org/students-teachers/student-resources/research-starters/research-starters-worldwide-deaths-world-war

"Return of the Beatles." *The New York Times*, November 4, 1963.

Richmond, Ben. "The Strange Album That Topped the Charts After JFK's Assassination." *Vice*, November 23, 2013.

Roberts, Michael James. *Tell Tchaikovsky the News: Rock 'n' Roll, the Labor Question, and the Musicians' Union, 1942–1968*. Durham: Duke University Press, 2014.

Rorabaugh, William. *Kennedy and the Promise of the Sixties*. New York: Cambridge University Press, 2002.

Schrum, Kelly. *Some Wore Bobby Sox: The Emergence of Teenage Girls' Culture, 1920–1945*. London: Palgrave Macmillan, 2004.

"Singers: The New Madness." *Time*, November 15, 1963.

"Singing Nun of 1960s, Friend Commit Suicide." *Los Angeles Times*, April 2, 1985.

Spitz, Marc. "Still Tingling Spines, 50 Years Later." *The New York Times*, August 16, 2013.

Weir, William. "A Little Bit Softer Now, a Little Bit Softer Now . . ." *Slate*, September 14, 2014.

Yagoda, Ben. *The B-Side: The Death of Tin Pan Alley and the Rebirth of the Great American Song*. New York: Riverhead Books, 2015.

# Mr. Tambourine Man and the Raindrops on His Head

Altschuler, Glenn. *All Shook Up: How Rock 'n' Roll Changed America*. Oxford: Oxford University Press, 2004.

Barry, Dave. *Tricky Business*. New York: G.P. Putnam's Sons, 2003.

Breihan, Tom. "The Number Ones: The Byrds' 'Mr. Tambourine Man.'" *Stereogum*, August 7, 2018.

Chung, Evan, and Josh Levin. "The Day The Music Stopped." Produced by *Slate*. *One Year: 1942*. November 3, 2022. Podcast. https://slate.com/podcasts/one-year/s4/1942/e3/recording-ban-1942-james-c-petrillo-the-american-federation-of-musicians-and-the-creation-of-bebop

Grimes, William. "Art Rupe, Who Brought Rhythm and Blues to the Mainstream, Dies at 104." *The New York Times*, April 16, 2022.

Guesdon, Jean-Michel, and Philippe Margotin. *All The Songs: The Story Behind Every Beatles Release*. New York: Black Dog & Leventhal, 2013.

Hentoff, Nat. "Bob Dylan." *Playboy*, November 1966.

Hoberman, J. "Like a Complete Unknown: I'm Not There and the Changing Face of Bob Dylan on Film." *The Village Voice*, November 13, 2007.

Leslie, Ian. "A Rocker's Guide to Management." *The Economist 1843 Magazine*, November 14, 2018.

Merton, Robert. "The Matthew Effect in Science, II: Cumulative Advantage and the Symbolism of Intellectual Property." *Isis* 79, no. 4 (1988): 606–23.

Merton, Robert. *The Sociology of Science: Theoretical and Empirical Investigations*. Chicago: University of Chicago Press, 1973.

Roberts, Randall. "Art Rupe, Pioneering Rock 'n' Roll Mogul Who Helped Launch Little Richard, dies at 104." *The Los Angeles Times*, April 17, 2022.

Rosenthal, Arthur. "The History of Calculus." *The American Mathematical Monthly* 58, no. 2 (1951): 75–86. https://doi.org/10.1080/00029890.1951.11999628

Sanneh, Kelefa. *Major Labels: A History of Popular Music in Seven Genres*. New York: Penguin, 2021.

Sisario, Ben, Alexander Alter, and Sewell Chan. "Bob Dylan Wins Nobel Prize, Redefining Boundaries of Literature." *The New York Times*, October 13, 2016.

Stanley, Bob. *Yeah! Yeah! Yeah!: The Story of Pop Music from Bill Haley to Beyoncé*. New York: W. W. Norton & Company, 2014.

Stone, Sly. *Thank You (Falettinme Be Mice Elf Agin)*. New York: AUWA, 2023.

Yagoda, Ben. *The B-Side: The Death of Tin Pan Alley and the Rebirth of the Great American Song*. New York: Riverhead Books, 2015.

Zollo, Paul. *Songwriters on Songwriting*. New York: Da Capo, 2003.

# I Want You Back in the Sweet Sunshine on My Shoulders

Associated Press. "Jury finds that Ed Sheeran didn't copy Marvin Gaye Classic 'Let's Get It On.'" *NPR*, May 4, 2023.

Bright Tunes Music Corp. v. Harrisongs Music, Ltd., 420 F. Supp. 177 – Dist. Court, SD New York 1976.

Bronson, Fred. "U.S. Pop Stars Go 'Over' The Top." *Billboard*, March 31, 2001.

Byrne, David. *How Music Works*. New York: Three Rivers Press, 2017.

Emerson, Ken. *Doo-dah!: Stephen Foster and the Rise of American Popular Culture*. New York: Da Capo, 1998.

"Exclusive: The Complete Text of Bruce Springsteen's SXSW Keynote Address." *Rolling Stone*, March 28, 2012.

Folds, Ben. *A Dream About Lightning Bugs: A Life of Music and Cheap Lessons*. New York: Ballantine Books, 2019.

Grand Upright Music v. Warner Bros. Records, Inc., 780 F. Supp. 182 – Dist. Court, SD New York 1991.

Griffin et al v. Sheeran et al, No. 1:2017cv05221 – Dist. Court, SD New York 2020.

Hamilton, Jack. *Just around Midnight: Rock and Roll and the Racial Imagination*. Cambridge: Harvard University Press, 2016.

Izundu, Chi Chi. "Ed Sheeran Sued over Claims He's Ripped Off a Marvin Gaye song." *BBC*, August 10, 2016.

Kenneally, Tim. "Ed Sheeran Off the Hook in Marvin Gaye Copyright Case (for Now)." *The Wrap*, February 3, 2017.

MCIR. "Cases." George Washington University Law School. Accessed February 14, 2020. https://blogs.law.gwu.edu/mcir/cases-2/

Marcus, Greil. *Mystery Train: Images of America in Rock 'N' Roll Music*. Boston: E.P. Dutton, 1975.

Meschino, Patricia. "Harry Johnson, Legendary Jamaican Producer of Harry J Studios Credited with First Reggae Single, Dead at 67." *Billboard*, April 8, 2013.

Milner, Greg. *Perfecting Sound Forever: An Aural History of Recorded Music*. New York: Farrar, Straus and Giroux, 2009.

"Music: James Taylor: One Man's Family of Rock." *Time*, March 1, 1971.

Parsons, Gerald. "How the Yellow Ribbon Became a National Folk Symbol." *Folk Center News* 13, no. 3 (Summer 1991): 9–11 https://maint.loc.gov/folklife/ribbons/ribbons .html

Philips, Chuck. "Songwriter Wins Large Settlement in Rap Suit: Pop Music: Following a Court Ruling, Biz Markie and Warner Bros. Agree to Pay Gilbert O'Sullivan for Rapper's 'Sampling' of 'Alone Again (Naturally).'" *Los Angeles Times*. January 1, 1992.

Sisario, Ben. "Ed Sheeran Won His Copyright Trial. Here's What to Know." *The New York Times*, May 4, 2023.

Springsteen, Bruce. *Born to Run*. New York: Simon & Schuster, 2016.

Steele, Anne. "Who Wrote 'Stairway to Heaven'? Music Industry Braces for Copyright Suits." *The Wall Street Journal*, August 4, 2019.

Structured Asset Sales, LLC v. Sheeran et al, No. 1:2018cv05839 – Dist. Court, SD New York 2021.

United States Copyright Office. "A Brief History of Copyright in the United States." https:// www.copyright.gov/timeline/ (accessed October 1, 2019).

Vaidhyanathan, Siva. *Copyrights and Copywrongs: The Rise of Intellectual Property and How it Threatens Creativity*. New York: New York University Press, 2003.

Wang, Oliver. "20 Years Ago Biz Markie Got The Last Laugh." *NPR*, May 6, 2013.

Yoo, Noah. "Ed Sheeran Sued for $100 Million for Allegedly Copying Marvin Gaye." *Pitchfork*, June 28, 2018.

# When You're Hooked on Feeling with a Dancing Queen

"Barry Levine: 'Father of Rock N Roll' also Credited with Rise of Payola." *Albany Herald News*, January 21, 2017.

Breihan, Tom. "The Number Ones: ABBA's 'Dancing Queen.'" *Stereogum*, October 14, 2019.

Brewster, Bill, and Frank Boughton. *Last Night a DJ Saved My Life*. New York: Grove Press, 2014.

Covach, John. "Why Casey Kasem Mattered." *Time*, June 19, 2014.

Dannen, Frederic. *Hit Men: Power Brokers and Fast Money Inside the Music Business*. New York: Knopf Doubleday, 1991.

Dunham, Will. "U.S. Radio Deejay, 'Shaggy' Voice Casey Kasem Dead at 82." *Reuters*, June 15, 2014.

Federal Communications Commission. "Payola and Sponsorship Identification." *FCC .gov*. Modified October 7, 2014. https://www.fcc.gov/general/payola-and-sponsorship -identification

Fong-Torres, Ben. "Clive Davis Ousted; Payola Coverup Charged." *Rolling Stone*, July 5, 1973.

Harris, Larry. *And Party Every Day: The Inside Story Of Casablanca Records*. Lanham: Backbeat Books, 2009.

"In the News." *Billboard*, January 26, 2002.

Kangas, Chaz. "Paul Anka's 'Having My Baby': Disgustingly Misogynist or Unfairly Maligned?" *The Village Voice*, May 24, 2013.

Kelly, Kim. "A Brief History of American Payola." *Vice*, February 14, 2016.

Manly, Lorne. "How Payola Went Corporate." *The New York Times*, July 31, 2005.

Matos, Michaelangelo. "Larry Harris." *AV Club*, December 8, 2009.

Meisler, Andy. "After 29 Years, Still Counting Down the Hits." *The New York Times*, May 2, 1999.

"The Nation: Takeoff." *Time*, December 10, 1973.

Prince. *The Beautiful Ones*. London: Oneworld, 2019.

Proulx, Brenda Zosky. "Paul Anka Has a Dark Side – but He Won't Talk about It." *The Montreal Gazette*, August 13, 1982.

Pruter, Robert. *Chicago Soul*. Chicago: University of Illinois Press, 1992.

Simpson, Kim. *Early '70s Radio: The American Format Revolution*. London: Bloomsbury, 2011.

Shaprio, Peter. *Turn the Beat Around: The Secret History of Disco*. New York: Faber and Faber, 2005.

Tannenbaum, Rob. "Stayin' Alive." *Los Angeles Times*, December 10, 2020.

Trounson, Rebecca. "Casey Kasem Dies at 82; Radio Personality Hosted Top 40 Countdown Show." *Los Angeles Times*, June 15, 2014.

Trust, Gary. "How the Charts Have Evolved Across Billboard's History: The Hot 100, Billboard 200 & More." *Billboard*, November 14, 2009.

Vitello, Paul. "Casey Kasem, Wholesome Voice of Pop Radio, Dies at 82." *The New York Times*, June 15, 2014.

von Appen, Ralf, and Markus Frei-Hauenschild. "AABA, Refrain, Chorus, Bridge, Prechorus: Song Forms and Their Historical Development." *Samples: Online Publication of the German Society for Popular Music Studies* 13 (2015): 1–83. http://dx.doi.org/10.22029/jlupub-850

"Willis Wardlow Obituary." *Los Angeles Times*, January 5, 2002.

Zehme, Bill. "Barry Manilow." *Rolling Stone*, November 1, 1990.

Zhito, Lee. "Billboard Launches Super Singles Chart." *Billboard*, June 9, 1973.

# Don't Give Up On Us Just as It's Time for a Celebration

"Bill Veeck, Executive." *National Baseball Hall of Fame*. Accessed April 8, 2020. https://baseballhall.org/hall-of-famers/veeck-bill

Behrens, Andy. "Disco Demolition: Bell-Bottoms be Gone!" *ESPN*, August 11, 2004.

Bradshaw, Melissa. "'Imagery, and a Little Bit Of Satire': An Interview With Frank Ocean." *The Quietus*, November 22, 2011.

Brewster, Bill, and Frank Boughton. *Last Night a DJ Saved My Life*. New York: Grove Press, 2014.

Chow, Andrew. "Lil Nas X Talks 'Old Town Road' and the Billboard Controversy." *Time*, March 30, 2019.

Doerschuk, Bob. "When Drums Went Country." *DRUM!* March 2018.

Easlea, Daryl. *Chic: Everybody Dance: The Politics of Disco*, London: Helter Skelter, 2004.

Feldman, Brian. "Before 'Old Town Road,' Lil Nas X Was a Tweetdecker." *New York*, April 5, 2019.

Gage, Jeff. "Alice Cooper on Unlikely Bond With Glen Campbell: 'We Were Survivors.'" *Rolling Stone*, August 10, 2017.

Hickey, Walt. "Why Classic Rock Isn't What It Used to Be." *FiveThirtyEight*, July 7, 2014.

John, Derek. "July 12, 1979: 'The Night Disco Died' — Or Didn't." *NPR*, July 16, 2016.

Leight, Elias. "Lil Nas X's 'Old Town Road' Was a Country Hit. Then Country Changed Its Mind." *Rolling Stone*, March 26, 2019.

Lynskey, Dorian. "The 1979 Riot That 'Killed' Disco." *BBC*, September 22, 2023.

Marsh, Dave. "The Flip Sides of 1979." *Rolling Stone*, December 27, 1979.

Miller, Karl Hagstrom. *Segregating Sound: Inventing Folk and Pop Music in the Age of Jim Crow*. Durham: Duke University Press, 2010.

Millman, Ethan, and Brendan Klinkenberg. "Tyler, the Creator on His Grammy Win: It 'Feels Like a Backhanded Compliment.'" *Rolling Stone*, January 26, 2020.

Payne, Ogden. "Meet YoungKio, The 19-Year-Old Netherlands Producer Behind 'Old Town Road.'" *Forbes*, May 30, 2019.

Petridis, Alexis. "Disco Demolition: The Night They Tried to Crush Black Music." *The Guardian*, July 19, 2019.

Sclafani, Tony. "When 'Disco Sucks!' Echoed Around the World." *Today.com*, July 10, 2009.

Shaprio, Peter. *Turn the Beat Around: The Secret History of Disco*. New York: Faber and Faber, 2005.

Terry, Josh. "'Disco Demolition Night' Was a Disgrace, and Celebrating It Is Worse." *Vice*, June 12, 2019.

Vognar, Chris. "The Day Disco Was Demolished." *The New York Times*, October 29, 2023.

Waleik, Gary. "Forty Years Later, Disagreement About Disco Demolition Night." *WBUR*, July 12, 2019.

Wiser, Carl. "Rupert Holmes ('Pina Colada Song')." *Songfacts*, January 13, 2017.

Young, Julius. "Country John Rich Speaks Out on Lil Nas X's 'Old Town Road' after Billy Ray Cyrus Hops on Remix: 'Let The Fans Decide.'" *Fox News*, April 5, 2019.

# Rocking from 9 to 5 with My Buddy Amadeus

Bakker, Gerben. "Adopting the Rights-Based Model: Music Multinationals and Local Music Industries since 1945." *Popular Music History* 6, no. 3 (2011): 307–43. https://doi.org/10.1558/pomh.v6i3.307

Bliss. Karen. "Michael Jackson's 'Thriller' at 35: A Look Back at the Iconic Music Video By Those Who Made It." *Billboard*, December 2, 2018.

Breihan, Tom. "The Number Ones: Michael Jackson's 'Beat It." *Stereogum*, July 10, 2020.

Dannen, Frederic. *Hit Men: Power Brokers and Fast Money Inside the Music Business*. New York: Knopf Doubleday, 1991.

Heller, Steven. "Alex Steinweiss, Originator of Artistic Album Covers, Dies at 94." *The New York Times*, July 19, 2011.

Hill, Michael. "Bill Haley". From the Rock & Roll Hall of Fame, Hall of Fame Essays. https://rockhall.com/inductees/bill-haley/

Hirschberg, Lynn. "Hall and Oates: The Self-Righteous Brothers." *Rolling Stone*, January 17, 1985.

Mamo, Heran, Anna Chan, and Hannah Dailey. "A Timeline of Ye & Taylor Swift's Relationship." *Billboard*, August 5, 2024.

"Obama Goes on Record to Call Kanye West a 'Jackass." *Rolling Stone*, April 12, 2012.

Pareles, Jon. "MUSIC; Post Mergers: A Modest Proposal." *The New York Times*, February 6, 2000.

Passman, Donald. *All You Need to Know About the Music Business*, 11th edn. New York: Simon & Schuster, 2023.

Puterbaugh, Parke. "Anglomania: The Second British Invasion." *Rolling Stone*, November 10, 1983.

Quan, Denise. "Eddie Van Halen Deconstructs His Collaboration on 'Beat It." *CNN*, November 30, 2012.

*Quincy Jones: The Many Lives of Q*. Produced by Paul Bullock and Deborah Perkin. Aired 2008, on BBC.

Reed, J.D. "Music: New Rock on a Red-Hot Roll." *Time*, July 18, 1983.

Swedien, Bruce. *In the Studio with Michael Jackson*. New York: Hal Leonard, 2009.

Tannenbaum, Rob, and Craig Marks. *I Want My MTV: The Uncensored Story of the Music Video Revolution*. New York: Plume, 2012.

Thompson, Derek. *Hit Makers: The Science of Popularity in an Age of Distraction*. New York: Penguin, 2018.

"What Goes around: America's Corporate World Alternates between Competition and Consolidation." *The Economist*, September 15, 2016.

Wilson, Dan (@danwilsonmusic). "Tom Petty Was a Huge Inspiration to Me." *Instagram*, April 13, 2022. https://www.instagram.com/danwilsonmusic/p/CcTNf0eJpZA/

# You Already Got My Kiss, So Don't Forget My Number

Adams, Douglas. "How to Stop Worrying and Learn to Love the Internet." *The Sunday Times*, August 29, 1999.

Augustenborg, Ned, dir. *The Ballad of Don Lewis*. 2020; Pottstown, PA: MVD Entertainment, 2020, DVD.

Dalla Riva, Chris. "Spotify's Former Data Guru Tells All: A Conversation with Glenn McDonald." *Can't Get Much Higher.* May 26, 2024.

Dunn, Alexander, dir. *808.* 2015; Cupertino, CA: Apple Films, 2016, VOD.

"Electric Rhythm: The History of the Drum Machine." Posted October 4, 2018, by *Reverb.* YouTube, 15 min. 57 sec. https://www.youtube.com/watch?v=4d89S-jOsfY

"Evening News." *CBS*, April 14, 1984. https://tvnews.library.vanderbilt.edu/programs /296383

Heimlich, Russell. "Wikipedia Users." *Pew Research Center*, January 13, 2011.

Horkins, Tony. "'I Murdered the Drummer!'" *International Musician & Recording World*, June 1985.

Linn, Roger. "Museum." Accessed May 15, 2020. https://www.rogerlinndesign.com/about /about-museum

Mack, Bob. "Down with Milli Vanilli." *Entertainment Weekly*, November 30, 1990.

National Labor Relations Board, Petitioner, v. Musicians Union, Afm Local 6, Affiliated with the American Federation of Musicians, Respondent, 960 F.2d 842 (9th Cir. 1992)

Pareles, Jon. "Ikutaro Kakehashi, Engineer Behind Revolutionary Drum Machine, Dies at 87." *The New York Times*, April 3, 2017.

Philips, Chuck. "Milli Vanilli's Grammy Rescinded by Academy: Music: Organization Revokes an Award For the First Time after Revelation That the Duo Never Sang on Album." *Los Angeles Times*, November 20, 1990.

Philips, Chuck. "'We Sold Our Souls to the Devil': In a Wide-Ranging Interview, the Duo Tell the Whole Story About What It Was Like to Live a Lie." *Los Angeles Times*, November 21, 1990.

Roediger, Henry L., and K. Andrew DeSoto. "Forgetting the Presidents." *Science* 346, no. 6213 (November 2014): 1106–9. https://doi.org/10.1126/science.1259627

Roediger, Henry L., and K. Andrew DeSoto. "The Power of Collective Memory." *Scientific American*, June 28, 2016.

Tannenbaum, Rob, and Craig Marks. *I Want My MTV: The Uncensored Story of the Music Video Revolution.* New York: Plume, 2012.

Williams, Alex. "Frank Farian, the Man Behind Milli Vanilli, Is Dead at 82." *The New York Times*, January 23, 2024.

Zaromb, Franklin, Andrew C. Butler, Pooja K. Agarwal, and Henry L. Roediger. "Collective Memories of Three Wars in United States History in Younger and Older Adults." *Memory & Cognition* 42 (2014): 383–99. https://doi.org/10.3758/s13421-013-0369-7

# It's a Damn Good Thing We Danced the Macarena

Caramanica, Jon. "Prince Be, Who Infused Rap With Mysticism, Dies at 46." *The New York Times*, June 19, 2016.

Clary, Mike. "Jurors Acquit 2 Live Crew in Obscenity Case." *Los Angeles Times*, October 21, 1990.

Coscarelli, Joe, and Ben Sisario. "With R. Kelly on Trial, What Has Become of His Music?" *The New York Times*, August 18, 2021.

"Delegates' Macarena Dance." *C-SPAN*, August 26, 1996. https://www.c-span.org/program
/vignette/delegates-macarena-dance/58774

"Dolly Parton Goes Undercover on Reddit, Twitter and Instagram." Posted November 11,
2020. *GQ*, 6 min. 4 sec. https://www.gq.com/video/watch/actually-me-dolly-parton
-goes-undercover-on-reddit-twitter-and-instagram

Green, Abel. "Leer-ics: Part II." *Variety*, March 2, 1955.

Green, Abel. "Twilight of Leer-ics." *Variety*, April 6, 1955.

Green, Abel. "A Warning to the Music Business." *Variety*, February 23, 1955.

Hall, Alison. "Celebrating Women Through Their Copyright Story: Dolly Parton and
Whitney Houston." *Library of Congress* (blog), March 27, 2023. https://blogs.loc.gov
/copyright/2023/03/celebrating-women-through-their-copyright-story-dolly-parton
-and-whitney-houston/

Harris, Keith. "Phil Spector, Famed 'Wall of Sound' Producer Convicted of Murder, Dead
at 81." *Rolling Stone*, January 17, 2021.

Heath, Chris. "Praise Be." *Details*, August 1993.

Hochman, Steve. "Two Members of 2 Live Crew Arrested After X-Rated Show." *Los
Angeles Times*, July 11, 1990.

Hunt, Dennis. "P.M. Dawn's New Day: Rappers' Return to '60s Spirit Leads to Hit Single."
*Los Angeles Times*, November 30, 1991.

"Jim Morrison & The Doors on The Ed Sullivan Show." *Ed Sullivan Show* (blog),
November 9, 2010. https://www.edsullivan.com/jim-morrison-the-doors-on-the-ed
-sullivan-show/

Joyce, Mike. "'Freak' Accident of Silk Success." *The Washington Post*, December 23, 1993.

Martin, Linda, and Kerry Segrave. *Anti-Rock: The Opposition to Rock 'n' Roll*. New York:
Da Capo, 1993.

McWhorter, John. "How Dare You Say That! The Evolution of Profanity." *The Wall Street
Journal*, July 17, 2015.

McWhorter, John. *Nine Nasty Words: English in the Gutter: Then, Now, and Forever*. New
York: Avery, 2021.

Miller v. California, 413 U.S. 15 (1973).

Milligan, Glenn, and Rob Campbell. "An Interview with Motorhead's Lemmy Kilmister
& Phil Campbell." *Metalliville Zine*, October 8, 2003. http://www.metalliville.co.uk/
bankup/INTERVIEWS%20Folder/Lemmy%20and%20Phil%20C%20of%20Motorhead
.htm

Mohr, Melissa. *Holy Sh*t: A Brief History of Swearing*. Oxford: Oxford University Press,
2013.

Philips, Chuck. "Album Sales Pact Averts Omaha Case: Pop: Obscenity Charges Are
Dropped after Two Record Retail Chains Agree to Stop Selling Sexually Explicit 2 Live
Crew Music to Minors." *Los Angeles Times*, July 2, 1992.

Philips, Chuck. "Dallas DA Drops Obscenity Charges Against Chain: Law: Sound
Warehouse Agrees Not to Stock 2 Live Crew's Controversial 'As Nasty as They Wanna
Be.'" *Los Angeles Times*, November 10, 1990.

"Picks and Pans Review: The Bliss Album. . . (vibrations of Love and Anger and the
Ponderance of Life and Existence)." *People*, June 7, 1993.

Posner, Gerald. *Motown: Music, Money, Sex, and Power*. New York: Random House, 2005.

Reed, Dan, dir. *Leaving Neverland*. 2019; New York: HBO Documentary Films, 2019, VOD.

Regina v. Hicklin, L.R. 2 Q.B. 360 (1868)

*The Rolling Stone Encyclopedia of Rock & Roll*. s.v. "P.M. Dawn." 3rd ed. New York: Rolling Stone Press, 2001.

Roth v. United States, 354 U.S. 476 (1957)

Sanneh, Kelefa. *Major Labels: A History of Popular Music in Seven Genres*. New York: Penguin, 2021.

Sharkey, Joe. "NEW JERSEY DAILY BRIEFING; PM Dawn Singer Faces Charges." *The New York Times*, September 22, 1995.

"Show Business: Sex Rock." *Time*, December 29, 1975.

Thompson, Derek. "1991: The Most Important Year in Pop-Music History." *The Atlantic*, May 8, 2015.

Wyman, Bill. *Stone Alone: The Story of a Rock 'n' Roll Band*. New York: Viking, 1990.

# I Mean It, No Diggity, I Like the Way You Move

A&M Records, Inc. v. Napster, Inc., 239 F.3d 1004 (9th Cir. 2001).

Albinsson, Staffan. "A Costly Glass of Water: The Bourget v. Morel Case in Parisian Courts 1847–1849." *Swedish Journal of Music Research* 96, no. 2 (2014): 59–70.

Alderman, John. *Sonic Boom: Napster, MP3, and the New Pioneers of Music*. New York: Basic Books, 2001.

Borland, John. "RIAA Settles with 12-Year-Old Girl." *CNET*, September 9, 2003.

Brown, David. "Kool Herc and the History (and Mystery) of Hip-Hop's First Day." *Rolling Stone*, August 11, 2023.

Brown, Harley. "'We've Crossed the Threshold': How Ricky Martin's 'Livin' La Vida Loca' Became the First No. 1 Song Made Entirely in Pro Tools." *Billboard*, May 10, 2019.

Chang, Jeff. *Can't Stop Won't Stop: A History of the Hip-Hop Generation*. London: Picador, 2005.

Daley, Dan. "Recordin' 'La Vida Loca': The Making OF A Hard Disk Hit." *Mix*, November 1, 1999.

de Reydellet, Jean. "Pierre Schaeffer, 1910-1995: The Founder of 'Musique Concrète.'" *Computer Music Journal* 20, no. 2 (Summer 1996): 10–1. https://www.jstor.org/stable/3681324

Dunn, Jancee. "Madonna Can't Stop the Music." *Rolling Stone*, September 28, 2000.

Eckard, Greg. "How an Oil Engineer Created Auto-Tune and Changed Music Forever." *Vice*, February 25, 2016.

Farley, Christopher John. "Radioactive." *Time Europe*, October 23, 2000.

Healey, Jon. "Another File-Sharer Faces Costly Day of Reckoning." *Los Angeles Times*, September 2, 2008.

"Historical Background." *SACEM*, https://societe.sacem.fr/en/history

*History Detectives*. Season 7, episode 7, "Hindenburg Artifact/John Adams Book/Birthplace of Hip Hop." Aired April 10, 2029, on PBS.

Hogan, Marc. "How Much Is Music Really Worth?" *Pitchfork*, April 16, 2015.

"How Sampling Transformed Music." Posted March 2014. Ted, 16 min. 40 sec. https://www.ted.com/talks/mark_ronson_how_sampling_transformed_music

Jones, Sarah. "Dr. Andy Hildebrand Honored with Recording Academy Special Merit Award." *Grammy.com*, February 23, 2023.

Katz, Mark. *Capturing Sound: How Technology Has Changed Music*. Berkeley: University of California Press, 2010.

Knopper, Steve. *Appetite for Self-Destruction: The Spectacular Crash of the Record Industry in the Digital Age*. New York: Free Press, 2009.

Kravets, Dave. "Supreme Court OKs $222K Verdict for Sharing 24 Songs." *WIRED*, March 18, 2013.

Labaton, Stephen. "5 Music Companies Settle Federal Case On CD Price-Fixing." *The New York Times*, May 11, 2000.

Law, Sam. "Metallica vs. Napster: The lawsuit That Redefined how We Listen to Music." *Kerrang!* April 13, 2021.

Lewis, Peter H. "STATE OF THE ART; Napster Rocks The Web." *The New York Times*, June 29, 2000.

Linn, Roger. "About Roger Linn Design." https://www.rogerlinndesign.com/about/about-roger-linn-design (accessed October 12, 2021).

Linn, Roger. *MPC3000 MIDI Production Center Software version 3.0 Operator's Manual*. Akai, May 1994.

Manning, Kara. "Madonna Wraps Video As 'Music' Leaks Online." *MTV News*, May 31, 2000.

Martin, Linda, and Kerry Segrave. *Anti-Rock: The Opposition to Rock 'n' Roll*. New York: Da Capo, 1993.

Milner, Greg. *Perfecting Sound Forever: An Aural History of Recorded Music*. New York: Farrar, Straus and Giroux, 2009.

"Napster Debate." *Charlie Rose*, May 12, 2000. https://charlierose.com/videos/19757

Palacio, Debbie. *Dennis Miller Live*. Season 8, episode 6, "The Music Industry." Aired February 22, 2021, on HBO.

Palmer, Robert. "The Pop Life; Tom Petty: Ready to Fight the Good Fight." *The New York Times*, May 6, 1981.

Parker, Lonnae O'Neal. "A Hit That Bashes Single Guys' Nerves." *The Washington Post*, April 14, 1999.

Passman, Donald. *All You Need to Know about the Music Business*, 11th ed. New York: Simon & Schuster, 2023.

Reynolds, Simon. "How Auto-Tune Revolutionized the Sound of Popular Music." *Pitchfork*, September 17, 2018.

"RIAA v. The People: Five Years Later." Electronic Frontier Foundation, September 30, 2008.

Samuels, Allison. "The Doctor's in the House." *Newsweek*, November 21, 1999.

Senate Hearing 106-1060: Music on the Internet: Is There an Upside to Downloading?, Before the Committee on the Judiciary, 106th Cong. 2 (2000) (statement of Jim Griffin, Director of Technology at Geffen Records from 1993 to 1998).

Stravinsky, Igor. *Chronicle of My Life*, London: Gollancz, 1936.

Thompson, Clive. "How the Phonograph Changed Music Forever." *Smithsonian Magazine*, January 2016.

Vanhorn, Teri. "Napster to Sponsor Free Tour by Limp Bizkit, Cypress Hill." *MTV News*, April 24, 2000.

Waldfogel, Joel. *Digital Renaissance: What Data and Economics Tell Us about the Future of Popular Culture*. Princeton: Princeton University Press, 2018.

Weisbard, Eric. "Napsternomics." *The Village Voice*, August 1, 2000.

Whiteman, Paul, and Mary Margaret McBride. *Jazz*. New York: J.H. Sears & Co, 1926.

Williams, Stereo. "Outkast's 'Aquemini' Is the Pinnacle of the Duo's Art & the Culmination of Atlanta's 1990s Spirit." *Billboard*, September 18, 2018.

Witt, Stephen. *How Music Got Free: The End of an Industry, the Turn of the Century, and the Patient Zero of Piracy*. New York: Viking, 2015.

# Slow Jamz Run Down to the Deepest Part of Me

Aniftos, Rania. "Chris Brown's Legal Problems: A Timeline of Trouble." *Billboard*, July 24, 2024.

Bennett II, James. "Stereotyping Instruments: Why We Still Think Some Are for Boys, Others for Girls." *NPR*, April 19, 2018.

Castiglione, Baldassare. *The Book of the Courtier*. Translated by George Bull. New York: Penguin, 1976.

Christgau, Robert. "The Velvet Underground." http://www.robertchristgau.com/get_artist .php?name=The+Velvet+Underground

Chu, Jeff. "The Music Man." *Time*, March 19, 2001.

Conger, Bill. "Taylor Swift Talks about Her Album Speak Now, Her Hits 'Mine' and 'Speak Now,' And Writing Her Songs." *Songwriter Universe*, October 11, 2010.

Coscarelli, Joe. "Pink Quietly Became Pop Royalty. Here's How She Made It Last." *The New York Times*, October 5, 2017.

Dalla Riva, Chris. "The Death of the Key Change." *Tedium*, November 9, 2022.

Dalla Riva, Chris. "One Song, Many Writers." *Tedium*, February 4, 2023.

Drumming, Neil. 'Yeah,' Lil Jon Came through Again." *Entertainment Weekly*, May 14, 2004.

Iasimone, Ashley. "Kelly Clarkson Says She Gave Up 'Millions' in Songwriting Royalties to Show How Much She Dislikes Dr. Luke." *Billboard*, September 13, 2017.

Kornhaber, Spencer. "Kesha's Legal Paradox." *The Atlantic*, April 7, 2016.

Kreps, Daniel. "Lady Gaga Defends Kesha in Unsealed Deposition from Dr. Luke Defamation Lawsuit." *Rolling Stone*, January 30, 2019.

Lewis, Randy, and Joel Rubin. "Led Zeppelin's Three Surviving Members Briefly Share Courtroom at 'Stairway to Heaven' Trial." *Los Angeles Times*, June 17, 2016.

Lustig, Jay. "50th Anniversary For Velvet Underground's Landmark Launch at Summit High School." *NJArts.net*, November 19, 2015.

"Max Martin Master Class – Interview Polar Music Prize 2016." Posted February 12, 2018, by *puntapie*. YouTube. 1 hr. 9 min. 26 sec. https://www.youtube.com/watch?v=ehI0h63qlXk

McKenna, Kristine. "Eno: Voyages in Time & Perception." *Musician*, October 1982.

McLeod, Kembrew, and Peter DiCola. *Creative License: The Law and Culture of Digital Sampling*. Durham: Duke University Press, 2011.

"Music and Theatres in Paris." *The Music World*, August 4, 1860.

"NE-YO & Stargate on the Making of 'So Sick' – ASCAP EXPO." Posted April 23, 2013, by *ASCAP*. YouTube, 1 min. 27 sec. https://www.youtube.com/watch?v=ICzlxxp6Ta0

Peltz, Jennifer. "Kesha and Dr. Luke Reach a Settlement over Rape and Defamation Claims." *NPR*, June 22, 2023.

Power, Tom. "Pop Hitmaker Max Martin on His 1st Jukebox Musical & Juliet." Produced by CBC. *Q with Tom Power*. July 21, 2023. Podcast. https://www.cbc.ca/listen/live-radio/1-50-q/clip/15921970-pop-hitmaker-max-martin-1st-jukebox-musical-and

Reardon, Jim, and Chris Clements. *The Simpsons*. Season 14, episode 18, "Dude, Where's My Ranch?" Aired April 27, 2003, on Fox.

Reddington, Helen. *She's at the Controls: Sound Engineering, Production and Gender Ventriloquism in the 21st Century*. Sheffield: Equinox, 2021.

Repacholi, Betty, and Samantha Pickering. "Modifying Children's Gender-Typed Musical Instrument Preferences: The Effects of Gender and Age." *Sex Roles* 45, no. 9 (November 2001): 623–43. https://doi.org/10.1023/A:1014863609014

Reuters. "Expert Testifies Stairway to Heaven Chord Progression Used 300 Years Ago." *The Guardian*, June 17, 2016.

Seabrook, John. *The Song Machine: Inside the Hit Factory*. New York: W. W. Norton & Company, 2015.

"SHOF Talk: Max Martin." Posted July 13, 2017, by *SongwriterHallofFame*. YouTube, 2 min. 58 sec. https://www.youtube.com/watch?v=j0Rf_yMf3To

Skidmore v. Led Zeppelin, No. 16-56057 (9th Cir. 2018).

"Sophia Somajo Talks Private Dancer, Women in Pop and Writing with Max Martin." *Pop Justice*, September 17, 2018.

Staley, Oliver, and Amanda Shendruk. "Here's What the Stark Gender Disparity among Top Orchestra Musicians Looks Like." *Quartz*, October 16, 2018.

Stutz, Colin. "Max Martin Talks Lessons From Prince, Trying to Stay Anonymous & How Pharrell Nearly Ruined His Career in Rare Interview." *Billboard*, February 27, 2017.

Tingen, Paul. "The Stargate Writing & Production Team." *Sound on Sound*, May 2010.

Upton, George. *Woman in Music*. Chicago: A.C. McClurg and Company, 1892.

Wang, Amy. "Inside Garageband, the Little App Ruling the Sound of Modern Music." *Rolling Stone*, March 16, 2019.

Ware, Jessie. "Max Martin." *Table Manners with Jessie & Lennie Ware*. December 1, 2021. Podcast. https://podcasts.apple.com/ie/podcast/max-martin/id1305228910?i=1000543573827

Wrape, Elizabeth, Alexandra Dittloff, and Jennifer Callahan. "Gender and Musical Instrument Stereotypes in Middle School Children: Have Trends Changed?" *Update Applications of Research in Music Education* 34, no. 3 (December 2014). https://doi.org/10.1177/8755123314564255

# All I Know is that We are Young, Dumb Suckers

Baauer (@baauer). "Harlem Shake Turns 10 Today.." *Instagram*, May 21, 2022. https://www
.instagram.com/baauer/p/Cd1NqtPvUhz/

Bertoni, Steven. "How Spotify Made Lorde a Pop Superstar." *Forbes*, November 26, 2013.

Brand, Charlotte, Alberto Acerbi, and Alex Mesoudi. "Cultural Evolution of Emotional
Expression in 50 years of song lyrics." *Evolutionary Human Sciences* 1, no. 11 (2019).
https://doi.org/10.1017/ehs.2019.11

Caramanica, Jon. "The Rowdy World of Rap's New Underground." *The New York Times*,
June 22, 2017.

Carlsson, Sven, and Jonas Leijonhufvud. *The Spotify Play: How Daniel Ek Beat Apple, Google,
and Amazon in the Race for Audio Dominance*. New York: Diversion Books, 2021.

Chesman, Donna-Claire. *Crybaby: The Artists Who Shaped Emo Rap*. New York: Permuted
Press, 2025.

"Creativity." *Mainliner Magazine* (United Airlines), July 1977.

Dalla Riva, Chris. "tHiS is a p0$t ABOUT Song t!tl3s." *Can't Get Much Higher*, September
7, 2023.

Farber, Jim. "Music Review: Three Stars for Mark Ronson's 'Uptown Special.'" *New York
Daily News*, January 12, 2015.

Garcia, John. "Lollapalooza Sees Huge Crowds, Great weather; Performer Travis Scott
Arrested, Charged with Disorderly Conduct." *ABC*, August 1, 2015.

Goodman, J. David. "'Someone's Going to End Up Dead': Settlements over Fatal
Astroworld Concert." *The New York Times*, May 8, 2024.

Green, Mark Anthony. "How to Rage with Travis Scott." *GQ*, August 3, 2015.

Interiano, Myra, Kamyar Kazemi, Lijia Wang, Jienian Yang, Zhaoxia Yu. and Natalia L.
Komarova. "Musical Trends and Predictability of Success in Contemporary Songs in
and out Of the Top Charts." *Royal Society Open Science* 5, no. 5 (May 16, 2018). https://
doi.org/10.1098/rsos.171274

King, Ashley. "Major Architect behind SoundCloud's 'Fan-Powered Royalties' Departs."
*Digital Music News*, July 14, 2023.

Kirkpatrick, David. "With a Little Help from His Friends." *Vanity Fair*, September 6, 2010.

Kolchinsky, Artemy, Nakul Dhande, Kengjeun Park, and Yong-Yeol Ahn. "The Minor
Fall, the Major Lift: Inferring Emotional Valence of Musical Chords Through Lyrics."
*Royal Society Open Science* 4, no. 11 (November 15, 2017). https://doi.org/10.1098/rsos
.170952

Konstantaras, Antonis. "The 'Harlem Shake' Walked So TikTok Could Run." *Vice*,
December 28, 2022.

Kornhaber, Spencer. "The Bleak Lessons of the Astroworld Nightmare." *The Atlantic*,
November 10, 2021.

Lau, Melody. "Justin Bieber Gives Singer Carly Rae Jepsen a Boost." *Rolling Stone*, March
12, 2012.

Lee, Christina. "2 Chainz Explains Why 'Pretty Girls Like Trap Music,' Talks His Bucket
List and Benihana." *Rolling Stone*, June 16, 2017.

Lozano, Kevin. "'Nice For What.'" *Pitchfork*, April 7, 2018.

Mason, Kerri. "Baauer's 'Harlem Shake': Billboard Cover Story." *Billboard*, February 22, 2013.

McNeal, Bria. "I Asked a Music Psychologist Why Gen Z Loves Sad Songs." *Esquire*, September 1, 2023.

"Me at the Zoo." Posted April 23, 2005, by *Jawed*. YouTube, 19 sec. https://www.youtube.com/watch?v=jNQXAC9IVRw

"Most of the Dead Astroworld Festival Victims Were in One Highly Packed Area | Visual Forensics." Posted November 24, 2021, by *Washington Post*. YouTube, 13 min. 38 sec. https://www.youtube.com/watch?v=LGXwJnZSIkQ

"Music: the Stampede to Tragedy." *Time*, December 17, 1979.

Napier, Kathleen, and Lior Shamir. "Quantitative Sentiment Analysis of Lyrics in Popular Music." *Journal of Popular Music Studies* 30, no. 4 (December 2018): 161–76. https://doi.org/10.1525/jpms.2018.300411

Page, Will. *Pivot: Eight Principles for Transforming Your Business in a Time of Disruption*. New York: Simon & Schuster, 2023.

Patel, Vimal, and Sophie Kasakove. "What to Know about the Houston Astroworld Tragedy." *The New York Times*, November 15, 2021.

Price, Garret, dir. *Woodstock 99: Peace, Love, and Rage*. 2021; New York: HBO Documentary Films, 2021, VOD.

"The Rolling Stones Disaster at Altamont: Let It Bleed." *Rolling Stone*, January 21, 1970.

Setaro, Shawn. "How Trap Music Came to Rule the World." *Complex*, February 14, 2018.

Skelton, Eric. "Meet Desiigner's Biggest Influence: His Legendary 'Guitar Crusher' Grandpa." *Complex*, October 19, 2016.

"The Story Behind Mark Ronson's Hit Song 'Uptown Funk.'" *NPR*, April 16, 2015.

Thompson, Derek. "The Anti-Social Century." *The Atlantic*, January 8, 2025.

Trust, Gary. "Baauer's 'Harlem Shake' Debuts Atop Revamped Hot 100." *Billboard*, February 20, 2013.

Turner, David. "Look at Me!: The Noisy, Blown-Out SoundCloud Revolution Redefining Rap." *Rolling Stone*, June 1, 2017.

Victor, Daniel. "Mannequin Challenge Is the New Viral Video Sensation You Probably Can't Avoid." *The New York Times*, November 7, 2016.

Weiner, Jonah. "How Dozens of People Own a Slice Of a Hit." *The New York Times Magazine*, March 10, 2019.

# On that Dusty Old Town Road, I Died with a Smile

Beaumont-Thomas, Ben, and Laura Snapes. "Has 10 years of Spotify Ruined Music?" *The Guardian*, October 5, 2018.

Caramanica, Jon, Jon Pareles, Giovanni Russonello, and Caryn Ganz. "Holiday Hits, Christmas Comebacks and Some Jingle Bell Schlock." *The New York Times*, November 29, 2017.

Cheong-mo, Yoo. "Go Master Lee Says He Quits Unable to Win Over AI Go Players." *Yonhap News Agency*, November 27, 2019.

Chinoy, Sahil, and Jessia Mia. "Why Songs of the Summer Sound the Same." *The New York Times*, August 9, 2018.

Coscarelli, Joe. "Clairo's 'Pretty Girl' Went Viral. Then She Had to Prove Herself." *The New York Times*, May 23, 2018.

Douglas, Adam. "'All Subscription Models are From Satan and There is a Special Place in Hell for Those People in Charge That Went for This Business Model': Are Music Software Subscriptions Really as Bad as Some People Say?" *MusicRadar*, November 8, 2024.

Eggertsen, Chris. "Why Aren't More Pop Stars Being Born?" *Billboard*, August 23, 2023.

"Exclusive: The Complete Text of Bruce Springsteen's SXSW Keynote Address." *Rolling Stone*, March 28, 2012.

Gioia, Ted. "How Many New Songs Are Released Each Day?" *The Honest Broker*, April 1, 2023.

Glicksman, Josh. "Jason Derulo Still Wants You to Want Him—And Thanks to His TikTok Reinvention, More People Do Than Ever." *Billboard*, August 21, 2020.

Hiatt, Brian. "A ChatGPT for Music Is Here. Inside Suno, the Startup Changing Everything." *Rolling Stone*, March 17, 2024.

Hiatt, Brian (@hiattb). "The More I listen to "Not Like Us" the More I'm in Awe of Its Combination of Pop Accessibility, Virtuosity, Lyrical Density, and Brutal Attacks. It Should Win Record of the Year in a Just World." *Twitter*, July 9, 2024. https://x.com/hiattb/status/1810708324570083686

Hirway, Hrishikesh. "Glass Animals - Heat Waves." Produced by Radiotopia. *Song Exploder*, March 10, 2021. Podcast. https://songexploder.net/glass-animals

"The History of Muzak." MoodMedia. https://moodmedia.com/en/blog/inside-mood-media/history-of-muzak/ (accessed January 2, 2025).

"How 'Savage Love' Happened | Interview | Capital." Posted July 7, 2020, by *Capital FM*. YouTube, 5 min. 19 sec. https://www.youtube.com/watch?v=3JWJXXXTRE0

Kwaak, Jeyup. "Inside the Business of BTS—And the Challenges Ahead." *Billboard*, August 26, 2021.

Lanza, Joseph. *Elevator Music: A Surreal History of Muzak, Easy-Listening, and Other Moodsong*. Ann Arbor: University of Michigan Press, 2004.

Lamarre, Carl. "Drake & Kendrick Lamar's Rocky Relationship Explained." *Billboard*, February 14, 2025.

Leight, Elias. "Pop Stars Aren't Popping Like They Used To—Do Labels Have a Plan?" *Billboard*, August 2, 2023.

Martin, Rachel, and Vince Pearson. "More Than 'Kind Of Blue': In 1959, A Few Albums Changed Jazz Forever." *NPR*, April 29, 2019.

Millman, Ethan. "Conservative Fans Tried to Push Jason Aldean to Number One. They Just Missed." *Rolling Stone*, July 24, 2024.

Millman, Ethan. "'Rockin' Around the Christmas Tree' Is Now a Spanish AI Song." *Rolling Stone*, October 25, 2024.

Millman, Ethan. "Tekashi 6ix9ine: A Timeline of Terrible Behavior." *Rolling Stone*, January 18, 2024.

Page, Will, and Chris Dalla Riva. "'Glocalisation' of Music Streaming within and across Europe." The London School of Economics Europe in Question Discussion Paper Series, no. 182 (2023). https://www.lse.ac.uk/european-institute/Assets/Documents/LEQS-Discussion-Papers/EIQPaper182.pdf

Pelly, Liz. *Mood Machine: The Rise of Spotify and the Costs of the Perfect Playlist.* New York: Simon & Schuster, 2025.

Peoples, Glen. "Conservatives' Tendency to Buy Downloads Could Send 'Rich Men North of Richmond' to No. 1." *Billboard*, August 18, 2023.

Portwood, Jerry. "The Breakdown: Billie Eilish and Finneas on 'Bad Guy.'" *Rolling Stone*, December 16, 2019.

Serrà, Joan, Álvaro Corral, Marián Boguñá, Martín Haro, and Josep Ll. Arcos. "Measuring the Evolution of Contemporary Western Popular Music." *Scientific Reports* 2, no. 521 (2012). https://doi.org/10.1038/srep00521

Stebbings, Harry. "Mikey Shulman, CEO @Suno: The Future of Music, What is Gonna Happen?" *20VC*, January 10, 2025. Podcast. https://www.thetwentyminutevc.com/mikey-shulman

Strauss, Neil. "THE POP LIFE; Rap Is Slower Around Houston." *The New York Times*, November 23, 2000.

Tencer, Daniel. "10,000 AI Tracks Uploaded Daily to Deezer, Platform Reveals, as It Files Two Patents for New AI Detection Tool." *MusicBusinessWorldwide*, January 24, 2025.

Tencer, Daniel. "As Suno and Udio Admit Training AI with Unlicensed Music, Record Industry Says: 'There's Nothing Fair about Stealing an Artist's Life's Work.'" *MusicBusinessWorldwide*, August 5, 2024.

Tiday, Joe, and Sophia Smith Galer. "TikTok: The Story of a Social Media Giant." *BBC*, August 5, 2020.

Wakabayashi, Daisuke, and Jin Yu Young. "Defeated by A.I., A Legend in the Board Game Go Warns: Get Ready for What's Next." *The New York Times*, July 10, 2024.

# *Index*

Note: If you are looking for a specific song, please consult the entry for the band or artist that performed it.

Aaliyah   218
ABBA   106, 287, 298
Abdul, Paula   155, 179–80, 186
AC/DC   126
Ace, Johnny   8
Ace of Base   197, 234
Acker Bilk, Mr.   25
Adams, Bryan   152, 199–200
Adele   151, 242, 252, 255, 263, 296
Aerosmith   215, 247
Afrojack   255
Aguilera, Christina   202, 218, 228, 237
a-Ha   138
Aiken, Clay   224–5
Air Supply   140
album artwork   147–50
Aldean, Jason   112, 293, 302 n.8
All-4-One   186 n.3
Allen, Rick   168
Alpert, Herb   52, 68, 117, 141, 218
America (band)   69, 110
American Federation of Musicians
      (AFM)   28, 55, 164, 169
*American Idol* (TV show)   180, 225, 253
Analog sound   166, 202–4, 209
Andrews, Julie   238
Andrews Sisters, The   36
Angels, The   33 n.8
Animals, The   32, 162
Anka, Paul   11–12, 109, 162

Anthony, Oliver   293
Apple music products   213–15, 222,
      259–60, 267
Archies, The   63
Armstrong, Billie Joe   9 n.6
Armstrong, Louis   38, 85
artificial intelligence   290–2, 304
Ashanti   223, 226
Association, The   52, 62
Astley, Rick   162, 176
Atlantic (record label)   55, 76, 81, 145,
      147, 149
Audiomack   259, 264, 274, 282, 292
Austin, Patti   141
Auto-Tune, *see* pitch correction
Avalanches, The   222
Average White Band   100
Azalea, Iggy   272

B.o.B   1, 255
Baauer   263–4, 289
Bach, Johann Sebastian   265
Bacharach, Burt   239
Bachman-Turner Overdrive   98, 298
*Back to the Future* (film)   143
Backstreet Boys   234
Bad Bunny   270
Bad English   178, 179 n.1
Baez, Joan   9 n.6
Baker, Roy Thomas   229

Ballard, Hank 6
Bananarama 165
Bangles, The 98, 158
Bangs, Lester 30
Barenaked Ladies 214 n.4
Bar-Kays, The 221
Barry, Jeff 53
Basil, Toni 144
Beach Boys, The
  "Good Vibrations" 57, 58 n.9, 162
  "I Get Around," "Help Me,
    Rhonda" 42
  "Kokomo" 176
  Surf rock 22, 24, 38
Beatles, The
  "All You Need Is Love" 61
  Arriving in America and initial
    popularity 10–11, 28–32, 37–8,
    139, 198, 276
  Break-up 73, 77 n.6, 96, 109, 175
  "Come Together" 60
  "I Feel Fine" 40
  impact on music and
    songwriting 44–5, 53–7, 251
  "Hey Jude" 58, 180, 203
  "Let It Be," "The Long and Winding
    Road" 75
  "Love Me Do" 42
  "Paperback Writer" 50–1
  "Revolution 9" 217
  "Stars on 45" 153
  "Ticket to Ride" 39
  Twists 6
  "We Can Work It Out," "Penny Lane,"
    "Hello, Goodbye," "Get Back" 62
Bee Gees 109–10, 117, 120, 127, 130,
  143, 275–6, 289
Beethoven, Ludwig van 110, 224, 264
Bellamy Brothers, The 102
*Ben* (film) 86
Bennett, Tony 238
Berlin (band) 170
Berry, Chuck 10–11, 56, 85
Beyoncé 133, 214, 228–9, 240, 255,
  294, 296

Bieber, Justin 263–5, 270, 278–9, 295
  n.5, 304
Big and Rich 113
Big Boi 222
Big Bopper, The 8
Big Three, The 75
Biggie Smalls, *see* Notorious B.I.G., The
*Billboard* (magazine)
  chart methodology 91–6, 112–13,
    121–2, 178–80, 186–7, 262–3,
    293–4, 304
  charts and number ones 1–3, 13, 22,
    25–6, 35, 117, 141, 147
  magazine reporting 81, 296–8
  magazine history 4
BitTorrent 212, 259
Biz Markie 77
Black Eyed Peas 239 n.2, 255
*Blackboard Jungle* (film) 141
BLACKstreet 220
Blige, Mary J. 221 n.7
Blondie 121, 123, 131, 135, 162, 166, 170
Bloodshy and Avant 247
Blossoms, The 39
Blue Swede 98
Blues (musical style) 46, 89, 113, 192,
  273, 303
Blunt, James 247
Bobbettes, The 36
Bogan, Lucille 192
Bolton, Michael 193 n.6, 199
Bon Jovi 159, 199, 234
Bonds, Gary U.S. 31
Bone Thugs-N-Harmony 189
Boney M. 156
Bono 173
Boone, Debby 126, 180–1
Boone, Pat 2, 4, 17, 80, 162
Boston (band) 175
Bourget, Ernest 204–6, 209, 212
Bowie, David 95 n.2, 106 n.14, 153
Boyz II Men 181, 198, 227
Brandenburg, Karlheinz 207
Brandy 215, 227
Braxton, Toni 190, 215

Bread (band)   74
*Breakfast Club, The* (film)   143
British Invasions   11, 37, 139–41, 184
Bronson, Fred   147, 227
Brothers Johnson, The   222
Brown, Bobby   176, 186
Brown, Chris   249, 298
Brown, James   104, 251, 277
Browns, The   11, 13, 68
Brubeck, Dave   281
Bryan, Zach   293
Bryon, Dennis   108–9, 127 n.9
BTS   293 n.3, 296–7, 304
Buffalo Springfield   73
Buggles, The   135
Busta Rhymes   257
*Butch Cassidy and the Sundance Kid*
      (film)   141
Byrds, The   50–1, 57 n.8
Byrne, David   67

C+C Music Factory   186
Cabello, Camila   279, 298
California, Randy   232
Campbell, Glen   102, 112
Capaldi, Lewis   284
Capitol (record label)   30, 91, 175
Captain and Tenille   110, 128
Cara, Irene   142, 170
Caray, Harry   114–15
Cardi B   270, 273, 278, 292, 304
Carefrees, The   29
Carey, Mariah   181–2, 196–9, 214, 227,
      246, 255, 304
Carlsson, Andreas   234
Carmichael, Hoagie   16
Carnes, Kim   153
Carpenter, Sabrina   286, 298
Carpenters, The   69, 87, 108
Carter, Ron   219
Casablanca (record label)   94–5, 149
Cash, Johnny   192
Castiglione, Baldassare   248
censorship   8, 79, 189–93, 202
Chainsmokers, The   278–9

Chance the Rapper   265
Chandler, Alfred D., Jr.   144
Change (band)   220
Chantels, The   36
Charles, Ray   1 n.1, 16, 41–2, 252
Cheap Trick   176
Checker, Chubby   6, 14, 38, 162
Cheiron (studio)   234, 237, 247
Cher   62, 87, 226
Chic (band)   116
Chicago (band)   104, 110, 152, 176
Chiffons, The   36, 76
Child, Destiny's   222, 227–8
Childish Gambino   270 n.3
Chordettes, The   36
Christgau, Robert   251
Clapton, Eric   77, 110
Clarkson, Kelly   225, 234–5, 250
classic rock (musical style)   122–4
Clovers, The   80–1, 192
Coates, Odia   109
Cochran, Eddie   8, 56, 245
Cocker, Joe   141
Coldplay   52, 251 n.8, 296
Coleman, Ornette   281
Collins, Phil   140, 146, 149, 154, 166,
      175, 189
Coltrane, John   238, 281
Columbia (record label)   55, 91, 130, 144,
      147, 149
Combs, Sean   221, 226, 228
Commodores   121–2
compact disc (CD)
      history of physical media   5, 202, 209,
         214–15, 260, 269, 299
      record contracts   212
      royalties and revenues   79, 195,
         206, 213
computer algorithms   261, 270, 286, 295
Coolidge, Calvin   3 n.3
Coolio   189
Cooper, Alice   112 n.1
Cortez, Dave "Baby"   14, 162
Costello, Elvis   13
Cougar, John   150

Count Basie 65 n.1
country (musical style) 55, 112–14, 121–2, 186 n.3, 293–5
Country Joe 202
court cases 75–83, 192–3, 209, 213
cover songs 13, 79–81, 217–18
CR-78, 166
Crane, Stephen 172
Crazy Town 210 n.3
Creed (band) 223 n.10
Croce, Jim 68, 87, 124 n.7
Crosby, Bing 27
Crosby, Stills, Nash, and Young 73
Cross, Christopher 131, 151
Crystals, The 39, 128
Cudi, Kid 304
cultural memory 2, 159–63, 223 n.10
culture club 140
Current (band) 117
Curtis, Eddie 81
Cutting Crew 159
Cyrus, Billy Ray 112
Cyrus, Miley 238, 279, 304

DaBaby 286
Daddy Cool 80
Daddy Yankee 270
Daft Punk 120, 279
Dahl, Steve 114–16, 119
Dale, Dick 22
Damian, Michael 173
dance and dancing
    1960s dance crazes 6, 41
    disco 103–5, 118
    films 143–4
    music videos 137–8
    TikTok 286
Danja 247
Darin, Bobby 14
Davis, Mac 73
Davis, Miles 281
Davis, Sammy, Jr. 85, 126
Dawes, Charles C. 3 n.3
De La Soul 222
Dean, Ester 240, 246

Dean, Jimmy 29 n.7
DeBarge 223
Decca (record label) 55, 144, 147–8
Dee, Joey 38
Dees, Rick 108
Deezer 259, 264, 292
Def Jam (record label) 145, 149
Def Leppard 57 n.8, 168, 237
Del Río, Los 182
Del Shannon 16
Dem Franchize Boys 240 n.3
Denniz PoP 233–8, 244
Denver, John 73, 97, 110
Depp, Johnny 302 n.9
Derulo, Jason 230, 289
DeShannon, Jackie 245
Desiigner 273
D4L 240
Diamond, Neil 73, 80, 94, 130, 158 n.1, 183
Diddy, *see* Combs, Sean
digital audio workstation 202, 238–44, 282
digital sound 5, 78, 164, 202–4, 209, 219–22, 226, 299
DiMucci, Dion 36
Dinning, Mark 8, 18
Dion, Céline 200, 225, 234, 292
Diplo 263
Dire Straits 138
disco (musical style)
    backlash and homophobia 108, 114–20, 125
    dance clubs 90
    DJs and mixing 102–5, 167, 217
    sexism 123
    Wadlow, Bill 91–2, 95
Disco Demolition Night 114–20
distribution 146–7, 292–3
Dixie Cups, The 36
DJ Jazzy Jeff 177, 221
DJ Khaled 265
DJ Kool Herc 215–19
DJ Screw 288 n.2
DJs (dance clubs) 90, 103–5, 167, 215–17

DJs (radio)   37, 90–6, 114, 130, 175
Doja Cat   250, 288, 294
Donaldson, Bo   106
Doobie Brothers, The   100, 130
Doors, The   62, 189–90
Doo-wop (musical style)   14, 22, 34, 192
Dorsey, Jimmy   25, 27
Dorsey, Tommy   27
Douglas, Carl   96
Dowell, Joe   39–40
Downes, Geoffrey   135 n.2
Dr. Dre   1 n.1, 220–2, 253
Dr. Luke   235, 237–8, 247, 250
Drake   166, 210 n.2, 257, 272, 276, 279, 286, 301–4
Drifters, The   6, 16 n.9
Driftwood, Jimmy   17
drum machine   86, 104, 140, 164–72, 219–22, 235
Dupri, Jermaine   220
Duran Duran   136, 140, 143
Dylan, Bob   1, 10–11, 44–9, 51–2, 58, 72 n.5, 109, 301

Eagles   1 n.1, 108, 110, 129, 131, 162
Earth, Wind and Fire   107, 298
*Ed Sullivan Show, The* (TV show)   30, 189–90
Edwards, Tommy   3, 181
*808* (film)   166
Eilish, Billie   9, 282
Ek, Daniel   259–60
Elegants, The   14, 162
Elliman, Yvonne   117
Ellington, Duke   113
Elofsson, Jörgen   234
Eminem   9, 13, 223, 253, 255, 257, 279
emo rap (musical style)   274
Emotions, The   126, 182
Eno, Brian   251
Eric B.   218
Ertegün, Ahmet   81
Estefan, Gloria   174, 199
Europe (band)   237
Eurythmics   140

Evans   60
Evans, Faith   221
Everly Brothers, The   19
Extreme (band)   197

Faces (band)   73
Faith, Percy   12, 180–1
Falco   134, 152 n.10
Falsetto   31, 39, 80, 104, 107–8, 117 n.5, 174
Fanning, Shawn   208
Farian, Frank   156–7
Fats Domino   10
Fender, Freddie   98
Fergie   239 n.2, 255
5th Dimension, The   61–2, 220
Fifty Cent   201–2, 221 n.7, 235, 253, 267 n.2
file-sharing   202, 207–15, 222, 259–60
Film and music   55, 141–4
Finneas   282
Flack, Roberta   69, 87, 110
*Flashdance* (film)   142–3, 170
Fleetwood Mac   127, 162, 288
Fleetwoods, The   9, 19
Flo Rida   255, 277
Flock of Seagulls   140
Flood, Dick   13
Floyd, Eddie   128
Folds, Ben   71
folk (musical style)
    literary lyrics   51–2
    1960s   14, 30, 44, 49, 75
    tragedy songs   7
Fonsi, Luis   270
Fontana, Wayne   40
Foster, Stephen   75, 83
Four Preps, The   29
Four Tops   42, 62, 149
Fox, Michael J.   143
Foxx, Jamie   252, 255
Frampton, Peter   77, 174
Francis, Connie   19, 42, 162
Frank Ocean   113
Franklin, Aretha   50, 58 n.9, 175

Freddie and the Dreamers 41, 162
Freedom Williams 186
The Fresh Prince, *see* Will Smith
Fuentealba, Victor 169
fun. 265
Funky Meters, The 219
future 303–4

Gabriel, Peter 175
Gamble, Kenny and Leon Huff 251
Gangsta rap (musical style) 271
Garfunkel 51, 62, 75, 98, 141, 162
Gates, David 74
Gaudio, Bob 130
Gaye, Marvin 58, 82, 117, 166,
    187, 272
Gaynor, Gloria 116, 127 n.8
Geffen (record label) 146, 212
gender and gender issues
    girl groups 34–7
    lyrics 5, 50, 224
    radio 122–6
    rock 'n' roll 11
    violence 18, 195, 245–50
*General Hospital* (TV show) 141
Genesis (band) 175
Gentry, Bobbie 51–2
Ghost, Amanda 247
Gibb, Andy 116–18, 130
Gibb, Barry 117 n.5, 120, 127
Gibson, Debbie 176
Gilder, Nick 121
Gilmer, Jimmy 23
Gioia, Ted 9, 281
Glass Animals 302 n.9
Glover, Henry 53
Goffin, Gerry 40, 47, 151
Goldsboro, Bobby 59
Gomez, Selena 284
Goodman, Benny 3
Gordy, Berry 35, 37, 254
Gotye 262
*Graduate, The* (film) 141
Grammy Awards 17, 125, 155–6, 281
Grand Funk 68, 110

Grande, Ariana 100 n.7, 234, 265, 277,
    296, 298, 304
Grandmaster Flash 226
Grant, Amy 175, 199
Grasso, Francis 103–5
Grateful Dead 117
*Grease* (film) 117
Green, Al 87, 275
Greenberg, Florence 36
Greene, Lorne 29
Greenwich, Ellie 53
Griffin, Jim 212
Grohl, Dave 210
Guess Who, The 68
Guns N' Roses 173
Guthrie, Gary 130

Haley, Bill 10, 141
Hall, Daryl 103 n.11, 136–7, 150, 166
Hall, Tom T. 50 n.6
Halsey 274, 278–9
Hamilton, Joe Frank 92–3
Hammer, Jan 143
Hammer, MC 177, 303
Hammerstein, Oscar, II 238
Handsome, Charlie 294 n.4
hard rock (musical style)
    1970s 68, 117 n.4
    1980s 137 n.4, 159 n.2, 173
    1990s 197, 199, 210, 258
Harlow, Jack 294 n.4, 297
Harris, Larry 94–5
Harrison, George 29, 68–9, 75–7, 96,
    162, 175
Harrison, Wilbert 1 n.1
Harry J 81
Haskell, Jimmie 52
Hayes, Isaac 67, 193
Hazlewood, Lee 50 n.6
Heap, Imogen 230
Hefner, Hugh 92, 93 n.1
Hendrix, Jimi 38 n.10, 47
Henley, Don 108–9
Herman's Hermits 40, 60
Hiatt, Brian 301

Hicklin and Miller Tests    193
Hicks, Taylor    253–4
Hi-Five    199
Higgenson, Tom    242
Hildebrand, Andy    225–6
Hill, Lauryn    220, 276
hip-hop/rap (musical style)
    drum machines    166
    emo rap (musical style)    273–4
    history of genre    215–17
    lyrics    186–7, 189, 193–4
    1990s    177–8
    relationship to country    112, 294
    sampling    77, 215–17, 230–1
    snap (musical style)    240 n.3
    track-and-hook    240
    2000s    235
    2010s    257
Holland-Dozier-Holland    251
Holly, Buddy    8, 11, 45, 56
Hollywood Argyles, The    5
Holmes, Rupert    129–30
Honey Cone    86
Horn, Trevor    135 n.2
Hornsby, Bruce    166
Horton, Johnny    17, 181, 191
Houston, Thelma    130
Houston, Whitney
    "Didn't We Almost Have It All," "So
        Emotional," "Where Do Broken
        Hearts Go"    176
    "Exhale (Shoop Shoop)"    200
    "Greatest Love of All"    175
    "Higher Love"    163
    "How Will I Know"    149
    "I Wanna Dance With
        Somebody"    166
    "I Will Always Love You"    181, 196,
        243 n.4
    "I'm Your Baby Tonight," "All the Man
        I Need"    199
    New Jersey    65 n.1
    "Saving All My Love For You"    151
Hues Corporation    98
Hugo, Chad    235

Human League, The    140, 175
Hyland, Brian    17

Idol, Billy    176
Iglesias, Enrique    227
Ingram, James    141, 199
Ini Kamoze    200
Instrumentals    12, 21–2, 25–8, 100, 281,
    283–4
Intellectual property and copyright    75–
    83, 204–6
Interpolation    80–1, 218
INXS    176
Isaac Newton, Sir    43

J. Cole    301
J Balvin    270
J Dilla    222
J. Geils Band    154
Ja Rule    226, 228
Jacks, Terry    77 n.7
Jackson, Andrew    17
Jackson 5, The    75, 84, 87
Jackson, Janet    165, 190, 198–200,
    220, 227
Jackson, Michael
    "Bad," "The Way You Make Me
        Feel"    171
    "Ben"    73, 86
    "Beat It"    103 n.11, 150 n.8, 152
    "Black or White"    187 n.4
    "Don't Stop 'Til You Get
        Enough"    127
    "I Just Can't Stop Loving You," "Dirty
        Diana"    175–6
    "Man in the Mirror"    158–9
    Music videos    137–8
    "Rock With You"    119
    "Say Say Say"    150
    "You Are Not Alone"    195
Jam, Cult    163
James, Harry    27
James, Rick    303
James, Tommy    53
Jan    23

Jawsh 685  289
Jay-Z  214, 235, 254–5, 257
jazz (musical style)
    big bands and instrumentals  3, 14,
        25–8, 55, 214
    improvisation  67, 238
    1959  281
    quotes about genre  113, 276
Jelly Roll  298
Jepsen, Carly Rae  264
Jett, Joan  142 n.5
Jimin  304
Jimmy Jam  198, 220
Jobs, Steve  213–14
Joe  227
Joel, Billy  131, 149, 187
John, Elton  2, 80, 102, 103 n.11, 110,
        150, 152, 199, 202
Jonas Brothers  265
Jones, Quincy  137 n.4, 170
Joplin, Janis  69, 124 n.7
Jordan, Montell  189
Josiah and the Bonnevilles  303
Jungkook  297

Kabaka, Remi, Jr.  166
Kaempfert, Bert  12, 37, 162, 214
Kakehashi, Ikutaro  170
Karim, Jawed  262
Karol G  298
Kasem, Casey  90, 95
KC and the Sunshine Band  102, 104,
        110, 130–1
Kelly, R.  195, 225
Kendricks, Eddie  73
Kennedy, John F.  24, 28–31, 49
Kennedy, Robert F.  49–50
Kerker, Gustave  248
Kesha  238, 247, 250, 279
Keys, Alicia  212, 247, 254–5
Keys and chord changes  153, 242–3,
        272–3
Kilmister, Lemmy  199
Kim, Andy  94
King, Carole  40, 73

King, Martin Luther, Jr.  49
Kingsmen, The  31
Kingston Trio, The  7
Knack, The  121
Knight, Glady  1 n.1, 87, 150
Kool and the Gang  120, 177
Kostal, Irwin  238
Kriss Kross  189
Kroeger, Chad  227
KRS-One  194
Kygo  163

LaBelle (band)  98, 162
labor and labor issues  28, 55, 163–4,
        169–71
Lacy, Steve  288
Lady Gaga  234, 250, 278, 289, 298
Lamar, Kendrick  265, 279, 296,
        300 n.7, 301
lang, k.d.  265
Latin (musical style)  33, 270
Latto  297
Lauper, Cyndi  146, 175
Lavigne, Avril  238
Lawrence, Vicki  1 n.1, 70 n.3
Lawrence, Vince  116
Led Zeppelin  89, 104, 123, 139, 232
Lee, Brenda  14–15, 162, 303
Leeuwen, Robbie van  75
Legend, John  275
Leiber, Jerry  36
Leibniz, Gottfried  43
Lennon, John
    Beatles, The  29, 32, 53, 56, 61–2, 238
    "Fame"  95 n.2
    "(Just Like) Starting Over"  124 n.7
    "Whatever Gets You Thru the
        Night"  96
Lewis, Don  163–4, 170
Lewis, Huey  143, 175
Lewis, Jerry Lee  11
Lewis, Terry  198, 220
Lil Jon  240 n.3, 243–4
Lil' Kim  218
Lil Nas X  111–12, 121, 294, 297, 304

Lil Wayne   255, 257, 265, 298
LimeWire   202, 214, 260
Limp Bizkit   210
Linn, Roger   167, 170, 220
LinnDrum   166–7, 170
Lipa, Dua   120
Lipps Inc.   119–20
Lisa, Lisa   163
Little Brother Montgomery   113
Little Richard   11, 44, 56
Live music   202, 257–9
Lizzo   288, 304
LL Cool J   221
LMFAO   254
Lobos, Los   166
Loeb, Lisa   189
Loggins, Kenny   149
Lopez, Jennifer   221, 227–8
Lorde   261, 276 n.7
Lorentzen, Martin   259
*Los Angeles Times* (newspaper)   90,
      156, 178
Love, Mike   57
Love Unlimited Orchestra   67
Lovin' Spoonful, The   62
Ludacris   221 n.8, 255
Lukather, Steve   152
Lulu   46
Lynyrd Skynyrd   174
Lyrics and lyrical trends   7–9, 46–52, 70
      n.3, 186–93, 270–1

M (artist)   121
McCall, C.W.   106
McCartney, Paul
   "Band on the Run"   57, 97
   Beatles, The   29, 53, 56, 238
   "Coming Up"   131
   "Ebony & Ivory"   153–4
   "Junior's Farm"   96
   "My Love"   69 n.2
   "Listen to What the Man Said"   104
   "Say Say Say"   150
   "Silly Love Songs"   109
   "Uncle Albert/Admiral Halsey"   87

"With a Little Luck"   130
McCoy, Van   104
McCrae, George   104
McGuire, Barry   50
McKee, Bonnie   236, 246, 253
Macklemore   267, 279
McLean, Don   87, 162
Madonna
   "Crazy for You"   146
   "Like a Prayer"   173
   "Live to Tell," "Papa Don't
      Preach"   167–8
   "Music"   210
   Music videos   138, 190, 289
   "Open Your Heart"   175
   "Take a Bow"   200
   Relationship to disco   120
   "Vogue," "This Used to Be My
      Playground"   199
   "Who's That Girl"   174
MAGIC!   265
*Major Labels* (book)   54, 57, 187
Mamas and the Papas, The   45 n.3
Mancini, Henri   63
Manilow, Barry   100, 109, 130, 298
Mann, Manfred   26, 102
Mannequin Challenge   264
Marcels, The   14
Mario   239
Maroon 5   237, 255, 277–8
Marsh, Dave   116
Martika   189
Martin, Dean   38, 85
Martin, George   154
Martin, Max   224, 234–9, 242, 247, 249,
      251–3, 276, 296
Martin, Ricky   202
Marvelettes, The   36, 108
Marx, Richard   162–3, 199
Matthew Effect   45, 49
Mauriat, Paul   62
Mayer, John   298
Meat Loaf   9, 182
Meco   117
Meek, Joe   21 n.1

Megan Thee Stallion   286, 292, 304
Mellencamp, John, *see* Cougar, John
Men at Work   144
Mendes, Shawn   298
Mercury, Freddie   229
Merton, Robert K.   43–5, 49
Metallica   210
MFSB   101
M.I.A.   302
*Miami Vice* (TV show)   143
Michael, George   140, 166–7, 175–7, 199
Migos   273
Miller, Glenn   3, 27, 61
Miller, Steve   80–1, 110, 154, 218
Milli Vanilli   155–7, 178, 199
Mingus, Charles   276, 281
Miracles, The   36, 87, 102
*Mission: Impossible* (TV show)   141
Missy Elliott   235
Mitchell, Guy   15
Modugno, Domenico   2, 37, 181
Monica (artist)   218, 220, 227
Monica (friend)   74, 222
Monkees, The   50, 57
Montgomery, John Michael   186 n.3
Moroder, Giorgio   117, 170
Morrison, Jim   189–90
Motown (record label)   31, 35–8, 104,
      145, 149, 187, 251, 254
Mozart, Wolfgang Amadeus   80, 134
MPC (sampler)   220, 221 n.7
MP3   202, 206–8, 214
Mr. Mister   143, 154
Mullen, Larry, Jr.   171
Multiple discovery   43–5
Musgraves, Kacey   293
music industry evolution   14, 52–6,
      144–50, 206–9, 259–64, 293
music streaming   196, 206, 212–13,
      259–70, 282–4, 293–9
MTV   134–44, 147, 155, 175, 190, 194,
      262–3, 289
music videos   111, 133–47, 149–50, 161,
      175, 190, 202, 263, 270 n.3, 289
Musique concrète (musical style)   216–17

Muzak   283–4
Mýa   218
Myles, Alannah   199
Mystikal   227, 243

Napster   208–15, 222, 259–61, 292, 299
Nelly   112, 228, 255
Nelson, Ricky   2, 4–5, 181, 245
Neptunes, The   235
New Jersey   1, 65–6, 106 n.13, 157, 159
      n.2, 226–7, 251, 274 n.6
New Kids on the Block   174, 197, 199
*New York Times, The* (newspaper)   10,
      24, 29, 149, 194–5, 250, 290, 295–6
Newman, Randy   79
Newton-John, Olivia   106, 110, 130–1,
      152, 181
Next (band)   202
Ne-Yo   239–41, 250, 255
Nickelback   227
Nicki Minaj   111, 234, 302–3
Nicks, Stevie   127, 222
Nilsson, Harry   69
Nine Inch Nails   111
Nixon, Richard   94
Noone, Peter   61
Notorious B.I.G., The   218, 221, 257, 281
NPR   37, 116, 281
NSYNC   224 n.11, 234
N.W.A   177, 194

O'Connor, Sinéad   98, 199
O'Day, Alan   130
O'Sullivan, Gilbert   77
Oakey, Philip   140
Obama, Barack   133
Oates, John   103 n.11, 136–7, 150, 166
Ocean, Billy   154, 167, 175
*Officer and a Gentleman, An* (film)   141
Ohio Players   103, 110
OMI   267
One Direction   234
112 (band)   221
Orbison, Roy   16–17, 21, 42
Orlando, Tony   85, 110

Osmond, Donny   73, 85
Outkast   218, 222, 228
Outsyders, The   247
Owen, Richard   76
Owl City   253

Paak, Anderson   301
P. Diddy, *see* Combs, Sean
P.M. Dawn   177–8, 187, 193–4
Page, Jimmy   232
Page, Larry   54
Page, Will   262, 282, 293
Palmer, Robert   166
Parker, Ray Jr.   152
Parker, Sean   208, 259–61
parlor music (musical style)   125
Parr, John   152
Parton, Dolly   9 n.6, 134, 154, 196
Passion Pit   126
Paul, Sean   228, 240, 272
Payola   93
Peaches and Herb   130
Pelczynski, Michael   268
performance rights and publishing   55,
      78, 205
Perry, Katy
   "California Gurls"   1 n.1, 236
   "Dark Horse"   279
   "E.T."   255
   "Firework"   230
   "I Kissed a Girl"   237
   "Last Friday Night (T.G.I.F.)"   242
   "Part of Me"   236
   "Roar"   261
   "Teenage Dream"   252–3
   Toplining   246
   "Waking Up in Vegas"   234
Pesci, Joe   38 n.10
Pet Shop Boys   166
Peter, Paul, and Mary   50
Petey Pablo   244, 255
Petras, Kim   250, 286
Petrillo, James C.   28, 169
Petty, Tom   151, 213
Philips (record label)   30, 209

Pink   218, 236–7, 250, 279
Pink Floyd   98, 117
pitch correction   164, 225–6
Pittman, Bob   134, 140
Plain White T's   242
Plant, Robert   89, 104, 232
Platters, The   2
Playboi Carti   297–8
Poison (band)   167
Poke and Tone   221
Police, The   149, 221
Polo G   291
Porcaro, Jeff   152
Posse cut (musical style)   265
Post Malone   269, 274, 279, 289, 294, 304
Powfu   9
Powter, Daniel   254
Presley, Elvis   3, 5, 10–12, 39, 42, 44, 47,
      73, 134, 196
Preston, Billy   69 n.2, 94
Preston, Johnny   5, 8
Price, Lloyd   9, 56
Prince   89–90, 138, 149, 171 n.6, 174,
      183, 199, 202
Public Enemy   177, 194, 222
Puff Daddy, *see* Combs, Sean
Puth, Charlie   263

Quavo   265
Queen   2, 57, 117, 122, 229
Queen Pen   220

R&B (musical style)
   "I Swear"   186 n.3
   "Leave the Door Open"   301
   "Peaches"   295 n.5
   Race and racism   35, 113–14,
      122–6
   "So Sick"   239
   Songwriting   55
race and racial issues
   disco   92, 114, 116–18
   lyrics   5, 50, 188–9
   motown   34–7, 187
   music videos   137 n.3

R&B   35, 113–14, 122–6
Rock music   10–11, 71, 122–6
radio
 *American Top 40* (radio show)   90–6
 censorship   8, 190
 deregulation   14 n.8
 disco   114–15
 fade out   32
 legal disagreements   28, 55, 164, 169
 Muzak   283
 programming and race   121–6
Radiohead   211
Rae Sremmurd   264
Rakim   218, 257
Rami   224, 234
Rascals, The   50, 62
Ravon   218
Rawling, Brian   226
RCA (record label)   55, 144
recording contracts   39, 145–7, 211–12
recording technology
 analog to digital transition   5–6,
  202–4, 299
 digital audio workstation   238–
  44, 282
 drum machines   164–71
 microphones and
  amplification   27, 70
 sampling   219
 studio as an instrument   45
Redding, Otis   50 n.6, 58, 124 n.7, 128
Reddy, Helen   87, 110
Reggae/Dancehall (musical style)   80,
  123, 197, 240, 265, 272, 277
REO Speedwagon   154
Replacements, The   126
Reynolds   92–3
Rhythm Heritage   105, 117
RIAA   206–7, 210, 261
Rich, Charlie   87
Rich the Kid   297
Richie, Lionel   122, 149, 150, 152, 154
Right Said Fred   198
Righteous Brothers, The   24 n.3, 62
Riley, Jeannie C.   50

Ringtones   240 n.3, 289
Robbins, Marty   6
Robinson, Smokey   38, 87
Robyn   234
Rock 'n' roll (musical style)   10–11, 14,
  24 n.3, 56, 71 n.4, 190
*Rocky* (film)   117
*Rocky III* (film)   143
Rodgers, Jimmie   8
Rodrigo, Olivia   3, 297
Roe, Tommy   40, 62
Rogers, Kenny   121–2, 154, 238
Rogers, Nile   116, 154
Rogers, Richard   238
Roland Corporation   166, 170, 219
*Rolling Stone* (magazine)   109, 112, 116,
  139, 150, 210, 273, 291
Rolling Stones, The
 aging   4 n.5
 Altamont Speedway Free Festival   258
 Arriving in America   11, 139
 "Brown Sugar"   71 n.4
 "Honky Tonk Women"   63
 lyrics   51
 "Miss You"   123
 "Ruby Tuesday"   62
 "Start Me Up"   195
Ronettes, The   24
Ronson, Mark   219, 276–7
Ronstadt, Linda   110
Rose, Axl   173
Rose, David   25
Rose Royce   103
Rosner, Alex   118
Ross, Diana   59, 72, 102 n.9, 110, 120,
  150, 220–1
Roy, Harry   191
royalties
 fair use   291
 federal regulations   78–9, 81
 performance   195–6, 205
 recording contracts   146, 211–12
 streaming   266–70, 283–4
Ruby and the Romantics   27
Run-DMC   186

Rupe, Art　56
Rutherford, Mike　175

Sadler, Barry, SSgt.　59–60
Sakamoto, Kyu　37
Sampling　77, 215–22, 230–1
Sanneh, Kelefa　54, 57, 187
Santana　202
Santo and Johnny　11
*Saturday Night Fever* (film)　117, 127,
　　142–3
*Saturday Night Live* (TV show)　136, 235
Savage Garden　215
Schaeffer, Pierre　216
Scott, Travis　57, 257–9, 269, 296,
　　302, 304
Sean, Jay　242
Second World War　8, 27, 37, 55, 144
Sedaka, Neil　34, 110
Seeger, Pete　50 n.7
Seger, Bob　168
Seitzer, Dieter　207
Selby, Sidney "Guitar Crusher"　273 n.5
Sembello, Michael　142
Semisonic　151
sexuality and homophobia　92, 114,
　　116–18
Shaboozey　297
Shaggy　218
Shakira　248 n.6
Shangri-Las, The　41
Shaw, Artie　27
Shaw, Charles　156
Sheeley, Sharon　245
Sheeran, Ed　82, 263, 278
Shellback　237–8, 249, 276
Sheriff (band)　175
Shirelles, The　6, 16 n.9, 36, 50
Shocking Blue　74–5
Shore, Dinah　28
Shuggie Otis　222
Shulman, Mikey　290
Sia　272
Silk (band)　193
Silk Sonic　301

Silver Connection　100
Simon, Paul　49, 110
Simon　51, 62, 75, 98, 141, 162
Simple Minds　143
Sinatra, Frank　3, 6, 27, 56–7, 65 n.1,
　　85, 117
Sinatra, Nancy　50
Singing Nun, The　30–1, 37
Sir Mix-a-Lot　190
Sister Sledge　221
6ix9ine　302
Slash　173
Sledge, Percy　62
Smeezingtons, The　255
Smith, Bessie　192
Smith, Sam　286
Smith, Will　177, 221
Snoop Dogg　1 n.1, 13, 235, 255
Snow (artist)　197
Socrates　15
Sodel, Lee　290, 292
Soft rock (musical style)　68–74
Somajo, Sophia　249
song structure　9–10, 57, 96–102,
　　105, 237
songwriting　45, 53–6, 102, 230–44, 246
Sonny　62
Sony (record label)　145, 209, 213
Soul, David　130
Soul, Jimmy　41, 162
*Soul Train* (TV show)　136
Soulja Boy Tell'em　240 n.3
Souls of Mischief　74
*Sound of Music, The* (film)　238
SoundCloud　112, 259, 263–4, 268, 274,
　　282
SoundScan　178–88, 230, 297
Southern Tones, The　252
Spandau Ballet　177
Spears, Britney　223, 234, 237, 247, 249,
　　251, 255
Spector, Phil　18, 24, 38–9, 77, 195
Spice Girls　227, 289
Spinners, The　94
Spirit (band)　232

Spotify
  data   33, 69, 73, 167, 183, 190, 271
  fake artists   282–5, 292
  playlists   1, 168, 284
  service history   258–62, 299
  Spotifycore   295–6
Springfield, Rick   154
Springsteen, Bruce   2, 65–7, 72 n.5, 102
  n.10, 126, 300
Squier, Billy   149
Squire, George Owen   282
Staples Singers, The   80–1, 110, 162, 183
*Star is Born, A* (film)   278
*Star Wars* (film)   117
Stargate   239–41, 247
Starland Vocal Band   100
Starr, Edwin   75
Starr, Ringo   2, 29, 77, 79–80, 96
Stars on 45 (band)   153
Starship (band)   152, 154, 175
Stefani, Gwen   255
Steinman, Jim   182
Steinweiss, Alex   147
Stevens, Ray   75, 108
Stewart, Amii   128
Stewart, Rod   73, 110, 115, 200
Stoller, Mike   36
Stone, Sly   49–50, 86–7, 165
Storch, Scott   235
Stories (band)   71 n.4
Storz, Todd   91
Stravinsky, Igor   203
Strawberry Alarm Clock   60
*Streets of Fire* (film)   182
Streisand, Barbra   87, 110, 120, 130–1,
  183, 278
Studdard, Ruben   225
Styles, Harry   304
Styx   121
Sully, Susan Ann   140
Summer, Donna   117, 123, 131, 170, 202
Suno   282, 290–2
Supremes, The   25, 31, 34, 36, 42, 51,
  58–9, 62–3, 72, 171
Surf rock (musical style)   22–3

Survivor (band)   143
Swae Lee   269
*S.W.A.T.* (TV show)   105
Swift, Taylor   133–4, 249, 266–7, 274,
  276, 279, 284, 290, 300–1, 303–4
SWV   200
SZA   286, 302

Taio Cruz   242
Talking Heads   67
Tartikoff, Brandon   143
Taste of Honey, A   118
Taupin, Bernie   152
Taylor, Chip   54
Taylor, Derek   57
Taylor, James   68
Taylor, Johnnie   110
Taylor, Mark   226
Tears for Fears   140
Teddy Bears, The   18
Teddy Swims   296
Teenage tragedy songs (musical style)   7–
  9, 17–18, 41, 59, 274
television and music   30, 57, 61, 133–44,
  167 n.3, 189–90, 225, 253
Temptations, The   38, 63, 73, 84, 86, 289
Tems   303
Terror Squad   235
Theater and music   10, 12, 38, 55
Thicke, Robin   272
Thomas, B. J.   63, 105 n.12, 141
Thomas, Timmy   165
Three Dog Night   71 n.4, 79, 87
T.I.   255, 272
Tiffany   166–7
TikTok   111, 282, 285–9, 292, 297,
  299, 303
Timbaland   218, 235, 255
Timberlake, Justin   120, 235, 255, 265, 298
*Time* (magazine)   29, 68, 90, 108, 190
time signatures   61, 103–4, 151, 166–7
Timmer, Jan   209
Timmy T   197
TLC   189, 196 n.7, 200, 224, 227
Tornados, The   21

Toto   152–3, 289
Townsend, Ed   82–3
Townsend, Pete   75
T-Pain   240 n.3, 255
TR-808, 166–7, 197, 273
Trap (musical style)   112, 273–4, 277, 303
Travolta, John   117, 127, 130, 143
Troggs, The   54
*Turn the Beat Around: The Secret History
    of Disco* (book)   90, 103
Turtles, The   57 n.8
Twista   255
2 Chainz   273
2 Live Crew   193
2Pac   1 n.1, 190 n.5, 281
Ty Dolla $ign   297
Tyler, Bonnie   140
Tyler, the Creator   125, 298
Tymes, The   33, 275

UB40   158 n.1, 197
Ulrich, Lars   210
Underwood, Carrie   234
Universal (record label)   145, 213
Upton, George   249
Usher   166, 227–8, 237, 243–4, 252
    n.9, 254
U2   140, 171–2, 251 n.8

Valens, Ritchie   8
Valli, Frankie   31, 42, 105, 106 n.13, 117
Vampire Weekend   74–5, 77
Van Halen, Eddie   112 n.1, 137 n.4
Vanilla Ice   186
Vaughan, Stevie Ray   154
Veeck, Bill   114
Velvet Underground, The   251
Velvetettes, The   36
Vera, Billy   167
Verne, Larry   9, 162
Vertical Horizon   225
Video Music Awards (VMAs)   133–4
Vietnam War   49–50, 59–60, 75, 85
    n.11, 189
Vinton, Bobby   33, 37, 42, 50, 68, 162

Violence songs and artists   18, 21 n.1,
    115, 195, 249–50, 257–8

Wahlberg, Mark   186
Waite, John   143
*Wall Street Journal* (newspaper)   81, 190
Wallen, Morgan   294–304
War (band)   218
Ward, Anita   130–1
Wardlow, Bill   91–2, 94–5
Warner (record label)   145–7, 213
Warnes, Jennifer   141, 176
Warren, Diane   179 n.1, 215, 247
Warwick, Dionne   94, 150, 239, 294
Washington, Grover   74
*Washington Post, The* (newspaper)   193, 224
Weeknd, The   263, 274, 279, 286, 304
Welk, Lawrence   14
Wells, Mary   38, 149
Wesley, Fred   104
West, Kanye   13, 133–4, 221 n.8, 234 n.1,
    252, 255, 289, 297
*West Side Story* (film)   141
Wham!   99 n.4, 140, 154
Whitburn, Joel   147
White, Barry   67, 100
White, Karyn   198
Whiteman, Paul   203
Who, The   11, 75, 139, 166, 258
Wikipedia   34, 86, 107, 159–63
Wild Cherry   110
Wild Pair   186
Wilde, Kim   171
Will to Power   174
will.i.am   239 n.2, 254
Williams, Deniece   130, 154
Williams, Hank   8
Williams, Maurice   1, 31
Williams, Pharrell   235, 255,
    271–2, 298
Wilson, Brian   24, 57
Wilson, Dan   151, 252
Winter, Edgar   68
Winwood, Steve   163
Withers, Bill   87, 221

Wiz Khalifa   255, 263
*Wizard of Oz, The* (film)   10, 99
Wonder, Stevie
  "Ebony & Ivory"   153–4
  "Fingertips Pt. 2"   42
  "I Just Called to Say I Love You"   149
  "I Wish"   107, 222
  "Part-Time Lover"   154
  Relationship to Bob Dylan   47
  "Sir Duke"   113 n.2
  "Superstition"   84
  "That's What Friends Are For"   150
  "You Are the Sunshine of My Life"   69
  "You Haven't Done Nothin'"   94
Wray, Link   202
Wrecking Crew, The   57
Wyman, Bill   195

XXXTentacion   2, 9, 272, 274

Yes (band)   135
Yorke, Thom   211
Young, Neil   69, 73, 209
Young Jeezy   243 n.5
Young Thug   112, 157, 250, 279, 302, 304
YoungKio   111
YouTube
  comments   106
  "Harlem Shake"   263
  "Savage Love (Laxed—Siren
    Beat)"   289, 299
  service history   262–4

Zagar   60
Zappa, Frank   217

# *About the Author*

**Chris Dalla Riva** lives at the intersection of music and data. Playing in bands and recording music since his teenage years, Dalla Riva is currently a senior product manager at Audiomack, where he focuses on data analytics and personalization. Outside of his job, he writes the popular newsletter *Can't Get Much Higher* and has had his work featured by *The Economist, Business Insider*, and NPR, among many others. His original claim to fame was setting off an internet-wide debate about the decline of key changes in popular music. He currently lives in Hoboken, New Jersey, with his four guitars and future wife, Devin.

## About the Illustrator

**Caileigh Nerney** is a graphic designer and artist with a passion for transforming complex information into compelling visual narratives. Her expertise spans infographics, branding, and visual identity, with a focus on making information both accessible and engaging. Her work has been featured in *The Wall Street Journal*, NBC, and exhibited at the Connersmith Gallery. She lives in New Jersey with her husband, her greatest supporter and creative sounding board, and is deeply grateful to her family for their unwavering encouragement of her artistic journey.